Richard Cornell is a member of the Department of Political Science at York University.

The monolithic nature of the communist movement during the Stalinist period overlay pluralist tendencies. These were suppressed in the 1920s, though they were to re-emerge after Stalin's death.

The history of the Communist Youth International is revealed in this volume as an important example of the 'autonomist' tendencies in the communist movement after the First World War. The experience of the CYI also demonstrates that differences between the Leninist and Stalinist eras were of degree, rather than of kind. Under Lenin, organizational principles and practices were introduced that gave to the new communist movement a distinct, authoritarian cast.

Cornell considers the relevance, in the development of radical movements among the young, of such qualities as untempered idealism, a predisposition to embrace the most radical alternatives for social change, and a self-assertiveness or rebelliousness directed against traditional adult teachings. He shows how these qualities were to lead, after the First World War (and more recently), to conflicts between radical, ideologically orthodox youth and more pragmatic adult party leaders.

In introducing their new kind of radicalism, the young communists of Europe in 1919 considered themselves to be the most revolutionary element among revolutionaries – the highest form of 'revolutionary vanguard.' Moscow did not agree.

RICHARD CORNELL

Revolutionary
Vanguard: The
Early Years of
the Communist
Youth International
1914–1924

University of Toronto Press
Toronto Buffalo London

© University of Toronto Press 1982
Toronto Buffalo London
Printed in Canada

ISBN 0-8020-5559-1

Canadian Cataloguing in Publication Data

Cornell, Richard, 1927-
  Revolutionary vanguard.

  Bibliography: p.
  Includes index.
  ISBN 0-8020-5559-1

  1. Communist Youth International - History.
  2. Socialism and youth - History - 20th century.
  I. Title.

HX547.C67   324'.1   C82-904036-4

This book has been published with the help of a grant from
the Social Science Federation of Canada, using funds provided
by the Social Sciences and Humanities Research Council of
Canada, and a grant from the Publications Fund of the
University of Toronto Press.

Contents

Preface

During the Stalinist period, centralization and ideological
uniformity were the most striking features of the communist
movement. Communism appeared to be a more or less monolithic
phenomenon. Thus, it is not surprising that the diversity
that emerged after World War II, and particularly from the
late 1950s, was interpreted as something quite new. In fact,
communism acquired its characteristic Marxist-Leninist definition only by the suppression or uprooting at an early stage
of other, less authoritarian conceptions of communism.

The communist movement, as represented in the Communist
International (Comintern) and its auxiliary organizations,
was another phase in a continuing effort by 'left-wing social democrats' to implement an orthodox interpretation of
Marx's ideas on revolutionary social change. The Russian
Bolsheviks were indeed the predominant factor within the
new, revolutionary International. Because they had been successful, their ideas carried great weight. But just as before
1917, even before 1914 and the outbreak of war, socialists
had been divided over many crucial matters of theory, strategy, and tactics, the early communists were not really in
agreement on several basic issues. New differences had arisen
over how to interpret the prospects for revolution, what a
revolution meant, and which strategies and tactics were to
be followed. It was over mundane, but critical, questions of
organizational structure and process, however, that the
'revolutionary solidarity' of these first communists broke
down. Enthusiasm for 'action' was not to prove strong enough
to keep them together. Coming from different countries, with
different traditions and different historical and cultural
experiences, the various communists brought with them

different conceptions of what was an appropriate basis for
a revolutionary organization. These differences over organization reflected a deeper disunity over the purposes of the
new communist movement.

What it meant to be a communist was under debate and in
the process of definition in the years immediately after
World War I. It was at this time that the Russian party
not only acquired its authoritarian, Marxist-Leninist features, but also went on to shape the entire communist movement in its image. It did so by imposing an organizational
structure through which it could determine the purposes the
communist movement was to serve. The first signs of this
development were apparent in the Communist Youth International (CYI), which was founded several months after the
Comintern in 1919. Both internationals were dissolved by
the Russian party in 1943. That which was soon to come
within the communist parties and the Comintern was seen
first within the youth movement and its organizations, and
in a clearer and less ambiguous form.

The history of the youth international can tell us a great
deal about the nature of communism, seen as a political movement. It provides an important example of how the communist
movement developed *in practice* in the early post-war years.
Young communists exercised a significant influence on this
development. Among the most devoted supporters of the Russian
Bolsheviks, they played an active part in the creation of
many communist parties. Mostly situated on the extreme left
of the socialist political spectrum, they served also as a
moral and idealistic spur to all revolutionary forces. Above
all, they raised, as few other communists did, the fundamental issue of the nature of the new communist movement.
What was the revolution to be for? What were the values to
be in the new socialist society?

This study of the youth international emphasizes the close
relationship that existed between the early communist movement and the 'socialist mainstream.' The Communist Youth
International, like most other communist organizations, was
not a completely new phenomenon; it was neither grafted onto
the old socialist movement, nor did it take root in different soil. Rather it grew out of a previously united (if
only formally) socialist movement and flourished in its way
as a new branch. One cannot understand the history of communism, or more recent developments within the movement,
without recognizing that its separation from the 'socialist

mainstream' has in many ways been an artificial one. The
youth international's history demonstrates that the diversity now flourishing openly within what traditionally is
called the international communist movement is *not* new,
but has deeper historical origins. This diversity should
be seen as the reappearance of an earlier pluralism whose
roots go back into the 'socialist mainstream,' a pluralism
that had been suppressed under Lenin, Trotsky, and Stalin
without destroying its sources. The insistence of the young
communists on autonomy, on a less restrictive definition
of democratic centralism, and the Russian Bolshevik response to these pressures were an important indication of
the course the new communist movement was to take and a
precursor to the imposition of Marxism-Leninism as the
only permissible conception of communism.

This exploration of the Communist Youth International
helps to clarify another misunderstanding concerning the
development of communism. As Helmut Gruber notes in his
International Communism in the Era of Lenin, it is 'equally
distorting to subordinate the continuity between the era
of Lenin and that of Stalin to differences between these
two periods of communism.' Differences between the Leninist
and Stalinist eras were of degree rather than of kind. It
was under Lenin that new organizational principles and
practices were introduced, giving to the new communist
movement even in Lenin's time a distinct, authoritarian
cast. The suppression of other, less centralized, conceptions of communism already was well on its way to completion. The Leninist criteria have provided a continuing
raison d'être ever since for all communist organizations.
This was not accomplished, however, without the transformation of these principles and practices into dogmas - that
is, democratic centralism was not seen simply as a rational
means for the effective functioning of communist organizations (to be revised or perhaps abandoned if its application proved to be ineffective or harmful), but became instead a matter of faith, of the 'true' interpretation of
Marxism, to which one must subscribe unquestioningly if
one is to remain a member of the movement. Although cautious in his introduction of the new norms to the Comintern, Lenin did so knowingly and without reservations.
Stalin only carried Lenin's work to its conclusion. Thus,
it is a misconception to assume that the Stalinist period
was in some way an impure or perverted version of the 'true'

communism inspired by Lenin. The organizational and decision-making norms, and the relationships between communist organizations, indeed the very nature of these organizations themselves, were already set in Lenin's time, before the imposition of Stalin's particularly intensified form of authoritarianism. The experience of the Communist Youth International highlights the fact that the hegemonic aspirations of the new, Leninist interpretation of Marxist orthodoxy began with its founder. In fact, the communist youth movement was the arena in which the first in a long line of unsuccessful communist challenges to Leninist principles emerged.

This study also demonstrates the broad historical relevance of certain qualities found, perhaps in greatest abundance, in young people: untempered idealism, a predisposition to embrace the most radical alternatives for social change, and a self-assertiveness directed against traditional adult tutelage. These qualities were to lead, both then and more recently, to conflicts between radical, ideologically orthodox youth, and more pragmatic adult party leaders. The first young communists manifested an almost pristine devotion to their idealistic visions, and a dedication to 'revolution' unmatched within the movement. Introducing a new kind of radicalism, the young communists considered themselves to be the most revolutionary element among revolutionaries, the highest form of 'revolutionary vanguard.' The notion, still in high fashion in many circles, that young socialist activists are more revolutionary than their elders thus has an important historical precedent.

This work is not intended to be a history of the communist youth movement, or even of the youth international. It is the more fundamental question of the nature of communism, as reflected in the experience of the CYI, and not the development of the youth organizations, the Comintern, or the national communist parties, or the communist position on the political and moral issues of the time that is at the centre of the story. The Comintern and the parties are important here only in the context of their relationship to the youth movement. As to the major issues facing the communist movement as a whole, the CYI and the youth organizations took positions on many events and developments, and adopted various programs as the basis for their agitational and propaganda activities. The CYI also said little, if anything, about many events and issues.

On some things it was strongly of one mind; on some it was
divided; on others the CYI central apparatus was very concerned and took strong positions, while the individual
youth organizations were quite indifferent. Finally, there
were many local issues that absorbed the attention of the
individual organizations, but which were of peripheral interest, at best, to the central apparatus and to the other
youth organizations. The issues dominating the whole movement, certainly at the level at which the future of the
movement was to be determined (through the corps of activists
and functionaries, those who held some kind of office or were
delegates to conferences and congresses), were *internal*
ones: relations with the parties and the Comintern, and
with 'Moscow,' and questions of strategy and tactics. The
fate of the young communists in the conflict engendered
by these issues was an omen of what was to come for other
communists. It also was in many ways a tragic consequence
of the unreality of the youthful 'revolutionary vanguardism.'

Acknowledgments

A debt of gratitude is owed to a number of people for their
assistance and advice in the planning, research, and writing
of this study. First, to Alexander Dallin, Richard Lowenthal,
Joseph Rothschild, Peter Juviler, Henry Roberts, Paul Noyes,
Grey Hodnett, and Henry Krisch, all of whom went through
the draft manuscript in great detail sharpening my approach
to the issues. Second, to the directors and staffs of the
Schweizerisches Sozialarchiv in Zurich, the International
Institute for Social History in Amsterdam, the Arbeiderbe-
vegelsens Arkiv in Oslo, and the Bibliothek, Institut für
Marxismus-Leninismus beim Zentralkomitee der Sozialistische
Einheits Partei Deutschlands in East Berlin who provided
considerable and gracious assistance in locating materials
and in relaxing regulations so as to enable me to utilize
available sources more conveniently; and the Arbejderbevae-
gelsens Arkiv in Copenhagen, the Arbetarrörelsens Arkiv in
Stockholm, the Deutsche Staatsbibliothek in East Berlin,
the Istituto Gramsci in Rome, the Biblioteca Nazionale in
Florence, the Zentralbibliothek in Zurich, the Maurice
Thorez Institute in Paris, and the library of the Hoover
Institution, Stanford. Third, to Theodor Pinkus, who found
source materials for me which were most difficult to obtain,
and who arranged an important interview; to all those who
gave so willingly of their time to share with me their ex-
perience or knowledge; to Magister Knut Langfeldt, Dr Agne
Gustafsson, Mr Albert Dienaar-Kok, Marty Fletcher, Fred
Fletcher, Alfred Senn, and many others for their assistance;
and to Robert Bass for his encouragement. Fourth, to the
Inter-University Committee on Travel Grants (predecessor
of the International Research and Exchanges Board); the
Research Foundation, State University of New York; the

Russian Institute, Columbia University; the Minor Research
Grants Committee, Faculty of Arts, York University; and the
Social Science Federation of Canada for the financial assistance necessary to complete the study. Finally, to E.H.
Carr in whose work (a footnote in the third volume of *The
Bolshevik Revolution, 1917-1923)* I found the idea for a
study of the Communist Youth International. Needless to
say, the interpretations set forth, and all inadequacies
therein, are my own.

R.C.

Abbreviations

AJ	Zentralstelle für die arbeitende Jugend Deutschlands; Verband der Arbeiterjugendvereine Deutschlands
AJI	Arbeiter Jugendinternationale
CAP	Comité Administratif Permanent
Comintern	The Communist International or the Third International
CYI	Communist Youth International (Kommunistische Jugendinternationale - KJI; Kommunisticheskii Internatsional Molodezhi - KIM)
ECCI	Executive Committee of the Communist International
ECCYI	Executive Committee of the Communist Youth International
FGS	Federatione Giovanile Socialista
FSJ	Freie Sozialistische Jugend
IASJ	Internationale Arbeitsgemeinschaft sozialistischer Jugendorganisationen
ISB	International Socialist Bureau
ISC	International Socialist Commission or Zimmerwald Commission
IJK	*Internationale Jugendkorrespondenz*
IUSYO	International Union of Socialist Youth Organizations (Internationale Verbindung der sozialistischen Jugendorganisationen)
JC	Fédération Nationale des Jeunesses Socialistes-Communistes de France, which became Fédération des Jeunesses Communistes
J-I	*Jugend-Internationale*
JG	*Die Junge Garde*
KAJ	Kommunistische Arbeiter Jugend
KAPD	Kommunistische Arbeiterpartei Deutschlands

KIM	(see CYI)
KJD	Kommunistische Jugendverband Deutschlands
KJK	(see CYI)
Komsomol	Kommunisticheskii soiuz molodezhi
KPD	Kommunistische Partei Deutschlands
NKU	Norges Kommunistiske Ungdomsforbund
NLP	Norwegian Labour Party (Det norske Arbeiderparti)
PCF	Parti Communiste Français
PCI	Partito Comunista Italiano
SED	Sozialistische Einheitspartei Deutschlands
SFIO	Section Francaise de l'Internationale Ouvrière
SPD	Sozialdemokratische Partei Deutschlands
SPJ	Verband der freien sozialistischen Proletarier-Jugend
USPD	Unabhängige Sozialdemokratische Partei Deutschlands
VKPJ	Verband der kommunistischen Proletarierjugend
VSAJ	Verband der sozialistischen Arbeiterjugerd

The groups and organizations noted above were often quite inconsistent when referring to themselves and to their journals. Various shorter versions of their full, formal titles were used frequently. They were also referred to by others in various ways. These abbreviations constitute an effort to provide a list of titles that is as representative as possible of the alternative usages. Some abbreviations (e.g. AJ) refer to the organizations that followed one another within a particular political/ideological tendency.

REVOLUTIONARY VANGUARD: THE EARLY YEARS OF THE
COMMUNIST YOUTH INTERNATIONAL, 1914–1924

1

A tradition of independence

The socialist youth movement came to life relatively quietly
in the late nineteenth century. Although this was a time of
intense social and political turbulence, it was still an
era when young people were kept firmly in their place. In
general, the younger generation followed adult initiatives.
Thus, the growing trend within the European working class
toward organizational unity and increased political activity
came in due course to have its effect on the apprentices and
young workers. Nevertheless, there were distinctive features
to the socialist youth movement as it developed into the
twentieth century, characteristics which were to give it a
personality of its own, and which were later to lead to
serious problems in its relationships with the adult organizations.

Young workers and apprentices, the latter a product of
persisting pre-capitalist economic institutions, certainly
were fertile ground for socialist ideas. Still forced to
accept adult tutelage in most areas of their lives, often
exploited quite shamefully in the work-place, products of
an educational system that forced most young people into
the labour market in their early teens, denied voting rights,
and remaining a natural manpower reservoir for the military,
it was almost inevitable that the natural discontent and
rebelliousness of youth would be accentuated by their position near the bottom of an established economic and political order. Idealism, frustration, and impatience led many
into the socialist movement.

4 Revolutionary vanguard

Formation of youth organizations

Developing as it did across diverse conditions and historical traditions, it is not surprising that the emerging socialist youth movement displayed considerable heterogeneity. The result was a varied pattern of national movements differentiated according to focus of activity, form of internal organization, and degree of involvement in political affairs.[1] Two common themes, however, ran through this diversity: anti-militarism and economic discontent. While both factors were present, the activities and orientation of each youth organization tended to be shaped by one or the other. Thus, two types of youth organization began to be seen.

In some countries the military played a direct role in stifling social protest. This brought forth a bitter resistance, especially among younger workers. Increasingly, the military was seen as a major obstacle to social change. The immediate cause of the formation in 1886 of the first socialist youth organization, the Belgian La Jeune Garde/ De Jonge Wacht, was the use of the military to put down labour demonstrations. The gradual coming together of young workers was accelerated and given a particular focus by agitation within military units to prevent their use against strikers and demonstrating workers. Belgium was long considered 'the classic country of anti-militarist propaganda through the socialist youth organization.'[2] Other such groups were formed in the more open societies of Europe at the turn of the century.

In other countries, authoritarianism limited the possibilities for anti-militarist agitation. Strong anti-militarist sentiments could be translated into actions only at great risk and thus economic considerations became of more direct importance for the establishment of socialist organizations. The desire to improve their economic condition led young workers and apprentices in Austria to form the Verein Jugendlicher Arbeiter in 1894. Neglected by the trade unions and the socialist parties, and chafing under adult paternalism, the younger generation of Austrian workers sought its own way to material betterment and social improvement. The Austrian organization soon became a model for other socialist youth organizations.

1 Thaller, *Die Internationale* ... 2
2 Münzenberg, *Die sozialistische Jugendorganisationen* ... 2

5 Tradition of independence

Anti-militarism and economic and social discontent provided the environmental context within which socialist
youth organizations developed. The objective of those who
joined, of course, was to do something about existing conditions. Positive, direct action was always the immediate
concern of all socialist youth leaders. The possibilities
for action, however, varied from country to country - partially due to legal restrictions or harassment, partially
because of opposition from party leaders, and in part the
result of differences in strength of the national labour
movements. In all cases, before effective 'actions' and
'campaigns,' and strikes and demonstrations could be carried out, the youth organizations had to develop sufficient
size and strength. Thus, from the outset the deeper and
more fundamental interest of the young socialists was in
politicizing, 'educating,' and organizing the vast mass of
young people. As the strength of the young socialists grew,
so too did their involvement in economic and political confrontations with established authority. Missing, however,
was any appreciable awareness of the philosophical or theoretical issues that occupied the party theorists. Members
of the younger generation were guided, for the most part,
by a simplistic commitment to socialism gleaned from the
more popular writings of Marx, such as the *Communist Manifesto*.
The problem of how to promote their cause most effectively
was by no means confined to the first young socialists. It
continues to be, even today, the most persistent and contentious issue within the entire socialist movement. For the
young socialists at the turn of the century, this problem
gradually took form in three interrelated issues: 1) the
relationship between the generations: between young socialists and the socialist parties, 2) the meaning of socialism
and the commitments that socialists had assumed, and 3) the
role the youth movement was to play in the struggle for
socialism. They were not always immediately and clearly
perceived as issues. They formed, none the less, the substance of an ongoing debate that was to have a profound
effect on future developments. It was, indeed, out of the
responses to these incipient issues that the traditions and
identity of the socialist youth movement crystallized.
Quite consciously the young socialists, right from the
formation of the first youth organization in Belgium, struggled to assert a separate identity. Impelled toward unity by
ideology and the rigours of existence in a hostile political

environment, the young socialists nevertheless drew apart
from the socialist parties. In the early years this independence from the parties created little conflict. There were
sufficient similarities in the views of both the parties
and the youth organizations to maintain a degree of harmony.
The parties often were important sources of financial support to the youth organizations. However, as time went on
sources of conflict began to develop. An estrangement betwee
the generations set in that was to reach the brink of schism
by 1914.

For the most part, the young socialists had their own
leaders, organizations, and independent existence. The
socialist parties encouraged the formation of separate
youth organizations, rather than enrolling the young workers
directly into the parties in youth sections or departments.
It was understood that it would be easier to reach and mobilize young workers if they had been recruited into their
own organizations. Winning the younger generation was very
important to the parties, for they recognized that youth
was the future. If there were to be prospects for the eventual construction of a socialist society, a new, Marxist
'Weltanschauung' had to be implanted in the coming generations. This involved not only efforts to counteract the
influence of prevailing middle-class ideas as propagated
by the educational system, but also positive indoctrination
in Marxist notions of class, class consciousness, and class
conflict. On more practical grounds, the more traditional
and established parties were seeking to develop a reservoir
of potential recruits, a body of convinced and committed
young workers that would in time swell the ranks of socialist parties in each country. The parties also thought that
separate organizations would be more useful for conducting
propaganda among soldiers and young recruits. Organizing
young workers and educating them politically were recognized
as vital tasks by the international socialist congresses in
Paris (1900) and Stuttgart (1907).

The most important reason for the formation of independent
youth organizations, however, was the rejection by the young
workers themselves of the 'spiritual tutelage of the older
generation, no matter whether well- or ill-intended.'[3]
Whether tutelage was in the form of a master dominating an
apprentice, a foreman exploiting a young worker in shop or

3 Danneberg, *Die Rekrutenschule* ... 6

factory, or an adult socialist leader presuming to guide or
lead young socialists, it was rejected. The search for a
distinct identity and an opportunity to go their own way
led those who joined the socialist youth organizations to
struggle, if not always successfully, to preserve the independent existence of their organizations. The Austrian
youth organization, more than any other, was considered as
typical of an independent socialist youth organization ad-
ministering itself.[4]

Not all socialist youth groups succeeded in establishing
and maintaining their independence. Youth organizations
formed after 1907, such as those in France and Germany,
were controlled by their parties. Where local party and
trade-union leaders in these countries supported the notion
of autonomous or independent youth groups, the young socialists had more freedom. Elsewhere young socialists increasingly grew restive under party-adult tutelage.

The tendency in the youth movement to form independent
organizations was accelerated by the political and ideological differences that emerged within the socialist movement.[5] Dissension over the meaning and interpretation of
doctrine was tearing apart the facade of party unity. Socialists were being split gradually into different camps
by disagreements over what socialism meant, what a commitment to Marxian socialism entailed in terms of practical
work, and how socialists were to carry out their commitment
to fight militarism and imperialism. The youth movement
could not avoid being swept up in the maelstrom of these
party controversies. Clearly, young socialists had a role
to play in bringing socialism about. But exactly what was
this role to be? Were they to be a direct political force,
or was their political strategy to be indirect and essentially confined to 'youth tasks' (Jugendaufgaben)?

The issues of the parties' educational activities became
the focal point of political/ideological controversy within
the youth movement. As socialists sought to persuade workers
and intellectuals to accept socialist doctrine, they also
turned to the young workers in an effort to provide them with
a socialist education. Yet there were differing conceptions of
what constituted a socialist education. The reformists or revis-
ionists believed that socialism could be achieved through the
reform of capitalist society from within. They did not envisage

4 Tschitscherin (Chicherin), *Skizzen aus der Geschichte* ... 16
5 See Schorske, *German Social Democracy, 1905-1917*, 97-108

the violent 'overthrow' of capitalist society and even less the participation of the younger generation in such radical activities. The young workers were to be imbued with the Marxist 'Weltanschauung,' but political decisions and 'actions' were to remain the concern of the party. For the democratic reformist socialists of the right, political action meant first and foremost voting and parliamentary manoeuvring. As the young workers were not yet of voting age, their activities acquired a political character only in the sense that socialist education had a clearly political basis. The efforts of the party leaders to limit the activities of youth groups primarily to non-political work became a major point of dispute between factions in the international socialist movement.

The radicals, or orthodox Marxists, within the socialist movement remained convinced that the evils of capitalist society could be eliminated only by the overthrow of that society. All elements of the working class were to be mobilized for this end. This meant that active participation in the 'revolutionary struggle' was to be an essential element in the socialist education of the younger generation. The radicals, however, were divided into the uncompromising revolutionaries on the left (like Lenin) who thought in terms of violent confrontations, and those who remained orthodox Marxists but thought that revolution meant any change that put capitalists out of power and the proletariat into power. This latter group, which came to be known as the centre, was very reluctant to resort to violence despite its apparent aggressiveness and its support of militant actions such as strikes and demonstrations.

In the years before World War I the younger generation of socialists found the radical arguments increasingly more appealing. A complete overthrow of existing society through confrontation, rather than its gradual transformation, was more in tune with youthful impatience. Direct participation in political affairs, in anti-militarist activities and the 'revolutionary struggle,' was more in accord with the youthful urge for action. A conflict thus developed between young socialists committed to revolutionary activity and reformist or pragmatic party leaders unwilling to commit their parties to radical action. The situation was only worsened when the more radical, revolutionary, and anti-militarist socialists turned to the independent youth organizations as sources of support. An excellent example of this occurred in Germany

where the radical leaders, Karl Liebknecht and Klara Zetkin,
saw the youth movement as an asset in their efforts to radicalize the party. In return, the youth organizations believed
it was in their interests to encourage and aid the radicals.
For their part, the party leaders sought with limited success
to control the youth organizations and to bring them under
party supervision. In Germany, the most important country
for the development of the socialist movement in those years,
party leaders did succeed in maintaining organizational control over the youth movement. However, serious tensions and
conflicts remained. These were temporarily suppressed during
World War I, but burst forth everywhere to reshape the socialist youth movement quite drastically as the war drew to a
close.

Creation of a youth international

Inevitably, the universalistic, internationalist character
of Marxian socialism had impelled the socialist parties to
try and form a united international organization. The founding
of the Second International in 1889 found a belated echo in
the youth movement. International unity and solidarity were
as important - and as logical - for the young socialists as
for the parties. After abortive attempts in 1889 and 1904
to form a union of socialist youth organizations, a conference was convened in Stuttgart in May 1907 in connection
with the meeting of socialist parties. It was natural that
this youth meeting reflected the major subjects of concern
in the socialist movement.
    From the turn of the century through World War I, the two
associated issues of militarism and colonialism were of paramount importance to both young and old in the international
socialist movement. Not only were the international congresses preoccupied with these problems, but there were ongoing
debates within each national socialist movement. Socialism
and anti-militarism came together for a number of reasons:
the idealistic pacifism of many of those attracted to socialism; doctrinal association of capitalism and bourgeois society with conflict; belief that the observable militarism
of the era was a product of, and a prop for, capitalist society; and more practical reasons such as the threat to peace
posed by colonial rivalries of the European powers, and fears
of the more nationalist socialists that war would worsen the
position of their own countries vis-à-vis others.

By the time of the 1907 congress of the Second Internationa
anti-militarism had become the predominant issue of the socia
ist movement. Reflecting an inability to achieve a consensus,
the congress resolution, 'On Militarism and International Con
flict,' was purposely vague on the subject of anti-militarist
tactics. By omission, however, the parties intentionally denied the young socialists an active role. They were quietly
put in their place when the resolution went no further than
to state that it was the duty of the working class 'to see to
it that proletarian youth be educated in the spirit of the
brotherhood of peoples and of socialism and is imbued with
class consciousness.'[6] The debate on anti-militarism spilled
over into the proceedings of the first international socialis
youth conference, held immediately afterwards. Imbued with
a strong anti-militarism, the young socialists did not follow
silently the parties' lead.

The dominant figure at the youth conference was the German
left-socialist, Karl Liebknecht. After 1907, Liebknecht serve
as an inspiration and 'elder statesman' for young socialists
throughout Europe. His anti-militarist views had a deep impact on the younger generation and inevitably brought him
into conflict with the German government. At the party congress in Mannheim in 1906 he had made an impassioned speech
against militarism, which was published soon afterwards.[7]
In April 1907 the publication was confiscated and Liebknecht
charged with treason. He was convicted in October 1907 and
sentenced to eighteen months in prison. His presence at the

6 The resolution of the Second International is cited in
  Gankin and Fisher, *The Bolsheviks and the World War*, 57-9
7 *Militarismus und Antimilitarismus* ... An admirer of
  Liebknecht remarked some years later on the sources of
  his influence on the younger generation: 'We found in
  Karl Liebknecht the qualities of a revolutionary youth
  who, with an aversion to all compromise, is pushing forward with the older generation. He has left behind as an
  inheritance to the socialist youth his energy and readiness to take action. If one could only prove worthy of
  this legacy and follow in the footsetps of this pioneer.
  If also the older ones in the labour movement could feel
  the touch of his spirit it would be much better!' (*Basler
  Vorwärts*, 14 January 1921, 13), organ of the left in the
  Swiss Social Democratic Party. In 1907 Liebknecht was in
  his mid-thirties.

meeting in Stuttgart thus occurred while he was awaiting
trial. Liebknecht was to be imprisoned again in May 1916
for participating in anti-war demonstrations. After his
murder in Berlin in January 1919, the communists made
Liebknecht, who had been one of the founders of the Communist
Party of Germany (KPD), into a symbol of radical anti-war
activities, a martyr to 'capitalist militarism.' At the 1906
conference, Liebknecht had urged the young socialists into
political action, contrary to the intent of the socialist
parties, in the form of systematic anti-militarist propaganda.
The conference resolution followed Liebknecht and not the
party leaders, who believed political activities were best
left to their own organizations.

The Stuttgart conference of young socialists was important
for what it portended for the future: its mood of anti-war
activism, and the search for an independent political role
for the youth organizations. Another decision the conference
took that was to have future consequences was to found an
International Union of Socialist Youth Organizations (Internationale Verbindung sozialistischer Jugendorganisationen),
or IUSYO. While the 'international solidarity' of the emerging
socialist youth movement was institutionalized formally in
the IUSYO, the leaders of the Second International were able
to determine the direction of the new youth international by
influencing the selection of its executive organ, the five-
man International Bureau.[8] Under the leadership of the
international secretary, the Austrian youth leader, Robert
Danneberg, the International Bureau was as opposed to seeing
the IUSYO develop into a politically active, independent
youth international as were the leaders of the Second

8 Elected to the International Bureau were Leopold Winarsky
(Austria), Henri de Man (Belgium), Karl Liebknecht
(Germany), Gustav Möller (Sweden), and Henriette Roland-
Holst (Netherlands), of whom only de Man and Möller were
from the younger generation (Münzenberg, *Die sozialistische
Jugendorganisationen* ... 48). The Austrian youth organization performed all of the secretarial functions. The
charge was made at the congress that some of the trade-
union leaders had attempted to get the youth to tone down
their anti-militarist fervour by dangling promises of
much-needed financial aid in front of the delegates
(ibid., 54).

International.[9] The youth movement was to be only a recruiting ground for the parties, under their general supervision if not outright control. Thus, at its inception and much like the Second International itself the IUSYO was a loose association with no central authority. The International Bureau, through its secretariat in Vienna, did little more than act as a central clearing house for the gathering and exchange of information. All communications between the International Bureau and individual youth organizations had to be channelled through either a national party or an individual approved by that party.[10] The International Bureau, which seldom, if ever, met formally, did publish reports from time to time on the activities of national organizations.

This state of affairs did not suit everyone in the youth movement. The tendency of the youth organizations to assert or demand their independence, and their eagerness to be involved in political activity, were not long in manifesting themselves in the youth international. Several youth organizations, most notably the Italian, the Swiss, and the three Scandinavian, began to press for an independent, centralized, politically active international organization more in their own image.[11] In order to put an end to these efforts, the party leaders in the Second International's executive organ, the International Socialist Bureau, proposed that the youth international be dissolved. The more pliant International Bureau of the IUSYO would be incorporated directly into the Inter-

9 See also the resolution, approved with Second International encouragement at the international socialist youth conference in Copenhagen in September 1910. The youth movement 'in every country [was to] work in *continuous agreement* with the socialist party and the trade unions. It should ... decide upon its areas of activity in agreement with the party and the trade unions' (Münzenberg, *Die sozialistische Jugendorganisationen* ... 103). A new International Bureau was elected at Copenhagen, consisting of De Man, Zeth Högland (Sweden), Emanual Skatula (Bohemia), Sverre Krogh (Norway), and Robert Danneberg (Austria), with the latter serving as international secretary.
10 See Tschitscherin (Chicherin), *Skizzen aus der Geschichte* ... 42-51
11 See the Italian position in Münzenberg, *Die sozialistische Jugendorganisationen* ... 106-7

national Socialist Bureau as one of its sections, where it
would continue to perform its clearing-house functions.[12]
While a lively and controversial, although inconclusive,
discussion about the future of the youth international was
taking place in the years preceding the oubreak of war, the
IUSYO continued its formal and inactive existence as an international organization. Its future was to have been decided
at a congress in Vienna in August 1914, but these plans were
frustrated by the war. In 1914 the International Union of
Socialist Youth Organizations, as distinguished from its
member youth organizations, remained an ineffective non-
political body whose limited functions suited socialist
party leaders. Under the chaotic conditions of war, however,
the revolutionary anti-war elements of the centre and left
breathed new life into it and converted it into an important
political instrument.

Reaction to the outbreak of war

Although the anti-militarism of the youth movement had been
genuine, it was not strong enough in the belligerent countries to withstand the outbreak of war in August 1914. The
youth organization in Germany, by far the largest and best
organized, had never belonged to the IUSYO. Led by the future
president of the Weimar Republic, Friedrich Ebert, it was
from its inception in 1908 subordinated to the social democratic party (SPD). A majority of the youth orgnization's
members followed the majority in the SPD (called the Majority
Socialists) in 1914 and supported the government and the
war effort. Nationalist sentiment and fear of the consequences
of a victory by the semi-feudal Russian autocracy outweighed
any idealistic anti-capitalist, anti-militarist notions. The
young socialists for the most part joined with the rest of
the German young people in taking up arms for the fatherland.[13]
Young French socialists likewise accepted the decision of
the French socialist party to support the war, nationalism

12 See Münzenberg, *Die Dritte Front*, 119. See also the draft
   reglement to govern the relations between the Second International and the IUSYO prepared by the IUSYO secretariat
   and circulated for discussion in 1913, the text of which is
   in ibid., 105-6.
13 See Laqueur, *Young Germany*, chapter 10

and anti-German sentiment prevailing. The first reaction
of the Austrians was one of support for the party and its
belief that a victory for the Central Powers over tsarism
would be in the best interests of the working class. It
soon changed its position and, following Robert Danneberg
and Friedrich Adler, came out in total opposition to the
war and in favour of a negotiated peace (Verständigungs-
frieden). Thus, with the complete disintegration of the
Belgian socialist movement under the impact of the German
occupation, and the lack of any significant socialist youth
organizations in Great Britain and Russia, socialist youth
in all of the belligerent countries, with the exception of
Austria, were at least formally behind their national
governments. Military mobilization and strict wartime con-
trols made it impossible for those young socialists who
did remain opposed to the war to function effectively.

Perhaps the young socialists in the neutral countries
also would have given way to the pressures for national
defence had their countries been engaged. As it was, the
anti-war spirit of the Stuttgart conference was kept alive
in the non-belligerent countries, where it in fact flourished
and grew. Thus, leadership of the opposition to the war
within the socialist youth movement came from Switzerland,
Scandinavia, the Netherlands, and Italy, even after it had
joined the war.[14]
Both the Second International and the IUSYO were shattered
by the war. Socialists were in the trenches fighting one
another. Socialist internationalism had given way to traditional nationalist animosities. The Second International
lost even the appearance of unity, as well as any capacity
to act effectively. The socialists in the belligerent
countries refused even to talk to each other. The socialists
in the neutral lands tried in vain, through the International
Socialist Bureau after it had been moved to the Netherlands,
to find a common ground on which the socialist parties
could bring an end to the fighting. The IUSYO, however, was
able to regroup itself and become the focal point for socialist anti-war activities and propaganda. As the war went on,

14 There are numerous accounts of these efforts, including
  Schüller, *Von den Anfängen der proletarischen Jugendbewegu*
  ... 82-107; Münzenberg, *Die Dritte Front*, 152-65; idem,
  Die sozialistische Jugendorganisationen ... 204-11; and
  Sie ist nicht tot! ...

it was the International Bureau and the youth organizations
and groups cooperating with it that gave the anti-war opposition its most broadly based support.

The secretariat of the IUSYO in Vienna had been forced
to end its activities when the war broke out. Moreover,
Robert Danneberg, the international secretary, was a supporter of Kautsky's view that the International could function only in peacetime. He believed that in order to function effectively the youth international had to represent
the young socialists of all countries and all political
tendencies. The war obviously made this impossible. Furthermore, he endorsed the pre-war concept of the youth
movement as primarily an educational movement, with politics
to be left to the socialist parties. He opposed the war,
and supported the efforts of socialist youth in the neutral
countries to demonstrate against the war. He saw in these
demonstrations an expression of solidarity against capitalism and its wars, but he was not willing to go beyond that.

Meanwhile, the young socialists in Zurich were searching
for ways to revive the youth international and turn it into
an independent, politicized organization. They engaged in
an active correspondence with both the secretariat in Vienna
and socialist youth organizations in other neutral countries.
The central figure in these efforts was Willi Münzenberg,
the dynamic secretary of the Swiss youth organization. In
taking the initiative to arrange a conference of young socialists opposed to the war, Münzenberg and the Swiss re-
sponded and gave direction to a broader desire for the intensification of anti-war action. This was centred in the
Swiss, Scandinavian, Italian, and Dutch youth movements,
and within the small youth groups opposing the policies of
their socialist parties in Germany and France.[15]

The Bern conference of the international socialist youth
movement opened on the evening of 4 April 1915, at a joint
session with the national congress of the Swiss youth organization.[16] The conference was to see one of the first

15 Unless otherwise noted, reference to the Swiss socialists
   means those in the German-speaking cantons. They were
   more numerous and politically active than the socialists
   in the French-speaking cantons. The two did not merge
   until after the war.
16 This was the first open international socialist conference since the outbreak of the war. The International

tests of strength between the militant views of Lenin and the conciliatory, pacifist approach of the centre.[17] It was thus a prelude to the dissolution of the international socialist movement, which was to begin at Zimmerwald in September 1915 and culminate in the formation of the Communist International in March 1919. Under the leadership of Robert Grimm and Angelica Balabanova, the views of the centrists carried the day.

Socialist Women's Conference, held a few weeks earlier, had not been held publicly. A conference in Copenhagen in January 1915 had been limited to the socialist parties of the Netherlands and the Scandinavian countries, and another in London in February had been restricted to the socialist parties of the entente countries. While the Bern conference was by no means representative of all members of the IUSYO, it did have a wide constituency and in fact represented the currents within the anti-war opposition as a whole. For a list of the delegates, who came from Bulgaria, Denmark, Germany, Italy, the Netherlands, Norway, Sweden, Poland, Russia, and Switzerland, see *Sie ist nicht tot!* ... 21

17 The Russians apparently attached great significance to the Bern conference. Alexandra Kollontai, at this time a Menshevik-Internationalist, wrote in February 1915 from Stockholm to Lenin's wife, Krupskaya. Referring to the plans for the conference, Kollontai noted that the youth organizations constituted the revolutionary wing of the socialist movement in all the neutral countries. 'It seems to me,' she want on, 'that [the young socialists] can more quickly than any others serve as the basis for a revived revolutionary International' (from a letter in the Central Party Archives, Institute of Marxism-Leninism, cited in M.M. Mukhamedzhanov, 'V.I. Lenin i mezhunarodnaia sotsialisticheskaia molodezh' v gody pervoi mirovoi voiny,' *Novaia i novyeshaia istoriia* no. 2 (1967): 3-13.

The Bolshevik representatives left the conference soon after it began, apparently over voting procedures. The discussion on this point was never set forth in detail, but it would appear that the Bolshevik-Menshevik split in the Russian delegation, as well as the presence of Polish representation, made agreement impossible on how to cast the delegation's one vote. The Menshevik dele-

The conference was moderate in the sense that it refused
to endorse Lenin's call for an 'international civil war'
and a break with the right-socialists. In accordance with
centrist views, the delegates were willing to politicize
the youth movement only to the extent that it served the
anti-war movement. Young socialists were not otherwise to
intervene in, or be occupied with, party affairs. The decisions of the conference, however, did reflect the basic
difference between both left and centre, and the right.
The conference not only supported 'revolutionary socialism,'
but re-created the youth international as an active, independent organization free from party or Second International
control. This marked a critical turning point in the history of the socialist youth movement. After the Bern conference, the youth movement became absorbed in finding an

---

gate remained at the conference with an 'advisory' vote.
While the conference was proceeding, discussions went on
with the Bolshevik delegates. New voting arrangements
were agreed upon and the Bolsheviks returned. Each
country was to have two votes, Poland being considered
a separate country for the purpose of the voting.
    Münzenberg reports that Lenin, while dissatisfied with
the resolution adopted by the conference, encouraged the
Bolshevik delegation to remain (*Die Dritte Front*, 163).
Evidently Lenin felt that the resolution was the best
that could be hoped for under the circumstances, and
while certainly not as revolutionary as he would have
liked, it was a step towards his views. According to
Angelica Balabanova, Lenin sent Inessa Armand to the
conference to represent the Bolshevik view, and to win
the conference to the Bolshevik position. 'He did not
dare to come himself, sat downstairs in a little adja-
cent café drinking tea, getting reports from her, giving
her instructions' (Bertram Wolfe, 'Lenin and Inessa
Armand,' *Encounter* XXII, 2 [February 1964]: 83-91).
    Balabanova also says that Lenin himself prepared the
resolution offered by Armand and rejected by the conference. The text of this resolution is not available,
but it would appear most likely to have followed the
position of Lenin outlined in his letter to the 'Nashe
Slovo' group of 9 February 1915 (*Sochineniia* XXIX [1932]:
318-25, and discussed in Gankin and Fisher, *The Bolsheviks*
... 163).

organizational structure with which it could first preserve itself, under the difficult conditions that prevailed, and then expand into an effective force for ending the war and promoting radical social change.

By 1918 all the existing socialist youth organizations except the large German Zentralstelle, the Dutch Arbeider-Jeugd-Centrale, and the French National Committee (all three of which were the representative socialist youth organizations in their country and still under party control) had joined the reconstituted IUSYO.[18] This growth in support was not, however, accompanied by a corresponding growth in membership. Military and other governmental restrictions (especially the 'Reichsvereinsgesetz' in Germany) kept the size of the potentially large socialist youth organizations in the belligerent countries extremely small.

The Bern conference had moved the secretariat to Zurich, and elected Willi Münzenberg as international secretary. He plunged immediately into the affairs of the youth international, developing contacts with those socialist youth organizations not represented at Bern.[19] In addition, he began the important task of editing *Jugend-Internationale*, by which the youth international was to become known throughout Europe. Its first issue appeared in September 1915.[20]

18 Münzenberg, *Die Dritte Front*, 196-7. See Humbert-Droz, *Mon Evolution* ... 166, for the opening of communications with the young French opposition socialists.

19 Münzenberg, *Die Dritte Front*, 192ff

20 *Jugend-Internationale* (cited hereafter as *J-I*) was not only the first international socialist youth periodical, but aside from the *Periodical Bulletin of the International Socialist Bureau*, it was the first international socialist periodical (Grünberg, *Die Internationale* ... 439). During the war, *J-I* was published in German in Zurich as a quarterly (ten issues in all) and distributed illegally in Germany (see Münzenberg, *Die Dritte Front*, 204-7, for a discussion of these activities). On 1 May 1918 it was prohibited in Switzerland, but a last, eleventh issue was published after prohibition under the title *Brot, Frieden, und Freiheit*. Individual issues were published in Swedish, Danish, and Norwegian translations, and all eleven appeared later in Russian and German in a reprinted version. Altogether some 300,000 copies were printed during the war (Münzenberg, *Die*

He was also active in Zurich as a member of the Zimmerwald Commission (International Socialist Commission), a body created in
September 1915 at the first meeting of representatives from the
anti-war opposition groups in the various socialist parties.[21]
   Of great importance to the newly organized youth international were the series of demonstrations it sponsored.
These served to spread its ideas among wider circles of

Dritte Front, 203). Frequent contributors during this
period were Roland-Holst, Radek, Balabanova, Kollantai,
Trotsky, Zinoviev, Bronski, Liebknecht, Rühle, van Amstel,
Edwin Hörnle, Höglund, Olaussen, Danneberg, and of course
Münzenberg. Edward Bernstein also contributed several
articles. To succeed *J-I* after its prohibition, the international secretariat brought out a 'circular letter'
(Zirkularschreiben). An attempt was made to resume publication in Stuttgart in the fall of 1918 after Münzenberg
was released from jail and expelled from Switzerland.
This proved abortive, however, as Münzenberg was soon
re-arrested in Germany. It was not until the following
July, when he was released again, that it became possible
to resume publication. The twelfth issue appeared in
July 1919, and it continued as a monthly, becoming the
organ of the Communist Youth International with the
November 1919 issue.

21 The youth international was not invited to the Zimmerwald
conference. The presence of the Swedish and Norwegian
delegates, who were leaders of their youth organizations,
was thought to be sufficient (Schüller, *Von den Anfängen*
... 145). Upon the urging of the Bolsheviks, Münzenberg
was invited to the second conference, in Kienthal in
April 1916, as representative of the IUSYO. Münzenberg
apparently had become peeved at the Russians and would
not let a representative of the Bolsheviks participate
in the first session of the International Bureau in
Zurich, 1-2 February 1916. It was reported to Lenin in
January that Münzenberg could not forgive the Bolsheviks
because they had 'behaved badly' since the Bern conference (Mukhamedzhanov, 9, quotes a letter of 30 January
1916 from Lenin to M.M. Kharitonov, and the latter's
response, concerning the forthcoming meeting of the youth
international's International Bureau). On 5 February the
International Bureau met in a joint session with the
Zimmerwald Commission (International Socialist Commission).

young people, as well as to associate the youth international with the cause of peace. A series of annual International Youth Days was held, the first in early October 1915, and the succeeding ones in early September of each year.[22] These took the form of demonstrations, rallies, meetings, and speeches designed to generate enthusiasm among youth. In 1915, socialist youth in all countries were called upon to take part in the 'revolutionary struggle for peace and freedom' by participating as speakers in meetings, distributing publications, and agitating in schools, factories, and elsewhere. Demonstrations were to be held for peace and socialism. In 1916 the slogans urged that the only way to end the war and prevent a new one was through revolutionary mass actions and the acquisition of political power by the working class. Support for disarmament was regarded as the best anti-militarist tactic. Acquiring a still more radical tone, the call in 1917 asserted that peace could be obtained only by the sharpest kind of revolutionary struggle against capitalist governments. While socialist youth in the belligerent countries were to redouble their propaganda efforts and prepare for great demonstrations and mass actions, socialist youth in the neutral countries were to form the core of the youth international. In these countries, young socialists were to attempt to sharpen class antagonisms, demand demobilization, give financial support to socialist youth in the belligerent countries, and work for the 'practical realization of socialism.' This propaganda was directed as much against the socialist parties supporting the war as against the war itself.[23]

World War I was a turning point in the development of the socialist movement. Not only was an established way of life to be damaged beyond repair, but the credibility of the existing system barely survived. These weaknesses were to enable socialism in Europe to develop, in spite of its many inner conflicts, into the powerful political force of today.

22 This was continued in later years by both the Communist Youth International and its rival socialist youth internationals. See Schönhaar, *Der Internationale Jugendtag* (Berlin 1922; Vienna 1925)
23 The manifestos issued for these occasions are in Münzenberg, *Die sozialistische Jugendorganisationen* ... 219-21 224-7, 227-9.

The war was also to lead the young socialists to the conclusion that if their ideals were to be realized, they must
take the initiative themselves. They could not rely on the
socialist parties to remain true to the revolutionary pre-
scriptions for social change inspired by Marx. The spontaneous tradition of independence from before the war was
thus strengthened and reinforced. On the foundation of this
tradition, which found its most symbolic expression in the
youth international, a strong, independent, politicized,
and orthodox Marxist youth movement was to develop in Western
and Central Europe. This was to become the communist youth
movement in 1919, when the IUSYO was transformed into the
Communist Youth International. All that is past may not
necessarily be prologue. Nevertheless, it is clear that
when it was formed, there were strong ties between the
Communist Youth International and what had gone before.

2

Factional struggles and the socialist youth

Opposition to the war and a general commitment to 'revolutionary socialism' formed the basis for the development of the socialist youth international after 1915. Several basic issues of principle, however, lay behind these broad points of agreement. Left for the most part unarticulated or unexplored was what it meant, in terms of strategies, tactics, and organization, to be a revolutionary socialist, and what the role of the youth movement was to be after the war.

Political neutrality

Debilitating doctrinal and factional conflict had not disappeared from the socialist movement, in fact the war only intensified it. The youth movement, however, succeeded until the end of the war in remaining essentially apart from it. Action rather than issue oriented, the young socialists had little interest in doctrinal questions. Their attention was occupied by demonstrations against the war, efforts to spread the gospel of revolutionary socialism, and the struggle to preserve or maintain organizational and political independence from the parties. The leadership was unwilling to confront these questions forthrightly for fear of disrupting the 'revolutionary solidarity' that had developed among the young socialists. It was pointless to do so in any event, for as long as the war continued there were no opportunities for pursuing the struggle for sociali~

The centrists encouraged this aloofness from the contentious doctrinal questions. Robert Danneberg, the Austrian centrist youth leader, wrote in the first issue of *Jugend-Internationale* in September 1915 that 'hard necessity will bring the workers together after the war, and the new

International will stand on a firmer basis than ever before. It does not lie with the proletarian youth to mix in the conflicts of the parties. The youth movement can only suffer damage by so doing.' The left, however, was pushing the young socialists continuously towards involvement. Lenin was particularly astute in this regard. He won a sympathetic audience for his views by encouraging the young socialists' insistence on organizational independence. In order to separate the youth from the 'bad' (reformist) and 'confused' (centrist) ideas of the adults, 'we must advocate the unconditional *organizational independence* of the youth organizations, not only because the opportunists fear this independence, but also because ... without full independence the youth will neither be in a position to become good socialists, nor prepared to carry socialism forward.'[1] Lenin omitted deliberately any reference to *political* independence, for the young socialists were expected to fall obediently into place behind the leadership of the Bolsheviks and their supporters.

Although the youth movement for the most part refused to be drawn into these controversies within the anti-war movement, it could not ignore them. Too many of the issues impinged upon the activities or aspirations of the young socialists. One of these that had emerged already at Bern was the question of how to prevent future wars. A long discussion on anti-war tactics took place after Bern in the pages of *Jugend-Internationale*. The new organ of the youth international became the major outlet for the divergent views of the entire anti-war movement. The debate on tactics focused on the future: on how peace could be maintained after the war.

The Bern conference had approved, over the opposition of a sizable leftist minority, a demand for complete disarmament.[2] Nothing was resolved by this decision, however. On the extreme left, Lenin was condemning disarmament and compulsory international arbitration because they assumed the continued existence of capitalist states and 'imperialist diplomacy.' Only through the revolutionary overthrow of capitalism and the ending of imperialist wars could real peace be established. The vast majority of socialists from the right and centre, however, supported compulsory arbi-

1 *Sotsial-Demokrat* 2 (December 1916): 116-20
2 *Berner Tagwacht*, 17 April 1915, 1

tration and measures for limiting armaments. The right did
so because it saw these measures as steps toward the reform
of capitalist society. The centre's position was determined
by the pacifist nature of its adherents, and an unwillingness to accept the *violent* revolutionary tactics of the left.
In the middle were those who, because of strong pacifist influences, supported disarmament and were somewhere between
left and centre. The Scandinavian left, the Swiss youth organization, Henriette Roland-Holst and a minority in the
Dutch left (the Tribunists), and some of the Polish left
were included in this group.

Lenin recognized the youth international publicly for the
first time at the end of 1916 in the context of this debate
on disarmament. In an article in *Sotsial-Demokrat* (December
1916) he said that because the 'social patriots' dominated
most socialist parties, 'the task of struggling for revolutionary internationalism ... has fallen to the union of socialist youth organizations.' While praising the revolutionar
attitude of *Jugend-Internationale*, he criticized it for its
'incorrect' position on disarmament, a view that failed to
appreciate the role of civil war in the future socialist
revolution. In an article in the September 1917 issue of
Jugend-Internationale, Lenin, now back in Russia, condemned
all disarmament schemes, and presented his arguments for
arming the proletariat and initiating a revolutionary civil
war. In the same issue, the Dutch revolutionary, van Amstel,
also argued against the advocates of disarmament on the
grounds that only when the proletariat comes to power would
disarmament become possible and peace assured.

As the war dragged on many young socialists, including
Willi Münzenberg, shed their pacifist inclinations and
turned away from disarmament. Münzenberg recognized, however,
that behind the arguments for disarmament lay an antipathy
to violence that was deeply rooted and persistent within
the socialist movement. Strong opposition remained in the
youth international to the militant tactics derived by the
left from its violence-laden perception of the revolutionary
process. One could not have avoided discussing future anti-
war tactics, but to have insisted on a decision, on conformity, would have been to split the youth movement. Lenin
was obviously not averse to splits and divisions. In fact,
he encouraged them so as to separate out the 'genuine' revolutionaries. Münzenberg saw things differently. He cast his
net far wider than Lenin in defining who was a revolutionary

and who not. His main criterion was psychological. Lenin put
great weight on finding those who would support the 'correct'
strategy, tactics, and organizational forms; Münzenberg always looked first and foremost simply for revolutionary ardour and an enthusiasm for 'action.' Thus, Münzenberg was
preoccupied during the war with holding all young revolutionaries together in the youth international, preparing to
take advantage of the possibilities for action when the war
finally ended.[3]

As the political divisions crystallized gradually during
the war into three main factions - right-socialist, Zimmerwald majority (centrist), and the leftist minority at
Zimmerwald (Zimmerwald left) - the pressure on the socialist
youth to become involved politically became intense.[4] In the
fall of 1916 an incident involving Ernst Christiansen,
leader of the Danish youth organization and later one of the
founders of the Danish communist party, brought the tension

3 Münzenberg apparently was won away from disarmament at
   the second conference of the anti-war opposition, in
   Kienthal, Switzerland, in April 1916. While the conference resolution on peace rejected general disarmament
   and pacifism, it did not subscribe to the leftist view
   of revolutionary civil war. The majority of the opposition as a whole remained advocates of some form of arms
   limitation. The Kienthal resolution appeared shortly
   after the conference in *Jugend-Internationale* (*J-I*),
   along with an article criticizing it and arguing for the
   leftist position. No mention was made of disarmament.
      In February 1917, before the return to Russia, Lenin
   and Radek sought to pressure Münzenberg into having the
   Swiss youth organization adopt officially the standpoint
   to which he himself had been converted: a social transformation through an armed uprising as the best means
   for assuring peaceful relations among states. Münzenberg
   resisted, however, feeling that the time was not yet
   ripe for such a step. He endeavoured to convince Lenin
   and Radek that the youth movement would be destroyed if
   it were pushed too fast in this direction (Fritz Brupbacher,
   Zürich während Krieg und Landesstreik, 53-4).
4 Discussion of the factional rifts in the socialist movement during and after the war can be found in Fainsod,
   International Socialism and the World War, and Cole,
   Communism and Social Democracy, 1914-1931.

within the youth movement into the open. In September the
reformist Danish social-democratic party had voted overwhelmingly to approve the participation of socialists in a
national government. Christiansen had taken what to Münzenberg was an irresolute attitude. Why had the young Danish
socialists not blocked, or opposed more vigorously, this
action by the party? In view of the youth international's
support for revolutionary socialism, and its adamant opposition to any socialist cooperation with bourgeois governments, Münzenberg asked for an explanation. Christiansen
apparently had felt that spirited opposition to the party
decision might well have led to a split in the socialist
movement in Denmark. Accepting the position of the Zimmerwald majority, he was not willing to take this step. Although an inter-Scandinavian conference of young socialists
declared that it could not approve in principle 'the attitude of Comrade Christiansen towards "minister-socialism"
at the last Danish party congress,' it nevertheless recognized that the 'current situation inside the international
socialist movement ... requires the unconditional unity of
all organizations and tendencies which really stand on the
principles of the socialist class struggle.'[5]

The strains imposed by the factional controversies surfaced once again the following spring. By this time various
peace efforts were under way within the socialist movement
to which the young socialists had to respond. For some,
such as the Danes, ending the war took precedence over all
other considerations. An extremist position reflected the
influence of Lenin and an erosion of the political neutrality that had been maintained so assiduously by the young
socialists. It was held by some of the leaders of the Swedish
movement and Münzenberg, who by now had moved close to the
Bolsheviks. This view not only rejected the pacifism of the
Danes, but insisted on a break with the International
Socialist Bureau in the Hague and the erection of a new
International. The large majority, however, was not willing
to go quite so far against the Zimmerwald majority (centrist
position. The majority of young socialists remained at this
time committed to 'revolutionary socialism' and to a struggle
against the 'social patriots.' But, it could not as yet see
any benefit from openly shattering the tradition of 'proletarian internationalism' by creating a new International.

5 *J-I*, 1 March 1917, 10

The International Bureau in May 1917 was thus able to preserve the status quo within the youth international, despite
the increasing penetration of leftist ideas. Although not
appreciated at the time, the International Bureau took a
position on the activities of the youth movement that was
to have the most serious of consequences. The IUSYO was to
continue as an independent political movement engaged in
'international actions' and supporting with all means 'the
revolutionary elements ... [in each country in their] struggle
against the [bourgeois] governments and the social patriots,
with the youth assuming the lead in this struggle.'⁶ One
may note here the incipient 'avant-gardism' which was by
1919 to characterize the way in which the young revolutionaries defined their role and mission, and which was to lead
to the sharp confrontation between the generations (a focal
point of this study).

6 Schüller, *Von den Anfängen* ... 150. A report of the
International Bureau meeting is in *J-I*, 1 September 1917,
15-20. After the transfer of ISC (International Socialist
Commission, or Zimmerwald Commission) to Stockholm in
1917 and the resignation of Robert Grimm as secretary,
the youth international began to receive considerable
financial assistance. With Zeth Höglund in control of
the ISC, and with the International Bureau of the IUSYO
moving closer to the Zimmerwald left, the two bodies enjoyed more cordial relations than had been the case when
the centrist Grimm had run the ISC.
    The resolution of the International Bureau session is
in Schüller, 149-50; *J-I*, 1 September 1917, 18-19; and
Münzenberg, *Die sozialistische Jugendorganisationen* ...
218-19. Münzenberg's views on the negotiations for an international socialist conference reflected his association
with Lenin in Zurich, and were an extension of efforts
he had been making for some time to promote a third conference of the Zimmerwald movement. As far back as January
1917 he had sent letters to Grimm calling on the ISC to
adopt a more radical, anti-'social patriot' policy, and
to convene a conference to discuss the attitude to be
taken toward the various parties. Supported by the Swedes,
he called for an open break with the International Socialist Bureau in The Hague (see the relevant correspondence
in the papers of Robert Grimm in the International Institute for Social History, Amsterdam).

Looking ahead, the International Bureau had decided at
its first meeting in Zurich in February 1916 to convene a
genuine international youth conference in Brussels immediately upon cessation of hostilities. In preparation for this
post-war conference, the secretariat was directed to work
out a draft Declaration of Principles and to submit it to
member organizations for discussion.[7] The draft, prepared
by Münzenberg, was first published in the December 1916
issue of *Jugend-Internationale*. It was intended by the
International Bureau to be a provisional program. Adoption
of a final version was to await the post-war conference of
all socialist youth organizations.

This program for the most part confined itself to the
traditional concerns of the youth movement - economic protection, anti-militarism, recruitment, and education. Indi-
cative of the politicization of the movement, however, and

Münzenberg travelled with Grimm through Germany to
Stockholm in late April 1917, on his way to the meeting
of the International Bureau. Grimm was going to work out
the details of the transfer of the ISC from Switzerland
to Stockholm (Buber-Neumann, in *Von Potsdam nach Moskau*,
wrongly states that Münzenberg travelled with Lenin in
the 'sealed car;' Münzenberg, in *Die Dritte Front*,
wrongly puts the International Bureau session in August).
Münzenberg was thus caught up in the backwash of the
'Grimm affair' in June 1917. He was linked with Grimm
in some Swiss papers as an agent of the German government. The central committee of the Swiss Social Democratic Party cleared Münzenberg at a meeting in June.
He defended himself against the charges in an article
in the 1 September 1917 issue of *J-I*.

7 Münzenberg, *Die sozialistische Jugend-Internationale*, 48.
The International Bureau decided to expand its membership
by adding representatives from Sweden and Austria, with
Zeth Höglund and Robert Danneberg to fill these positions.
Representatives from Denmark, Norway, Italy, Switzerland,
and the German anti-war opposition (Bertha Thalheimer)
participated, in addition to Münzenberg. It also was
agreed unanimously that the emphasis in the work of the
youth organizations was to be on revolutionary anti-
militarist propaganda and the struggle to protect the
young workers economically (Münzenberg, *Die Dritte Front*,
210).

the success of the pre-war radicals, was the insistence that
education of young socialists must include participation in
political activities such as strikes, demonstrations, and
electoral campaigns. The youth international would be reshaped
after the war so as to assure 'the introduction and carrying
out of common actions to strengthen international solidarity
[among socialist youth] and [the revival of] the capacity
for struggle [against capitalism] in individual countries
... and the education and preparation of young workers for
the social revolution.[8]

The declaration was clearly an expression of a point of
view around which almost all members of the youth international could unite. Emphasizing principles and generalities
on which all revolutionary, anti-war socialists could agree,
its purpose was to preserve the centre/left coalition.
Münzenberg, while moving closer to the Bolsheviks, remained
convinced that differences over ways and means should not
be allowed to disrupt the newly formed revolutionary unity.
This solidarity was crucial to Münzenberg for it would,
after the war, make it possible for the youth movement to
play a key role in the anticipated social revolution. By
mid 1918 all members of the IUSYO had accepted the declaration except for the Austrians, and even their hesitation was
on procedural, not substantive grounds.[9] As could be expected,
Lenin was not at all pleased that the declaration avoided
any trace of factional controversy, apart from its clear but
general support for 'revolutionary socialism' against the
dominant reformism in the movement. Tartly rebuking Münzenberg, Lenin expressed his displeasure because the declaration, as well as the editorial policy of *Jugend-Internationale*,
failed to make a clear distinction between party tendencies.
It did not come out clearly for the left against the right
and centre.[10]

The Russian revolution in March 1917 only heightened the
factional tensions. It was greeted with great enthusiasm by
Jugend-Internationale in its May 1917 issue. Prominently
featured was Karl Radek's assertion that the era of social

8 *J-I*, 1 December 1916, 3
9 Münzenberg, who agreed that the final decision on a program would have to await the end of the war, saw no reason for pressing for Austrian agreement. See *Der Jugendliche
Arbeiter*, January 1920, 8
10 *Sotsial-Demokrat* 2 (December 1916): 116-20

revolution in Europe had now begun. This, of course, was just what the young socialists wanted to hear. The same issue also contained the first article by Lenin, a reprint of his 'Parting Letter to the Swiss Workers.' While *Jugend-Internationale* continued to maintain a neutral position after the March revolution in Russia, and particularly after the second session of the International Bureau in May, it now began to feature articles by leading Bolsheviks, including Lenin, Trotsky, Radek, Kollontai, and others.

In November 1917 the Bolshevik revolution reverberated throughout the European socialist movement. Greeted with enthusiasm by the extreme left, it also was looked upon with favour, in varying degrees, by a broad spectrum of socialists extending even into the right. Developments in Russia aroused the hopes and elevated the aspirations of other socialists, and emboldened them to more aggressive action. The result, of course, was sharp conflict with governmental authority. Münzenberg and his fellow anti-war activists in the secretariat were arrested for their part in demonstrations in support of the Bolsheviks, and against the war, which took place in Switzerland in and after November 1917.[11] Although the Swiss youth organization eventually provided other functionaries to man the secretariat, the youth international was without any effective leadership until the middle of 1918.

As the tragedy of war drew to its bitter end, the socialist youth movement was emerging as a vital force. Much of the younger generation, by nature critical and skeptical, increasingly had lost faith in the prospects for social change from within the existing system. The youth organizations in all countries grew enormously as hostilities ceased. Young socialists, now politicized and radicalized, vehemently anti-capitalist and anti-militarist, were engaging directly, through their own organizations, in the struggle to shape post-war society. They were determined to have a say in shaping their own future. Under these conditions, the political neutrality cultivated so carefully by the youth international could not persist. As political activity, now free from wartime restraints, intensified and interest turned to the shape of post-war society, the substance of the doctrinal

11 See *Bericht des Ersten Staatsanwaltes A. Brunner* ... for these events. See also *Staatsarchiv des Kantons Zürich* ... for these events and biographical material on Münzenberg.

and factional disputes became more immediately relevant. No
longer were the divisive issues theoretical and abstract;
they were now concrete political questions. In addition to
a commitment to action, a radicalized young worker or student had to come to some decision over what it meant to be
a revolutionary socialist. He had to decide how and for what
immediate purposes, he was to be active. One had to choose
between conflicting interpretations and demands.

Divisions had become even more acute at the end of the
war than ever before. The Bolsheviks had succeeded in com-
pleting a revolution in Russia. Rejecting Bolshevik tactics
completely, and denouncing the notion of a dictatorship of
the proletariat, the right-socialists supported parliamentary democracy and became vehemently anti-Bolshevik. In the
eyes of the left, the right-socialists remained 'lackeys of
capitalism.' In the middle remained the centrists, still a
far from homogeneous group of basically pacifist socialists
who wished to maintain the traditional solidarity of the
working class. The irreconcilable antagonism between right
and left, however, eventually split the centrists. Disagreement with the Bolsheviks on tactics and organizational questions caused the 'right-centrists' to de-emphasize the dictatorship of the proletariat. They were for revolution, but
only as a spontaneous expression of a united and class-
conscious proletariat. When such a condition failed to develop they began to turn to the right. The 'left-centrists,'
on the other hand, had become more revolutionary as the war
went on and, impressed by the successes of the Bolsheviks
in Russia, were moved towards militancy. The larger number
of centrists, however, remained in the middle, supporting
revolution in principle, but not necessarily approving
Bolshevik tactics, and still hoping for reconciliation between
all the factions.

The final, and inevitable, break came when the Bolsheviks
moved to implement their long-sought project for a new
Third International that would effectively exclude all right-
socialists. With communist parties beginning to form in many
countries, and in fear of losing the initiative to the right-
socialists, the Bolsheviks hastily founded the Communist
International (Comintern) in Moscow in March 1919.

The young socialists were now pitched headlong into party
debates. Neutrality was no longer possible. It was not certain, however, that the young socialists would be able to
agree on doctrinal issues, or unite in support of one faction.

It remained to be seen if enthusiasm for revolutionary change was sufficient to keep the youth movement together. More concretely, the youth international had to make a decision concerning membership in the new International. On 29 May 1919, the Executive Committee of the Communist International (ECCI) had appealed to all socialist youth organizations to unite and join the new International.[12] Could all members of the youth international heed this call?

Resolution of these uncertainties depended upon developments within the individual youth organizations themselves. It was especially on events within the revived socialist youth movements in Austria, France, and Germany, all of which had been relatively quiescent before November 1918 because of their countries' participation in the war, as well as within the Italian youth movement, that attention now focused. It was in these countries that political and social unrest gave the greatest hope for an extension of the 'international proletarian revolution' begun in Russia.

Status of youth organizations

Austria
By the time the efforts to convene the long-awaited conference of the IUSYO were coming to a head in the fall of 1919, the Austrian socialist movement had been split irreparably.[1] The large majority of young socialists remained in the existing youth organization (Verband der sozialistischen Arbeiterjugend Deutsch-Österreichs - VSAJ) and accepted the politics of the centrist Austrian socialist party. The centrists conceived of the revolutionary struggle for socialism essentially as one without violence and with full respect for democratic procedures and civil rights. Much educational or 'consciousness-raising' work had yet to be done before the mass movement necessary for a socialist revolution could be established. A very small minority of leftists, eager to

12 *Die Kommunistische Internationale* 2 (1919): 109-10. 'Now the hour has arrived to organize a [new, communist] youth international.' The left wing of the IUSYO was included by the new Executive Committee of the Comintern (ECCI) with those (Spartakists, Bolsheviks, Dutch 'Tribunists') it considered as constituting the core of the new Third International (ibid., 1 [1919]: 40-5).
13 *Der Jugendliche Arbeiter*, December 1919, 10

impose a revolution on Austria, rejected any accommodation
with the new bourgeois republic and formed a communist youth
organization (Verband der kommunistischen Proletarierjugend
- VKPJ).

The young Austrian centrists sympathized with the intention of the new Bolshevik regime in Russia to build a socialist society. In principle they accepted most of the *aims*
of the Communist International. They had serious doubts,
however, about the prospects for immediate implementation
of the revolutionary goals, as well as about the methods
the Bolsheviks were using, methods which the Austrians
feared the Bolsheviks were in the process of imposing upon
the revolutionary movement everywhere. Whatever the inadequacies of Hapsburg rule, the Austrian socialist movement
never developed a taste for violence or a readiness to force
a revolution through to completion in the Leninist fashion.
The members of the VSAJ separated themselves quite sharply
from the communists. They insisted that the youth organization be an independent supplement to a united socialist
party, and not a 'young party' in competition with it.[14]
The primary mission of the youth organization was to help
prepare the way for revolution by developing the revolutionary class consciousness of the young workers.

The doctrinal and factional controversies that had led
to the formation of two revolutionary socialist youth organizations were to complicate the question of Austrian
membership in the youth international. The VSAJ had been
a founding member of the IUSYO. Nevertheless, the VKPJ
claimed to be the only youth organization in Austria that
fit the requirements for membership in the Communist International. Even those preparing for the conference of the
IUSYO remained uncertain if, by following the Communist
International, the other socialist youth organizations
would be expected to choose between the VSAJ and the VKPJ.
As events were to show, membership in the youth international was to be determined strictly on the basis of factional considerations.

14 Ibid., January 1920, 8. See also *Proletarier-Jugend*, 1
   January 1920, 4-6, and Thaller, *Die Internationale* ...
   especially 13 and 19

France

By July 1918 the majority in the national committee of the
French party (SFIO) was for ending the war. It also condemned intervention against the new Bolshevik regime in
Russia. This attitude had been anticipated by the youth
organization in June, when its national congress had elected
an anti-war national committee.[15]

The transformed youth organization was centrist in character. A large majority at the second congress in April 1919
voted for continuing the close association with the SFIO,
in which Jean Longuet and the centrists were the dominant
faction. Representatives from the left had advocated autonomy, primarily to allow the youth organization to dissociate itself from party policy and join the new Third International. The supporters of the Comintern in the youth organization soon formed a 'Committee for Autonomy' (Comité
pour l'autonomie des Jeunesses socialistes et leur adhesion
a la IIIe Internationale) to work for independence of the
youth organization from the party.[16] Thus, by the end of
1919 the communists were still a minority within the French
socialist youth movement, seeking to transform it into a
communist youth organization and win it for the Comintern.

Italy

The socialist youth organization in Italy was formed in
1901 on the Belgian model.[17] It was, in the pre-war years,
independent of the party and trade unions, although it received their support. The conflict between youth organization and party over independence for the former did not become acute in Italy. An attempt in July 1912 by the reformist

15 *Die Jugend der Revolution* ... 480-1
16 The 'Committee for Autonomy' was an offshoot of the
'Committee for the Communist International' within the
SFIO, which in turn was the successor to the 'Committee
for the Resumption of International Relations' established by those French socialists (Merrheim, Bouderon)
who had participated in the Zimmerwald conference in
1915. The 'Committee for Autonomy' drew most of its
strength from the Paris area.
17 Münzenberg, *Die sozialistische Jugendorganisationen*
... 17-20, 142-6

in the party to dissolve the youth organization was defeated. Acting independently, young socialists participated in the continuing struggle between the reformists and the revolutionaries in the party, supporting only those parliamentary candidates who had an active anti-militarist policy.

After the entry of Italy into the war the socialists continued their anti-war activities. This resulted in harassment and repressive measures by the government and a serious disruption of the work of the youth organization. In the summer of 1917 the central committee of the socialist party, the trade-union leadership, and the socialist parliamentary faction met in Milan to work out a program of action for the post-war period. The central committee of the youth organization, supported by the membership, disagreed with the decision of the Milan conference to work for a republic.[18] Its continued support of revolution and a dictatorship of the proletariat quickly led to conflict between the youth organization and the party leaders.

These differences were sharpened when the party parliamentary faction refused to send a representative to the September 1917 youth congress in Florence on the grounds that the youths were 'Bolshevik.'[19] A joint session of the youth organization central committee and the secretariat of the party in early February 1918 simply 'agreed to disagree.'

After the war, and particularly at the national congress in Rome in October 1919, several tendencies appeared in the Italian socialist youth movement:[20]

1) the 'pure' communists or abstentionists (communist astensionisti), led by Giuseppe Berti, who followed the 'ultra-left' position of Bordiga and abstention from participation in parliamentary elections and trade-union activity;
2) the maximalists (massimalisti elezionisti), led by the secretary of the youth organization, Luigi Polano, and

18 *J-I*, 1 September 1917, 12-13
19 *Zirkularschreiben der internationalen Verbindung sozialistischer Jugendorganisationen* 1 (15 March 1918)
20 *Die Kommunistische Internationale* 4/5 (1920): 143, and *Internationale Jugend-Korrespondenz*, 20 September 1921, 3-4 (hereafter cited as *IJK*)

following Serrati in the party, who were for seizure of power by the proletariat, the formation of soviets, and maximum unity in the socialist movement, and were followers of the Comintern in economic and parliamentary tactics[21];
3) the youth group associated with the newspaper *l'Ordine nuovo* in Turin, which emphasized the importance of factory councils; and
4) the centrists (massimalisti unitaria), led by Masotti, who - following the positon of Lazzari in the party - were for workers' soviets and the dictatorship of the proletariat, but against violence and any split in the socialist movement.

There were no right, or reform socialists, followers of Turati, to speak of in the youth movement. In 1919 there was still wide support from all the factions for the Third International and a commitment to 'revolution.' It was not until early 1921 that the factional controversies began to resolve themselves with the expulsion of all who did not support the Comintern unconditionally.

Germany
The outcome of the factional conflict in the German youth movement was to have a decisive impact on developments within the youth international. The first national social-ist youth organization had been formed under party and trade-union aegis in 1908: the Zentralstelle für die arbeit-ende Jugend Deutschlands. It functioned under the control of party and trade-union leaders up to, during, and after the war, and it never joined the youth international (IUSYO). Centres of opposition to its policy of non-involvement in politics existed primarily in Berlin, Hamburg, Dresden, and Stuttgart, but until World War I they remained within the organization as disunited and dissident voices.[22]

21 Polano is mistakenly identified as an abstentionist in one source (Cammett, *Antonio Gramsci* ... 69, 143). More accurately, he was a maximalist who moved to a left-maximalist position in 1920 in accord with Bombacci and Misiano in the party
22 *J-I*, 1 October 1917, 12-13. See Schorske, *German Social Democracy, 1905-1917*, 97-108, for the independent, radi-cal character of the youth movement in 1908. In 1912 a discussion flared within the youth movement on the issue of independence from the party (SPD). The opposition,

During the war, the anti-war opposition was divided into two factions. One, the more radical left wing, favoured an immediate break with the old 'Zentralstelle' (AJ) and the formation of an independent revolutionary youth organization despite restrictions imposed by law and military authorities.[23] The other, and by far the larger, followed the centre; its emphasis was on unity of the opposition as a separate faction within the movement.

Both left and centre rejected the paternalistic 'recruiting school,' educational nature of the pre-war German socialist youth movement. They wished to form a political organization active in improving the conditions of young workers and conducting anti-militarist propaganda. The centre, however, did not believe that youth organizations should intervene in party matters, or involve themselves in disputes over strategy and tactics. Both factions were able to cooperate at the beginning of the war, despite their differences, on the basis of an anti-war, anti-government, anti-majority socialist program.[24]

---

arguing that the youth must of necessity become involved in party affairs, sought freedom from what they considered to be the confining policies of the party and trade unions. The discussion was carried on between the then leaders of the youth organization in the pages of the party theoretical journal, *Die Neue Zeit*. See also Heinzelmann, *Die Organisation der sozialistische Jugend*

23 In 1907 the Reichstag drafted a law regulating political associations (Reichsvereinsgesetz), which applied to all of Germany. Paragraph seventeen prohibited all under eighteen from belonging to political groups and attending political meetings. This draft was passed into law in April 1908.

24 The secretariat in Zurich supported, after the Bern conference, the German opposition groups both morally, and financially, *Jugend-Internationale* was smuggled into Germany and distributed illegally. It became the organ of the entire opposition movement within the German socialist party, with contributions coming from various opposition leaders in Germany. Much correspondence was passed secretly back and forth between Germany and Switzerland. See *Deutschlands Junge Garde* ... and Sieger, *Die junge Front*

By the end of October 1918 the opposition had agreed to
split from the 'Zentralstelle' and join in forming the Free
Socialist Youth of Germany (Freie Sozialistische Jugend
Deutschlands - FSJ). Rather than resolving the tensions,
this step paradoxically marked the beginning of a period
in which the differences among the young anti-war socialists
intensified to the point where they finally split into
several competing organizations. Just as the opposition
group in the youth movement was uniting, the opposition in
the party was breaking apart. Centre and left in the party
had joined in April 1917 to form a new party, the Independent Social Democratic Party (USPD). The formation of the
Communist Party of Germany (KPD) in December 1918 forced
the youth movement to face for the first time strategic and
tactical questions, and created a crisis within the FSJ.
The young revolutionary socialists now had to decide if they
should affiliate with one of the two existing revolutionary
parties - KPD and USPD. This meant coming to grips with the
question of what it meant to be a revolutionary socialist.

The revolution in Germany had overthrown the monarchy and
installed, provisionally, a socialist government. The factional differences within the socialist movement now took
on a new form and the labels left, centre, and right acquired new meanings. These were concerned with the nature
of the system that was to replace the overthrown monarchy,
and how it was to be achieved. The majority socialists, who
included almost all of the old right, were reform socialists.
They were pleased with the overthrow of the old system,
wished for a democratic republic, and supported the early
convening of a constituent assembly to ratify the new order.
The left, advocating the overthrow, violently if necessary,
of the entire 'bourgeois' state, was itself divided. Most
of the left, including most of the Freie Sozialistische Jugend,
were for dispensing with a constituent assembly and, optimis-
tically and enthusiastically, for carrying out the revolution, as a minority if necessary. The spontaneously formed
workers' and soldiers' councils would assume full powers. A
small minority on the left, most notably Rosa Luxemburg and
most of the Spartakist movement, opposed in principle this
anarcho-syndicalist 'ultra-left' and its refusal to participate in the trade unions and the elections to parliamentary
institutions. Nevertheless, even Rosa Luxemburg was swept
along the path to open revolution in January 1919.

The centre was the most heterogeneous of all the factions.
Composed as it was of pacifists, anti-militarists, revolutionary socialists, and sympathizers of the Bolsheviks in
Russia, it was never a unified movement. Most supported the
idea of 'proletarian revolution,' while eschewing violence
and supporting democratic procedures. A majority favoured
fundamental reforms, a new social order based on workers'
councils, and ultimately the convening of a constituent
assembly. Under no circumstances was it ready to join the
left in an armed uprising should that be the only way to
bring about the desired goal. Some on the left wing were
inclined to join the communists in an armed struggle for
power. It was this segment that the communists later courted
as it grew in strength. The majority, however, continued to
resist calls for revolutionary action when it became clear
that there was no widespread support for such action within
the working class or the population at large. This new right/
centre/left configuration tended to mirror the three socialist parties: SPD/USPD/KPD.

It was the reluctance of the USPD to press for continuation of the revolution that led the second FSJ congress in
February 1919 to declare its support for the KPD.[25] Under
the powerful anarcho-syndicalist influence of Otto Rühle,
the majority of participants were led to anticipate a
sharpening of the revolutionary situation, despite earlier
defeats. It supported the workers' and soldiers' councils,
the immediate violent overthrow of the bourgeois state,
and the establishment of a dictatorship of the proletariat.
This decision, however, did not reflect a unanimity of outlook within the FSJ. Thus, the period from February to
October 1919 was one of struggle at the local level between
supporters of the KPD and supporters of the USPD; among the
KPD supporters, there was a struggle for control of the organization.[26]

The FSJ flourished in the months following the end of the
war. It grew into a strange collection of all young people
who considered themselves revolutionary, and who were in

25 The best sources on the congress are *Die Jugend der
Revolution*, 365-6, which contains the resolution on the
relations with the parties and the basic theses, and
Die Junge Garde, 5 March 1919 (hereafter cited as *JG*).
26 *Die Jugend der Revolution*, 367-80

any way rebelling against the existing order. The members
were exposed to a mélange of ideas and calls to action.
Anarchism, syndicalism, Marxism, bolshevism, and the
ideas of Luxemburg, Liebknecht, Rühle, Kautsky, and others
all had some effect on the young socialists in Germany.
The older leaders and functionaires, in their twenties,
and those coming from the schools and universities, were
probably able to arrive at more reasoned decisions when
comparing the ideas competing for influence over the working
class and the socialist movement. Committed to revolution
and some notion of socialism, the political views of the
large majority were rather unsophisticated. They remained
divided on the same contentious issues that had existed
during the war - the necessity for violence, the role of
the youth movement, and organizational forms - as well as
the new issues of strategy and tactics. Thus, encompassing
as it did the most politicized and radicalized elements in
the younger generation, a large majority in the FSJ was
drawn naturally to the KPD, which at this time demonstrated
the most aggressive commitment to revolution among all
German socialist parties.

During these months of great internal stress in 1919,
members of the FSJ were active in various ways. The FSJ was
seeking to publicize its ideas, develop 'revolutionary class
consciousness,' and win more members.[27] A major effort was
made to secure the election of FSJ supporters as local
leaders (jugendliche Vertrauensleute) in the factories,
schools, and shops. A program of 'demands,' which the FSJ
leadership hoped would incite the mass of young workers and
students to struggle for a proletarian dictatorship, was
widely propagated. The strike movement in the Berlin continuation schools (Fortbildungschule) during the summer of
1919 was a focal point of FSJ attention. In July, the
national committee emphasized the importance of strikes as
a weapon in the struggle for social demands. The FSJ grew
rapidly in early 1919, with the age group 14-17 soon becoming a majority.[28] This rapid growth ended later in 1919
as the anticipated revolution failed to materialize and the
Weimar republic was established instead. There was a loss

27 For these activities see *Deutschlands Junge Garde* ...
and Pietschmann, *Der politisch-ideologische Klärungsprozess* ... 60-88.
28 Ibid., 158-9

of interest among those whose hopes for an immediate revolution were not fulfilled. Furthermore, the right-socialist
SPD was beginning to revitalize its activities among young
workers.

While the leaders of the FSJ were defending the decision
to support the KPD, and to become active in party affairs,
they were also faced with a lively internal debate over the
use of parliamentary tactics. Some were for using parliamentary methods so long as the final struggle, 'the period
of direct revolutionary action,' had not begun. Many others,
however, perhaps most, rejected utilization of the existing
'bourgeois institutions.' Although the national committee
(Reichsausschuss) decided in mid July to treat the issue
as a tactical problem and not to make it part of a declaration of principles, it was within a year to lead to a bitter
split within communist ranks.[29]

29 The structure of the leading organs of the FSJ underwent
   some change over the years. A central executive committee
   (Zentralausschuss) of seven equal members, and a
   national committee (Reichsausschuss) formed out of the
   central executive committee and one delegate from each
   of the districts (Bezirke) and to meet quarterly, were
   included in the first statutes adopted by the second
   congress in February 1919 (see Richter, *Die Jugend und
   die sozialistischen Parteien*, 30-1). These organs super-
   seded the national executive committee (Reichsarbeit-
   sausschuss) that had been established at the first congress in October 1918. The only conditions for membership in the FSJ at this time were recognition of the
   Jena resolution of April 1916 (by which the revolutionary
   anti-war opposition agreed to form a loose faction
   within the 'Zentralstelle') and the theses as adopted
   by the FSJ. The fifth FSJ congress in December 1920 revised the statutes (*JG*, December 1920). The national
   committee was retained, and a new executive body
   (Reichszentrale) of nine replaced the central executive
   committee. The centralizing of the KJD after the second
   CYI congress in the summer of 1921 began at the sixth
   congress of the KJD in Halle in September 1921 (see
   Resolutionen und Richtlinien des 6. Reichskongress ...
   21-3). The two leading organs - Reichszentrale (or
   Zentrale) and national committee - remained, but the
   size of the former was now to be determined by each

Meanwhile, as the third FSJ congress met illegally in
Weimar in October, the process of 'clarification' within
the FSJ was reaching a climax.[30] An important leader of
the Russian Komsomol, Lazar Shatskin, was clandestinely
in Germany at this time. He brought to bear on the delegates the enormous prestige of the Bolshevik party. Following the Leninist line, he condemned the centrist views
of the USPD. He put the official Russian imprimatur on the
KPD as the only truly revolutionary party in Germany. The
FSJ should thus 'go with' the KPD, even though the anarchist and syndicalist elements, which he condemned, still
exercised a strong influence on the party. His insistence
on a break with the centre ran counter to the policy of
the new KPD leader, Paul Levi, who sought to broaden the
basis of communist support by appealing to the left wing
in the USPD.[31]

The second FSJ congress in February had declared that
it sympathized with the KPD, but it had not adopted the
KPD program as its own, nor had the leftists (communists)
broken completely with the centrists.[32] By October the
situation had changed. The Comintern had been formed and
was calling for all 'real' revolutionaries to break with

---

congress. The national committee was now to be formed
by representatives from the districts on a proportional
basis according to membership. In each delegation there
were to be some chosen by the district committee, and
some chosen by the district leadership (Bezirkszentrale).
Adopting the Russian terminology, a central committee
(Zentralkomitee) was created at the ninth congress in
1925 to replace the Reichszentrale.

30 *Die Junge Garde* (*JG*) was prohibited and the FSJ subjected to harassment as a result of the demonstrations
sponsored by the FSJ on 7 September, International
Youth Day.
31 See Lowenthal, 'The Bolshevization of the Spartakus
League,' in Footman (ed.), *International Communism*, 30ff
32 There had been some effort, primarily from the Bremen
Left Radicals and *Arbeiterpolitik*, to have the FSJ merge
with the forces of the left within the party even before
the founding of the KPD. It continued for some time
thereafter (Pietschmann, *Der politisch-ideologische
Klärungsprozess* ... 49-50).

both the right and centre.[33] Plans were well under way for the formation of a clearly communist youth international. Thus, by the time of the third FSJ congress, the FSJ leadership was determined to purge the organization of all non-communist elements. The congress indicated its support for the KPD as long as it pursued a clearly revolutionary policy. It called for a sharp struggle against the 'unclear' policies of the USPD.[34] The split was completed by the expulsion of all who opposed this position. By the time the international youth conference opened in early November, German socialist youth had been split and a mass organization committed to the new Third International had come to occupy a prominent place within the German socialist youth movement.

33 See the platform of the Comintern adopted at the first congress in Degras (ed.), *The Communist International* ... I, 23.
34 *J-I*, January 1920, 13-14; *Die Kommunistische Jugend*, 20 November 1919, 135; *Abriss der Geschichte der deutschen Arbeiterjugendbewegung* ... 232-3: and Pietschmann, *Der politisch-ideologische Klärungsprozess* ... for the divisions among the delegates. The proposal was made at the congress to change the name to Freie Kommunistische Jugend, but was rejected as many delegates could not work legally under an openly communist name. A name change would also have made it easier for the USPD leaders to mobilize opposition to the now communist FSJ.

3

Radicalism and revolution

The most important threads in the early history of the
Communist Youth International are those of political and
ideological conflict and the struggle for the control of
organizations. A closer look at the young socialists involved in these activities provides a more human dimension
to impersonal theoretical argumentation and formal institutions. It was not my intention to create a psychological
or sociological profile of the first young socialists. What
can be described, however, are the conditions that led
enormous numbers of young people to join socialist youth
organizations at the end of the war, as well as the personal histories of several of the movement's leaders. The
experiences of these individuals dramatize the forces at
work within the younger generation in Europe after World
War I.

During 1917 and 1918, the increasing hardship brought
on by the war was turning the population in belligerent
countries, especially the workers, in a more radical direction.[1] Demonstrations and strikes became more frequent and
more violent, and finally culminated in revolutions in
Germany and Austria in October/November 1918. Shortly there
after the war ended, leaving a situation of crisis and
political unrest in its wake throughout Europe.

Radicalization of the young

On 10 November 1918, a young munitions worker, Erich
Habersaath, was shot and killed during the German revoluti

1 For radicalization of the working class in France see
  Wohl, *French Communism* ... 114-22, 127-31.

45 Radicalism and revolution

He had only just been elected to the leadership of the
newly formed revolutionary youth organization, the Freie
Sozialistische Jugend (FSJ). In his eulogy, Karl Liebknecht,
soon himself to be martyred in the revolutionary cause,
spoke of new struggles and new victims. He urged all young
people to continue the struggle for a social revolution and,
if necessary, to die 'with the same firm resoluteness' as
had Habersaath.[2] His audience, both those present and those
to whom the message quickly spread, needed no encouragement.
They were already girded for battle, for the struggle to
carry through a socialist revolution.

There were several general reasons for the intensification
of political involvement and activism within the ranks of
young workers and socialist intellectuals. First and deepest
was the traumatic experience of World War I. Increasingly
severe economic conditions brought on by the war, especially
in the defeated countries, had the most disturbing effect
on daily life. Beneath the difficult problems of finding
work and daily bread, however, lay deeper and far longer
lasting influences. The unbelievable slaughter and carnage
that had occurred was to have a scarring impact on the
younger generation. It intensified the tradition of intense
anti-militarism and pacifism among the young socialists.
This anti-militarism was both a cause and an effect of the
bitter reaction of so many young people to the humanly de-
grading consequences of the war. It led to further condemnation of the captialist system and to bitter recriminations
against those socialists who, for whatever reasons, had
supported the war effort. It also led many young people,
primarily young workers and apprentices, but also many sons
of 'bourgeois intellectuals,' to join socialist youth organizations and support their radical leaders and programs.
The notion that if you destroyed capitalist society you
would also destroy the sources of war had a wider appeal
than ever before. This placed many who had developed within
a pacifist tradition, socialist or religious, in a para-
doxical position. Proponents of non-violence were committing
themselves to revolution and violence for the sake of peace.
For many, however, this seemed inevitable. To be effective,
pacifism had to be revolutionary. Later on, in 1919, the
creation of the Third International (the Comintern) provided
a universal, internationalist image that appealed to those

2 Fritz Globig, ... *aber verbunden sind wir mächtig*, 249

committed to the 'brotherhood of man' and to the 'joining
of hands' for peace; these were commitments that originally
had led many to pacifism. Perhaps for the first time a program and a justification for political action was provided
to those impatient 'to do something for peace.' In such a
way did pacifism and revolutionary socialism draw together.

The impact of the Russian revolution was a further source
of youthful radicalism. Tsarist Russia had been for years
the symbol of reactionary repression in European socialist
and liberal-democratic circles. To many young socialists
the Bolsheviks represented the most organized and committed
elements on the Russian scene. They *acted*, and did not just
talk, about peace and social justice. The Bolsheviks had
taken Russia out of the war. They had issued their Decree
on Peace, calling for a peace without annexations and in-
demnities and denouncing the imperialism of the secret
treaties between the entente powers. This affected many
young pacifists - for example, in the French-speaking areas
of Switzerland.[3] Once in power, the Bolsheviks had acted
according to their internationalist principles in contrast
to the right-socialists in 1914. Youthful enthusiasm for
'action,' for change, swept many into support of Bolshevik
promises and visions of a better world, in Russia and
throughout Europe. Soviet Russia came to be equated with a
clean, fresh start, and with the destruction of the old and
a turn to new forms and new values. The hostility of the
conservative regimes of the victorious powers, and their
intervention in support of the old Russian forces, produced
a wave of sympathy for the Soviet regime (but not necessaril
for the party as such) among the working classes in Europe.
Such expressions of sympathy came most easily from the youn{

Developments within the national labour and socialist move
ments also provided a stimulus to the radical turn after the
war. The association of most of the socialist and labour
leaders with reformism in practice, if not in theory, tendec
to discredit these leaders' more pragmatic, less apocalyptic
views of social and political change. Each to a greater or
lesser degree had been committed to working within the capitalist system and had been responsible for the general support that the socialist movements in the belligerent countr
had given to the national war effort. The Bolshevik charge
that the pre-war and wartime socialist leaders had been

3 Interview with Jules Humbert-Droz

traitors to the cause of proletarian internationalism and
the interests of the proletariat found considerable response
in the socialist youth movement.

Of much less importance for the formation of the attitudes of youth were the purely doctrinal or ideological disputes of the time. The fine points of these disputes reached
only a very thin layer of youth leaders who were also active
in the parties. The typical young radical was moved more
by a personal emotional experience, than by a reasoned intellectual decision on the merits of one or another doctrinal issue.

Thus, many turned to radical socialism from a deep moral
and spiritual rebellion against the social reality in which
they developed to young adulthood. Ignazio Silone (who was
known under his real name, Secondino Tranquilli, while in
the youth movement) has provided us with a revealing self-
portrait of a young man who in 1917, at age seventeen,
joined the Italian socialist youth movement with a view of
society that originated in his early childhood and 'which,
as it later on assumed a political form, was bound to re-
veal itself as radical.' The cruelty of existing social
distinctions in the mountainous district of southern Italy
where he grew up, the observed hypocrisy and deceit in the
separation of moral values from daily social relations,
the corruption of liberal principles and democratic processes by those social relations, the association of the
State with 'swindling, intrigue, and privilege,' and the
unwillingness of adults, even those in whom he saw high
moral qualities, to become 'involved' - all led Silone to
a 'moral mutiny against an unacceptable long-established
social reality.' Joining the socialist movement 'meant a
conversion, a complete dedication' by which

the Party became family, school, church, barracks; the
world that lay beyond it was to be destroyed and built
anew. The psychological mechanism whereby each single
militant becomes progressively identified with the collective organization is the same as that used in certain
religious orders and military colleges, with almost
identical results. Every sacrifice was welcomed as a
personal contribution to the 'price of collective redemp-
tion'; and it should be emphasized that the links which
bound us to the Party grew steadily firmer, not in spite
of the dangers and sacrifices involved, but because of

them. This explains the attraction exercised by Communism
on certain categories of young men and of women, on intellectuals, and on the highly sensitive and generous
people who suffer most from the wastefulness of bourgeois
society.[4]

Finally, harassment and repression by the authorities
helped to radicalize socialist youth. This was true even
before the war when, as in Germany, work among youth by
socialists was restricted by law.[5] Under conditions of
illegality or harassment, moderation had a hard time findin
a receptive audience. Whereas before the war the induced
radicalism was limited primarily to anti-militarist propaganda and demonstrations, in the wartime and post-war years
it turned to wider political objectives and a belief that
the old system had been weakened to the point where positive action by the committed could destroy it.
The German example shows that this process of radicalization was not restricted to the socialist movement or the
young workers. The whole of that rather unique phenomenon,
the German youth movement (Jugendbewegung), had become
politicized during the war.[6] By the time the war ended,
those who remained in the movement had been polarized into
a right and a left. This was especially so of the older
members, who in 1913 had formed the Freideutsche Jugend.
An incoherent move of a considerable part of the Freideutsc
Jugend towards a vague 'leftism' and internationalism had
taken place during the latter part of the war. After the
German revolution of October/November 1918, many more were
drawn into politics. More of the moderates now became ex-
tremists, and more among the indifferent became activists.
Those elements in the Freideutsche Jugend that moved fur-
thest to the left, to the communists, were 'the product of
a mood of despair and pessimism, a nihilistic attitude
towards the world in general.'[7]

4 Crossmann (ed.), *The God That Failed*, especially 72-88
5 See Schorske, *German Social Democracy, 1905-1917*, 97-10
  271-2
6 For the German youth movement see Laqueur, *Young German*
  chapters 10-13, for this period.
7 Ibid., 114. The movement of those on the left in the
  Freideutsche Jugend to the communists was not without
  its problems. While in 1919 those on the extreme left

Of particular interest as an example of this extension
of radicalization beyond trade-union and socialist circles
is Norway. From the end of the war, especially from 1919,
'one can note a new and strongly radical trend in academic
circles and especially among students.'[8] This was associated
with Erling Falk, who organized dissident intellectuals
into the group called Mot Dag. Among students there was
also considerable sympathy for the new regime in Russia,
and an increasingly critical attitude toward the Versailles
peace treaty. This coincided with a growing anti-capitalism
and disgust with the behaviour of those who had profited
from the war, which facilitated the turn by students and
intellectuals to radical socialism. 'Although it is hardly
possible to speak of any generally held political theory
at that time, there was a blend of attitudes, moods, and
ideas coalescing into feelings of unrest.'[9] Mot Dag was to
play a prominent role, together with radical socialist
trade-union leaders, in bringing the Norwegian Labour Party
both into, and later out of, the Comintern.

Three young radicals

Each individual turned to radicalism, to the communist
movement, on the basis of a slightly different combination
of influences and motives. Illustrative of this differentiated process of radicalization are the experiences of
three important communist youth functionaries of those
early years: Willi Münzenberg, Henri Barbé, and Gabriel Péri.

---

were in sympathy with the communist movement and its
aims, they did not equate the communist movement with
the KPD. 'Most of them were unwilling to adopt the party
line on all questions ...' (ibid., 124). They differed
with the KPD on several points: their pacifism, but
above all, over their belief that while the struggle for
socialism would one day be successfully completed, the
struggle of the young versus the old would continue. It
was not until 1921 that the left in the Freideutsche
Jugend joined the communists. A few, such as Alfred
Kurella, had joined earlier. Most soon left the communists.
8 Christophersen, '"Mot Dag" and the Norwegian Left,'
Journal of Contemporary History 1, no. 2 (1966): 137
9 Ibid., 138

Péri became an important member of the French communist
party in the 1920s and 1930s. After working within the
socialist youth movement in Marseilles, especially in anti-
militarist activities, he became secretary of the French
communist youth organization in 1922, and editor of *l'Avant
Garde*.[10] In 1924 he became foreign editor of *Humanité*, and
in 1932 was elected to the National Assembly. There he became very influential as a vice-chairman of the foreign
affairs committee. He had also become a member of the party
central committee. He was shot by the Germans in December
1941 as a hostage.

Péri joined the socialist movement in 1919 as a seventeen
year-old from a petit bourgeois family in Marseilles.

My adherence to socialism [he later wrote] was not the
result of a revolt inspired in me by the spectacle of
social injustices. Nor was it the influence of my friends
or of my family upbringing ... I grew to intellectual
maturity in a world that was still at war. War was *the*
event; one met it at every turn of the road. It arose
every time one began to think; and it molded my reflections, my conception of life.[11]

In searching 'to discover the meaning of life and an expla-
nation of the events around me,' Péri came across a few
lines in a philosophy text devoted to historical materialis
'I felt in this summary description a kind of premonition.'
He read the *Communist Manifesto* and commentaries on *Das
Kapital*, and then further in the writings of Marx and Enge1

A sense of order and harmony came of itself ... Now the
world was explained to me ... [but] I could not be content with the intellectual satisfaction which socialism
had given me. I realized that I had to render a service,
fulfill a task, that it was impossible to separate what

10 He became a full-time functionary at this time, with the
further responsibility of relations between the French
JC and other communist youth organizations, especially
the German. He was a delegate to the third CYI congress
in December 1922.

11 *Toward Singing Tomorrow. The Last Testament of Gabriel
Péri*, 18

the philosophy of socialism taught me from the great
movement to which I felt drawn.[12]

The Russian revolution and the revolutionary unrest of
1918-1920 also played a great role in Péri's development.
He later referred to the feeling that the Bolshevik revolution would spread as having been important, noting that
in 1919 when he joined the young socialists, Budapest was
in the hands of the Hungarian Soviet, a Soviet regime was
in power in Bavaria, the Italian workers were occupying
their factories, and there were revolutionary outbursts
in various places in France. 'The fight for socialism, for
the Revolution, could not be "on the periphery" of one's
main activity. It was *the* main activity; it was destined
to be my life.' Those with whom he associated, fellow students mostly, reasoned as he did. To remain aloof from
earth-shaking events was humiliating. 'Instinctively we
had entered the camp of revolt: revolt against bourgeois
law and order, against bourgeois morality on which we
pinned responsibility for everything we hated.' The setbacks received by the socialist party at the polls in
November 1919 were attributed by Péri to the party's inability to abandon its wartime policies of collaboration
with the bourgeoisie, and to the absence of a 'revolutionary
general staff' comparable to the Bolshevik party in 1917.
For Péri there was only one road to travel: the road taken
by the victorious Bolsheviks. The revolutionary movement
had to adapt itself to national conditions in each country,
but gain inspiration from the lesson of Bolshevism. Socialism could not develop if it stood aloof 'from an experience which had replaced or was in the process of replacing
the capitalist order by the socialist order of society.
That is why I went along with the extreme left of the socialist party.'[13] Thus, a combination of motives led Péri
to the most radical forms of political activity: the effects
of the war and the post-war unrest as observed at an im-
pressionable age; the ideas of Marx; the Russian Revolution;
a craving for action, for participation, for something to
which he could commit himself; and a faith in the power of
a unified, committed, dedicated group of militants.

12 Ibid., 19
13 Péri's remarks here are from ibid., 20-3.

Henri Barbé was to become for a short time from 1929 to 1931 the effective leader of the French communist party. His early years had been spent in the communist youth organization. He had joined the socialist youth organization (Jeunesses socialistes - JS) of St Denis, an important working-class suburb of Paris, in 1917, at about the same age as Péri. In his memoirs, he writes that the reasons tha attracted him to the young socialists were various and of unequal importance.[14] There were the militant traditions of his family. The social climate of extreme leftism that pervaded his home and early adolescence encouraged him to move in the direction of the JS. At that time there was no other place to go for anyone with such a background.

For many young people, revolt against the war or against the authoritarianism of the government, 'against restrictions of any kind,' could find an outlet only among young socialists. As with Péri, Barbé found in the JS an opportunity to satisfy a need for action and participation in the promotion of social change. His drift toward the young socialists was encouraged by the fall of the tsar and the socialist nature of the new political order in Russia. Only at socialist gatherings could he obtain information on events in Russia. Barbé also notes that the social activities, the games and entertainment provided, were an important reason why many joined the young socialists. For a long time, the Jeunesses socialistes was the only association for young people in existence in St Denis.

Developments in French society served to reinforce Barbé' decision to join the young socialists. The big Paris strike in early May 1918 had a marked effect on him, and, he says, on many others. Although the strike was put down quickly, it 'had given to the workers (men and women) self-confidenc in their capacity for action.' During the strike the Jeunesses socialistes played an important and *active* role. Its members provided liaison between the factories and the delegates on the strike committee, they organized concerts and other entertainment for the workers, and helped to raise funds to help those in need. Barbé himself participated in the meetings of the strike committee. This active involvement of the young socialists was repeated during the big mass strikes in 1919 and 1920. This was especially so for the youth of St Denis, a worker's district at the centr

14 Barbé, 'Souvenirs de militant ...' 6-7

of the strike movement. The young socialists had become
'militants.'

All the militants [activists] of the Jeunesses socialistes
in St Denis were at the same time militants in the trade
unions. We were then right in the middle of all these
actions - the fighting against both the employers and
the state. These impressive movements formed my way of
thinking; they were my social and political education.
They also oriented us against reformism, conciliation,
social collaboration, and submission in the face of repressive violence on the part of the public authorities.
We could not understand why the socialist party and the
leaders of the CGT trade-union federation were preaching
good faith and dialogue, and rejected the direct revolutionary action of the workers who were fighting with
vehemence and stubbornness.[15]

Action, commitment, participation, enthusiasm, no compromise - these were what characterized the young socialist
militants.
Not all young workers joined, of course; and not all who
joined became militants. For many, radicalization, to the
extent it occurred, was only a patina that soon rubbed off
as conditions changed, or as age and the passing of time
brought other means of satisfying their needs. For the
committed, however, like Barbé, the 'way of living was the
same as for the other militants of the movement in St Denis.
I leave for the factory at six in the morning. I organize
meetings at night until ten or eleven. I live with my
parents and am completely involved with the problems of
living and revolutionary action.'[16]
Much of the bitterness towards the reformists was due to
the young socialists' anti-militarism. This led to an
acceptance of the Leninist condemnation of wars as imperialist manifestations. Anti-militarism meant struggle not
against violence as such, but rather against the use of
workers and peasants by the capitalists for their own sel-
fish ends. On political issues, the majority of the members
of the Jeunesses socialistes were after 1919 among the

15 Ibid., 10-12
16 Ibid., 19

strongest supporters within the French socialist movement
of unconditional adherence to the new Third International.

By far the most interesting example of the evolution of
socialist youth to radical socialism during and after World
War I is Willi Münzenberg. From the spring of 1915 until
the summer of 1921, Münzenberg was the leading figure in
the international socialist (after November 1919, the communist) youth movement. His experience differed from the
average member of the socialist or communist youth organizations only in degree. He was from the outset not only an
activist, but a leader. He thus exhibited a greater degree
of commitment than many in whom radicalism flared up at the
end of the war, only quickly to die down or out. The kinds
of forces and circumstances that led to radicalism were
the same, however, in both the highly and the transiently
committed.

Münzenberg was not yet twenty-six when he became international secretary of the International Union of Socialist
Youth Organizations (IUSYO) at the Bern conference in 1915.

17 A full biography of Münzenberg would be a significant
contribution to the history of European communism in
the inter-war period. Unfortunately, it has been possibl
to reconstruct only a tantalizingly incomplete picture
of the man. He died under mysterious circumstances in
1940, leaving only a fragmentary legacy of written work.
His personal papers were apparently destroyed when he
hurriedly left Germany in 1933, and his closest confi-
dant died in 1938. For his earlier years up to 1921, of
greatest interest here, there is an autobiographical
study that he published in 1930 - *Die Dritte Front*. It
is more the history of the Swiss and international socia
ist youth movements after he became associated with ther
than a self-declaration or personal history. Furthermore
it is coloured by a somewhat apologetic portrayal of his
attitudes and behaviour in terms of the accepted values
and perspectives of a member in good standing in the
international communist movement in 1930. A more recent
study by Babette Gross (*Willi Münzenberg*), who lived
with Münzenberg from 1922 until their separation by the
war and his death in 1940, provides little new about his
early life. The first third of her book is devoted to tl
years before 1921, and relies heavily on *Die Dritte Fror*
and interviews with a few of the individuals who knew

One might have expected him at that age to be active in a
socialist party. At the time, however, European society,
including the socialist movement, favoured age. An aggressive, dynamic, and ambitious young man found only limited
opportunities to display his talents. Münzenberg thus did
not see the socialist party as an outlet for his interests.
He had been an active participant in the developing socialist youth movement since he was sixteen, and this made
him part of an independent movement with which he still
identified.

He was born in 1889 in Thuringia in Germany of a farmer's
daughter, who died when he was not yet five, and the il-
legitimate son of a baron. A thin and delicate child with
a stubborn will, he suffered under his father's rule and
from his periodic drunkenness. Like his father, he was
restless by nature. As an eleven-year-old boy he was influenced by the prevalent German myth concerning the Boer
War. He ran away from home intending to join the Boers

Münzenberg at that time. The discussion of the Communist
Youth International is brief and comes from contemporary
sources. Münzenberg apparently later reflected to some
extent on his boyhood in her presence, but little new
on his years in the international socialist youth movement is presented. The man himself - his thoughts, the
development of his political ideas, his evaluations of
developments, and most importantly, the growth of his
personality - remains a shadow. Buber-Neumann, in her
Von Potsdam nach Moskau (197, 448-9), has some references
to Münzenberg's career. She provides a somewhat longer
description of Münzenberg in her *Kriegsschauplatz der
Weltrevolution*. There are in addition several brief sum-
maries of Münzenberg's career available in English, all,
however, concentrating on the post-1921 years: Carew-
Hunt, 'Willi Münzenberg,' in Footman (ed.), *International
Communism*; Gruber, 'Willi Münzenberg: Propagandist For
and Against the Comintern,' *International Review of
Social History* X, part 2 (1965): 188-210; Fischer,
Stalin and German Communism, 610-15; and Schleimann,
'The Life and Work of Willi Münzenberg,' *Survey*, no. 55
(April 1965). An interesting biographic sketch by Arthur
Koestler is to be found in his *The Invisible Writing*.
There are also some comments on Münzenberg in Ypsilon,
Pattern for World Revolution, chapter 13.

in their freedom struggle but, as with most such boyish
escapades, did not get very far before returning. This was
his first, but not last, identification with an 'exploited
people.'

His experience as a barber's apprentice at age fourteen
was also to have an effect on the development of his views.
The conditions in which most apprentices laboured were op-
pressive and demanding; twelve- to fourteen-hour days, six
and a half days a week, under the personal control of the
master. It was about this time that efforts to organize a
socialist youth and apprentice movement were beginning in
Germany. With his independent spirit and restless energy,
Münzenberg soon left for a job in a shoe factory in Erfurt
and it was here that his intellectual horizons began to
broaden. He had always been an avid reader, but mostly of
cheap fiction. Under the guidance of the worker whom he
helped in the factory, a member of the socialist party,
Münzenberg began to read political works and more serious
literature. His long association with socialist organizations began in the summer of 1906, when he was brought int
the socialist education club in Erfurt. He quickly became
absorbed in the discussions and his reading. In 1907, as
a seventeen-year-old, he became chairman of the club, whic
he turned into a youth group and the core of the first
young workers organization in Erfurt.

Münzenberg and the Erfurt group joined the north German
socialist youth organization formed in 1907, although also
attracted to the more radical south German group and impressed by Liebknecht's *Militarismus und Antimilitarismus*.
It was this incipient radicalism, especially on the issue
of anti-militarism, that led the socialist party leadership to place the independent youth movement under party
and trade-union control.[18] Münzenberg, as leader of the
Erfurt group, accepted subordination at a youth conference
in 1908. He later said that he and many others had been
very naive.[19]

In early summer 1910 Münzenberg went to Switzerland.
He has said that the restrictive policies of the central
leadership of the new youth organization led him to give
up any hope of accomplishing anything and he 'hit the road

18 See Schorske, *German Social Democracy, 1905–17*, and Kor
   Die Arbeiterjugendbewegung ...
19 Münzenberg, *Die Dritte Front*, 34–42

with no specific objective.[20] He does seem to have developed a certain 'Wanderlust,' having hiked through Germany
for several weeks in the fall of 1909. Welcomed heartily
into the more open atmosphere of the Zurich socialist
movement, he decided to stay and become active there. For
Münzenberg, Zurich must have been a wonder after his
German experiences. The political and intellectual climate
of pre-war and wartime Zurich has been characterized as a
'magnificent chaos.'[21] Emigrants and exiles from all over
Europe had found a refuge there. Russian Bolsheviks and
Mensheviks, revolutionary syndicalists and anarchists from
Italy, Poland, Germany, Russia, and Austria all mingled
with each other and with Swiss socialists. The ideas of
Marx, Bakunin, Kropotkin, Max Stirner, and others were in
the air. The newcomers gathered at the meetings of the
social democratic youth organization, which had become the
centre for theoretical debate. Although the older socialists
tended to dominate the discussions, the younger members
remained, absorbing all the ideas that heatedly were flung
out in debate.[22]

At first Münzenberg was influenced by anarchist views.
He read Kropotkin, Max Stirner, Bakunin, and others, and
was part of the Schwänli-Klub formed by Fritz Brupbacher
to influence young socialists. He later said that he was
influenced above all by the anti-authoritarian mood and
anti-militarist thrust of these works. Münzenberg also had
the feeling that now he was 'together with people who did
not always limit themselves to making speeches, conducting
courses, and explaining history, but who demanded activity,
who were driven to action, who wanted themselves to make
history.'[23] Brupbacher, a close friend of Kropotkin and
all the well-known French and Spanish anarchists, and long
at odds with the Swiss party and trade-union bureaucracy,
provided Münzenberg with his first exposure to the harsh-

20 He wandered for a few weeks in Switzerland, expecting to
   push on to Marseille and further (ibid., 56-7). Gross says
   (34) he was thinking perhaps of going to the United States
21 The Swiss anarchist, Fritz Brupbacher, in his introduction to *Die Dritte Front*
22 See Tschitscherin (Chicherin), *Skizzen aus der Geschichte*
   ... 63-5
23 Münzenberg, *Die Dritte Front*, 67-77

ness of tsarist Russia. He brought him into contact with many of the Russian students in Switzerland.

This association with anarchism was only a phase in Münzenberg's development. However, a certain anti-authoritarianism was to remain and later affected his image of a centralized communist movement. How much this was due to his early exposure in Switzerland to anarchist ideas, how much to his resentment of the German party leaders' interference in the youth movement, and how much to his own independent personality is impossible to say.

Soon he began searching beyond anarchism for something to which he could commit himself. In the spring of 1911 he travelled in Italy and met the Italian socialists in Milan. He was impressed not only by the radicalism and anti-militarism of the Italians, and by the fact that in Italy, as in Germany and Switzerland, the party leaders had sought to curb the radicalism and independence of the youth, but above all by the degree to which the Italian socialist youth had organized themselves. A born organizer, if perhaps not the best administrator, Münzenberg was becoming disillusioned with the negativism of anarchism. Perhaps he failed to find in anarchism that sense of inner security that conformity to a formal organization can bring to some. Given his later independent attitude toward the Comintern, however, both while in the youth movement, and later in his publishing activities, one cannot in any way view Münzenberg as just another Comintern 'apparatchik' or 'organization man.' On his return from Italy, he plunged headlong into the task of transforming what was essentiall a debating club into a firm socialist youth organization, expelling the anarchists in the process.

Münzenberg viewed those whom he gathered around him as having found their life's work in the socialist youth movement. This also applied to Münzenberg himself.

Each day, each free hour belonged to the socialist youth organization. We were filled with youthful idealism and wanted to revolutionize the world ... A powerful urge to action animated us, we used every opportunity to arrange great political rallies, meetings, and demonstrations so as to be able 'to do something.' But some of us were not satisfied with that. For hours we pondered what one coul

do in order to push forward the impotent Social Democratic
Party. We were weary of theory, and eager for action.[24]

This craving for action, the desire 'to do something,' was
typical of those who joined the radical organizations
during and after the war. 'Anything better than nothing'
could have been their slogan. When in an increasingly polarized post-war political environment the traditional
socialist leaders continued to advocate negotiation and
compromise, the impatient younger generation sought refuge
with those who promised a chance to act and to participate
in the making of a new world.

After what he described as a 'relapse' for a short time
at the end of 1911 and early 1912, Münzenberg rose quickly
to the leadership of the socialist youth organization in
the German-speaking areas of Switzerland, becoming a full-
time functionary as of 1 January 1914. This 'relapse' referred to the despondence that had taken hold of Münzenberg
and his associates. The socialist youth movement did not
seem to be going forward.[25] Reading the Russian classics
for the first time, as well as Ibsen and Strindberg, he
found himself in a period of 'Weltschmerzlichkeit,' pon-
dering the mysticism and radical pessimism of these authors.
But he soon shook this off and moved on to his aggressive
organizing activities, arranging protest groups, setting
up new sections, and instilling an enthusiasm in the movement that had not been there before.

In the spring of 1914 he took a trip to Germany, meeting
all of the left-radicals in the socialist movement in
Stuttgart, many of whom were to become activists in the
communist party of Germany, as well as in the SPD (social
democratic party) opposition in Dresden, Leipzig, and elsewhere. The outbreak of war and the failure of the socialist
leaders to prevent it shocked Münzenberg. He refused to
obey the order from the German authorities to report for
military duty, remaining in Switzerland as a 'Refraktär'
(one who refused to do military service, or 'draft dodger').[26]
He opposed emotionally and outspokenly the Swiss party
leaders when they argued, justifiably, that they had no

24 Ibid., 89-90
25 Ibid., 92-5
26 Böhny, 'Die sozialistische Jugendbewegung ...' *Der
Öffentliche Dienst* ... 57. Jahr., no. 46 (1964)

means to stop the war.[27] Münzenberg pleaded for the use of all means to end the war, a general strike if necessary. He refused to accept the fact that events had gone far beyond any possibility for direct action by the socialist movement, especially one in a neutral land. Yet, he refused to give up and this coloured his attitude throughout the war. As the war went on and its tragic consequences became increasingly obvious, he turned further away from the socialist leaders and to the radicalism of Lenin and the Bolsheviks.

Münzenberg met his first major Russian figure in 1914, when Trotsky came to Zurich and immediately occupied a position in the leadership of the Eintracht club, the social democratic discussion circle.[28] His biographer, Babette Gross, says that he soon met and became good friends with Karl Radek, who had fled from Bremen.[29] Münzenberg came up against Lenin and his ideas for the first time at the Bern conference in April 1915, but did not immediately accept Lenin's views and become a member of his circle.

There was a strong pacifist influence in the Swiss socialist youth movement at this time which did not leave Münzenberg unaffected. This was clearly observable in French-speaking Switzerland, where Jules Humbert-Droz led a pacifist opposition to the war based on Christian principles, while the young Swiss socialists in Zurich came under the influence of Professor Leonhard Ragaz and his 'religious socialism.' How important this influence was is a matter of dispute. Gross says that Ragaz exercised a deep influence

27 Münzenberg, *Die Dritte Front*, 142-4
28 The Arbeiterbildungsverein Eintracht (Eintracht workers' education club) was founded in 1840, and in 1869 it joined the German SPD. The socialist party was then, and remained for a long time, a loose association of grou of various kinds that went beyond the boundaries of the German Reich. Eintracht was the centre of the socialist movement in the German-speaking parts of Switzerland. During World War I, the Zimmerwald left in Switzerland formed their own group, the Kegelklub, within which Lenin soon became active after his move from Bern in 1916.
29 Gross, *Willi Münzenberg*, 65

on Münzenberg and the other young socialists.[30] Münzenberg
earlier had dismissed his association with Ragaz as short
and not significant.[31] It has been suggested that in 1919
the young Swiss socialists 'were influenced by the severity
of the ethical demands of the religious socialists, who
contrasted with the readiness for compromise of the official party leadership. The young socialists also wanted,
after the break-up of the International, to find a new and
deeper socialism.'[32] Contributing to socialist pacifism was
the fact that before the war the Swiss military had been
used on occasion against striking workers.[33] Clearly, at
the Bern conference, Münzenberg had supported the pacifist
disarmament position of the Scandinavians. He was neither
for Lenin (revolutionary arming of the proletariat), nor
for Grimm (armed neutrality for Switzerland). It is not
known whether Münzenberg's position was the result of basic
opposition to violence developed out of his encounter with
'religious socialism,' or was adopted for other reasons.
If he had a commitment to non-violence at this time, he
soon abandoned it when he became active in the Zimmerwald
left movement at the Kienthal conference in 1916. Certainly
by the spring of 1916 'at least the leading personalities
of the youth organization had shed the idealist and religious influences.'[34] and had given up support for the slogan of disarmament.

While Münzenberg increasingly became sympathetic to
Lenin's views, he did not identify himself clearly with
Lenin until after the Bolshevik revolution. Even then he
retained certain reservations: on the issue of relations
with the centrists and with which socialists it was necessary to split, and on the crucial issue of independence
for the youth organizations. While fully in agreement with
Lenin's insistence on a complete split with the old party
and trade-union leaders, Münzenberg long remained committed

30 See also Mattmüller, *Leonhard Ragaz und der religiöse
Sozialismus*, especially vol. II, where it is suggested
that Münzenberg in *Die Dritte Front* was projecting his
later development to earlier times.
31 Münzenberg, *Die Dritte Front*, 148–52
32 Mattmüller, 154
33 Böhny, 'Die sozialistische Jugendbewegung ...'
34 Mattmüller, 154ff

to developing a genuinely mass revolutionary movement.[35]
Münzenberg was willing to tolerate a far wider variety of
opinions within the communist movement than was Lenin.
Despite the later claims of Soviet historians,[36] the influence of Lenin on the international socialist youth movement during and after World War I was marginal. Still, after
he moved from Bern to Zurich in February 1916 Lenin did influence Münzenberg. Münzenberg, who became part of the
group that gathered around Lenin, found Lenin a dedicated,
purposeful, committed revolutionary who, at least until
1920-21, approved of independence for the youth organizations. For the mass of young workers in Switzerland and
elsewhere, however, Lenin was of no significance. They were
not exposed to the doctrinal arguments, so knew almost
nothing of him. Even the leaders in many countries, such
as Scandinavia, had only a dim, if indeed any, acquaintance
with Lenin and his ideas until after the Bolshevik revolution. To the extent thereafter that he offered a radical
action program and radical solutions to youth in a radical
mood, he attracted followers. As the leader of the successful 'socialist revolution' in Russia he was accorded considerable respect, even though there was certainly not at the
time any cult of adulation such as was to develop later.
The large majority of those who came into the socialist
youth movement, then the communist youth movement, in those
early post-war years did so not because they were disciplin
followers of Lenin, his ideas, or the Bolshevik party, but
the reasons cited earlier. Lenin's major contributions appe
to have been his unequivocal commitment to 'revolution,' hi
condemnation of the old socialist leaders, and his call for
unity and discipline within the ranks of those 'truly' comn
to revolution. Lenin's arguments for discipline and central
ation generally found enthusiastic response among the young
socialists. What Lenin, and especially his successor, meant
these terms in practice was not fully understood at the
beginning. Above all, Lenin and the Bolsheviks offered an o
let for the youthful desire for action.
For most of the period November 1917 to July 1919 Münzenberg was in prison. Only after the summer of 1919 was he
able to resume his role as international secretary of the

35 Interviews with Jules Humbert-Droz, Giuseppe Berti,
   and Ernst Christiansen
36 See especially Privalov, 'Bor'ba V.I. Lenin i Bolshevikc
   ...' and 'Vlianie Bolshevikov na mezhdunarodnoe dvizheni
   molodezhi ...'

youth international. By now a Spartakist active in the
German communist party and a supporter of the new Communist
International (Comintern), Münzenberg sought to reap the
harvest of radicalization and win a wide mass following for
the Communist International and world revolution.[37]
  Willi Münzenberg was a young man in search of a vision, of
something to which he could devote his life. 'One must dismiss the trivialities and steer for the ultimate goal,' he
had exclaimed after he had first arrived in Zurich.[38] In
contrast to many others for whom early rebelliousness was
but a passing phase, Münzenberg remained dedicated.[39] He

37 See Münzenberg, *Nieder mit Spartakus!*
38 Quoted by Brupbacher in Münzenberg, *Die Dritte Front*, 5
39 Various witnesses have testified to Münzenberg's dedication and commitment and his many talents. Brupbacher saw
   in him a 'wild passion and desire joined with an eminently
   practical intelligence and an inexhaustible energy'
   (Münzenberg, *Die Dritte Front*, 8). Several of those active
   with him in Zurich have left impressions of him. 'Equipped
   with a good intellect and, for his age and considering his
   occupation, extensive learning, he was a remarkable agita-
   tor, a stirring and zealous speaker, and an exceedingly
   intensive worker' (Böhny, 'Die sozialistische Jugendbewegung
   ...'). 'Willi Münzenberg exercised a strong influence on
   the youth organization and was its spiritual leader. The
   members did whatever he said' (letter from Altstadtrat
   Jakob Baumann, Zurich, 7 November 1969, displayed at the
   exhibition on the occasion of the hundredth anniversary
   of Lenin's birth, 23 April - 17 May 1970, Helmhaus Zurich,
   and deposited with the Schweizerische Sozial-Arkiv,
   Zurich). 'He knew how to arouse them and was a brilliant
   organizer' (letter from Anny Klawa-Morf, 21 October 1969,
   ibid.). Ernst Christiansen, the Danish socialist youth
   leader and later minister in a social democratic government, knew Münzenberg well from their meetings during and
   after the war. He has emphasized Münzenberg's qualities
   as an orator and organizer, and as a very idealistic young
   man in those years, one who remained at the same time very
   practical (interview with Christiansen). Giuseppe Berti,
   the Italian youth leader, has emphasized the commitment
   and dedication of Münzenberg and his leadership qualities
   (interview with Berti). Another Italian, Luigi Polano, be-
   lieves that Münzenberg had a certain 'lust for power'
   (introgante) (interview with Polano).

remained dedicated in a way that separated him from the many who, out of opportunism or blind dogmatic faith, gave themselves to whomever held power in the communist movement, or who remained so committed to the utopian ends that they lost sight of the consequences of various means. Münzenberg could never completely come to grips, however, with the logical consequences of his commitment to Lenin and democratic centralism. One can perhaps best place him in a vague and ambiguous position between Lenin and Luxemburg, torn between, on the one hand, a belief in the need for decisive commitment to revolution and firm unity within the movement, and on the other, an instinctive fear of bureaucratization and the substitution of the will of a small group for that of the working class as a whole.

By the time the Communist Youth International (CYI) was formed in November 1919, war-weariness, economic privation, a discredited capitalist system, nationalist antagonisms, the appeal of the new Bolshevik regime in Russia, and the inherent ease with which younger people accept change all had contributed to turn many young workers, former soldiers, and students to the more revolutionary socialist organizations.[40] Resisting these influences were the traditions scorned and denounced by the socialists as 'bourgeois,' the desire for peace and an end to conflict, the appeals of reform socialists, and general apathy. The socialist youth movement was certainly the most vigorous manifestation of the radical mood that swept Europe at the end of the war. This youthful radicalism was to prove to be less enduring than anticipated. It led to unrealizable expectation, and to a conflict that could not be won with the leaders of the new communist movement. Nevertheless, the heady experience of independent participation in stirring events left its mark. As time has shown, it was a precursor of things to come.

40 See Engelhardt, *Die deutsche Jugendbewegung* ... 71-4

4

The Berlin congress

The delegates to the founding congress of the Communist
Youth International (CYI) gathered in Berlin illegally and
under constant threat of discovery by the police on 20
November 1919. Enthusiastic and dedicated, with grand visions and great expectations, the young socialist leaders
met 'in the dark, dirty, narrow backroom' of a shabby and
inconspicuous tavern in the working-class suburb of Neukölln.
Because an invitation to the congress had been intercepted
by the German police, many of the foreign delegates had to
enter the country clandestinely. As a precaution against
discovery, the participants moved to a new location each
day, including, on one occasion, the large studio of the
sympathetic German artist, Käthe Kollwitz.[1]

1 Originally scheduled for Weimar on 5 November, the conference was moved to Berlin because of fear of discovery
by the police. The main organizer of the week-long
meeting was Leo Flieg, who later was to become an important functionary in the German communist party (see the
Comintern journal, *Internationale Presse-Korrespondenz*,
11 November 1924, 1980-81). For the conference setting
see *Die Jugend der Revolution*, 7; Münzenberg, *Die Dritte
Front*, 302; Kurella, *Gründung und Aufbau der Kommunistischen Jugendinternationale*, 21; and Schüller's comments
in *Die Junge Garde*, November 1924.
  Käthe Kollwitz built a considerable reputation as a
graphic artist. Living in the poorer district of North
Berlin, she drew her themes from the labour movement, to
which she gave much support. For her role at this time
see Jahnke and Pietschmann, 'Zur Gründung der Kommunistischen Jugendinternationale ...' *Beiträge zur Geschichte
der Arbeiterbewegung* 12. Jahr., no. 1 (1970): 3-22.

Despite the unprepossessing circumstances, an aura of anticipation permeated the meetings. Everyone accepted as self-evident that the revolutionary process had begun, inevitably to end in a socialist society. The old order had brought itself to its knees by a fratricidal war. The Bolsheviks in Russia had delivered the initial thrust and brought socialism to power for the first time. All that remained was to unite and smite the old order a final blow.

The developments within the youth movement during the preceding year makes it clear that the organizers of the congress intended it to fulfil several purposes. This is confirmed by the reports of the preparations for the congress, as well as the discussions at the congress and the resolutions adopted. The participants were first to affirm a commitment to revolutionary socialism: to the 'proletarian revolution,' to the overthrow of bourgeois society, and to the creation of a dictatorship of the proletariat in each country. Specifically, this commitment was to mean support for the new, spontaneous revolutionary institutions – the workers' councils, or soviets – as the organs of working-class power. There was to be no doubt on this point. The purpose of the revolutionary struggle was a revolutionary transformation of society, with power residing in the hands of the working class. All revolutionary socialists were expected to acknowledge that this power could be exercised only in the image of Russian experience, that is, in the form of the soviets apparently serving as the basis of the socialist society being built in Russia. There was little difficulty in eliciting a positive response from the delegates on these points. If all issues could have been kept on this elevated level of principle, the future of the Communist Youth International, indeed of the entire communist movement, might well have been quite different.

There were, however, specific problems that could not be put off by reducing them to abstractions and generalities. One was the problem of who were to be members of the new youth international. Few difficulties would have arisen if it simply had been a case of accepting any and all youth organizations willing to make the necessary commitments. There were to be demands, however, that additional requirements be fulfilled. Some decision with respect to the factional controversies had become inevitable. The organizers believed that in light of the changes wrought in the struct

of capitalism by World War I and the Bolshevik revolution,
the 'truly' revolutionary forces had to be separated from
the traitors, slackers, and vacillators if the revolutionary will and strength of the proletariat was to be brought
to the point of successful action. This view mirrored that
of the first Comintern congress the preceding March, which
called for the break-up of the centrist forces so as to
make it easier to capture the 'really revolutionary' elements for communism. The delegates to the Berlin congress
must have faced some confusion on this point, for the
Comintern had just accepted the adhesion in October of the
Italian socialist party, an extremely heterogeneous group
covering the socialist spectrum from right to extreme left.[2]
Nevertheless, the general point was not disputed. All 'true'
revolutionaries had to be identified and mobilized behind
an agreed program.

There was yet another objective of the organizers, the
determination of appropriate strategies and tactics. But,
before this issue could be faced it was necessary to make
certain judgments. How severe a blow had capitalism received? What were its prospects for revitalizing its energies and restoring itself to its position of dominance?
What were the weaknesses that could be exploited? How ready
was the proletariat to take advantage of the possibilities
for revolutionary advance? Thus, a clear evaluation of the
existing situation, with all its opportunities and obstacles,
had to be agreed upon.

Finally, and most importantly, the delegates were to
create a youth international which, in contrast to the pre-
1915 period, would be politically active. All young revolutionary socialists agreed that they would play an important role in the coming transformation of society, but it
was not clear what this role was to be. Also yet to be decided was how the youth organizations were to engage in
political affairs, what the priorities to be accorded to
the various activities of the youth organizations were to

2 The Berlin congress was one of the few instances of
   communication between the Russian party and the Italian
   socialists at this time, It was only in *'Left-Wing'*
   Communism: An Infantile Disorder, written in April 1920,
   that Lenin first intervened directly in Italian socialist party affairs (see Urquidi, 'The Origins of the
   Italian Communist Party, 1918-1921').

be, and what sort of relationship would exist between the youth organizations and the parties, and between the youth international and the new Third International (Comintern). These were all issues the congress was expected to resolve.

The character of the new youth international

The character of the Berlin congress turned out to be quite different from that which had been anticipated throughout the war. The Bern conference in 1915 had been convened on the understanding that a final decision on the future of the youth international would have to await the end of the war. Only then would a broad conference of all socialist youth organizations be possible. It was assumed that this conference would be a massive demonstration of support for revolutionary social change. It would also demonstrate the solidarity of a new, younger generation of socialists that had finally succeeded in liberating itself from the stulti- fying effects of adult tutelage. These plans ran afoul of the rapidly developing factional conflicts. 'Revolutionary solidarity' became such an exclusive category that it left out almost as many young socialists as it included.

Isolated in Switzerland during the war, Münzenberg gradu- ally built up an extensive network of links between the socialist youth organizations through his correspondence as international secretary of the International Union of Socialist Youth Organizations (IUSYO). At Bern and Kienthal he had met those young socialists active in the anti-war opposition, especially the Scandinavians, with whom he was to maintain a long and warm relationship. Arrested in 1917 for participating in demonstrations celebrating the Bolshe- vik revolution, he finally was expelled from Switzerland in November 1918. Arrested and in jail again in Germany in January 1919, he was free to resume his activities in the youth international only in the early summer. While in jail he had used his time to write several books and to maintain a correspondence with various socialist youth organizations

Meanwhile, the remaining members of the international secretariat were busy in Zurich in late 1918 and early 1919 attempting to arrange the long-awaited conference of the IUSYO. All who considered themselves to be supporters of a socialist revolution - most organized young socialists at

3 Münzenberg, *Die Dritte Front*, 285

this time - were to be invited. By the spring of 1919 Lenin
apparently had been informed of the efforts of the international secretariat to convene a conference, but he was
interested only in a meeting capable of creating a new,
purely leftist or communist youth international.[4] Only
through such an organization did he see the youth movement
being useful in radicalizing the socialist movement and
assisting in the formation of communist parties. Expectations that a new youth international would be established
already had been voiced at the founding congress of the
Russian communist youth organization, the Komsomol, in
October/November 1918.[5] Münzenberg and the young socialists
in the West, however, believed that they already had created
a new and sufficiently revolutionary youth international at
Bern.

Münzenberg returned immediately to party and youth international affairs upon his release from prison in July. He
was busy in Stuttgart until late August, when he went to
Vienna to prepare for the IUSYO conference. Returning to
Germany, he moved on to Berlin to escape re-arrest and
settled in to a precarious illegal existence.[6] In contact
with the various factions and leaders in the German communist party (KPD), as well now with the Russian representatives to the pending youth conference, Münzenberg moved to
the Leninist position on the composition of the new Inter-

4 See Kurella, *Unterwegs zu Lenin*, for his trip to Moscow
  in April 1919 and his meeting with Lenin.
5 Cited in Fisher, Jr, *Pattern for Soviet Youth*, 51
6 It seems quite likely that Münzenberg had some communication with Radek in his prison cell, probably through
  Karl Moor. Moor, in Berlin in 1919, was a friend of
  Münzenberg from his years in Switzerland, as well as a
  frequent visitor to Radek (see H. Schurer, 'Karl Moor:
  German Agent and a Friend of Lenin,' *Journal of Contemporary History* 5, no. 2 [1970]; Carr, 'Radek's "Political Salon" in Berlin, 1919,' *Soviet Studies* 3, no. 4
  [April 1952]' and Haas, *Carl Vital Moor* ...). Bronski
  was also in Berlin at this time and in the circle of
  German communist leaders to which Münzenberg had access.
  Strangely, Münzenberg has nothing to say about his activities during these crucial months, either in his auto-
  biography or through Babette Gross.

national, and on which youth organizations were to be invited to the IUSYO conference. The Russians wished to invite to the conference only those organizations that had participated in 'international actions' against the war, or that had expressed their will to carry out the revolutionary program of the youth international 'in other ways.' These terms in effect meant that there could be no room for the centrists, much less the right-socialists. One could be considered a revolutionary socialist only if one joined the left unreservedly and was active on its behalf.

At the end of May, the Executive Committee (ECCI) of the new Comintern issued its call for the formation of a clearly communist youth international, and Lenin saw to it that a program and statutes were drafted. Despite this, and despite the fact that he himself had moved much closer to the Bolsheviks, Münzenberg remained reluctant to abandon his vision of a broad movement of all 'revolutionary young socialists.' However, events within the German Free Socialist Youth (FSJ), and the arguments of the Russian Komsomol representatives, were soon to lead Münzenberg and other supporters of a broad conference to accept the Russian position.

Relations between left and centre in the FSJ came to the breaking point in October. It had become evident that the centrist leaders were not committed to decisive revolutionary action, or to a firm break with the right-socialists. As a result, Münzenberg now accepted Lenin's argument that the young centrist socialists had to be separated from their leaders as quickly as possible. This could best be done by forming a tightly organized youth international, one which supported unconditionally the 'revolutionary activism' of the Comintern, from those 'youth organizations which were politically most progressive and capable of action.'[7] Münzenberg and the other organizers of the conference thus decided not to invite any right-socialists or centrists.[8] With this decision, all possibilities for a broad, democratic youth movement committed to a radical, socialist transformation of European society vanished.

7 Kurella, *Unterwegs zu Lenin*, 99
8 Kurella, *Gründung und Aufbau* ... 20. For discussion of the efforts to organize the international conference see ibid., 11ff; *Der Jugendliche Arbeiter*, February 1920, 4; *Zirkularschreiben* ...; and Jahnke and Pietschman

When the Berlin conference convened, the delegates agreed almost unanimously with this decision to exclude the centre and to create a communist youth international.[9] The youth organizations they represented were by this time infused with the 'revolutionary activism' upon which the communist movement was built. This led to a common antipathy to the centre, but it also led to serious differences over the attitude to be taken toward the anarchists and syndicalists. The anarcho-syndicalists had been invited to participate in the founding of the Comintern earlier in 1919 because they had welcomed the Bolshevik revolution and had indicated a willingness to accept the dictatorship of the proletariat. Lenin regarded them as actual or imminent converts to his views and as a source of support for his revolutionary politics. Thus, Comintern policy at the outset had been to form a bloc with all such groups. This was reaffirmed in the circular on tactics distributed over Zinoviev's signature, as chairman of the Comintern executive committee (ECCI), in September.[10] By the latter part of 1919, however, it had become clear that a 'syndicalist question' had emerged in the revolutionary movement.

Anarchist and syndicalist ideas persisted among adherents to the new communist parties. This was especially so in

---

'Zur Gründung der Kommunistische Jugendinternationale ...' Present at Berlin were representatives of the so-cialist youth organizations or groups in Italy, Spain (Madrid), Russia, Russia (Volga Germans), Hungary, Switzerland, Romania, Poland, Austria (VKPJ), Germany (FSJ), Sweden, Norway, Denmark, and Czechoslovakia (Kladno), as well as the Comintern representative (see *Unter dem roten Banner*, 6, for the delegates and the distribution of the number of votes per country).

9 The refusal of the provisional bureau, set up to organize the conference, to invite the Austrian centrists (VSAJ) was the subject of some opposition from the Italian delegate, Luigi Polano, after his delayed arrival on the second day (*Unter dem roten Banner*, 23-4; *Pervyi kongress KIM* ... 75-9).

10 For the circular see 'Rundschreiben des Exekutiv-Komitees der Kommunistischen Internationale' in *Die Kommunistische Internationale* (Petrograd edition) no. 3 (1919): 73-4. For reference to its appearance at Berlin see *Die Kommunistische Jugend*, 25 December 1919, 154-5.

Germany, where it was a source of a split in the KPD. It was also an issue in Italy, France, Norway, and elsewhere. Anarcho-syndicalist ideas had led to differences over the role and structure of the party in the revolution, over the attitude to be taken toward the State before and after the revolution, and over the question of 'direct action,' as opposed to 'political activity,' as the substance of revolutionary struggle.

The delegates at the Berlin congress disagreed about how to respond to the anarchist and syndicalist views. Some thought that the youth international should oppose only those anarchists and syndicalists who were against the dictatorship of the proletariat.[11] To fail to make this point clear would be to confuse those anarchists and syndicalists with whom the communists could collaborate. 'We must say clearly that we are against them,' argued one participant, '[only] as long as they are against the dictatorship of the proletariat.'[12] Nothing more was to be done that might disrupt the developing cooperation between all distinctly revolutionary forces, at a time when revolution seemed imminent.

The Russian Bolsheviks, however, remained ever vigilant in defence of what they saw as correct, ideologically orthodox principles. There could be compromises in practice, especially where there were expectations of conversion, but there could be no compromises over ideological principle. Thus, the ECCI representative, Mieczyslaw Bronski (Braun), spoke out against anarcho-syndicalist rejection of the importance of the party. The Russian delegate, Lazar Shatskin, condemned the West European anarchist and syndicalist ideas. While he did not reject cooperation with anarcho-syndicalists the thrust of his argument was to put the ECCI circular in ideological perspective. He spoke of the 'danger of penetration into our ranks of anarchist and syndicalist ideology,' and the emergence in Germany of syndicalist tendencies, 'even in the communist movement.'[13] This was a reference to the impact of the ideas of Wolffheim and Laufenberg

11 *Pervyi kongress KIM* ... 160
12 Ibid., 143
13 Ibid., 98. For criticism of syndicalist ideas from the Germans see ibid., 109. Carr notes that an unnamed 'representative of the Third International' was present at the Heidelberg congress of the KPD in October 1919

and the 'ultra-left.' The delegates barely approved a statement declaring that the youth international 'clearly fights against' syndicalist ideology and the anarchists,[14] rather than a more mildly worded resolution preferred by the minority sympathetic to the activism of the 'ultra-left.'[15]

The Berlin congress reflected an abandonment of the political neutrality of the war years.[16] Acceptance of the new orthodoxy of the left, as represented in the Comintern, although by no means universal, did represent the prevailing orientation within the socialist youth movement in 1919.

---

arguing against a federal structure for the party (*The Bolshevik Revolution, 1917-1923* III, 138, fn. 2). This could have been Shatskin, for he was arguing in this vein also at Berlin (see *Pervyi kongress KIM ...* 99), but more likely was Bronski.

14 *Pervyi kongress KIM ...* 160; Münzenberg, *Die Dritte Front*, 377-8

15 Ibid. Polano, the Italian delegate, and Oskar Samuelsen representing the three Scandinavian countries, remained unhappy with the congress decision on this point (*Pervyi kongress KIM ...* 160-1; *Unter dem roten Banner*, 57).

16 Another basic break with the policies of the old youth international concerned the issue of anti-militarism. The Scandinavian-influenced Bern decision in favour of general disarmament was for all practical purposes buried by the Berlin congress, and approval given to a policy of arming the proletariat and the formation of Red Guards. However, because of strong Scandinavian resistance to the abandonment of disarmament the discussion of specific anti-militarist tactics was put off. Despite the persistence of the Scandinavians, the International Bureau in June 1920 rejected and condemned as 'bourgeois pacifist' the Scandinavian proposals for disarmament and compulsory arbitration. The most pressing task for communist youth organizations as a time of great revolutionary expectations was 'to prepare and educate the proletarian youth for the necessary military conquest of power by the proletariat, and for the defence of the proletarian dictatorship' (*Bericht über die erste Sitzung des Büros der Kommunistischen Jugend-Internationale abgehalten am 9. bis 13. Juni 1920 in Berlin,* 23.)

This did not, unfortunately, remove the young socialists once again from doctrinal and factional controversy. Other, even more serious differences among the participants were to emerge. The delegates represented movements with a wide variety of traditions, experiences, and levels of development. The delegates were all committed to 'revolutionary action' and the formation of a strong, centralized youth international. But not all of them came with the same understanding of what a revolution involved, or what it meant to centralize the 'proletarian movement.' Distinct differences in perception were overshadowed by the enthusiasm of the delegates and the pervasive mood of revolutionary euphoria. Nevertheless, they were the source of some serious disputes, and led many participants to misunderstand what had been accomplished in the way of doctrinal unity.

Differences persisted until mid 1921, when the ebbing of revolutionary expectations tempered CYI anti-militarist tactics. Scandinavian resistance to these proposals to arm the workers was on two grounds. First, they did not have the expectations of social revolution in Scandinavia that all communists apparently had with regard to Central Europe. Although their hopes were high for Scandinavia, they anticipated success coming only in the aftermath of broader revolutionary developments in Central Europe. In such circumstances, the need for violence might well be minimal. Thus, the Scandinavians wished to tailor their agitation and propaganda to fit their own national conditions. Emphasis would be placed on peaceful development of the social struggle so as to put on the capitalists the onus for the use (or threat of use) of force, an anathema in Scandinavia. By 1921, the CYI, while still calling for disarming of the bourgeoisie and arming of the proletariat, had in fact abandoned preparations for revolutionary action and come to emphasize destruction of the bourgeois armies from within through agitation and propaganda, and the formation of revolutionary groups. The Scandinavians could accept the necessity of destroying the existing bourgeois military organizations for reasons of social revolution.

Political evaluations of the prospects for revolution

One must remember that the purpose of this furtive gathering
of young revolutionaries known as the Berlin congress was
to promote a revolution. Unfortunately for the delegates,
there were no obvious steps that would assure success. Thus
the thorny question of what to do persisted. The differences
observed in the debates over strategy, tactics, and even
over organizational issues, can ultimately be reduced to
differences in the evaluation of the prospects for revolution. Some saw the political, economic, and above all,
social, destruction in Europe in more cataclysmic terms
than did others. All saw the old bourgeois order as having
been mortally wounded. The question at the end of 1919 was
not whether it could be toppled and destroyed, but rather
how much resistance was left. The delegates had different
estimates of how strong the old order remained. They also
had different ideas about how to accelerate its demise.
  These differences reflected various understandings of
what the revolutionary process meant. One's notion of what
a 'proletarian revolution' was, of what behaviour the revolutionary process entailed, and of what had to be accomplished before one could say that 'the revolution' had been
achieved tended to shape interpretations of reality, and
thus evaluations of the prospects for revolution. To a
certain extent, an emotional and almost mindless enthusiasm
for action and for change underlay, or overrode, the more
rational images of existing circumstances.
  One would have expected the new Communist International
to provide some guidance for its youthful supporters. It
had been in existence only since March, however, and was
'international' in not much more than name and intent.
There had not yet been an opportunity for its adherents to
meet and agree on a 'Comintern line.' In the absence of a
shared, agreed Comintern evaluation of the situation, the
Bolshevik-inspired activities of the executive committee
in Moscow, the views of the various ECCI representatives
in Europe, and events in the German communist movement all
served as potentially divergent guidelines for individual
groups and organizations in deciding on how (or, indeed,
whether) to interpret or apply the very general statement
adopted at the first congress that served as a program for
the Comintern.

Still in his privileged cell in Berlin's Moabit prison, the Bolshevik emissary, Karl Radek, sent a message to the delegates. His views reflected not only approved Bolshevik revolutionary strategy, but also the caution with which he approached the prospects for revolution in Germany at that time.[17] Although Radek saw the period as one of economic misery, disintegration, and world revolution, he warned against rash optimism. There was always the danger of the capitalists uniting in the face of the revolutionary wave. Young communist activists had to be prepared for a pro-tracted struggle. Thus there would be no benefit derived from extreme measures. On the contrary, such measures could weaken the proletariat and play into the hands of the bourgeoisie. At the same time, all communists must combat the various influences deflecting the proletariat from the path of revolution and hindering the formation of communist parties. Vacillating elements such as the German Independents (USPD), and on the other side 'the "left" elements attempting to circumvent or shorten the very long route by means of brief, spectacular actions with no lasting result (vspyshko-puskatel'stva) and all kinds of other magic recipes ...'[18] were seen to be equally at fault.

In terms of specific day-to-day activity designed to 'push forward' the masses, Radek, supported by Münzenberg, believed that a mass working-class organization dedicated to revolutionary change had to be built. The communists had to become the 'motive force' within the existing trade unions, from which position they could expand and control the factory councils (Betriebsträte). Conquer the trade unions and the factory councils and the communists would conquer the masses; conquer the masses and the communists would seize power. But this effort could only be success-ful if all communists were united in disciplined communist organizations.

Another Bolshevik emissary, Bronski (Braun), took a similarly cautious line in his remarks to the delegates.[19]

---

17 *Pervyi kongress KIM* ... 15-22. See also Carr, *The Bolshevik Revolution, 1917-1923* III, 139-40
18 *Pervyi kongress KIM* ... 21
19 Bronski was a Polish socialist who had been active in Zurich with Lenin and the Zimmerwald left. He was now in Germany as a founding member of the West European secretariat of the Comintern. Bronski not only visited

He was careful to make no specific prediction of when the revolution would occur. It was declared only to be inevitable because the hunger and misery produced by war and capitalism were promoting 'an unconscious revolutionary movement.' Communists could hope to accelerate and channel this development only by mobilizing broad support among the masses.

Münzenberg discussed the failure of the communist-led uprisings in Berlin and Munich in early 1919. In condemning the urge to precipitous armed action he echoed the note of caution expressed by Radek and Bronski. Political strikes, he said, were a legitimate weapon for the workers in the struggle to win power, but such actions had to be well planned and organized. In the case of the Berlin and Munich events, Münzenberg argued that the communists had not led the masses (as they must do), but instead had moved before sufficient support had been marshalled. It was his view that while the 'objective' factors for revolution existed in Germany, the will of the masses did not. In order to take advantage of this 'objective' situation and lead the revolution, communists had to establish a strong base of support among the 'proletarian masses.'[20] Münzenberg adhered to the Luxemburgist view that power should be taken only by a majority of the proletariat, represented through their own institutions, the soviets (Räte). The revolution was *not* to be an effort by some minority 'to remodel the world in its image.' He had defended the communist (Spartakist) position in mid 1919 by asserting that the Spartakists would take power 'only by the clear, unambiguous will of the great majority of the proletarian masses.'[21]

Thus, while what passed as the Comintern evaluation in remarks by Radek and Bronski did not see Europe on the verge of an imminent revolutionary conflagration, implicit was a faith that the highly unstable conditions would soon lead to one. Others, however, saw events differently. Those associated with the 'ultra-left' saw Europe as not merely on the verge of, but directly experiencing a revolution.

Radek in his confinement, but was in continuous contact with the leaders of the KPD, Paul Levi and Klara Zetkin. For his remarks at the Berlin congress see *Unter dem roten Banner*, 29-32.
20 For Münzenberg's views see *Unter dem roten Banner*, 39-49
21 Münzenberg, *Nieder mit Spartakus!*, 11

Direct political and armed action were the only appropriate tactics; only through such activities could the masses, who were assumed to be eagerly searching for leadership, be mobilized and organized.

These evaluations were not remote or esoteric exercises. All communists wished to be active, in the most productive way possible, in the anticipated revolutionary transfer of power. This meant reading the omens correctly, and deducing appropriate strategies and tactics. It also meant the creation of an ideologically unified organization. As various communists interpreted events differently, they understandably drew different conclusions as to what should be done. This situation was only exacerbated when individuals advocated strategies and tactics drawn less from a reasoned evaluation of circumstances, than from the application of certain a priori definitions of revolution and the revolutionary process.

The passionate debates over what to do, and why, created the insuperable problem of how ideological unity, and thus unity in action, was to be achieved when apparently irreconcilable differences of view existed with respect to strategy and tactics. There would be little justification for separating 'truly' revolutionary socialists from the other socialist tendencies if unity could not be achieved even within the new communist movement.

Differences over strategy and tactics

The insistence by Radek, Bronski, and Münzenberg that a mass organization was essential *before* revolutionary action could be successful did not find favour with all of the delegates. An intense discussion developed over whether or not the masses were needed by the communists before they could expect to win power, and if so, what had to be done to win them. In an important way, these differences were related to those between the Leninist and Luxemburgist notions of how the party should be organized and how and when 'the revolution' would occur. These two conceptions, together with some elements of anarcho-syndicalist thought seem to have mingled in the minds of many of the participants at the Berlin congress.

Insisting that a socialist revolution could be accomplished only if the masses were led by an elite, disciplin conspiratorial party, Lenin rejected any suggestion that the masses themselves were capable of determining their own future.[22] Having been active in a quite different environment, however, Rosa Luxemburg increasingly grew critical of Léninist doctrine and Bolshevik practice. She believed that a genuinely socialist revolution could be achieved only by a mass party organized in essentially democratic forms. In this way the 'great working mass' could determine for itself the means for effecting the revolution, as well as the forms of political and economic life after the revolution.

For the delegates assembled in Berlin, the paramount question was how the revolution would come. Could a small, disciplined revolutionary party bring it about as it had in Russia? Or was it necessary to have much wider participation by workers, or of the population as a whole? This specific, yet crucial question had not been answered definitively in the fall of 1919. There was no agreement within the new International, no dogma or authority to which the young commumists at Berlin could refer. Richard Schüller, the Austrian communist youth leader and later a leading functionary in the youth international, represented the most militant of the young communists. He went even beyond Lenin and argued that

if we have an active minority that is energetic, we will be able, without a doubt, to capture for ourselves the majority of the proletariat. For the dictatorship of the proletariat in no way means that all of the proletariat commands. It means only that all questions are settled from the point of view of the proletariat without the participation of the bourgeoisie. For this, it is sufficient that a unified minority of the proletariat takes power in its hands, and by so doing prevents the indifferent masses from supporting our enemies.[23]

Schüller went so far as to suggest that the application of terror, without which it would be impossible to create the dictatorship of the proletariat, might, within limits

22 For discussion of Lenin's views of the role of the
masses see Carr, *The Bolshevik Revolution, 1917-1923*
III, 180-2, and Schapiro, 'Lenin's Heritage,' *Encounter*
XXXV, no. 1 (July 1970)
23 *Pervyi kongress KIM* ... 107

and if it were a matter of taking power, be directed even
against the mass of the proletariat.

The majority, however, while not quarrelling with the
need to have disciplined communist organizations that would
provide leadership, rejected Schüller's call for attempts
to take power before an adequate tie to the masses had been
developed. One of the German delegates, Hans Meyer, re-
sponded to Schüller by saying that

> of course the dictatorship is in practice led by an or-
> ganized minority. In this sense the assumption of power
> somehow depends on party decisions. But the actual con-
> struction of the dictatorship is possible only after the
> masses have been revolutionized and a majority is for the
> leadership of the party ... If the masses do not stand
> with us, it is true that we may be able to stir up mili-
> tary uprisings (of which, however, Hindenburg is also
> capable), but we will not be able to accomplish the so-
> cialist revolution, to transform the entire economic
> system.[24]

Valeriu Marcu argued that the Hungarian and Bavarian experiences had demonstrated that communists did not yet have
the base from which to erect a dictatorship of the proletariat outside Russia. Few, however, were willing to accept
his assertion that twenty or thirty years might pass before
the revolution could be consummated in Europe.[25]

The program adopted by the congress did not entirely
clarify this point. However, the clear implication was that
the Russian experience of a minority coup could not be repeated elsewhere – at least not in Central and Western Europe
The program affirmed the faith of the delegates that a socialist revolution was inevitable. Out of the 'contemporary
revolutionary epoch' would emerge a socialist society, but
there was no forecast as to when this would occur. It was
recognized, however, that much mobilizing and organizational
work remained ahead. While the material conditions for world
revolution were said to be at hand, 'the victory of the
revolution depends upon the will and energy of the international proletariat.'[26] Nevertheless, the tenor of the program

24 Ibid., 109-10
25 Ibid., 148
26 Münzenberg, *Die Dritte Front*, 375-6

reflected the feeling of optimism, anticipation, and inevitability that had gripped the young revolutionary socialists. It seemed to be taken for granted that the approaching revolution would achieve success 'soon.' Success was thought to depend on a broad revolutionary tide of mass support for communist leadership. All that was needed was for young communists to be active and success would be theirs.

Although for the most part agreed on the need to mobilize the masses, it was not clear how this was to be done. Some believed that they should be organized apart from existing institutions, such as parliament and the trade unions. Others insisted that communists had to go into and participate in these and all other organizations and institutions that had some tie to or influence over the masses. The first Comintern congress in March had accepted participation in bourgeois parliaments in principle, but subordinated such activity to extra-parliamentary mass actions.[27] This view was reaffirmed by ECCI in a circular letter issued by Zinoviev; it stated very emphatically that while communists could not renounce use of bourgeois parliaments in principle, the real solution to the question of acquiring power 'will occur under all conditions *outside* parliament, *on the streets.*'[28] Only strikes and uprisings would settle the conflict between capital and labour. ECCI thus rejected parliamentarianism as an end in itself, as a desirable form by which a society was organized politically. It did accept, however, the possibility of using existing parliaments for promoting revolution. Whether or not to participate in a given electoral campaign depended upon a series of concrete conditions in each country.

Supporters of a 'left opposition,' or 'ultra-left,' including the Dutch Tribunists, with strong backing in Germany, France, and Italy, were not willing to accept even this qualified use of parliamentary tactics. In their

27 This position in effect straddled the dispute within the new KPD in December 1918, when Luxemburg and Liebknecht argued for participation in the constituent assembly and caution in mass actions, while the majority rejected this position and set in motion the January actions that resulted in the death of the two leaders.
28 See *Die Kommunistische Jugend*, 25 December 1919, 154-5, and *Die Kommunistische Internationale* (Petrograd edition), no. 3 (1919): 74

view any participation in existing institutions would weaken fatally the revolutionary fervour of the masses.[29] They thus argued against using parliamentary methods and for a boycott of the reformist-controlled trade unions. This opposition was composed of several diverse elements. It included orthodox Marxists who refused to compromise revolutionary scoialist principles by working within bourgeois institutions. There were also many who simply overestimated the existing unrest, tension, and possibilities for revolution, as well as a considerable number of anarchists and syndicalists who had joined the communist movement after the war. These latter, while supporting communist activities designed to bring about a revolution, tended to bring their traditional anti-state, anti-parliamentary views with them.

The more militant views on tactics were represented at Berlin by Schüller and Felix Lewinsohn, a leader of the 'ultra-left' opposition in the German Freie Sozialistische Jugend. Defending extra-parliamentary action, Schüller expressed his unabashed militancy by arguing that

> our task is in no case to allow a rise in the capitalist mode of production. We must make use of all ways and means in order to prevent its restoration and the revival even if only temporarily, of bourgeois supremacy. An unceasing and most active struggle against capitalism on all lines - such is our task. By means of constant strikes, leading to a general strike; by means of the revolutionary destruction of the army and all other available means at our disposal we must keep economic life in a state of continuous turmoil. But [this] ... need not lead to a tactical line of brief, spectacular actions which in the end come to nothing (vspyshko-puskatel'stva) The creation of such 'labour unrest' must serve only to prepare for the seizure of political power.[30]

Schüller saw the 'ultra-left' as natural allies. Attacks on the 'ultra-left,' such as those mounted by Paul Levi and the other leaders of the KPD in Germany, should be abandoned. Yet, even Schüller was not against the use of

29 For the 'ultra-left' view see Gorter, *Offener Brief an Genossen Lenin.*
30 *Pervyi kongress KIM* ... 106-7

parliament in principle. In fact, he specifically referred
to the possibility, suggested in Zinoviev's circular, of
using deputies' immunity for conspiratorial purposes. He
only opposed parliamentarianism because he perceived the
situation to be much more conducive to revolution than did
Radek and Bronski and the congress majority. In particular,
he opposed this tactic for Austria because he believed a
viable structure of soviets was emerging. To use parliament
would undercut efforts to replace it in the course of a
socialist revolution with a system of soviets.[31]

Felix Lewinsohn, later to be a leader of the German
'ultra-left' youth organization, the Kommunistische Arbeiterjugend (KAJ), also supported using parliament in principle
as a forum for preparing the struggle for political power.[32]
But he, too, believed that possibilities existed for organizing the proletariat outside parliament for revolutionary
struggle. By participating in elections to the national
assembly, communists would only encourage democratic illusions in the masses. Representing the prevailing opinion
within the FSJ, he thus spoke against participation by
German communists in parliamentary elections at a time when
the revolutionary process was already underway. But here
was the critical question: had the revolution really begun
in Europe?

Münzenberg, also, was opposed to the use of parliament.
While in Stuttgart earlier in the year, he had been elected
chairman of the KPD district organization for Württemberg.
It was in this capacity that he participated in the party
conference that summer, and the party congress in the fall.
At the August conference of the KPD, held illegally in
Frankfurt, he had been for the revolutionary factory coun-
cils as the focal point of party work.

31 Ibid., 158-9
32 Ibid., 159. Lewinsohn opposed the call by the leader of
   the German FSJ, Friedrich Heilmann, for 'dissociation'
   from the 'left' elements in Germany (ibid., 136). Lewinsohn, like Münzenberg and the ECCI, wished to avoid a
   split in the German FSJ such as had already occurred in
   the German party (KPD). This exchange between the two
   German communist youth leaders was an early sign of the
   differences that were to prove irreconcilable.

Our entry [said Münzenberg] into this bankrupt ...
[parliament] would [falsely] fill the working class
with new hope ... Criticism of parliamentarism is much
more successful from outside than from within. The
masses who follow us today do so from disappointment
with other parties, especially the USPD which claims
to be represented in parliament only as 'dynamite' [to
destroy it].[33]

This position put him in opposition to the party leader,
Paul Levi, as well as to the Russian views. At the second
congress of the KPD in Heidelberg in October, just a few
weeks before the Berlin congress, Münzenberg led, with
George Schumann and others, what later came to be called
the 'middle group.'[34] This was a faction that opposed many
of the 'opportunist' theses, which the Levi-led party
executive (Zentrale) had placed before the congress, but
which also rejected the 'national bolshevism' of the
Laufenberg and Wolffheim group from Hamburg. Laufenberg and
Wolffheim were, among other things, against a centralized
party and emphasized the economic processes and work in the
factory organizations (Betriebsorganisationen) over direct
political activity. After the Hamburg group and those in
sympathy with it had been excluded from the debates,
Münzenberg acted as a 'left opposition.' This meant supporting a strong centralized party, but one in which certain rights were preserved for the members (Mitbestimmungs-
recht), and making the main speech in defence of the anti-
parliamentary position against Paul Fröhlich's speech in
favour of participation.[35]

33 Quoted from a report of the Reichskonferenz der KPD in
   Frankfurt on 16-17 August 1919 in Gross, *Willi Münzenberg*
   100
34 Ibid., 102
35 See ibid., 103; Fischer, *Stalin and German Communism*,
   118; and Münzenberg, *Die Dritte Front*, 287-8. Laufenberg
   and Wolffheim were two communist leaders from Hamburg
   who were in the forefront of the 'ultra-left' opposition
   to parliamentary institutions and the trade unions. They
   were the initiators of the phenomenon of 'national bolshevism,' an attempt to create a 'people's front' against
   bourgeois democracy and the Versailles settlement by
   bringing the extreme left and the extreme right together
   (see Schüddekopf, *Linke Leute von Rechts* ...)

Here in the debates at the Berlin congress, Münzenberg
argued that in times of open revolutionary action extra-
parliamentary means were the most suitable and could include
mass actions, demonstrations, strikes of all kinds, and in
the last resort and under specific conditions, uprisings.[36]
As his evaluation of the political situation demonstrated,
however, he was less sanguine than the 'ultra-left' about
the immediate prospects for 'open revolutionary action.'
Critical of extra-parliamentary actions that were prepared
poorly and not based on mass support, he believed that all
communist organizations should be active outside parliament
mobilizing the aroused masses and preparing them for the
time in the very near future when action would be possible.
   While believing the revolution to be imminent and sympathizing with the 'ultra-left,' he was not willing to be
party to a split in communist ranks. He therefore supported
the position of ECCI and the compromise on tactics worked
out by the Berlin congress.[37] The characterization of
Münzenberg as an 'optimistic revolutionary romantic,'
coined by the later right-wing of the KPD (Brandler,
Thalheimer, Zetkin, and others),[38] was not without justification, but it applied far more to other young communists
at the Berlin congress such as Richard Schüller, Felix
Lewinsohn, and the Romanian, Moscu.[39]
   The congress ended by adopting the equivocal position
set forth in Zinoviev's circular. Use of parliament, although only as a forum for agitation, was accepted. This
was a repudiation of the 'ultra-left.' Participation in
parliament, however, would depend on economic and political
conditions and the nature of the revolutionary movement in

36 *Unter dem roten Banner*, 45
37 See Buber-Neumann, *Von Potsdam nach Moskau*, 449, for
   her views on the imminence of revolution.
38 Gross, *Willi Münzenberg*, 103
39 It is not clear if the Moscu noted in the reports of the
   congress was the later Romanian communist party functionary, Ghitza Moscu. His biography in Lazitch and
   Drachkovitch, *Biographical Dictionary of the Comintern*,
   states that he was arrested in December 1918 and tried
   the following year. He then went to Moscow at the end
   of 1920. He could well have been out of custody in
   November 1919, and present at Berlin. In any case, the
   Moscu who was present was with the 'ultra-left' forces.

each country.[40] That in turn was a victory for those opposed to participation. No one was forced to make a clear decision for, or against, participation. Everyone, especially the 'ultra-left,' was left free to decide for themselves if conditions warranted such a policy.[41] Communist participation in parliament remained only a means to an end. After 1921, however, the main weight of Comintern tactics shifted from the streets and anticipation of imminent revolution to work within parliament. Little by little the communist parties began to play the game of parliamentary politics in order to further their revolutionary goals.

Neither Lenin, nor ECCI, nor any of the participants at the Berlin congress, including supporters and opponents of the 'ultra-left,' felt at the outset that the controversy over tactics was worth a split in the communist movement.[42] On the contrary, it was important that all groups and organizations willing to fight for the dictatorship of the proletariat in the form of soviet power unite as soon as possible and build a communist party, in spite of differences over tactics. As it turned out, it was not possible to avoid a split over these tactical questions.

Debate over the nature of the youth movement

The most controversial and emotional subjects discussed by the delegates concerned the very nature of the communist youth movement. Now that communist parties were being forme and the call issued for all 'truly' revolutionary socialist to unite, it was not evident that separate youth organizations remained necessary. A youth movement with its own traditions did exist, however, and this meant that some decisions had to be made about its future. Some in the parties did advocate fusion of party and youth organization into one revolutionary organization. They carried the argument for maximizing the striking power of the proletariat to its logical conclusion. This remained a distinctly minority point of view. Not only did Lenin

40 *Unter dem roten Banner,* 46; *Pervyi kongress KIM* ... 159
41 For 'ultra-left' approval of the Berlin line see *Kommunistische Arbeiter-Zeitung* (Hamburg), 18 December 1919.
42 See Lenin's letter to Sylvia Pankhurst in *Die Kommunistische Internationale,* no. 5 (September 1919): 681-4, and Zinoviev, ibid. (Petrograd edition), no. 3 (1919):

appreciate the continued usefulness of a separate youth
movement, but it was quite clear that the delegates accepted its existence and importance without question. It
was not clear, however, on what basis one justified the
youth movement remaining independent of the parties, or
what indeed 'independence' meant in the context of a unified movement of all 'truly' revolutionary socialists. As
a consequence, a disturbing uncertainty remained on several
points - namely, the specific role the young communists
were to play in the developing revolutionary struggle,
which activities the young communists were to be occupied
with, the priorities to be attached to these tasks, who
was to make these determinations (the parties, the Comintern, or the youth themselves), and the relations between
the youth international and the Comintern, and between the
communist youth organizations and the communist parties.

To understand the course of the debate on these questions,
one must first of all recognize the importance of the communist commitment to the idea of leadership. The notion of
leadership has been a basic and yet controversial aspect
of Marxist thought. For Marx, all communists, or all who
understood and accepted his theories, were leaders and in
the vanguard in the sense that they were 'the most advanced
and resolute part' of the proletariat. Leadership to Marx
meant being active in encouraging, educating, organizing,
and unifying the working class. Communists provided the
scientific and true definition of reality, of history. They
acted to awaken the working class so as to make it aware
of its degraded condition, and thus ready to act to effect
the transition from capitalism to socialism.

Lenin added a critical element to the Marxist idea of
communist leadership. From his own Russian revolutionary
heritage, and from his perception of working-class behaviour,
it was not enough for a Marxist, a communist, simply to be
one who aroused the working class. A socialist society
could be constructed only after the proletariat had acquired
political power, and it could do so only if it was led by
a disciplined, elite party of professional revolutionaries.
To be a communist, to be part of the 'vanguard of the proletariat,' was thus to be a member of this revolutionary
organization. It would not only prepare for and carry
through the revolution, with mass support, but would preserve the true faith against all deviants. During World
War I this came to mean a sharp split between the 'true'

revolutionaries on the left, and all other socialists. The latter were seen to have either betrayed the cause of proletarian revolution, or to be confused and vacillating.

An important refinement to Lenin's notion of an avantgarde emerged gradually and indistinctly from the wartime experience of the youth movement. It was given direct expression for the first time by the delegates to the Berlin congress.[43] Now, in effect, there was to be a vanguard within a vanguard. The delegates expected the new Communist Youth International to be the instrument through which a spontaneous mass movement of young workers, apprentices, and students would be mobilized. Aroused to action for revolutionary change, these young communists would be the vanguard of the revolutionary forces, that is, of those struggling for the dissolution of bourgeois parliaments and governments, and the transfer of power to the working class organized in revolutionary workers' councils. The young revolutionaries, it was said, would always be in the vanguard because they were more militant and dedicated. They would always be more committed, more impatient, more willing to cast out the old and the established and to bring in the new. They had not grown weary, or been tainted by a willingness to compromise. The young communists could be depended upon never to lose hope, or to slide into the egregious errors of 'opportunism' or 'reformism.' If not kept watch over, it was argued in the debates, even the elite communist parties would deviate from a clear and resolute revolutionary path. Even communist parties were not immune from 'calcification' or 'ossification.'

Youth organizations were said to demonstrate a healthy uniformity of outlook. It was extremely unlikely that their revolutionary character would be weakened from within by self-doubt. The parties, however, were seen as another matter. They were more heterogeneous and included individuals of all shades of enthusiasm and commitment. The members had joined for a variety of motives, some of which led the young communists to question their ability to resist the pressures to compromise. Although most party members still spoke of revolution, the young communists feared that their hopes for the future had been soured by

43 The first issue of *Jugend-Internationale* (*J-I*) in Septem 1915 had called upon the young socialists in all countr: to be the avant-garde of the 'proletarian peace fighter:

events, that their willingness to do battle with the bourgeois enemy had been eroded by the brutality of war. The
young communists doubted whether the party members would
have the strength to stand firm against all adversity,
avoiding the little compromises and concessions that led
to the breakdown of revolutionary resolve.

This image of the youth movement might well have satisfied certain needs of the young communists themselves. It
may also have in some significant way reflected the situation within the socialist movement during World War I. It
may indeed be a fact that young socialists are always
'more revolutionary' than older socialists. But the notion
that the young communists were the real leaders of the
revolution most certainly did not correspond to the way
in which party leaders saw the youth movement. The attitude of the socialist parties to the youth movement had
for the most part been one of neglect. It seldom had been
taken seriously as a political force. As has been noted
earlier, most socialists thought primarily of the future
when they bothered to think at all about the youth movement. That is, the youth movement was considered to be a
'recruiting school' in which future party members would
be raised within the framework of socialist ideas and
principles. Lenin and others in the left recognized at an
early point the useful role that the youth movement could
play in the factional conflicts within the socialist parties. Nevertheless, they, too, saw the youth movement
really only as an auxiliary institution.[44]

In his message to the congress, Radek had high praise
for the young supporters of the Comintern. They had performed admirably in the anti-war opposition. But, the
youth movement was only an auxilliary force,

44 See the preface by Kamenev to an early collection of
Lenin's articles and speeches that the party saw as
having reference to the role of youth in Soviet society
(*Inprekorr* 3, no. 68 [27 October 1923]: 776). See also
Lenin i Stalin o molodezhi. Frequently published and
often cited as a source of Lenin's views on the role of
youth is his speech at the third All-Russian Congress
of the Communist Youth Organizations of Russia, 4 October
1920. This was published by the CYI in 1920 in Berlin as
Die Aufgaben der kommunistischen Jugendorganisationen.

part of the entire struggling international proletarian
army. Its only justification as a special movement and
individual organization alongside communist parties of
the proletariat is that communist agitation among youth
needs to fit the latter's abilities to perceive reality,
that separate youth organizations contribute to the
growth of independent young proletarian revolutionaries.

This paternalistic attitude did not fit very well with the
image that young communists had of their place in the revolutionary process.

Bronski, too, saw a much more limited role for the young
communists. They could play a decisive role in efforts to
win over the masses, but he could not accept that they
would exercise a position of political, or even moral,
leadership. The main job of all young communists was to
conduct extensive propaganda work against all bourgeois,
'social patriot,' and 'unclear' [centrist] forces.[46]

The clandestine sessions of the Berlin congress were
thus the scene of a crucial debate. The young Lazar
Shatskin, sent by Lenin to impose the Leninist stamp on
the new youth international, was pitted against Münzenberg
and the older youth international leaders from Western
Europe. The Russians, in fact, had two representatives at
Berlin - Shatskin, and the young German, Alfred Kurella.
Although just a teen-ager, Shatskin was chosen by Lenin
for this assignment to influence the formation of a com-
munist youth international.[47] He was a leading figure in
the new Komsomol who also spoke good German. In the youth
international he became the voice of Lenin's centralism.[48]
As one of Münzenberg's successors in 1921 as leader of the
Communist Youth International, he played a key role in
Comintern efforts to 'bolshevize' the Norwegian Labour
Party in 1922 and 1923.

45 *Pervyi kongress KIM* ... 16
46 *Unter dem roten Banner*, 29-32
47 See Kurella, *Unterwegs zu Lenin*
48 See *Iunost'*, no. 7 (July 1965): 66-7 for a rehabilita-
tive reprint of reminiscences in 1923 by Shatskin. A
book of collected articles by Shatskin on the CYI has
not been available (*Pervyi gody Kommunisticheskogo
Internatsional Molodezhi* ...).

Alfred Kurella was the son of a well-known German scholar, and thus of 'bourgeois intellectual' origin.[49] Service in the German army had made him an opponent of the war by 1916. Having been declared unfit for duty he became engaged in anti-war propaganda. By early 1917 he had begun to organize a radical left wing within the Freideutsche-Jugend, an organization formed in 1913 by those who had outgrown the existing youth groups. He became exposed to Marx's ideas, and to the ideas of the revolutionary anti-war opposition. In October 1918 he fled from Berlin to Munich, where he had studied before the war, in order to avoid arrest. By this time he had been swept up in the revolutionary euphoria sparked by the Bolshevik revolution, and by the disintegrating political situation in Germany. By the middle of November Kurella had succeeded in founding a Munich section of the revolutionary Freie Sozialistische Jugend, and soon also joined the local section of the new KPD.

During the period of the Bavarian Soviet Republic (November 1918-February 1919), Kurella acted as censor for all telegraphic agencies in Munich. Stranded in Berlin after the fall of the Bavarian Soviet, he was assigned a task by chance that was to shape his future most dramatically. The leadership of the new KPD was in disarray after the ban on the communists in March. A courier was needed to take a report to Lenin and the Russian party on the state of affairs in the KPD. Kurella was picked for the job. Once in Moscow, Kurella was drafted by Lenin to participate in drawing the plans for the new youth international. He began to study Russian, became a member of the Russian Komsomol, and later played an important part in the Berlin discussions. He also served in the youth international leadership for some time and then moved into the area that was to occupy him for the rest of his career: ideological training and development.

Shatskin and Kurella had left Moscow in early summer expecting the conference to be held in Budapest as an expression of solidarity with the new communist regime. With Kurella travelling through Berlin and Shatskin through the Ukraine, neither got beyond Vienna after the fall of the Hungarian Soviet made it clear that the conference would

49 See Laqueur, *Young Germany*, and Kurella, *Unterwegs zu Lenin*, 14ff

have to be held elsewhere. In Vienna at a preparatory
meeting, and later in Germany, Shatskin and Kurella worked
with limited success to win Münzenberg and the West Europeans to the Leninist views on what the youth movement
should be and do. Drawing on two years of Bolshevik experience, Shatskin wished to divert the new youth international into educational work (kul'turno-prosvetitel'haia
rabota). By conducting propaganda in the schools, the
young communists could combat the influence of bourgeois
ideology. By being active in raising the educational level
of the individual worker, they could help to make him more
capable of participation in the administration of the
state after the revolution.
Shatskin insisted that

> it is out of the question to say that we have no time
> for such educational work. No one has said that we wish
> to discontinue political activity. This occupies first
> place in our program. But we cannot occupy ourselves
> only with street demonstrations, we must also deepen
> our work among the young people. A communist is not he
> who has read the *Communist Manifesto* and has learned
> by heart a few political phrases, but one who is able
> to carry his Marxist education into all aspects of life.

The Russians were prepared to assign only a limited
political role to the youth movement. The young communists
were to be active inside those socialist parties where
communist factions were struggling for control, but were
to engage in other political actions only when called upon
to do so by the party and/or Comintern. The youth movement
was to assist, certainly not to lead, the parties and the
Comintern. At a time when all communists believed that the
socialist revolution would soon engulf Europe (if it was
not already doing so), such political activity took 'first
place' in importance. In terms of time and effort, however
the Russians expected the youth movement to be occupied
primarily with development of the 'proletarian class-
consciousness' of the young workers. Only in such a way
could the youth movement contribute to the formation of a
mass revolutionary movement.

50 *Pervyi kongress KIM* ... 139-41

Shatskin's main concern was preparation of the youth movement for the anticipated revolutionary assumption of power in Europe. When this occurred, the youth organizations already would have a substantial background for their fundamental tasks after the assumption of power: the organizing and political education of all young people, and the control and direction of all youth activities.[51] They would have mobilized and 'educated' the larger portion of the young workers in the 'correct' Marxist principles, thus assuring ideological uniformity - the prerequisite for a disciplined movement, upon which the Russians placed such great weight.

Supporting Shatskin, and drawing on another if short-lived experience of communism in power, the Hungarian, Johan Lekai, argued that the dictatorship of the proletariat was not

a magic wand, with the help of which it is possible to change conditions at once ... Our Hungarian experience shows us how necessary it is that the youth be educated thoroughly. The young Hungarian workers did not have a proper education. They were inspired by our revolutionary words, but when hunger set in they left us ... Educational work is necessary also to prepare for the understanding of the decrees which must be issued during the dictatorship.[52]

Lekai was obviously somewhat less impressed with the revolutionary enthusiasm of the younger generation than was expressed in the prevailing mood of the delegates.

Münzenberg had quite different ideas. He rejected flatly the limited, auxiliary role envisaged by Radek, Bronski, Shatskin, and Lekai. On the contrary, the young communists would and should be found in the vanguard of all revolu-

51 See the debate on this subject between Shatskin (Pawlow) and the Hungarian, Johan Lekai (Köres) in Pawlow and Köres, *Die Aufgaben der kommunistischen Jugendorganisationen nach der Übernahme der Macht das Proletariat* ... Believing as they did in the imminence of revolution, the young communists devoted considerable attention to 'the tasks after the assumption of power,' both at Berlin and all during 1920.

52 *Pervyi kongress KIM* ... 144-5

tionary actions. He envisaged a far more direct and political role for communist youth than allowed for by the
Russians. Although he and most of the other delegates
agreed that it was necessary to combat bourgeois ideology
and to train class-conscious proletarians, they believed
that to accept the position of Shatskin and Lekai would be
to run the serious risk of turning educational work into
the primary aim of the youth movement. Schüller, Lewinsohn,
and the other more militant delegates thought that the role
of educational work in communist youth organization activities was overemphasized. Schüller agreed that 'a certain
level of education of the masses is a preliminary condition
for firm Soviet power. With illiterates and drunkards Soviet
power will not get very far. But the question to be decided
is whether we have in our organizations [sufficient resources to warrant expending energy on] educational activities.'[53] He was joined by others seeking to avoid diverting
limited resources from the political struggle.[54]

The wording of the program on this point was the result
of a compromise that did not really settle the matter.
'Building of conscious proletarian fighers and future build-
ers of communist society' was seen as a fundamental task
of the youth organizations.[55] Yet, of those tasks set forth

53 Ibid., 141
54 See the views of Lewinsohn (ibid., 145-6) and Samuelsen
(ibid., 155)
55 Münzenberg, *Die Dritte Front*, 379. The resistance of the
militants was only intensified when mention was made of
efforts in general education, beyond political propaganda, into the areas of art, literature, and science.
Countering 'bourgeois ideology' and widening the cultural perspectives of the young workers were seen to be
tasks not for the youth organizations, but for other
communist organizations. A further section of the program, over which there was also considerable dispute,
obligated the youth organizations to be concerned with
the physical development and well-being of the young
workers. Some felt that this, as general education, was
a luxury that could not be afforded at that time. The
militants supported the proposal, but linked it with
preparing the young workers for military actions against
the bourgeoisie. This went beyond the intentions of
those drafting the program, and was rejected.

in the program which were considered most important, youth
education was mentioned last. The delegates remained convinced of the need to place the priority on direct and immediate involvement of the youth organizations in the revolutionary process. Indeed, as has been suggested earlier,
they saw the youth organizations serving as a necessary
guiding force for the revolutionary movement.

One should not be surprised, then, to find that the issue
at the Berlin congress which was to have the most lasting
consequences for the communist movement concerned the relations between the generations. While the Comintern and
the youth international appeared to agree on the general
principles that were to govern their relations, it was not
until 1921 that this issue was finally settled. In the
meantime a bitter dispute arose between the youth international and the Russian leaders, a dispute over organizational norms that was to have serious consequences for the
future development of the entire communist movement.

Münzenberg, supported by the German FSJ, argued that the
new youth international should retain its autonomy.[56] This
meant that while the CYI identified with the basic principles and objectives of the Comintern, young communists
would not commit themselves to support or follow the Comintern on all tactical questions. The CYI therefore should
not join the Comintern as a constituent member, but 'must
consider itself to be on an equal (ravnotsennaia) footing
with its brother organization.[57] He pointed out that the
Swedish and Norwegian youth organizations had asserted
their independent position, and that this had been accepted
by the Comintern.

The Italians were even more outspoken. 'We must retain
our autonomy and our right of criticism,' said Luigi Polano.
'We wish to march shoulder to shoulder with the adults,
preserving the independence of our organization in order
to have the possibility of criticizing the mistakes of the
adults. Our adherence to the Comintern must be exclusively
in moral terms.'[58] He was adamantly opposed to including
the CYI and its executive in the Comintern.

56 *Pervyi kongress KIM* ... 168. See also *Die Junge Garde*,
   26 July 1919
57 *Pervyi kongress KIM* ... 168
58 Ibid., 169

The Russian position, again as expressed by Shatskin,
was that the young communists belonged inside the adult
organizations, which would lead the broad political struggle
of the entire proletariat. 'Youth is not some sort of exclusive universe,' said Shatskin. 'It does not consist of
a society within a society. It is part of the working class,
and its movement is part of the international workers' movement.' He was concerned about the challenge to centralism
that he saw at work in the new International. The 'opportunists' were agitating for federalism, and this had to be
opposed at all costs. The youth international had to come
out clearly for centralism. It should set an appropriate
and needed example at a time when the Comintern was
struggling to establish itself as the leader of the 'truly
revolutionary' part of the proletariat. 'By adhering to
the Communist International as a constituent part, we set
an example for the vacillating parties ... We must [accept
centralism] if we do not wish to destroy the Third International.' Despite variations in party structure, said
Shatskin, the international movement had to be united under
central leadership. In Soviet Russia it was necessary for
all communists to be organized on the basis of strict centralization. In Germany the situation was different, since
the communist party was not united or homogeneous. The
young German communists therefore were right to be cautious

But the Communist International as a whole has clear
policies and tactics, which we must accept unconditionally. [However], its executive committee is not some
kind of conductor, under whose baton we must dance.
Giving directives, it takes into consideration the
situation in the various countries.[59]

Shatskin was being disingenuous in those remarks, avoiding
a major issue. In November 1919 the Communist International
did *not* have 'clear policies and tactics.' Those parties or
groups that had joined, or were planning to join, the
Communist International had not had an opportunity to
gather together to discuss matters of principle, strategy,
or tactics. Although it was not put directly in such terms,
those advocating independence for the CYI were unwilling
to submit in advance to any and all decisions made by what

59 Ibid., 169-70

had to be considered a provisional executive in Moscow.
Most went much further and argued openly for independence
in principle, even from genuinely representative Comintern
institutions.

Shatskin at the end of his remarks injected an imperious
note, which perhaps foreshadowed things to come, when he
'once again insistently' proposed acceptance of his position. The only support for Shatskin noted in the records
came from Hans Meyer (Blank), who rejected the notion that
the CYI could conduct policies that did not fully conform
with those of the Third International.[60] Meyer was a vigorous opponent of the 'ultra-left.' Only by the application
of firm discipline could the youth movement be protected
from these and other misguided and dangerous views.

Richard Schüller rejected the Russian view of the CYI/
Comintern relationship. He opposed treating the youth international as if it were simply another party, no more
significant in the Third International than even the
smallest of parties. 'The youth international at present
already has acquired 300,000 members and, in fact, repre-
sents in itself a world movement and the association of
the most diverse groups of revolutionary youth in all
countries.' The youth international and the Third International had thus to be considered as equal organizations.
'The youth international is not a party,' admonished
Schüller, 'it is an International.'[61]

The congress voted 17-8 for adherence to the Comintern.
The decision, however, was an ambiguous compromise which
neither bound the youth international to the Comintern as
a constituent member, as demanded by the Russians, nor
accepted the concept of a completely equal relationship
between the two. As stated in the program:

> The Communist Youth International accepts (Steht auf dem
> Boden) the basic decisions of the first congress of the
> Third International and forms a part of this communist
> international. The central organs of the Communist Youth
> International are organizationally linked (verbunden)
> with the Third International and struggle in closest
> partnership with it.[62]

60 Ibid., 169
61 Ibid., 170-1
62 Münzenberg, *Die Dritte Front*, 380. Pietschmann (*Der*

With eight votes in opposition to even this limited con-
cession to the Russian view, as well as several abstentions,
and with Russian unhappiness about the continued challenge
to their notion of centralization from the youthful 'vanguardism,' it was evident that the issue had not been
settled definitively.[63]

Party/youth organization relations were as important to
participants at the Berlin congress as those between the
CYI and the Comintern. Münzenberg had stressed the need for
unity and firm discipline in his report on the draft program, but while unity demanded close ties between young
communists and the new communist parties, it would be wrong
to demand the dissolution of all youth organizations and
their merger with the parties.[64] Parties might lose 'the

---

politisch-ideologische Klärungsprozess ... 147) criti-
cizes Kurella for having erred (in *Gründung und Aufbau*
...) in saying that the Communist Youth International
was not subordinated fully to the Comintern at Berlin.
In fact, however, Kurella has a more sophisticated
recognition of the CYI/Comintern relations until 1921
than does Pietschmann.

63 *Pervyi kongress KIM* ... (172) gives the voting as 17-8,
with a Swiss abstaining. A more precise breakdown indicates that Austria, Italy, and a Romanian voted against,
and Switzerland and a Romanian abstained (*Der Kommunistische Jugend*, 25 December 1919, 154-5). Shatskin had
been accused of exhibiting a 'sectarian' attitude at
Berlin (interview with Luigi Polano). Coming from a
country where revolution was seen to be developing into
socialism, Shatskin believed others should follow this
experience. Polano says that he argued that one needed
to have a broader view. Each case must be decided on its
own merits. Shatskin was not heard without respect,
according to Polano, for he did bring some experience
of party/youth organization relations with him, and he
did have the prestige of the Bolshevik revolution behind
him. His views were not, however, accepted automatically
because Russian experience was seen to be most appropriate.

64 There was support for absorption of the youth groups by
the parties not only within the parties, and especially
in ECCI, but also in the youth organizations. Those
young communists who supported this position, usually

revolutionary way.' The fear persisted that 'revolutionary
purity' would be abandoned. The contention that the youth
organizations should simply write their programs in conformity with those of the parties was similarly rejected
categorically because 'the adherence of a party to the
Comintern still does not signify that this party is really
communist.'[65]

This position was challenged by Shatskin. The youth organizations were not political parties, he said.[66] Each
youth organization should be obligated to adopt the political program of its national communist party as its own
program. The hidden implications were not lost on the participants. What if a party no longer lived up to its revolutionary program? Who was to say, and by what criteria
when party behaviour ceased to conform to its revolutionary objectives? Those who spoke on this point tended to
echo Münzenberg's views: 'to accept the program of the
communist party does not mean complete acceptance of the
policies and tactics of the communist party.'[67] Thus, the
program of the CYI emphasized that the youth organizations
were independent of the parties, but worked in close contact with them in conditions of mutual assistance.[68]

---

the 'ultra-leftists,' believed that all communists
should, in the current situation of full-scale revolution, concentrate on political tasks. As the party was
the political leader, the young communists should join
with the party in a concentrated effort to push the revolution to its successful conclusion (Kurella, *Gründung
und Aufbau* ... 32). This assumed, of course, that the
parties would be 'ultra-leftist' parties.

65 *Pervyi kongress KIM* ... 161
66 *Die Kommunistische Internationale*, no. 11 (August?
   1920): 224-42
67 Quoted from *J-I* in Heinz, *Die Entwicklung der kommunistischen Jugendinternationale*, 10
68 Münzenberg, *Die Dritte Front*, 378. Shatskin was later,
   at the third Komsomol congress in October 1920, to
   claim that the Russian view had triumphed in all respects (Fisher, Jr, *Pattern for Soviet Youth*, 53), albeit not without a great struggle and as a result of
   'pressure (theoretical)' from the Russian side. He was
   somewhat premature in making this claim.

A major problem was left unsolved by this formula, however. The German delegates had to face the situation of two
parties claiming to stand on the platform of the Third International. Although the split was not yet final, the
excluded 'ultra-left' had already begun to organize the
Kommunistische Arbeiterpartei Deutschlands (KAPD). The
Comintern had not as yet indicated what it was going to do.
Lewinsohn, a strong supporter of the KAPD, proposed that
the 'youth organization stand on the platform of that party
in its country which most approximates the principles of
the Communist International and most clearly expresses the
will to proletarian revolution.' This would not only have
given complete freedom of choice to the youth organization,
but would have sanctioned support for the more militant
KAPD over the KPD. It was thus proposed that 'in its political struggle, communist youth stand on the platform of
that party or faction in its country the principles of which
are in agreement with the program of the Communist Youth
International and the Third International.'[69] This, again,
would have left it up to the youth group to decide if and
when the principles of a given party or faction were in
accord with the CYI and the Comintern.

The final decision, adopted 16-5, took most of the choice
out of the issue.[70] Youth organizations were to stand on
either 'the program of that party or faction in its country
which belonged to the Third International, or the program
of the Communist International.'[71] In either case, the youth
organization was obligated to support the Comintern position
over any individual communist party.[72] What the new program
did for the first, but by no means the last, time was to
place an obligation on communists to support the International above any national party.[73]

69 *Pervyi kongress KIM* ... 162
70 Ibid., 162. This report of the voting leaves twelve votes
   unaccounted for. There may well have been this many abster
   tions. The sixteen votes that passed the resolution are
   one short of a majority of the total votes available.
71 Münzenberg, *Die Dritte Front*, 378
72 The program thus did not really represent support for
   either side in the KPD/KAPD conflict. Although the KPD
   was a founding member of the Comintern, part of the dispute was over who truly represented the Comintern in
   Germany, and which the Comintern would support.
73 This was confirmed by Shatskin at the fifth Komsomol

A new youth international

An organization statute, endorsing centralization, was
adopted unanimously by the congress with little discussion.[74]
As the new leadership pursued its duties, it became evident
that centralization did not literally mean the giving and
enforcing of orders. That was not Münzenberg's style. It
was also not a style that lent itself to the independent,
assertive mood of those flocking to the communist youth
organizations. At this time the belief in centralism was
more an expression of faith and expectation that all good
young communists would behave spontaneously and naturally
in a disciplined and ordered manner. Evaluations and interpretations would be made, and policies determined, by consensus. The common commitment to revolution would bind all
participants together and smooth out any disputes. Directives would be followed simply because all recognized their
validity and appropriateness. Differences, such as those
that appeared at the congress, would smooth themselves out
somehow in the course of the revolutionary process. Serious
problems developed later as it became evident that centralism within the communist movement *did* mean that orders
would be given, and would be expected to be obeyed.

As in the Comintern, a great degree of authority was given
to the executive organ. An executive committee (ECCYI) of
five was to be elected by the congress. It would serve under
the formal authority of the congress and the International
Bureau. The composition of the executive committee reflected

---

congress in October 1922 (Fisher, Jr, *Pattern for Soviet
Youth*, 103). Young communists were obligated to obey the
party *only* when the party obeyed the Comintern.
74 *The Communist International* (London), no. 11/12 (1920):
2531. For the congress manifesto see *Pervyi kongress KIM
... 195-9. Several important differences are observable
between the draft statute circulated by Münzenberg in
1918 and the one adopted at Berlin. These indicate the
extent to which Münzenberg and the others had moved toward the Bolshevik position with the creation of the
Communist International. In the earlier draft, no mention had been made of only one member being permitted
from each country (Münzenberg, *Program und Aufbau der
sozialistischen Jugend-Internationale*, 14-16). This was
before Lenin's call for strict centralization expressed
in the invitation to the founding congress of the Comintern.

the relative importance of the various constituent organizations. Two members were from Germany, and one each from Scandinavia, the Slavic countries, and Latin Europe. Münzenberg, Leo Flieg, Oskar Samuelsen, Shatskin, and Luigi Polano were the first incumbents. The location of ECCYI in Berlin symbolized the independent existence of the new Communist Youth International. The German youth movement was the dominant influence in the CYI, as the Russian party was in the Comintern. It was in Central Europe that expansion of the revolution was anticipated; it was there that the young communists would be most active.[75]

The International Bureau was to meet between congresses and comprised members of the executive committee and one representative selected by each member organization. Already the hierarchically structured Bolshevik model of indirectly elected bodies was making its appearance.

The significance of the Berlin congress

In light of what was to happen over the next several years, the simplest way to interpret the congress might be to dismiss it as the petty wrangling of a handful of naive romanti

75 It has been suggested that in order to win Russian acquiescence in the location of the CYI executive organs in Germany, Münzenberg and the West Europeans had to pay a price: acceptance of the subordination in principle of the CYI to the Comintern (interview with Giuseppe Berti). Whether or not this was so, it was in any case more natural for leadership to reside in Western Europe. The West Europeans knew that the young Russian revolutionaries had begun to organize seriously only in 1917. The West Europe had long traditions and a degree of importance before the Russians even had a socialist youth movement. While Lenin Trotsky, Zinoviev, Bukharin, and other Russian party leaders had considerable experience and knowledge of a socialist movement in a capitalist system, this was not the cas with the Russian youth leaders. The young communists in Western Europe were quite unwilling to give up their position of leadership to the Russian organization. Apparently, both ECCI and the Komsomol recognized the impossibility of demanding a shift to Moscow at this time (interview with Alfred Kurella). For the composition of the new executive committee see *Pervyi kongress KIM* ... 211-1

who had an absurdly exaggerated notion of their importance.
Thus, the foregoing details of the proceedings could be of
little interest to those concerned with larger questions.
Such a judgment cannot be supported if one sees the proceedings in their proper perspective. Firstly, the delegates
at Berlin represented a political and social phenomenon that
had grown to significant proportions by this time. In most
of the European countries there was a large, and growing,
mass movement of young socialists willing and eager to work
for a revolutionary transformation of existing society.
These young socialists did, at this time, see themselves as
'more revolutionary' than the adults. The views expressed
in the proceedings had roots deep within the younger generation of socialists. One must turn to these proceedings
to discover the meaning the young socialists attributed to
their own movement.

Furthermore, the delegates were addressing issues whose
importance really went far beyond the youth movement. The
proceedings did not constitute some isolated, parochial
event. Although not recognized adequately at the time, the
debate over the role of the young communists was in reality
a debate over the nature of the communist movement itself.
These issues, it is true, ultimately were resolved outside
the youth movement. Nevertheless, it was at Berlin that the
critical questions of the communist movement were first
articulated and subjected to discussion and debate.

The Berlin program constituted a sharp break with both
the pre-war and wartime youth internationals. The Communist
Youth International encompassed the largest proportion of
the socialist youth movement, a movement that was now committed to revolution under the leadership, through the
Comintern, of the new Bolshevik regime in Russia. From an
organization that was closely tied to the socialist parties
and predominantly non-political in nature, the youth international moved during the war toward becoming an independent
revolutionary political movement. The Declaration of Principles drafted by Münzenberg in 1916 had rejected reformism
and the concept of 'national defence,' but it had not taken
sides between the left and the centre. At Berlin, the new
program affirmed support for the left, and a clear break
with all other tendencies.

The International Union of Socialist Youth Organizations
(IUSYO) had now become the Communist Youth International.
Lenin and the radical left had been forced by their minority

position and their inability to capture the International
Socialist Bureau, to set up a new, Third International. The
creation of the Comintern was the work of the Russian Bolsheviks, who exercised a controlling influence. The founding
of the Communist Youth International, however, was the work
of the young revolutionary socialists in Western Europe. The
Russian communists were in no position to assume the mantle
of leadership. The Berlin congress demonstrated quite clearly
that the initiative lay with the West Europeans. The Russians
through Shatskin and Kurella, could argue, cajole, and perhaps even threaten, but they could not exert a directing influence on the proceedings.

An important point to note about the Berlin congress is
that there *was* contact between the Russian Bolsheviks and
the extreme left in Central Europe prior to November 1919,
when Viktor Kopp arrived in Berlin as representative of the
Soviet government to negotiate an exchange of prisoners of
war.[76] The presence of the Russian emissaries had important
consequences at the Berlin congress and on the development
of the youth international. Furthermore, is it really true
that 'during the whole decisive period of civil war the
Russians hardly attempted to influence the policy of the
Western communist movement'?[77] Through Polano the Italian
left received a first-hand account of Moscow's views from
Shatskin. Shatskin also was active in discussions on parliamentary methods. He may well have supported or even encourage

76 Both Carr (*The Bolshevik Revolution, 1917-1923* III, 132-5
   and Borkenau (*World Communism*, chapter 8) emphasize the
   loss of contact, but the presence in Germany (from July i
   the case of Kurella, from August in that of Shatskin) of
   the Russian delegates to the Berlin congress enabled the
   latest thinking of the Bolshevik leaders in Moscow to be
   brought to the attention of the left in Central and Weste
   Europe. Shatskin had been personally instructed by Lenin
   before he left Russia. Radek had arrived in Germany in
   December 1918, but had spent most of the first half of
   1919 in jail and out of contact with events. It was only
   from August 1919 that he began to play a part in the affairs of the KPD. While there is no direct evidence that
   he received 'instructions' from Lenin through Kurella and
   or Shatskin, it is certainly most likely that he learned
   of Lenin's (and ECCI's) latest views on events in the Wes
77 Borkenau, *World Communism,* 165

Radek in his efforts to combat the anti-parliamentary, anti-trade-union elements, and to preserve unity in the German communist movement.[78]

Probably the most important result of the presence of Shatskin and Kurella in Berlin was the articulation in the youth movement rather earlier than in the Comintern of the view that the Russian model of organization was desirable and necessary for all communist groups. Shatskin's advocacy of strict centralization and subordination of the youth international to the Comintern, and of youth organizations to the parties, reflected the changed attitude of the Russian communist party to their new (October 1918) communist youth organization, the Komsomol. The Komsomol leaders, all party members, had called for closer party control at a meeting of their central committee in April 1919.

The Russian arguments for subordination of the youth organizations to the parties were much criticized after the Berlin congress as 'acceptable for Russia, but not Western Europe.'[79] The Russians may at this time only have meant to apply the principle of centralization to the youth groups, but it foreshadowed their application to the parties in 1920. Thus, the first phase in the transformation of democratic revolutionary parties into organs of Leninist dictatorship has its origins as early as the middle of 1919.[80]

78 There is no evidence that Shatskin ever visited Radek in his privileged cell. Certainly, the illegality of his presence in Germany precluded any such direct contact. Radek makes no mention of any communication with Shatskin in his later reflections (see Carr, 'Radek's "Political Salon" ...'), but there was a channel of communication available.
79 See chapter six, note 33.
80 See Lowenthal, 'Bolshevization ...' (24) for the suggestion that this occurred only beginning with the second Comintern congress in the summer of 1920. Furthermore, Carr's citation of both Lenin's *'Left-Wing' Communism: An Infantile Disorder*, and the stiffening of the Comintern attitude in the spring of 1920 (the dissolution of the Amsterdam bureau by ECCI in April and the attitude of ECCI towards the British Labour Party and the USPD in Germany expressed in May) as the points from which to date the change in Comintern organization (Russian experience should serve as an example to the Comintern

The participants in the Berlin congress dispersed as inconspicuously as they had assembled. Despite the defeats suffered by the revolutionary forces in Germany and Hungary in 1919, and the inauspicious circumstances in which they had deliberated, they left in an enthusiastic and buoyant mood. There was general expectation that a revolutionary transfer of power, and the task of constructing a new, socialist society, was just around the corner. In the meantime, it was necessary to translate the revolutionary solidarity within the socialist youth movement into specific support for the Communist Youth International and its program.

and the revolutionary movements in other countries) should be preceded by reference to the attitude of the Russian delegates to the founding congress of the Communist Youth International. Helmut Gruber also cites 1920 as the year in which the 'bolshevizaton' of the Comintern began (Gruber, *International Communism* ... 277). See also chapter eight, note 18.

5

'Clarity' in the socialist youth movement: the struggle for supremacy

The Communist Youth International (CYI) was built upon important traditions that had developed over the preceding
decades. At the outset, however, it was not much more than
an expression of the great expectations of those present
at the Berlin congress. The webs of loyalty that slowly
had given substance and continuity to the youth international had yet to be translated into support for the new
organization. The new youth international had to gain recognition by all young socialists, or at least by all those
'truly' committed to revolution. The revolutionary program
of the CYI needed to gain acceptance as the most appropriate
means of pursuing the younger generation's idealistic visions.
   The new CYI leaders had to build on existing strengths
and tie its supporters closer together, construct an organization capable of furthering the revolutionary goals of
the CYI, and help to resolve the political/factional conflicts within socialism once and for all in favour of the
new communist movement. These were not easy tasks. The last,
especially, was a difficult proposition, for the other
factional forces still exercised considerable influence
within the socialist youth movement. The new leaders thus
had to enter into an ideological and political struggle for
supremacy, the outcome of which would be critical for the
future of the Communist Youth International and its hopes
for revolution.[1]

1 As an organization, the youth international was expected
  by its founders to support the Bolsheviks in Russia,
  'the revolution,' and the Comintern. All young communists
  and supporters of the Third International were asked to

The young communists began this struggle from a relatively advantageous position. They were favoured by the post-war high tide of political radicalism that already had swept through several of the youth organizations represented at Berlin. The communist movement provided a framework for this youthful radicalism, as well as an ideological content and a sense of direction. When the CYI began operations, it could count as members large youth organizations in Soviet Russia, Germany, Italy, Sweden, and Norway. Although 300,000 members were claimed for the CYI at the Berlin congress, the figure was probably closer to 200,000.[2] Almost forty percent of these, however, came from the Russian Komsomol. Clearly, there was a need to expand support for the CYI outside Soviet Russia.[3]

---

assist the executive committee of the Comintern to become a body capable of exercising genuine leadership. As *Jugend-Internationale (J-I)* noted in its March 1920 issue, this had not yet happened. 'The only unifying factor in the Communist International until now has been the common program. An international organization with a united international leadership, the prerequisite for international action, is lacking ... Today there is in almost every land an international bureau or secretariat of the Communist International. This not only makes common, united action impossible, but impedes considerably the political activity of the Communist International.'

2 Kurella, *Gründung und Aufbau* ... 47. The approximate membership figures for the socialist or communist youth organizations in these countries at the time of the Berlin congress are as follows: Russia, 100,000; Germany (FSJ, 20,000; SPJ, 15,000; AJ, 30,000–50,000); Italy, 30–35,000; Sweden, 22,000; Norway, 13,000. In all of these countries except Germany, the youth organization represented at Berlin was by far the largest, if not the only, socialist youth organization in the country.

3 The situation only got worse. By 1921 the CYI counted 450,000 to 500,000 members, of which 250,000 (50–55 per cent) were Russian Komsomol members. At the time of its second congress in the summer of 1921 the CYI claimed a grossly inflated figure of 800,000 members. This was based on the membership figures for the socialist youth organizations at the time of assertion of communist

These first recruits to the communist youth movement had been radicalized by a number of factors. They also came from a variety of backgrounds. They included young veterans, alienated and guilt-ridden offspring of bourgeois families, rootless exiles from countries with authoritarian regimes, young workers, apprentices, and a large number of the unemployed. Although schools and universities were not encouraging sources for recruits to the revolutionary socialist cause, they were the scene of some radical activity. This was particularly so for those associated with vocational training. For instance, a series of strikes in the Fach- and Fortbildungsschule reached a peak in Berlin in the summer of 1919. Young communists sought to assert leadership of these expressions of dissatisfaction. Even here, however, the radicals could not establish a significant base of support.

Despite these circumstances, some of the leading young communists did come from the higher schools and universities. In several countries, socialist student organizations were formed in which there were strong communist sympathies. At an international socialist students' congress held in Geneva in December 1919, support for the communist parties was also strong.[4] The CYI wished to eliminate the distinction between young worker and young intellectual. Eventually the young communist intellectuals were absorbed into either the parties, or the youth organizations.

The most important sources of recruits soon came to be the factories and the shops - and during 1919, 1920, and 1921, the streets. Young workers and apprentices were the least organized element in the working class. The trade unions were not altogether responsive to their needs. Much child-labour legislation, and regulation of the master/apprentice relationship, it is true, was introduced under trade-union pressure. Still, the unions had a difficult enough time waging the struggle for their own interests.

----

control, before the centrists had left and before many others left due to the political activities of the communists. The figure 450,000 to 500,000 is more correct for 1921. By 1924 the percentage of the total CYI membership made up of Komsomol members was up to about 80 or 85 per cent due to the considerable growth of the Komsomol and drastic losses in the other youth organizations.
4 For a report on the congress see *J-I*, February 1920, 10-11.

As they were usually the first to be laid off in times of
economic stress, unemployment was always the highest among
the young. They were thus susceptible to communist appeals.
Many of the most militant supporters of the 'ultra-left'
and the 'revolutionary offensive' in 1919, 1920, and 1921
came from the ranks of the unemployed. Moreoever, revolutionary socialists of both centre and left were able to
win much support from young workers because of their vehement anti-militarism. There was a strong desire to revive
the traditional socialist commitment to struggle against
militarism, which had been broken by the outbreak of war.
Lenin had argued that only the left had been true to the
principles of international socialist solidarity, that
only it had fought against war, and that true peace could
be achieved only through revolution. Many young people
agreed with Lenin's further assertion that socialist and
trade-union leaders had betrayed the working class.

In contrast to the membership as a whole, the leaders
tended to come from a middle-class background. Some were
highly idealistic and committed to a broad internationalism
or universalism. Attributing (as Marx had) a high moral
value to 'the proletariat,' they found the Marxist notion
of class solidarity very appealing. Some were fundamentally
nationalist in their orientation. They had been driven to
revolutionary socialism and to the communist movement not
because of suffering humanity, but because of the evident
misery of their own countrymen. Some of the early leaders
were essentially rootless and nihilistic, working out their
own personal problems. The idealism of revolutionary social
ism provided a rationalization of their own emotional needs
Some had a rather well-developed dedication to revolutionar
change; others were more opportunistic and self-serving.[5]

After the Berlin congress, it was clear to the newly
elected executive committee (ECCYI) that its first task was
to establish the authority of the CYI. The new youth international was not exactly foremost in the consciousness of

5 One might cite as an example of the latter Milan Gorkic,
  a teen-aged socialist at the end of the war who became a
  leader of the Yugoslav communist party in the 1930s. He
  has been characterized as a 'cosmopolitan without revolutionary beliefs and without scruples, but smooth, ada
  able, and sufficiently literate' (Avakumovic, *History o*
  the Communist Party of Yugoslavia, 98, n. 31).

the average young worker. If the CYI was to be a leading revolutionary force, it had to be seen and accepted as such by all members of the constituent youth organizations. Understandably, therefore, the members of ECCYI were absorbed in publicizing the new youth international.

The difficulty of finding a permanent headquarters, poor postal communications, and the continuing 'state of siege' in Berlin and Germany as a whole handicapped the new leadership. Notwithstanding, ECCYI was slowly able to develop contacts with other revolutionary youth organizations.[6] This communications network was frequently used by the Comintern apparatus during these early years.[7] Much effort was devoted to the establishment of an extensive publishing operation. Regular publication was begun of *Jugend-Internationale* and *Internationale Jugendkorrespondenz*, in German and several other languages; and the *Internationale Jugend-Bibliothek*, a series of pamphlets and books for dissemination of CYI documents and propaganda, was started.

In the prevailing circumstances, the financing of ECCYI activities and those of the local communist youth movements became very difficult.[8] It took much effort and time to raise regular contributions from the national youth organizations. Poor economic conditions among young workers, domestic demands for limited resources, and strains between the youth organizations and the parties left the CYI in chronic financial difficulties.

The main source of support came from the Swedish, Norwegian, and Italian youth organizations.[9] Profits from publishing activities were of considerable importance, as were various collection drives by the Liebknecht Fund. These were undertaken at rallies and demonstrations held, when possible, each January on the anniversary of Liebknecht's death, on the first of May, and on each annual International

6 For these communications see *Am Aufbau: Dokuments des Exekutiv-Komitees*.
7 Kurella, *Gründung und Aufbau* ... 86
8 Ibid., 86-7
9 *Bericht über die erste Sitzung des Büros der Kommunistischen Jugend-Internationale* ... 8 (hereafter cited as *First Bureau Session); Die Jugend der Revolution*, 24. The Russian Komsomol collected money in Liebknecht Fund drives, but it is doubtful if this was put at the disposal of ECCYI in Berlin.

Youth Day in September. Still, ECCYI continued to experience serious financial problems during 1919, 1920, and most of 1921, and each issue of its publications carried appeals for funds. Apparently neither the Comintern, nor the Russian Komsomol gave financial support to ECCYI when, according to some who were active in its affairs, the Comintern was spending money lavishly elsewhere.[10]

Münzenberg and Leo Flieg were the only members of ECCYI to remain in Berlin. Most of the others were national leade and had to return home. Even Flieg, who was organizational secretary of the German Free Socialist Youth (FSJ) and active in the German communist party (KPD), was not always able to participate in the work of ECCYI. Münzenberg carried on with substitutes in lieu of several elected members: Alfred Kurella for Shatskin, Felix Lewinsohn for Flieg, and Willi Mielenz (from February 1920) for the Scandinavian representative. Several experienced young activists were co-opted to perform various tasks. Richard Schüller from Vienna and Sigi Bamatter from Basel were added right after the Berlin congress, and during 1920 the Yugoslav, Vuja Vujovitch, and the Lithuanian-White Russian youth leader, Viktor Greifenberger. Oskar Samuelsen became leader of an under-secretariat in Stockholm, one of several established to expand ECCYI influence. The members of ECCYI participated in many meetings of various socialist youth organizations. In addition, ECCYI also sponsored several regional conferences to win support for decisions taken at Berlin. In some cases this meant explanation and elaboration of the Berlin program as the memberships met to confirm the actions of their representatives. In others, it involved securing the support of a sympathetic youth organization or group that had not been able to have representation at Berlin.

The Communist Youth International in its first years was a highly personalized organization. To speak of the CYI

10 Ypsilon [Johan Rindl and Julian Gumperz (Rindl is a pse donym for Karl Volk, Gumperz for Jules Humbert-Droz)], *Pattern for World Revolution*, 71-2. In May 1921 ECCYI was refuting charges by the right-socialist and centris youth internationals that the CYI was dominated by Mosc by arguing that it had 'very little Soviet money at its disposal' (*Internationale Jugendkorrespondenz* [IJK], 10 May 1921).

after the Berlin congress is really to speak of Münzenberg
and the small corps of full-time functionaries who were
gathered around him. Periodically, at meetings of the International Bureau or the congress, a wider circle was
drawn in. Nevertheless, it was not the behaviour of the
ordinary young communist that gave meaning and substance
to the CYI. Rather, it was the activity of a few leaders
and activists at the top that shaped and formed the new
youth international. In no sense, however, can Münzenberg
and his fellow functionaries be considered as an all-
powerful elite leadership. They were leading only where
their followers in any event wished to go.

Ideological and political 'clarification' within the youth
movement

By mid 1920 ECCYI had overcome most of its organizational
problems. Yet, recognized and accepted arrangements between
the Communist Youth International and the Comintern, and
between national communist youth organizations and the communist parties, was lacking. This was due in no small part
to the fact that the socialist movement had not as yet been
fully split. The CYI leadership was pursuing the Leninist
policy of polarizing the socialist movement and enrolling
all 'truly' revolutionary young socialists under the banner
of the CYI. This meant weeding out 'ultra-left' influences
and 'clarifying' the centrist youth groups. In the communist jargon of the time, 'clarification work' was a euphe-
mism for efforts to split and break up the centrist organizations.
    Coping with 'ultra-left' influences was painful. Those
who were to do the remedial work were themselves part of
the problem. That amalgam of anarcho-syndicalism and 'left-
communism' that became known as the 'ultra-left' had a
strong hold on the youth movement.[11] Münzenberg and many
other leaders were swayed quite strongly by it. The new
CYI was thus not united ideologically. There was great
diversity of views as to what defined a communist. Indeed,
it was not evident that there was, or should be, *a* set of
beliefs and commitments that would define a 'true revolutionary.'

11 See Bock, *Syndikalismus und Linksradikalismus von
   1918-1923*

It was not that the anarcho-syndicalist groups themselves
were a major problem. There were only a few such groups in
Italy, France, Germany, Holland, and Portugal. They were
not perceived as a serious opposition by the CYI leadership.[12] It was the influence of anarcho-syndicalism and
'left-communism' on the membership of the youth organizations that created the difficulty. This hindered the development of ideologically unified communist organizations.
Many in the youth organizations emphasized 'direct action'
(especially the general strike), rejection of the parliamentary process and the trade unions, and decentralization
in organizational matters. All of these positions were the
precise opposite of those sanctioned by Moscow, and to be
accepted as a communist one was expected to follow officially approved strategies and tactics. In the circumstance
Lenin and the other Bolsheviks, by raising these issues to
questions of principle, unavoidably precipitated a split
within the new communist organizations.
Here once again could be seen the significance of differ
ent interpretations of existing reality. The 'ultra-left'
evaluation of the prospects for revolution was simply more
optimistic than Moscow's. It was this more expectant evalu
ation, and the unrestrained and unrealistic militancy that
derived from it, that had the greatest influence on the
young communists. With exceptions, the youth organizations
in 1919 were uncompromising in their refusal to treat the
existing bourgeois system as if it had any life left. Although Münzenberg was more skeptical, he too sympathized
with the militancy of the 'ultra-left' and its refusal to
deal with the existing order. Not to do so would be to
deny that there were *any* chances for revolution.
The first conference of the socialist youth organization
in south-eastern Europe, held in Vienna in mid May 1920,
represented the peak of unbridled support for 'ultra-lefti
within the CYI.[13] It had been called to secure the adherer

12 *Die Jugend der Revolution,* 17
13 See *Am Werk!* ... See also Kurella, *Gründung und Aufbau*
... 114-17. Of the twelve socialist or communist youth
organizations of varying political orientations in the
area, seven were members of the CYI (Yugoslavia, Roman:
Hungary, Slovak, Austria [VKPJ], Italy, and Greece); tł
adherence of two was seen as imminent (Bulgaria, Czech
and the German-speaking group in Czechoslovakia was va
lating. Only the Austrian centrists (VSAJ) were exclud

of these organizations, which were not well represented at
Berlin. Richard Schüller, a strong sympathizer of the
'ultra-left' and active in the southeast bureau of the
Comintern (a centre of 'ultra-leftism') was the major figure
at the conference.[14] He criticized the Comintern line in
its first months, and spoke against the KPD policy of participating in parliamentary elections. Münzenberg also was
unhappy with developments within the parties since the first
Comintern congress.[15]

It was not until the second Comintern congress in mid
1920 that the CYI finally accepted the Leninist position
on participation in parliaments and the trade unions. While
the delegates at Berlin had accepted participation in principle, there was no commitment in any specific sense. Thus,
opponents could continue to argue against utilization of
parliament and the trade unions in specific cases. By mid
1920, however, the Comintern executive (ECCI) had made
participation official policy for Germany and all other
countries. Even this did not end the matter, since the
Italian and French continued to refuse to accept the new
line. Insistence on acceptance of the Leninist position
led to the same split in the German youth organization
that had occurred within the party. The Kommunistische
Arbeiterjugend (KAJ) were gradually forced out of the communist FSJ during 1920. The final split occurred in
September 1920, when all who refused to accept the second
Comintern congress decisions were expelled.

14 Schüller was also the leader of the young communists in
   Austria (VKPJ). As early as May 1919 the organ of the
   VKPJ, *Die Kommunistische Jugend*, had been condemning parliamentary activity and advocating workers' councils as
   the best means for the erection of the dictatorship of
   the proletariat and the communist state (*Die Kommunist
   Jugend*, 1 May 1919, 46-7). In August the 'ultra-left'
   leadership of the VKPJ came out for the creation of a
   Soviet republic in Austria (ibid., 20 August 1919, 77).
   Schüller was a firm supporter in 1919-1920 of the KAPD
   in Germany. The VKPJ approved the anti-parliament, anti-
   trade union policies of the KAPD, with the result that
   Die Kommunistische Jugend and the Austrian party paper,
   Die Rote Fahne (Vienna), became embroiled in a conflict
   over the latter's attack on the KAPD.
15 Kurella, *Gründung und Aufbau* ... 115-16

At the second Comintern congress Münzenberg was very much on the left, opposing the 'opportunist' tendencies that he perceived in the International. His remarks indicated that he was concerned far less with growth in numbers, than he was in maintaining 'purity.' The fact that 'hundreds of thousands of workers ... fought with arms in their hands and shed blood for the program and aims of the Communist International' was considered by Münzenberg to be a great practical success for revolutionary propaganda and 'of more value for the proletarian revolution than thousands of new party cards.' He argued that it was too early to expand the Communist International, and repeated Zinoviev's comments on the different 'opportunist' tendencies in the Italian, Swedish, Norwegian, Danish, and Yugoslav parties. He spoke of 'enemies in our own house,' and of being unable to shake off the feeling that the Third International was threatened by a great danger obstructing and weakening revolutionary propaganda and action.[16]

Münzenberg also had doubts about the utility of the Twenty One Conditions for membership in the Comintern adopted by the second congress; not because they were too restrictive but rather because they were not severe enough if those 'who only a few weeks ago or even days ago fought against the Third International with all means [the Italian, Serrati, and representatives from the German USPD and the French socialist party], today say that they have no objection to signing the resolution on conditions.'[17] Parties wishing to become members of the Third (Communist) International shou prove themselves through their revolutionary deeds.[18]

Münzenberg and the Dutch 'ultra-leftist,' Wynkoop, were rebuked by Lenin for their 'sectarianism' and their uncompromising views.[19] Trotsky also argued in one of the commissions against the anti-parliamentary, anti-trade union

16 *Protokoly kongressov kommunisticheskogo internatsionala Vtoroi kongress kominterna, iiul'-avgust 1920g.*, 214, 215 (cited hereafter as *Vtoroi kongress*)
17 Ibid. For the Twenty-One Conditions see Degras, *The Communist International* ... I, 166-72
18 *Vtoroi kongress*, 216. See also the article by W.M. [Willi Münzenberg], 'Die Krise in der Kommunistischen Internationale und die Kommunistische Jugend,' *IJK*, 5 May 1921, 1.
19 *Vtoroi kongress*, 249

views of Münzenberg, failing, however, to get the latter to change his opinions.²⁰ A proposal by Münzenberg that the Communist International undertake 'at least the spiritual preparation of the broad masses,' and the 'technical-military-organizational preparation of the communist parties' for civil war was buried in a commission.²¹

Whatever his other differences with the Russians on tactics, Münzenberg personally still retained a general and as yet unspecified belief in the need for unity and discipline. He therefore accepted formally the Comintern line on tactics. Several of the most important youth organizations, however, refused to follow Münzenberg's lead. There was thus no slackening of 'revolutionary militancy' within the Communist Youth International. The youth organizations became a major source of support for the 'revolutionary offensive' after the second Comintern congress. This militancy was not entirely overcome until well after the change in the Comintern line instituted by Lenin in 1921. It was, as will be seen, a major source of Russian dissatisfaction with the youth movement. It was to be an important reason why the Comintern took steps in 1921 to deprive the youth movement of its traditional independence.

The founders of the new youth international had, at least from their own viewpoint, expelled a wide assortment of young people from the pale of progressive and moral respectability. The religious, nationalist, and non-political youth groups were considered hopeless. They reinforced retrogressive ideologies, they deluded and misled the younger generation, and were in general perceived as an enemy to be fought, rather than as sources of potential recruits. Having made a Faustian pact with the bourgeois system, the young right-socialists, or social democrats, had settled for the promise of progress and justice. They had sold the future to the bourgeois enemy in return for the illusion of freedom and democracy. They would never pay the price of their illusions, however, for the young revolutionaries would overpower the Devil before he could call for payment. In any event, they too were seen as having chosen to side with the forces of darkness.

It was to the broad mass of as yet unorganized youth, and to the young centrist socialists, that the communists

20 Gross, *Willi Münzenberg*, 110
21 *IJK*, 5 May 1921, 1

turned to build up a mass organization. Those not yet polit
icized were seen as virgin soil, waiting for the crust of
indifference to be penetrated and broken open by the sharp-
ness of communist ideas and the agility of communist agitation. As for the centrists, they wandered like a modern
Hamlet in overalls across the stage of working-class politics. They were an odd lot caught in the dilemma of wanting
a democractic revolution, but finding themselves unable to
act when the time came for decision. They would commit
themselves to use violence only as a last resort. They
would not abandon the bourgeois traditions of freedom and
pluralist democracy. Except for a militant left wing, they
would not consider an active struggle for power.

In 1919, however, the centrists wielded significant influence. In Austria, France, Finland, and Czechoslovakia
they were the dominant force within the socialist youth
movement. In Germany, they still existed as a serious
rival to the communists for the support of those young
people committed, or inclined, to revolutionary socialism.
Proclaiming a belief in the need for revolution and the
overthrow of the bourgeois state, and expressing a desire
to join the Communist Youth International, the young centrists were an obvious object of attention for the new CYI
leadership. The members of the centrist organizations were
as emotionally hostile to the existing order as were the
communists. If they could be persuaded that only the communist organizations represented any realistic hope for
change, the CYI goal of becoming the sole significant influence among the young workers, apprentices, and socialis
intellectuals would be much closer to realization. Certainly, the capture of large numbers of young centrists
was the quickest way for the communist youth organizations
to become mass organizations. The effort to woo and win th
young centrists thus became the foundation of CYI activity
during 1920.

From the beginning of the war, Lenin had been committed
to splitting the socialist movement. 'The task of socialis
he wrote in November 1914, 'cannot be fulfilled and the tr
international coalition of workers cannot be realized at
present without a ruthless break with opportunism...'[22]
Creation of a new, Third International was justified on th
basis of a clear separation between 'revolution' and

22 Gankin and Fisher, *The Bolsheviks and the World War*, 1:

'opportunism' or 'reformism.' By 1919 this meant gathering
all left forces together, ostracism of and hostility toward all right-socialists, and forcing a choice on the
centre: for the new Communist International, or for the
'social-patriots who have today gone over openly to the
camp of the bourgeoisie.'[23] As the Berlin congress demonstrated, the new CYI committed itself completely to this
policy.

It was not enough that the centrists should think in
terms of revolution. Nor was the willingness of most centrists to adhere to the Comintern sufficient to satisfy
Lenin's conception of a 'true international coalition of
workers.' The difficulty lay in the differing perceptions
of socialist internationalism, of revolutionary strategy
and tactics, of the dictatorship of the proletariat, and
of socialist organizational norms. Unconditional acceptance of the Comintern positions, of *his* positions, was
demanded by Lenin, and was the criterion by which the
'true revolutionaries' among the centrists were to be
identified.

ECCYI negotiated with the leaders of the centrist youth
organizations until mid 1920, hoping to persuade them to
accept the Berlin program as the best basis for achieving
socialism as their common goal.[24] Both sides were conscious
of the strong desire for 'proletarian unity' within the
centrist organizations. Formation of the new Communist
Youth International had been greeted with general approval
and some enthusiasm. It was some time, however, before the
membership at large became aware of the Berlin program and
its implications. The fine points of the dispute between
their leaders and the communists tended to be overshadowed
by the simple desire for united action.

The centrist leaders refused to abandon their principles.
As a result, the first session of the International Bureau
in June 1920 decided to play directly on this broad desire
for unity among the centrists. It decided that ECCYI would
'no longer follow the path of negotiations with the central
committees of the [centrist] youth organizations still outside the Communist Youth International.[25] The main effort

23 Degras, *The Communist International* ... I, 46
24 See *Am Aufbau* ..., *J-I*, and *IJK* for most of this correspondence.
25 *IJK* , 1 July 1920

now was to be directed toward strengthening the communist
opposition in the centrist groups in an effort to win the
membership away from its leaders. The International Bureau
hoped that sufficient pressure could be generated from the
membership at large to force either a change in policy, or
a new leadership. By putting the prospects for membership
on a take-it-or-leave-it basis, by stating that acceptance
of the centrist youth in the CYI was possible only through
unconditional acceptance of the Berlin program and the
'practical application of CYI directives,' the Internationa
Bureau believed the majority would come down against its
leaders. In any event, there would be a clear decision for
or against the Comintern, and those committed to revolution
ary action would be separated from those who were willing
only to talk of revolution.[26]

This Leninist approach to creating a revolutionary movement placed great weight on 'capturing' organizations. One
sees the beginnings in these years of the application of
the skilled, and often very successful, tactics by which a
communist minority asserts its control over an organization
The communists, including the CYI, went to great lengths in
this 'clarification' work to win majorities at various conferences and congresses. The takeover of an organization by
these methods can, at times, have considerable political
significance, and the communists did have some lasting
successes. More frequently, perhaps, they turned out to be
empty triumphs. Despite the willingness in practice to sett
for a clear separation between those who would accept the
Leninist perception of revolution (i.e. unconditional adher
ence to the Comintern), and those who would not, it is almost as if Lenin and his followers in these years expected
an ideological conversion to follow, once the leadership

26 The special question of the various Jewish revolutionar
youth organizations in Poland and elsewhere that had in
dicated a desire to join the CYI was discussed at the
International Bureau session. Following the Comintern
position, it was decided that Jews should join the exis
communist youth organizations (see *IJK*, 10 July 1920, a
30 July 1920). After much discussion, the Finnish young
socialists, while still under centrist influence, were
admitted to the CYI, as were the Bulgarian, Slovak, and
Lithuanian-Byelorussian communist youth organizations
(*First Bureau Session*, 12).

(the delegates to a congress, for example) had been won to the cause. One can imagine a certain resemblance to the time when an entire principality was expected to follow the ruler in his conversion - to Christianity or to Protestantism. The communists, however, did not have the means to compel their 'subjects' to follow. In a number of cases, the communists took over parties and youth organizations only to find that most of the membership soon disappeared.

Unable to see any legitimate alternative to their own prescription for successful revolutionary action, the young communists exhibited a rather myopic faith in their capacity to win the centrists to their position. The young communist leaders in 1919 believed that an overwhelming majority of the politically crucial young workers would come to the communist movement naturally. All that was required to win the young centrists was to clarify CYI positions, to attract their attention to communist arguments, and to expose the 'deceptive' arguments of centrist leaders. The majority committed to revolutionary action would thus see the need for unconditional acceptance of the Berlin decisions. The young communists simply could not or would not recognize the appeal of other images of the revolutionary process, and of socialism, much less their justification.

The decision of the International Bureau to break off negotiations was a prelude to the Twenty-One Conditions for membership adopted by the Comintern in July/August 1920. As early as the time of preparations for the Berlin congress the CYI had anticipated the second Comintern congress by defining more precisely which groups and factions were to be considered truly communist, and thus worthy of membership in the new revolutionary International. At the time of the International Bureau meeting in June 1920, however, the Comintern was still negotiating with the leaders of at least one very important centrist party, the Independent Social Democratic Party (USPD) in Germany, as well as with the still undecided and formally unified French and Italian socialist parties.

On 15 September 1920, after the second Comintern congress, ECCYI urged all communist youth organizations to be active participants in the controversy then raging over the Twenty-One Conditions.[27] The youth organizations were to assist in

27 For the ECCYI circular see *Am aufbau* ... II, 12-14. For a similar expression of views a month later after the split of the USPD in Germany see *IJK*, 10 October 1920.

accelerating the 'clarification' process. They were 'to be active everywhere and with all force for the unconditional acceptance and rapid realization of the Moscow decisions.' And, indeed, the young communists gave important support to those in the socialist parties working for the Comintern position.[28] This was especially so in Norway, France, and Italy. For the most part, however, they were busy within the various youth organizations. Those in which the centrists had a strong influence were subjected to a 'mechanical split,' as Paul Levi characterized it.[29] All 'unstable and irresolute elements' were rejected and eliminated.

Apart from excluding the centrists from the Comintern, the decisions of the second congress settled the simmering conflict with the 'ultra-left' by rejecting it on all essential points. The pro-Comintern leadership within the German Freie Sozialistische Jugend was now free to make the final break with the 'ultra-left' forces. The brief discussions of developments in Austria, France, Italy, and Germany that follow demonstrate how the effort to maximize the potential for revolutionary action, as well as to sustain ideological orthodoxy, only served to break up mass organizations and dissipate the revolutionary propensities of the young workers.

Austria
The Communist Youth International very much wanted to win the large and influential socialist youth organization in Austria (VSAJ). The Austrian group had been a founding member of the International Union of Socialist Youth Organizations (IUSYO), and its financial and spiritual leader up to 1914.[30] It still enjoyed wide respect. The denial of

28 See, inter alia, for Italy, *IJK*, 10 January 1921; for Norway, Sogstad, *Ungdoms Fanevakt*, 281-4; for Switzerland Egger, *Die Entstehung* ... 170-2; and *Die Jugend der Revolution*, passim
29 See Levi, 'The Beginning of the Crisis in the Communist Party and International,' excerpted in Gruber, *International Communism* ... 304-9
30 For the financial contributions from the various member organizations see *Bulletin der internationalen Verbindung der sozialistischen Jugendorganisationen*, published in Vienna by the secretariat from 1907 to 1914, as well as the reports by the International Bureau noted in the bibliography.

representation at the Berlin congress to the Austrian centrists (VSAJ), and the decision of the congress to recognize
only the communist youth organization (VKPJ) as the Austrian
section of the new youth international, had created an anom-
alous situation. The largest organization of young workers
and students in Austria thus remained outside the new youth
international, while the recognized member was a very small
sectarian group. The unconditional adherence of the VSAJ
would at once create a mass communist organization of young
workers. Such a move would have brought beneficial results
in other countries where centrist ideas were strong, such
as France and Czechoslovakia, since Austrian socialists
retained a position of influence within the socialist movement, despite the reduction of Austria to a minor state.
The capture of the VSAJ and its fusion with the tiny communist youth organization would also eliminate a formidable
competitor of the communists at one stroke.

The new CYI Executive Committee apparently entertained
some expectation that the VSAJ membership could be won to
the communist position. If so, it was totally unjustified.
The young socialists were rooted too deeply in the traditions of the Austrian labour movement. Their perspective
on revolutionary strategy was directly at odds with that
of the CYI. Where the communists sought ideological orthodoxy and 'revolutionary purity,' the Austrians constantly
pressed for as wide and as large a socialist movement as
possible. Only by maintaining a strong socialist opposition
to the bourgeois enemy could the working class, as a matter
of practical politics, protect itself. To divide the socialist movement, on whatever basis, was to weaken the working
class at a time when the bourgeoisie was ripe for overthrow.
Thus the VSAJ leaders bitterly criticized ECCYI for aiding
Moscow's efforts to turn the IUSYO into a tool of the
'party-political communist tendencies.'[31]

The VSAJ leaders were informed of the results of the Berlin
congress only in late December 1919.[32] The ECCYI letter was
not phrased so as to engender confidence and trust in communist intentions. The executive committee openly challenged
the good faith of the VSAJ central committee. The latter's
expressed desire to join the CYI was brushed aside as 'an
attempt to soothe the internationalism of its members so as

31 *Nicht wollen oder nicht können?* ... 28-38
32 For the correspondence between ECCYI and the Austrians
   see ibid.

to maintain [its] domination over [them].'[33] Furthermore,
at the same time that ECCYI was corresponding with the
central committee, asking for a reaction to the Berlin
decisions, it began to appeal over its head directly to
the membership. A 'circular to the sections of the socialist
youth organization of Austria' called upon members to accept
the Berlin decisions, press for a new national congress,
and join the CYI.[34]

Negotiations continued fruitlessly until the first bureau
session in June 1920. In May, while in Vienna for the conference of socialist youth organizations in south-eastern
Europe, Münzenberg and Flieg had met with the VSAJ central
committee.[35] The Austrians agreed to recognize the Berlin
decisions as the provisional program of the youth international, if ECCYI was ready to call a new conference to
reformulate the program, tactics, and relations of the
youth international to the party international.[36] This
meant, in effect, to abandon the decision to create a youth
international restricted to communists. The first bureau
session unanimously rejected further discussion on this
basis. There was no need for another conference, said the
CYI, since the majority of proletarian youth had already
made its decision.[37] The bureau session, as has been seen,
had decided to change its tactics from negotiations with
the centrist leaders to the bolstering of communist factions within the centrist organizations.

Having failed to win the leadership of the VSAJ to their
view in direct negotiation, ECCYI turned more intensively
towards the membership at large. Working through the VKPJ,
steps were taken to build an 'opposition' to the VSAJ leadership from within its own organization. The 'opposition'
that was formed, however, was never able to threaten the
position of the centrist leadership. It continued as a
very small minority until 1924, when its members all left
and joined the VKPJ. Instead of a mass organization with
deep roots in the traditions of the Austrian working class,

33 Ibid., 12-13
34 Ibid., 13-14
35 *Der Jugendliche Arbeiter*, June 1920, 7. See also Heinz,
   Kampf und Aufstieg
36 *Nicht wollen oder nicht können?* ... 24
37 See *IJK*, 12 August 1920

the CYI settled for a tiny 'gruppchen' without any influence among socialist youth. The belief in revolution persisted within Austrian socialism, even though qualified and conditional. It remained unmobilized and unsupported by the communists. They preferred to maintain the purity of their catacylsmic notion of revolution, even at the cost of political influence and mass support.

France
The strong hold that the Austrian social democrats had on the workers, especially in Vienna, was a source of strength and stability. As G.D.H. Cole has noted, 'Viennese socialism ... was an entire way of life: the activities of the party penetrated into everything ...'[38] Furthermore, the leadership in 1919 was relatively united around a point of view that corresponded to the spontaneous mood of the workers. It is thus understandable that the CYI found the Austrian youth movement impenetrable. In France, however, it was a different story. French socialism in 1919 was a confluence of several disparate trends. The various socialist organizations, from party to youth organization, were far from homogeneous. Intense factionalism meant considerable instability. The absence of a united leadership only intensified the slide into schism and sectarianism.

By the end of the war, the French socialist youth organization had, in effect, been transformed. With reformist socialism discredited, young socialists had become infused with revolutionary fervour. The new leadership was divided, however, into centrists and leftists. It thus did not give a unanimous vote of approval to the founding of either the Comintern, or the Communist Youth International. The attitude to be adopted toward the Bolshevik regime in Russia, and the whole issue of 'the International,' remained open and contentious within both party and youth organization. The majority in both followed a firm centrist line, refusing to commit French socialism unequivocally to the new Third International. The supporters of the Comintern in the youth organization could see only one way to overcome centrist hesitation. Only by making the youth organization independent of the party could they hope to capture it, and assure its adherence to the new revolutionary Internatonal. The

38 See Cole, *Communism and Social Democracy* I, 224

absence of party control or guidance, or a commitment to follow the party's lead, would permit far wider latitude to the pro-Comintern, pro-Bolshevik forces. In an open and fluid situation, the executive committee of the CYI proceeded to explore all options. It established relations both with the French centrist leaders in the national committee, and the opposition 'Committee for Autonomy.'

The youth organization's relations with the party and the new youth international were inevitably the major issue at the national congress at Troyes in April 1920. With the centrists constituting the largest group, as at the French socialist party (SFIO) congress in Strasbourg in February, the resolution adopted expressed a willingness to join the CYI on essentially the same terms as the Austrians. The organizational framework and freedom of action of the French youth organization were to be respected and a new international conference was to be arranged as soon as possible to formulate an agreed program for the youth international.[39] The communist minority failed to win acceptance for an immediate and unconditional acceptance of the Berlin program.

The voting on resolutions put forward by competing factions was important. It showed that considerable confusion and indecision remained. The centrist position of the national secretary, Pierre Lainé, received 3168 votes. Maurice Laporte and the communist 'Committee for Autonomy' drew 2350 votes. Holding a key position between the centrist and pro-Comintern forces was a group, led by Emile Auclair, trying to promote a compromise. The resolution of this group received 1881 votes. With 907 abstentions (mainly the communist-leaning delegates from Alsace-Lorraine), approximately one-third of the members had avoided making a choice.[40] Thus, while the centrists remained in control of the organizaton by virtue of their plurality, no one group could command a clear majority. The new national committee reflected these divisions: six centrists, four communists, and three Auclairists.[41]

39 *Die Jugend der Revolution*, 482
40 Ibid., 483. See also Kriegel, *Aux origines du communisme française* II, 720
41 Kriegel, *Aux origines* ... II, 720. One source says that the Auclair group, while not supporting the move for independence, did support unconditional adherence to the

The Troyes congress demonstrated an important difference between the socialist party (SFIO) and the youth organization. In the latter there was no counterpart to the social democratic right, to party figures such as Pierre Renaudel who condemned Bolshevism and wished to revive the Second International. Among the young socialists even the centrists wished to join with the Bolsheviks and their supporters in forming a new revolutionary International. What prevented the two factions from drawing together and uniting the socialist youth movement was, of course, the communist insistence that centrists were not 'really' revolutionary. Only by accepting the communist positions unconditionally, and by joining the CYI on the platform of the Berlin program, could the centrists give positive proof of their revolutionary bona fides.

After Troyes, the 'Committee for Autonomy' intensified its organizational and agitational work to win over the undecided and wavering elements. Despite an intense desire to split immediately and create a communist youth organization, its leaders reluctantly accepted the argument of the ECCYI representative, the young Serb, Vuja Vujovitch, that it was now possible to capture the youth organization from within.

While supporting the 'Committee for Autonomy,' ECCYI had been continuing to negotiate with the centrists. In May 1920 these negotiations led to a meeting in Milan between representatives of the national committee, ECCYI, and the Italian socialist youth organization.[42] Participating for the French were Lainé, and Renan Radi from the 'Committee for Autonomy.' Behind the apparent agreement that came out of this meeting lay a serious misunderstanding. Lainé had agreed that all revolutionary socialist youth organizations should be brought together. He was for 'drawing closer to

CYI (*Die Jugend der Revolution*, 483). Kriegel says that the Auclairists, while wishing to withdraw from the socialist youth organization and supporting in principle the Third International, had reservations about joining the new CYI. In her account of the youth movement, Kriegel relies heavily on the views and papers of one participant, Renan Radi.
42 The national committee had been commissioned by the Troyes congress to partipate in the ECCYI-planned meeting (*IJK*, 20 May 1920).

the CYI.'[43] This was interpreted by the ECCYI representatives to be an implied unconditional acceptance of the CYI position. ECCYI expected him to return to France, join forces with the 'Committee for Autonomy,' and bring the French youth organization into the fold of the Communist Youth International. Lainé, however, interpreted the Milan conference to have been an acceptance by the CYI of centrist views. The result was an intensification of acrimony between the factions. Each accused the other of deception and bad faith. Maurice Laporte later condemned ECCYI for having negotiated with Lainé.[44] He argued that it had weakened the efforts to defeat the centrists. Their views had acquired legitimacy among the undecided elements.

The first session of the CYI's International Bureau, in June, rejected the conditions for adherence to the CYI set by the congress at Troyes. Only unconditional acceptance of the Berlin decisions and their 'practical application' would do.[45] It had become clear by this time that there had not been an understanding with Lainé. The 'Committee for Autonomy' abandoned negotiations with the centrist leadership, attacked the national committee openly, and rapidly built up the opposition. The shift in tactics by the CYI produced a considerably more favourable turn in France than in Austria. In contrast with Austria, there was a significant opposition in the heterogeneous French socialist youth movement. There was not in France, as there was in Austria, broad general agreement within the socialist movement, or between the socialists and the working class, on the meaning of socialism and on which means were appropriate or inappropriate for achieving socialism.

Pressed by considerable sentiment for immediate formation of a separate communist youth organization, the 'Committee for Autonomy' could barely contain its impatience. Returning to France from the meeting of the International Bureau, Vujovitch succeeded in persuading the committee not to take precipitous action. The opposition

43 For the resolution adopted at the meeting see ibid., Kurella, *Gründung und Aufbau* ... 117, or *Die Jugend der Revolution*, 500-1.
44 *Zu neuer Arbeit* ... 26
45 *IJK*, 20 June 1920

groups that it represented were to continue to remain in
the youth organization until stronger and better organized.[46]
Vujovitch's arguments were buttressed by discussions, in
late July, between representatives of the 'Committee for
Autonomy,' the communist group in the party ('Committee
for the Third International' led by Fernand Loriot), the
group led by Auclair, and the communist students. Auclair
was now moving in the direction of support for the 'Committee for Autonomy.' It became clear that if Auclair went
over to the pro-Comintern opposition, it would have a
majority in both the national committee and among the membership at large. It was obvious to all that it would be
better to make a concerted effort to take over the existing
organization, rather than to separate and form another,
communist one.[47]

The reasons for the key shift of Auclair from a middle
position to outright support of the 'Committee for Autonomy'
are not clear. A strong probability is that he was influenced
by the views of the French delegation to the second Comintern
congress, Louis Frossard and Marcel Cachin. The telegram
that these two sent from Moscow in mid July, indicating
that they considered adherence to the Third International
necessary, was published just a few days before a conference
in Paris of the various opposition groups. The effect of the
telegram from Moscow on many centrists who leaned toward the
Third International was to remove their last doubts.[48] It
would appear that Auclair identified with the left-centre
in the party, which was to move with Frossard and Cachin
to form a majority for adherence, on the basis of the
Twenty-One Conditions, at the party congress in Tours in
December.[49]

46 Kurella, *Gründung und Aufbau* ... 102-3. With the representatives of the 'Committee for Autonomy,' Maurice
   Laporte and Boris Goldenberg (Marcel Ollivier), having
   been arrested at the border on the way to the Milan
   conference, Vuja Vujovitch went to Berlin in their place.
   See also *IJK*, 1 July 1920
47 *IJK*, 12 August 1920
48 Wohl, *French Communism in the Making, 1914-1924*, 179, 187
49 Ibid., 187. See *l'Avant-Garde ouvrière et communiste*,
   25 September 1920, 1 (cited hereafter as *l'Avant-Garde*),
   for references to the formation of the Laporte-Auclair
   alliance. For Auclair's opinions in August 1920 of the

130 Revolutionary vanguard

Despite agreement on unconditional acceptance of CYI terms,
the new pro-Comintern opposition was not without its own
differences. Apart from a dispute over when the separation
from the centrists should take place, the pro-Comintern
forces were at odds on organizational and programmatic questions similar to those that had developed elsewhere in the
communist youth movement. Should the 'action program' for
the soon-to-be communist youth organization be just for
'sincere' communists who had joined the CYI, or was it to
be broader, to serve a communist youth organization with a
wider membership? Was the youth organization to remain
'pure,' or was it to be more of a mass movement.[50] These
differences persisted for some time after the split with
the centrists and were a legacy of the imprecision with whic
the new communist movement was defined.

After intervention of the party general secretary, Frossar
in September, an extraordinary congress of the youth organization took place on 31 October to 1 November in Paris.[51]
By this time Frossard and Cachin had returned from Moscow,
apparently with acceptable terms on which SFIO could join
the Comintern as a communist party. When all of the Twenty-

---

centrists, of the 'reconstructors,' as 'verbally demagogi
super-revolutionary in their writings, and demi-reformist
in action,' see ibid., 9 October 1920, 2. Auclair was
speaking favourably of Charles Rappaport at this time
(ibid.). He seems to have faded very rapidly from the
scene after 1921, leaving the communist movement altogether. For crystallization of the opposition at a conference in the Paris working-class suburb of Puteaux see
also *IJK*, 12 August 1920; *Die Jugend der Revolution*, 484-
and *Die Kommunistische Jugend*, 20 August 1920, 132.
50 See the article by G. Vital in *l'Avant-Garde*, 9 October
1920, 5. See also Wohl, *French Communism in the Making,
1914-1924*, 194
51 *L'Avant-Garde*, 25 September 1920, 3. By this time the
opposition had become a majority in the national committee. *L'Avant-Garde* began publication as the official
organ of the new majority, now renamed the 'Committee
for the Communist Youth International.' Members of the
'Comité de l'Internationale Communiste des Jeunes' were
Maurice Laporte, L. Meriga, V. Radi, Calman, Lepetit,
Auclair, Camille Fegy, Humberdot (Jules Humbert-Droz?),
and Antoine Ker (*l'Avant-Garde*, 9 October 1920, 3).

One Conditions became known to the party membership, however, a storm broke over the head of Frossard.[52] With the decisive party congress scheduled to meet in Tours in December, Frossard and his supporters may well have encouraged the youth congress to meet and join the CYI on the basis of the Twenty-One Conditions. The pro-Comintern forces in the party could thereby gain some leverage for consolidating a majority for the Twenty-One Conditions at the party congress.

The extraordinary congress, attended by four representatives of ECCYI, rejected Lainé and the centrists and voted for unconditional union with the Communist Youth International on the basis of the Berlin decisions.[53] The delegates endorsed the broad revolutionary objective of the Comintern, which sought the substitution of a dictatorship of the proletariat, in the form of workers' councils (soviets), for the bourgeois-democratic parliamentary system.[54] They also discussed the question of how far the party organizations should intrude upon the activities of the soviets, once power was in the hands of the working class. This issue was soon to become important in the debates in 1921 over the so-called revolutionary offensive. By that time the changeover to a communist organizaton had been completed with a change in name, and the election of a new national committee and appointment of a new editor of *l'Avant-Garde ouvrière et communiste*. Maurice Laporte and Camille Fegy became the new national secretaries of the Fédération Nationale des Jeunesses Socialistes-Communistes de France (JC).[55]

52 Borkenau, *European Communism*, 96, and Wohl, *French Communism in the Making, 1914-1924*, 187ff
53 The key Seine department organization met a week before the congress and voted to join the CYI unconditionally (*l'Avant-Garde*, 23 October 1920, 1-2, and *IJK*, 10 December 1920). At the extraordinary congress, the centrists and the communists clashed from the very beginning. The areas of greatest centrist strength were Pas-de-Calais, Nord, Gironde, and l'Aube (*l'Avant-Garde*, 11 November 1920, 4). See the comments of Marcel Vandomme for the influence of Frossard and Cachin on many of the members (ibid., 23 October 1920, 1, and 11 November 1920, 3).
54 *L'Avant-Garde*, 11 November 1920, 6
55 *Die Jugend der Revolution*, 490, 496. See *l'Avant-Garde*, 11 November 1920, 8, for the composition of the new national committee and the election of Laporte and Fegy

With the struggle within their own organization won, the young pro-Comintern socialists immediately became active creating communist cells within the party and the trade unions. The JC did so, however, while retaining its full independence. The natural inclination of the members of the JC, as elsewhere among the young communists, was to assert themselves as a revolutionary vanguard by remaining separate from all parties. This attitude was underscored by the fact that JC leaders did not quite approve of the structure and work of the party 'Committee for the Third International.'

When the party met in Tours a few weeks after the young socialists' congress, the communists succeeded in winning a majority for unconditional adherence to the Comintern. This action was supported and applauded by the JC leaders present.[56] The minority at Tours, including the centrists and the right, departed to re-form the socialist party. The centrist minority at the Paris congress of young socialists followed this party minority and formed a new youth organization in close association with the new socialist party.[57]

---

as political secretary and administrative secretary. Members of the new leadership were: Auclair, Vandomme, Pontillon, Laporte, Vital, Calman, Perche, William, Schaub, Fegy, Kintz, Lacroisille, Wesziard, with (as candidates) Naze, Paratre, Honel, and Soufflot.

56 *IJK*, 1 February 1921
57 Organizational problems plagued the new leadership after the Paris congress. Acceptance of the congress decisions had to be won within the local groups. This was made difficult when Lainé and the centrists refused to accept the congress action and demanded in *Populaire*, the organ of the re-established socialist party, that the local group repudiate the communists. Lainé remained in physical possession of the records and assets of the secretariat, which he refused to give up to the new national committee. He was supported in this by the party leadership (Comité Administratif Permanent - CAP). Laporte and Vandomme reported on events within the youth organization to the CAP on 9 November, apparently receiving a cool reception (see *l'Avant-Garde*, 11 November 1920, 8, and 27 November 1920, 1, 4). The new leadership then broke with the party. After the congress of the SFIO in Tours and the formation of the PCF, relations between youth and party ceased to be one of coolness and hostility. Relations between the

The French socialist youth movement was to suffer the same fate as the socialist party. The communist forces captured the organization by winning more votes at congresses. They then purged all who refused to accept the Comintern line. The forces hoping for a radical change in French society were split. More seriously, the force of socialism as a significant obstacle to a reconsolidation of bourgeois society was broken. Surveying the condition of socialism in France in 1924, Robert Wohl concludes that 'ten years of war, revolutionary disturbances, and class conflict had not added one whit to the strength of the Marxist forces in France.'[58]

After 1920, the young workers in France were pawns in a factional power struggle, rather than a reservoir of potential recruits to a united and influential socialist youth organization. In the struggle with the centrists and right-socialists for supremacy, the JC could not capitalize on their advantage. It is true that at the outset the communists had more support among the young workers than the other factions. The anti-militarist opposition to France's policy in Germany maintained the JC as a significant force until the mid 1920s. As elsewhere, however, the organizational successes could not be translated into solid support for communism over the long run. When the communists failed to put forward a policy that all revolutionary elements could approve, they were left with the shell of a 'revolutionary, pure' organization.[59] When faced with the choice of working within the system for social change, or of remaining outside it without political influence, the young workers chose the former. The JC, like the PCF, found that the very split that enhanced its rise was to lead quickly to its isolation.

---

two communist organizations remained to be established firmly, however. All of the organizational activities of the JC, both among youth and within the party and trade unions, were hampered as a result of the anti-militarism campaign in early 1921.
58 Wohl, *French Communism in the Making, 1914-1924*, 395
59 See Lowenthal, 'Bolshevization ...' 42, for discussion of this point.

Italy
In both Austria and France, factional relations in the
youth movement reflected those in the party. In Austria the
young socialists for the most part were united behind the
centrist policies of the party. In France they were as
sharply divided between the centrists and communists as were
the members of the SFIO. In Italy, however, youth organization and party were at widely separated points on the socialist political spectrum. The former was extremely critical
of the party, and in sharp conflict with it. Deeply split
between revolutionaries and reformists, the party could not
develop an effective policy. The reformists preferred to
let 'the laws of capitalist development' take their course,
until the system fell of its own accord. Meanwhile, the
revolutionary elements which dominated the party apparatus
could not devise a coordinated and well-thought-out revolutionary strategy. Because of these differences, the party
could not agree on a program. Although it approved membership in the Comintern by a large majority in the fall of
1919, the party did not do so unconditionally.

The youth organization, by the spring of 1920, was overwhelmingly for unconditional adherence of the party to the
Comintern. It had joined the CYI at the Berlin congress.
Having no right-socialists and few centrists, the central
committee supported the Comintern call for exclusion of
these factions from the party.[60] Members of the central
committee worked within the leading party bodies for unconditional acceptance of the Comintern program, most
notably at the meeting of the national committee of the
party in Milan in April 1920.[61]

The dominance of the left in all its varieties (abstentionists, maximalists, and 'Ordine nuovo' supporters) was
evident at the session of the youth organization's national
council in Genoa at the beginning of June. The party was
condemned for its lack of 'revolutionary action and a real
revolutionary attitude.'[62] Its leadership was called upon
to adopt a precise, concrete program for the seizure of
power, and to create organs working outside parliament 'in
direct contact with the life of the masses' (factory counci.

60 *J-I*, May 1920, 14, and *Die Jugend der Revolution*, 311
61 *Die Jugend der Revolution*, 311
62 Ibid., 312, and *IJK*, 1 July 1920

and soviets).[63] The national council threatened to sever
all relations with the party if the 'non-revolutionary elements' gained the upper hand. As in France, there was a
large and impatient minority willing to break with the party
immediately. The maximalist majority, however, preferred to
wait until the forthcoming second Comintern congress had
settled the issues in dispute and decided who was, and who
was not, to be a member of the communist movement. If the
Italian party congress followed the anticipated Comintern
position and displayed sufficient revolutionary character,
there would be no need for a break.

The factions in the youth organization, while agreeing
on adherence to the Comintern, could agree on little else.
The maximalists and the youth group in Turin associated
with the newspaper *l'Ordine nuovo* could agree on a policy
of participating in parliamentary elections, but the former
were, at best, indifferent to the Ordine nuovo argument that
it was necessary to agitate among young workers so as to
kindle a desire to form factory councils and soviets. The
abstentionists were divided from both on the issue of participation in parliamentary elections, from the Maximalists
by the abstentionist call for the immediate expulsion of
the right-socialists and formation of a communist party,
and from the Turinese over the factory councils. What centrists there were became an increasingly isolated minority
at odds with all three left factions on the issue of unity
and the necessity for violence.[64]

The leading figure in the central committee in 1920 was
Luigi Polano, the political secretary. A follower of Serrati
at the time of the Berlin congress, Polano had sought then
to guide the youth movement in the maximalist direction.
He did so, however, within the context of the agreement
reached at the Rome congress in October 1919. This important meeting, just before the formation of the Communist
Youth International in November, had given its unconditional
approval to the Third International, but on the motion of
the respresentative of the Ordine nuovo group, Umberto
Terracini, the congress also had legitimized factionalism

63 *IJK*, 1 July 1920
64 The maximalist leadership, the Ordine nuovo youth, and
the abstentionists did agree in the fall of 1919 to move
the journal of the youth organization, *l'Avanguardia,* from
Rome to Turin and to open it to all of the left factions.

within the youth organization. Only 'revisionist' and 'social democratic' tendencies were proscribed. Each group associated with a faction in the party was free to organize itself on a national basis. Each individual was free to join that communist faction within the socialist party most congenial to his personal convictions.[65]

Most of the leadership had come to the youth movement during, or just after, the war. Polano, Secondino Tranquilli (Ignazio Silone), Giuseppe Berti, and Gino diMarchi were of the younger, wartime generation. Other leading participants were older 'youths' who had been active before the war. This was especially so of the Ordine nuovo group. Gramsci, Terracini, Tasca, and Togliatti had all been active in the socialist youth federation (FGS) while at the University of Turin from 1911 to 1915. After the war they all became active in the socialist party. All, in fact, became leading figures in the Italian communist party after 1921. Their earlier ties to the youth movement remained, even though all were in their mid-to-late twenties (Gramsci turned twenty-nine in January 1920).[66]

In the summer of 1920 Polano attended the second Comintern congress with one of the four votes given to the Italian socialist party, the others being held by Serrati, Bombacci, and Graziadei. By this time Polano had moved away from Serra and associated himself with the left-maximalists (Bombacci, Misiano).[67] He now supported the Comintern demand that all right-socialists, including Turati, be expelled from the Italian party.[68] In his remarks to the congress, Polano

65 *Vtoroi kongress*, 327
66 Tasca had been an active member of the FGS since 1908 (Cammett, *Antonio Gramsci* ... 75). The newly formed (1919 Ordine nuovo group found a receptive audience in the loca youth organization in Turin. It also found a promising reception for its ideas on factory councils within the youth movement more widely. It was the older, party-oriented leaders who represented the Ordine nuovo views in the councils of the socialist youth organization. Terricini and Mario Montagnana were active participants in the affairs of the youth movement in 1919 and 1920.
67 *Die Jugend der Revolution*, 312
68 At the Berlin congress Polano had argued against includir Turati with the German, Scheidemann, as a right-socialis to be villified. In fact, he succeeded in having Turati'

called on the Comintern to help the youth organization in its efforts to purge the party of its 'reformist elements.'[69] This was by way of attacking those who wished, or were considering, the admission of the French socialist party and the German USPD to the Comintern. For it would be contradictory, argued Polano, to ask the Italian socialist party to purge its 'opportunist' elements, while accepting these very same elements into the Comintern by admitting French and German centrists. While Polano was breaking with Serrati on the issue of party unity, he did not move completely to the position of what had by now become the majority in the youth organization, that of Bordiga and the abstentionist 'ultra-left.' He supported the ECCI theses on parliamentarianism, but declared that his position did not correspond to that of the Italian youth organization that he represented.[70]

After the second Comintern congress, the youth organization became a firm supporter of the Twenty-One Conditions. The central committee met in late October to hear reports on the first session of the International Bureau of the CYI, at which Polano and Mario Montagnana had represented Italy, and a report by Polano on the second Comintern congress. The decisions of the bureau session were approved unanimously, Polano's action at Moscow approved (including, apparently, his behaviour on the parliamentarianism question), and the Twenty-One Conditions accepted unanimously.[71] Even though Polano, a left-maximalist, and Montagnana, from Ordine nuovo, remained in the leadership, somewhere around

---

name removed from the list of right-socialists identified by name in the program of the CYI. While apparently accepting the call of the Comintern and the CYI to fight the right-socialists and the centrists, Polano and the young Italian maximalists at the end of 1919 still hoped (as Münzenberg had until only recently) to include as broad a spectrum of views as possible in the Italian socialist organizations joined to the Third International. Turati and Serrati did not become labelled as 'rightist' and 'centrist' until the first part of 1920.

69 *Vtoroi kongress*, 202-3
70 Ibid., 327. Polano declared that he would do all he could on return to win acceptance of the ECCI theses, and to change the ambiguous situation in the youth organization in which competing factions coexisted.
71 *IJK*, 20 November 1920

this time the central committee pledged the loyalty of the youth organization to Bordiga and his abstentionist faction.[7] The merger in August/September 1920 of the Bordiga youth groups into a communist 'astenstionista' (election-abstaining faction had consolidated their control over the central committee.[73]

These decisions of the central committee were not acceptable to everyone. Those who continued to follow Serrati, and an apparently larger group of centrist followers of Lazzari, became the core of a 'unitarian' opposition to the Twenty-One Conditions. This situation moved the youth organization toward an open split when the 'unitarian' minority rejected both the action of the central committee, and the provisions in the Comintern theses demanding discipline and conformity.

In December, the national council indicated its support for the 'communist faction' (abstentionists). There was to be 'no place for unity communism in the youth organization.'[7] It further commissioned the central committee to take action against the 'unitarians' in the youth organization. The session also decided that if the coming party congress did not produce a transformation into a communist party, the youth organization should join the abstentionists (Bordiga) to form a communist party.[75]

When the socialist party met in Livorno in January 1921 and favoured Serrati and Lazzari and the 'unitarian' communists, the communist groups left and set up a communist party (PCI) at a congress of their own.[76] Shortly thereafter

72 *Die Jugend der Revolution,* 312, and *Kommunismus* (Vienna), 15 January 1921, 49–59
73 *IJK,* 10 September 1920
74 *Kommunismus* (Vienna), 15 January 1921, 49–59. See also *IJK* 10 January 1920
75 Preparing the core of a new youth organization should the socialist party split, the opposition organized a formal 'unitarian' faction in Bologna in the first week of January 1921 (see *l'Avanguardia,* 23 January 1921 for Polano's report on the Bologna congress, and *J-I,* September 1923, 27–8).
76 Polano was elected a member of the central committee of the new party (*Die Kommunistische Internationale,* no. 16 [1921]: 755). Before the voting at the Livorno congress, Tranquilli had said that the youth federation would vote with the communists (Cammett, *Antonio Gramsci ...* 144).

the socialist youth met and settled the long controversy over which party faction to support.[77] A proposal that the youth organization leave the socialist party, declare its allegiance to the new PCI, and change its name was adopted overwhelmingly. Only a small minority supported the 'unitarian' position.[78] The new youth organization was to emphasize the development of young workers into 'conscious and clear communists.' Its political work was to concentrate on revolutionizing the trade unions by organizing a communist opposition in each union. Giuseppe Berti became the new political secretary. Tranquilli became editor of *l'Avanguardia*, and Luigi Longo, leader of the PCI after Togliatti's death in 1964, became a member of the new central committee.[79]

After the communists had driven out the 'unitarian' minority, the latter formed a new socialist youth organization

---

After the communists had lost, Polano indicated that the young socialists would follow the communist faction and break with the PSI (*l'Avanguardia*, 30 January 1921).

77 *IJK*, 15 March 1921. Vuja Vujovitch, the ever-active young Serb who had been co-opted into ECCYI, was present at both the party congress in Livorno and the youth congress in Florence as ECCYI representative (interview with Giuseppe Berti).

78 The minority of 'unitarians,' apparently not even having been allowed to speak, walked out after the vote. Most of the opposition had not been allowed into the congress hall by a decision of the central committee (*J-I*, September 1923, 27-8; see also Tranquilli's proposal in *l'Avanguardia*, 23 January 1921, that all who were in agreement with the Bologna principles be expelled from the youth organization). *J-I*, September 1923, mentions fifteen minority delegates; the report of the congress in *l'Avanguardia*, 13 February 1921, says that there were ten. For the congress proceedings see also *l'Avanguardia*, 23 January 1921.

79 The leading bodies of the youth organization were moved from Rome to Milan to be together with the communist party leadership. The new central committee included Berti, Longo, Tranquilli, Gorelli, Mangano, Cassita, de Marchi, Polano, Beltramelli, and Lembertini, with an inner executive committee to consist of Berti, Tranquilli, Cassita (as administrative secretary), de Marchi, and Gorelli. Polano was to remain as representative to ECCYI, but he soon moved into party affairs.

that continued to support the Serrati-led party. After expelling right (social democratic) elements in early 1923,
the 'unitarian' socialist youth merged with the communists
in May 1924 under the rising threat to the revolutionary
left from the fascists. There was now a clear separation
between Italian socialist and communist youth organizations.

Ironically, the exclusion of the centrists and the formation of a 'pure' revolutionary youth organization came just
when the Comintern was about to revise its strategy. The
split of the Italian socialist movement was not repudiated,
but the introduction of the united front policy in 1921 made
its logic questionable to many. Communists now were to pursue a policy of accommodation with those who had just been
expelled (the youth movement), or from whom the communists
had separated (PCI). The strength of the 'ultra-left' in
both the new PCI and the youth organization, however, made
acceptance of this change in line quite difficult. Those
most eager to promote the split, the 'ultra-left,' naturally
became the last to accept the justification for the new
policy.

These factional squabbles over who was, and who was not,
to be a certified member of the new revolutionary International were soon overshadowed by political events in Italy.
Despite its dominant position in the socialist youth movement, the new communist youth organization could not prevent
the rise of fascism and its appeal among young workers. The
communists saw a need for acquiring supremacy within socialist institutions. First secure leadership of those young
workers organized and committed to socialism, then go on to
organize and capture, ideologically, the vast uncommitted
masses. However, while the communists were struggling with
other socialist factions and tearing apart the socialist
movement, the fascists were reaching with great effectiveness many of the uncommitted. The fascists presented themselves as a united, cohesive force. Their call to action
apparently was perceived to be better suited to the immediate needs and expectations of young workers.

Germany
The centre of youthful turmoil and rebellion during 1919
and 1920 was in Germany. War, defeat, and revolution produced a situation of great instability, one that had a great
effect on the way in which the members of the younger generation developed their personal view of life. In addition,

the final break-up of the German Social Democratic Party
had released forces in the socialist youth movement that
had been pent up since well before the war. There was anger
at the traditional parties and politicians - at the older
generations for having failed their progeny. There was disillusionment with the prevailing conceptions of socialism,
and aggressive impatience with the pace and course of social
change. Not sure what to do but craving action and change,
hoping to build a new world while lashing out at the old,
idealistic youth looked for leadership.

Discussing strategies and tactics for revolutionary action
consumed the attention of all young socialists,and it was
almost inevitable that the heterogeneous character of the
Freie Sozialistische Jugend (FSJ) would lead to internal
conflict. There was, however, a great reluctance to destroy
the unity and broad appeal that had developed on the basis
of a commitment to 'revolution.' As long as the Comintern
itself continued to attempt to bring the warring German
factions together, tolerance of varying views in the FSJ
persisted and splits were postponed. Yet even the FSJ could
not withstand the forces tearing the German revolutionary
movement apart.

The first break occurred in October 1919 with the expulsion of the supporters of the Independent Social Democratic
Party (USPD), ten months after the left in the USPD had
split with the centre to form a communist party. The result
was a considerable decline in the effective strength of the
new communist youth organization. This was especially so in
Greater Berlin, Halle-Merseberg, Rhineland-Westphalia, East
and West Prussia, Leipzig, and Hamburg.[80] After their expulsion, the centrists formed the Verband der freien sozialistischen Proletarier-Jugend (SPJ).[81] Many points of agreement
remained between the centrists and the communists, which led
them to express general support for the program of the CYI.

80 *Die Jugend der Revolution*, 382-3
81 See *Proletarier-Jugend*, 1 January 1920, 7-10, for a discussion of the congress, at which Kurella represented
ECCYI. The newly elected central committee of the SPJ
(Schröter as chairman, Springer, Grossman, Brauer,
Hülder, Windau, and Mahlman) had its seat in Leipzig
and published the bi-weekly, *Proletarier-Jugend*. The SPJ
program and statute are in ibid., 4-6. See also ibid.,
15 June 1920

If the SPJ could be assured of 'freedom of movement' in the youth international, it said, there would be nothing in the way of the SPJ joining the Communist Youth International. But this was the very issue separating the centre from the communists. In late 1919 and all through 1920 the FSJ followed the policy of party leader Paul Levi, even though with some serious reservations. The leadership strove to forge a mass communist organization by playing on pro-Comintern, 'revolutionary solidarity' attitudes among the centrists. A growing left wing in the SPJ was encouraged to leave and rejoin the FSJ as members of the Comintern/CYI.

The expulsion of the centrists had been accepted as necessary. There was a desire in the FSJ, however, to avoid a further split within its own ranks. Levi's peremptory exclusion of those who differed with him (the 'ultra-left') found little acceptance in the FSJ.[82] The top executive body, the central executive committee (Zentralausschuss), was divided over the theses pushed through the Heidelberg party congress (October 1919) by Levi. Even the majority supporting him on strategy and tactics, however, did not all support his going so far as to exclude the 'ultra-left.'[83] The central FSJ paper Die Junge Garde, although under the editorial control of pro KPD forces, remained open to the views of the 'ultra-left' opposition until mid 1920. A conscious effort was made by the editorial board to stimulate discussion between the KPD 'Zentrale' and the opposition, with the hope that difference could be reconciled and unity re-established within the part and maintained within the youth organization.

82 For developments within the FSJ from October 1919 until the end of 1920 see especially Die Jugend der Revolution, 383-94. For the views of the 'ultra-left' see Protokoll der Reichskonferenz der Opposition der Freien Sozialistischen Jugend Deutschlands (28. und 29. August 1920 in Leipzig), n.p., n.d.
83 Pietschmann, Die politisch-ideologische Klärungsprozess ... notes that it is not possible to reconstruct the precise composition of the leadership. There are insufficie records and archival material remaining from the second FSJ congress and the central organs in the early years (see ibid., viii n. 1, for comment on the inadequacies in administrative work in the FSJ in these early years). Based upon discussions with former members of the leader ship he says that the following worked in the central

143 Struggle for supremacy

On one point there was no disagreement within the FSJ:
the definition of what a communist youth organization should
be. In keeping with the wartime view and the program of the
CYI, all agreed that the FSJ was to be both an educational
and a combat (Kampf) organization. The factories, schools,
and military organizations, rather than party-supervised
discussion clubs, were to be its fields of activity. It
would organize young workers and apprentices, supporting
their spontaneous radicalism and exploiting unstable and
difficult situations so as to radicalize an ever wider circle
of young people. Above all, the FSJ was to be an active
political organization independent of the party. Its members
would participate in all revolutionary actions of the German
working class. It would take its own positions on all critical questions affecting the German revolution. It would
make its own evaluations of the political situation and the
possibilities for revolutionary action and decide which
strategies and tactics were appropriate for each occasion.
It also would decide which faction or group within the party
could help the most to further these decisions. On these
points, there was no disagreement between the majority and
the opposition in the FSJ. The difficulty, of course, was
that the members of the FSJ could not agree among themselves
when making these independent decisions.
It was clear that major differences remained. Both sides
recognized the need for broadening the base of the communist
organizations, but differed over how to accomplish this: by
remaining true to 'pure' revolutionary principles and behaviour and staying out of all bourgeois and 'reformist' institutions, or by displaying a more pragmatic attitude and
utilizing all institutions in which 'the masses' were to be
found. There were differences over who were and were not
potential allies. The 'ultra-leftists' were sceptical at best

---

executive committee and the editorial board for *Die Junge
Garde* until the third congress (October 1919): Leo Flieg,
Fritz Globig, Willi Harth, Otto Oldenburg, Paul Schiller,
Willy Zimmerlich, Friedrich Heilmann, Günther Hopffe,
Marta Jogsch, Hans Meyer, Margot Ostler, Heinrich Papst,
and Max Kern, (ibid., 56). Elected to the central execu-
tive committee at the third congress were Hopffe, Jogsch,
Meyer, Ostler, Papst, Kern, and Felix Lewinsohn (ibid.,
108). Kern, Lewinsohn, and Schiller were leaders of the
'ultra-left' opposition.

of all moves to seek new ties to the centrists, especially
as the latter had only just been expelled from the FSJ. Of
more importance to the opposition were the syndicalist youth
groups that had emerged, especially in the Ruhr.[84] The
'ultra-left' was further estranged from the majority by its
opposition to democratic centralism. It insisted on a thoroughly decentralized and federalist organizational structure. On this point it had been joined before the split at
Weimar by many who supported the USPD. There was a mélange
of disparate influences behind this view: anarcho-syndicalism
the continued reaction to the pre-war socialist movement in
which reformist leaders had controlled a centralized movement, the ideas of Rosa Luxemburg, and budding resistance
to the imposition of Bolshevik norms of intra-party relations.[85] The young 'ultra-leftists' continued to argue for
building all communist organizations from the broad mass
membership because it, in contrast to the leaders, truly
had demonstrated the 'will to revolution.'

In 1919 the 'ultra-left' leaders did, perhaps, represent
the impatient, unstructured radicalism of the wider membership of the FSJ more correctly than did the majority in the
central executive committee. The average member was eager
and willing to engage the 'bourgeois enemy' at any time,
and in any place. After the failure of the revolutionary uprisings in early 1919, the leadership worked continuously
to avoid unprepared, and unsuccessful, actions. The results
of the elections in June 1920 only served to harden the opposition of the leadership to the anti-parliamentary, anti-
trade-union tactics of the 'ultra-left.' To justify its opposition, the central executive committee denied in *Die
Junge Garde* the correctness of the assertion [by the 'ultra-
left' forces] 'that the German proletariat has today the
will to take power and has been prevented from doing so only
by traitorous leaders. The results of the elections with 5.6
million votes for the reformists [SPD] and 4.8 million for
the compromisers [USPD], quite apart from the numerous labou
votes for the bourgeois parties, is plain enough.'[86] Much
yet needed to be done to 'bring the German proletariat to
the necessary level of ripeness.' This view turned out to be

84 *Die Junge Garde* (*JG*), 17 April 1920, 148
85 See Bock, *Syndikalismus und Linksradikalismus von 1918-
   1923* on the last point.
86 *JG*, no. 39 (July 1920): 218

the more persuasive one. The membership, while ready for
'action,' apparently in 1920 was not convinced that the op-
positions' tactics would be the most fruitful. A solid majority of the members certainly saw no need to split the movement over these issues. As events proved, neither uncontrolled
militancy nor the 'controlled radicalism' of the leadership
was feasible. The impatience of the young radicals could not
be curbed without a corresponding loss in their radicalism.
And yet, their aggressiveness could not be given free rein
without completely decimating the organization in losing
battles with the authorities. What was at fault, of course,
were the mistaken notions of both participants in the debate
about the prospects for revolution.

The structure of the youth organization was thus demon-
strably connected with issues of strategy and tactics, with
the question of how best to maximize and capitalize upon
the revolutionary enthusiasm of the membership. With its
scepticism of central authority, the opposition proposed
that the central executive body of the FSJ remain administrative in character (geschäftsführende). The press would be
decentralized by closing down *Die Junge Garde* and expanding
local FSJ papers and journals. By early 1920, however, it
was clear that the majority position in favour of a strong
central leadership would prevail. Decisive leadership in a
revolutionary period was considered essential. Thus, in the
spring of 1920 the pro-KPD leadership was emphasizing centralization, while at the same time still groping for a specific definition of the term in practice.

The immediate problem for the FSJ, of course, was how to
preserve its unity and avoid a split now that two competing
communist parties - KPD and KAPD - had emerged. The program
of the CYI required each member to support the party or
faction recognized by the Third International. But which
was the recognized party? Still hoping to effect a reconciliation of the two German communist groups, the Russians
had not yet excluded the secessionist KAPD from the International. Following the wishes of Lenin and the Comintern
to avoid a split, and themselves sharing many of the views
of the 'ultra-left,' Münzenberg and the leadership of the
youth international encouraged the pro-KPD forces in the
FSJ to proceed cautiously. Hopes were maintained that despite certain differences over tactics, unity with the
FSJ, in anticipation of reunion between KPD and KAPD, could
be preserved on the basis of the Comintern program and 'the

struggle for the dictatorship of the proletariat in the form of Soviet power.' Events were to show otherwise.

Although agreed on expelling the centrists, the delegates to the third FSJ congress in Weimar in October 1919 had not been able to reach any firm decision between the KPD and 'ultra-left' positions.[87] In mid February 1920 the national committee (Reichsausschuss) came down against the 'ultra-left' on all issues: the relationship between the FSJ and the parties, the attitude towards syndicalist and centrist youth, trade-union policy, and organizational questions.[88] Nevertheless, there was no formal split. The hope remained that the Comintern could solve the problem at its second congress in the summer. With compromise not possible in the FSJ, there was no common policy. There were two policies: the majority had one, the opposition another. These decisions, and the events surrounding the Kapp Putsch in March, only served to sharpen the crisis.[89]

In March 1920 right-wing elements from the military occupied Berlin, forced the government to flee, and installed a government of 'neutral experts' led by Wolfgang Kapp. Mass resistance turned into a general strike led by the trade unions. The members of the FSJ were among the most active of the communist forces in these events. Almost everywhere they undertook courier and communications (Nachrichtendienst tasks. Above all, they were active in disseminating revolutionary propaganda. The FSJ also was able to exercise some political influence through its representatives on the party 'action committees.' This participation by members of the FSJ in revolutionary activities deepened the political conflicts in their own ranks. The differences between the

87 The drafting of an official position, and a new program, were left to special commissions. For the program drafted by the program commission see *JG*, 10 January 1920, 77-8. For amendments made by the central executive committee see ibid., 17 January 1920, 87-8. For the theses drafted by the commission on the trade-union question see ibid.
88 See *JG*, 17 April 1920, 147-8; *IJK* 30 March 1920, 3-4; and *Die Jugend der Revolution*, 384-6, for discussions of this meeting. See also *The Communist International*, no. 11/12 (1920): 2537-9
89 For a discussion of events in the youth organizations during and after the Kapp Putsch see *Die Jugend der Revolution*, 386-9, and *Deutschlands Junge Garde* ...

'ultra-left' and the pro-KPD leadership showed up in the contradictory slogans used by the two factions. Those supporting the KPD leadership agitated for the election of workers to parliament and other political bodies, the entry of the communists into these institutions, and the arming of the workers through the workers' councils; the 'ultra-left' opposition was for the immediate proclamation of a Soviet republic, rejected the election of workers' councils at that time, and called for the mobilization of red armies. Each faction in the FSJ participated in the activities of the party group with which it sympathized. The majority went with the KPD leadership.[90] The refusal of the 'ultra-left' youth to follow the official FSJ position threatened to bring a split in various localities even during the course of the action.[91]

The central executive committee supported the majority in the KPD after the defeat of the Kapp Putsch. It accepted the argument that the situation had not been ripe for a seizure of power by the left, thus it had rejected the call by the 'ultra-left' for an armed uprising. But, it also condemned the support given by Levi and a majority in the KPD 'Zentrale' to the policy of forming a 'loyal opposition' to the projected SPD–USPD–trade-union government that Lenin and the Comintern later accepted as reasonable. When the German party and the Comintern sought to pick up the pieces after the Kapp Putsch, to assign blame and decide on future policy, the leaders and members of the FSJ were caught in the political cross-fire. The development of a clear programmatic and tactical position

90 See the circular letter (Rundschreiben) of the FSJ Berlin district leadership of 19 March against the immediate proclamation of a Soviet republic (*Die Jugend der Revolution*, 386), and the statement at the end of March 1920 from the central executive committee that the time was not yet ripe for a Soviet republic (ibid., 387).
91 *Kommunistische Arbeiter-Zeitung* (Berlin), no. 104 (June 1920). At a meeting of the central executive committee on 7 April, after the news that the 'ultra-left' in the party had constituted itself as the KAPD, the leaders of the FSJ sought the immediate expulsion of the KAPD followers. Only the 'energetic action' of the representatives of the opposition prevented this step, and brought the decision to put the matter before the next congress.

by the youth organization, without actually splitting, became even more difficult.

The controversy in the FSJ culminated at the fourth congress in May 1920. External events were shaping the course
of the dispute. On the one hand, conditions seemed favourable for a restoration of 'revolutionary unity' within the
socialist movement on essentially communist terms. As a result of the abortive Putsch, the workers were in a more radical mood. The KPD grew rapidly, and the USPD began to
move closer to it. This was also seen in the youth movement
when the FSJ and SPJ organizations in Berlin conducted a
joint May Day demonstration, with support for the Comintern
and the CYI as the slogan on which the two could agree.[92]
On the other hand, differences between the KPD leadership
and the KAPD had been strained even further and tensions
were acute within the youth organization.

It had proven to be impossible to fulfil the desire for
unity. A clear majority of the approximately 200 delegates
to the congress, representing almost 22,000 members, endorsed the position adopted in February by the national committee and came down on the side of the KPD.[93] Support was

92 *Die Jugend der Revolution*, 389
93 On the eve of the congress, *Die Junge Garde* carried a
lead article setting the tone for the deliberations (*JG*,
15 May 1920, 165). Notable was the 'anti-opportunism' of
the emerging 'left-opposition' in the KPD. This was a
product of dissatisfaction with Levi's support for the
policy of 'loyal opposition' to a proposed socialist
government after the defeat of the putsch. Levi had been
repudiated by a wide majority of the fourth KPD congress
in April. Thus, while still differing with the 'ultra-
left' on several issues, the majority in both the party
and the FSJ had drawn closer to it because of the events
in March. The militancy and dedication to 'action' of th
'ultra-left' found a sympathetic response from the
article's author (probably Münzenberg). The weakness of
the Weimar regime and the possibilities for revolution
were seen to have been highlighted by the events in Marc
The author was thus even more insistent that a split in
the FSJ (between 'orthodox' and 'ultra-left') on tactica
issues was to be avoided. For the congress see *Die Juger
der Revolution*, 390-1; *Kommunistische Arbeiter-Zeitung*
(Berlin), no. 104 (June 1920); and *JG*, 1 June 1920, 174

given to the KPD electoral campaign and the proposal to
struggle for 'minimum economic demands.'[94] The 'ultra-left'
delegates proposed that the program of the CYI be amended
to recognize both the KPD and the KAPD. This, too, was rejected. The delegates did, however, accept the view that a
final position on the party conflict was not yet appropriate,
since young communists were 'only beginning the clarification
process.'[95] This decision symbolized the hold that the notion
of 'unity' had on the young communists. It was also a response to the uncertain attitude of the Comintern regarding
German party developments. In a more pragmatic sense, the
refusal to push differences to a split reflected awareness
by the pro-KPD forces that the 'ultra-left' had considerable
support in the membership at large. Nevertheless, for their
opposition on all basic issues, the 'ultra-left' was excluded
from representation on the new central executive committee.[96]

94 Three resolutions on the party situation were put forward: for participation in the elections with the KPD,
   for the position of the KPD, but rejection of participation in the elections at that time, and for the KAPD
   position of complete opposition to parliamentary activity.
   See *Die Jugend der Revolution*, 390-1, for the resolution
   adopted. *Der Kommunist* (Dresden), no. 24 (June 1920) says
   that there were fifty-one votes for the third resolution,
   with sixty abstaining, when the congress approved the
   first resolution. *JG*, 1 June 1920, 174, gives the voting
   as 137-66-51.
95 *JG*, 1 June 1920, 175. For the activities of the 'ultra-
   left' opposition see *Der Kommunist* (Dresden), no. 33
   (mid-August 1920) and *Kommunistische Arbeiter-Zeitung*
   (Berlin), no. 114 (July 1920). For a statement of the
   position of the central executive committee towards a
   split, see *JG*, no. 30 (July 1920): 218.
96 An 'ultra-left' youth leader claimed later that while
   officially the communist youth had freedom and self-
   determination, with no authority imposed uopn them by
   the party, in practice the young communists were being
   used as an object of the 'egoistic needs of the party
   leaders' (*Kommunistische Arbeiter-Zeitung* [Berlin], no.
   106 [June 1920]). According to the KAPD youth, the attack
   by the supporters of the KPD on the young 'ultra-leftists'
   was inspired by the 'unscrupulous party-political activities' of the KPD. A list of those elected to the central

After the second Comintern congress, ECCYI changed its
view of the conflict among young communists in Germany.
Münzenberg now saw his hope for cooperation as illusory.[97]
At the Comintern congress, Münzenberg had supported the
Comintern leadership against the KPD leadership, being the
only member of the German delegation who was willing to re-
unite the KAPD with the KPD. He changed positions only after
the KAPD delegates left the congress because they could not
prevail on the question of tactics. He apparently also saw
the futility of further attempts to keep the supporters of

---

executive committee is not available. The following
apparently served at various times between the fourth
(May 1920) and fifth (December 1920) congresses: Heilmann
Hopffe, Meyer, Papst, Franziska Bergmann, Hermann
Bergmann, Hans Brüggemann, K. Ickert, Max Köhler, and
Walter Löwenhain.

97 Before the second Comintern congress, Münzenberg had
urged that both unity and discipline be maintained in
the FSJ. He expressed a belief, rather unrealistically,
that agreement could be reached on political questions
and the two communist parties could be reconciled. The
majority in the central executive committee should not
provoke a split, and the opposition should abandon its
separatist activities. (*JG*, no. 29 [July 1920]: 206-7).
In this article, Münzenberg apparently did not reflect
unanimity in ECCYI. In an editorial note in the next
issue it was stated that ECCYI had requested *JG* to note
that Münzenberg had been expressing his private opinions.
These corresponded to those of ECCYI and the FSJ leadership on the undesirability of a split, but not on the
attitude to be taken toward contemporary political questions and the communist parties (*JG*, no. 30 [July 1920]:
214). This same issue also contained a rejoinder to
Münzenberg from the anti-'ultra-left' majority in the
FSJ leadership (ibid., 215). In the first half of 1920,
until the second Comintern congress, *JG* gave considerabl
room to the opposition for the expression of its views.
A running 'debate' thus took place from about February
through July. The reports of the meetings of the FSJ
national committee and the congress sessions were relatively devoid of polemic, or at least the polemic on
both sides was reported equally.

the KPD and the 'ultra-left' together in the FSJ. Instead, the main effort should centre on splitting the centrist youth organization.[98]

Münzenberg parted company with the 'ultra-left' painfully, but firmly. Sympathizing with its activism and revolutionary élan, Münzenberg nevertheless could not condone the demand for decentralization. This insistence on discipline was to come back to haunt him in 1921. For the present, however, he recognized that there was no hope of keeping the 'ultra-left' within the movement. With Zinoviev, Münzenberg retained hopes for a future reconciliation. During discussions over the 'revolutionary offensive' before the third Comintern congress in 1921, Münzenberg expressed the hope that 'the great political-revolutionary work' of the Comintern would bring the 'ultra-left' groups back into the fold.[99] Tactical and organizational differences would be put aside in the heat and enthusiasm of a great 'revolutionary offensive.' Again, however, his wishes were to go unfulfilled.

Everyone refusing to accept the Twenty-One Conditions and the Comintern line was expelled from the FSJ in September 1920.[100] The commitment to unity that had bound the heterogeneous young German revolutionary socialists together in the fall of 1918 had proved too fragile to withstand the ideological passions of 1919 and 1920. The FSJ had finally been 'clarified.' The way was now open for those who remained in the FSJ to join with the left wing of the SPJ and

98 *JG*, 3 August 1920, 17
99 *IJK*, 5 May 1921, 1. For Zinoviev's views see *The Communist International*, no. 11/12 (1920): 2134
100 For the activities of the opposition groups see *Protokoll der Reichskonferenz der Opposition* ..., and *Kommunistische Arbeiter-Zeitung* (Berlin), no. 129 (September 1920), no. 126 (September 1920), and no. 158 (December 1920). See also *JG*, no. 5 (October 1920): 40, and *IJK*, 20 January 1921, 5-6, and 1 January 1921. The expelled groups constituted themselves as the *Kommunistische Arbeiter Jugend* (KAJ) at a conference in Braunschweig in late November 1920. Because of the difficulties that the KAPD was having in 1922, the KAJ decided to dissolve itself and enroll the membership in the KAPD. At the same time, the KAJ paper, *Die Rote Jugend* ceased publication (see *Kommunistische Arbeiter-Zeitung* [Essen], nos 5, 9, 12, 24, and 30 [1922]).

work to create a mass organization.[101] After a split in the USPD at Halle in October (after which the left-wing majority joined the KPD), a slim majority voted at the SPJ congress in Leipzig in November to leave the SPJ and merge with the FSJ and to adhere unconditionally to the CYI.[102]

With 8000 to 10,000 young left-wing centrists re-joining the FSJ, now renamed the Kommunistische Jugendverband Deutschlands (KJD) in compliance with the Twenty-One Conditions, the communist youth organization numbered about 30,000 to 35,000 at the end of 1920 - the SPJ retaining 6000 to 7000 and the 'ultra-left' KAJ only 2000 to 3000.[103] The right-socialist Arbeiter Jugend (Verband der Arbeiter Jugendvereine), rebuilt rapidly after the war, had by now become the largest young workers' organization with about 60,000 members. These figures show that the great majority of young workers and apprentices remained unorganized and unmobilized by the socialist organizations. At various times and depending on the issue, larger numbers could be gathered for demonstrations and protests. Those who were willing to make some formal commitment to one or another of the socialist youth organizations, however, remained relatively small. Apparently a considerable number had been brought into the trade-union movement at the local level, but the commitment called for by such activity was too parochial to satisfy the more politically oriented socialist organizations.

The failure of the revolutionary socialists to agree on what a socialist revolution meant was a major factor in, if not the decisive cause of, their inability to take advantage of the unstable conditions after World War I. Nowhere was this more evident than in Germany. The split with the centrists, and the expulsion of the 'ultra-left,' did not promote efforts to seize power. Nor did it lead to socialist organizations dedicated to and capable of working toward a radical change of society from within the Weimar Republic.

101 See *JG*, 1 June 1920, 180, and *IJK*, 20 May 1920, for SPJ-ECCYI discussions.
102 *IJK*, 10 and 30 October 1920. The voting was 145-141, with Bernhard Bastlein leading the majority, and Martin Brauer the minority (*Sozialistische Jugend*, February 1921, 22). The minority left the congress and continued as the SPJ in affiliation with the new USPD (*Der Jugendliche Arbeiter*, September 1921, 4).
103 *IJK*, 1 January 1921

The victory of 'revolutionary purity' within the German socialist youth movement was truly pyrrhic. The 'ultra-left'
was left to pursue the fruitless path of sectarianism, eventually to disintegrate. Those centrists who did not join the
KJD returned to the fold of the Social Democratic Party.
Although forming a more militant, ideologically orthodox
left wing, they were gradually absorbed into the mainstream
of party activity. The communists had lost the battle for
supremacy among young workers almost before they had begun.
While they were forging a 'revolutionary vanguard,' the
prospects for revolution in terms of a violent seizure of
power were slipping away rapidly. The young German communists nevertheless continued to hew to their conceptions of
revolution, revolutionary strategy, and proper forms of organization. As a result, they were unable to mobilize the
'young proletariat' for either a revolutionary seizure of
power, or for efforts to effect radical changes from within
the system.

The results of 'clarification'

By early 1921 the efforts of the Communist Youth International to destroy the influence of the centrist youth organizations had been completed for the most part. The results
were varied, from complete failure in Austria and Finland,
where the communists were forced to withdraw from the socialist youth organization, to initial successes in France,
Germany, and Czechoslovakia and fairly complete control over
the young workers' movement in Italy. The successes of the
communists appeared promising when seen in sheer numbers.
Measured in terms of delegates to congresses and the number
of members they were presumed to represent, the situation
appeared to show a wide commitment to the principles of the
Berlin program. However, these early successes were de-
ceiving. An increasingly stable and less revolutionary environment, and their internal political and organizational
problems, prevented the communists from consolidating and
expanding their influence. Internal difficulties especially
served to drain away much of the movement's vitality. One
of these was the delayed reaction to the strict centralism
of the Twenty-One Conditions (as their full import became
understood) and the increasing Russian dominance of the international communist movement.

Splitting and dispersing the corps of young post-war radicals blunted their effectiveness. Of even greater consequence was the impact of communist 'clarification' work on the extensive reservoir of uncommitted young workers. Most young workers were dissatisfied and hoping for something better. They were looking for leadership. Their attention and support was best obtained by simple and direct appeals from a united socialist youth movement. Instead, they became unwilling objects in an ideological and political struggle that they could not understand.

The communist youth organizations reached the high-water mark of their strength and influence (until the Popular Front, anti-fascist days of the 1930s) in late 1920 and early 1921, as a result of their disruption of the centrist youth organizations. But their gains only gave the illusion of success. The very raison d'être of all communist organizations was compromised from the outset. The doctrinal assumption that 'true' Marxists, 'true' revolutionary socialists, had to remain 'pure,' when – with only a very few temporary exceptions – the masses were not revolutionary in the communist sense, prevented them from gaining sufficiently wide support. This became clear in 1921 when the Comintern launched its united front policy. It sought alliances or cooperation with other working-class organizations and their leaders, while at the same time condemning and castigating them and attempting to woo individual workers to a revolutionary program in an increasingly non-revolutionary environment.

In 1920 and 1921, however, the young communists still looked to the future with great expectations. From its formation, the young communists were active participants in the struggle of the Comintern to develop into a force capable of bringing about the 'proletarian revolution' in Europe. Communist youth, especially in France, Germany, Britain, and Scandinavia worked to hinder the production and transportation of munitions to Poland during the Russo-Polish War; after the Heidelberg congress, the KPD recruited its most active workers from German communist youth, and often used the FSJ/KJD leadership to conduct propaganda where the local party groups were members of the 'ultra-left' opposition; in Sweden and Denmark the youth organizations provided the majority of the members of the left-socialist (communist) parties; in Norway it was the youth organization that took the lead in developing communist

influence in party and trade-union circles; in France and
Czechoslovakia the youth organizations had become known as
communist organizations and had accepted the program of the
CYI well before the socialist parties decided to join the
Comintern; in Switzerland, the youth organization was the
backbone of the new communist party, and in Belgium and
Spain the youth organization actually became the communist
party; in Italy, the communist-dominated youth organization
supported and often led all efforts to implement the Twenty-
One Conditions within the Italian socialist party.

After the political air had cleared in early 1921, there
were forty-nine various youth organizations and groups communist in nature that were members of the Communist Youth
International.[104] Some were openly communist, others retained
the name social democratic or socialist for tactical reasons.
Differences in size, composition, strength, structure, and
methods existed. Some were large mass organizations, others
were small insignificant sectarian groups located in only
one city or region. Some functioned quite legally. Many were
illegal, while others worked semi-legally and under severe
police harassment.[105] Sympathy or support for the militant
'ultra-left' persisted in many quarters, despite the expulsions. Often, as in the case of Willi Münzenberg, there was
only lukewarm support for the official Comintern positions.
Strong centrist influences remained. 'Clarity' had not been
achieved completely, and it soon was evident that the battle
for supremacy within the socialist youth movement had been
lost. Communist organizations were to experience further
conflict over revolutionary tactics, and to see serious splits
occur over the definition of centralism and discipline in
the Comintern.

During the rest of the 1920s, most communist youth organizations were reduced to relatively small sectarian groups too
involved in the factional struggles in their own and the
Russian party to have much influence among the mass of young
workers. The legacy of bitterness and ideological conflict
ultimately vitiated later efforts to sponsor cooperative actions with other youth and student groups in a common defence
against the growing threat from Nazi Germany. With the split
between 'socialists' and 'communists,' trust - that essential
ingredient to any effective cooperative endeavour - had
vanished.

104 For a list see Münzenberg, *Die Dritte Front*, 329-31
105 Ibid., 328-9

6

Conflict over the role of the youth movement

The glittering and evocative rhetoric of the nascent communist movement concealed a fundamental question of identity. The raison d'être of all communist organizations was asserted in doctrinal terms. They were said to be gatherings of all 'truly' revolutionary socialists, that is, of all who 'correctly' understood Marx's ideas and their application to existing realities. What the character of these new 'truly revolutionary' communist organizations was to be, however, was not self-evident. The first adherents to communism exhibited little more than a simple faith in the need for a 'disciplined' movement. It was not clear what this was to mean, concretely, in terms of organizational structure, decision-making processes, inter-party relations, or the relationship between the International's leading bodies and its constituent organizations. The young communists were the first to become involved directly with the difficulties in defining a communist identity. Inheriting a tradition of independent political activity, they knew precisely what they wanted the youth movement to be. However, a quite different view of the communist movement was emerging at the same time. The insistence by the Russian Bolsheviks that their conception of communism be accepted by all led to serious conflict and schism. It is in this context that the importance of the Communist Youth International (CYI) becomes evident.

The young communists made it clear quite early, certainly formally at the Berlin congress (1919), that they saw themselves as a revolutionary vanguard. Their wartime role of revolutionary leadership was to be maintained in the face of persistent weaknesses within the parties. Only when mass revolutionary communist parties had been created, and the young communists did not believe that this had as yet happened, could they abandon this position of leadership. Its leaders saw the youth movement as a natural and persistent source of pressure for maintaining revolutionary dedication and activism. Only complete independence from the parties could give the youth organizations sufficient opportunity for maximum application of this pressure. To become subservient to the parties and tied to their dubious commitments would be a fatal mistake. Some party leaders were thought to be weakening in their resolve to work for immediate revolution, and thus advocated 'opportunist' policies implying too much caution, an unwillingness to confront the bourgeois system, and an unhealthy pessimism about the revolutionary nature of the existing situation. Freedom from party control would enable the young communists to advocate and follow more militant policies, thus assuring the success of the revolution. An early sign of the direction the communist movement was to take can be found in the response of the Russian Bolsheviks to this definition of the communist youth movement.

Most adherents to the Communist International (Comintern), including members of the CYI, imagined themselves as part of 'the forerunner of the international republic of Soviets.'[1] They thought little about what organizational form the revolutionary socialist state would take. They put their faith in the spontaneous goodwill of a revolutionary working class. By means of workers' councils (soviets) the proletariat would create a system of mass participatory democracy. It was assumed that traditional national boundaries would be broken down. The Communist International would be the forum where transnational issues would be discussed. Decisions would be made on the basis of common interests and aspirations, and proletarian goodwill. Defence of the new Soviet Republic was considered essential, but was never justified apart from its importance in promoting world revolution. However, as revolution ebbed in the world and the new Soviet state struggled to consolidate itself, the question of the role and influence of the Russian party in the international movement became paramount.

As long as the expected revolution was seen as a universal phenomenon, questions relating to national differences were

1 Lenin as quoted in Carr, *The Bolshevik Revolution, 1917-1924* III, 125

thought to be of no importance. All nations would be swept
up by revolution at more or less the same time. When, however, it became apparent that this would not occur, the
prospect emerged of different parties reaching socialism
at different times and in different ways. Under these circumstances, it was hard to see on what basis a 'general
line' could be formulated for the movement as a whole. Some
criteria had to be found for deciding if national deviations
were to be permitted, and if so, which were acceptable and
which were not. This extensive diversity of condition called
for a more precise understanding of what centralization, in
the form of democratic centralism, really meant in the International. As it turned out, a viable reconciliation could
not be found between democracy and centralization. The
latter, by virtue of the dominant position of the Russian
party, was to prevail. The conflict in 1920 and 1921 between
the youth international and the Russian party leaders, who
also controlled the Comintern, provided the first evidence
of this.

After November 1917, the Bolsheviks began to give substance to the hitherto theoretical and ambiguous question
of the form of socialist rule. Application of the concept
of democratic centralism *after* the revolutionary seizure of
power was crucial. At first it was justified by the existing
conditions of civil war. It was later defended as necessary
in order to assure economic development. Thus, centralization and discipline were given specific content: party decisions on organizational questions were becoming part of
the Bolshevik experience, which was increasingly being insisted upon as a model to be emulated by other communist
organizations.

The second Comintern congress resolution on the role of
communist parties in the proletarian revolution (July 1920)
was based on the Bolshevik conception of the role and structure of *all* communist parties.[2] That structure was to be
based on the principles of democratic centralism that included the directly elective character of the lowest unit,
indirect election of other units, the absolute authority of

2 See Degras, *The Communist International* ... I, 127-35 fo
the resolution. See also *The Communist International*, no
11/12 (1920): 2137-50 for the draft theses presented to
the congress by ECCI; these were followed closely in the
adopted version.

higher bodies over lower ones, and a strong central party
body whose decrees were authoritative pending ratification
by the next party congress. There was to be only one communist party in each country, a principle adopted already by
the youth international at its founding congress in November
1919. The party was to create an organized nucleus, under
its strict control, in every non-political organization.
In short, the party was to direct the work of all organizations, including the youth organization and the soviets,
neither of which were to be thought of as in any sense replacing the party.

The Russian Komsomol came to define democractic centralism
for the international communist youth movement.[3] From its
inception in the fall of 1918, the Komsomol was subordinate
to the Russian party. Not having existed in 1917 when the
Bolshevik revolution took place, it had no tradition of
direct and independent participation in revolutionary activities. Over the opposition of a 'leftist' minority, it retained its separate organizational identity. A specific
statement on the manner in which the party would exercise
its guidance of Komsomol affairs was issued in mid 1919,
and ratified by the second Komsomol congress in October.
The Komsomol central committee was to be under the direct
control of the party central committee. The local Komsomol
organizations were to work under local party committee direction. Komsomol central committee members were also subject to party control in that as party members they were
subject to reassignment, despite the fact that they were
elected to their positions by the Komsomol congress. Thus,
by the time of the Berlin congress and the formation of the
Communist Youth International in November 1919, the Russian
Komsomol was itself committed to complete subordination to
the communist party. While considerable freedom of discussion continued for some time at Komsomol congresses, Komsomol
affairs nevertheless rapidly came under strict party control.
Deviants and non-conformists were quickly removed or forced
to recant.

Shatskin and other Russian youth leaders recognized that
the young West European communists had had experiences and
traditions that understandably led them to insist on independence from the parties. At the third Komsomol congress

3 See Fisher, Jr, *Pattern for Soviet Youth*, chapters 2 and
  3 for developments within the Komsomol.

in October 1920, Shatskin spoke sympathetically of the difficulties that young revolutionary socialists had had to
overcome in order to free themselves from the 'social-
patriot' and 'revisionist' socialist parties. What was important now, he said, was that all communist youth organizations accept the party/youth organization relationship
in Russia as the model for their relationship with their
own national communist parties. He made a distinction between
those communist youth organizations that had reached the
'most advanced' stage of full subordination to the communist
party (Russia); those that were in an 'intermediate' stage,
increasingly tying themselves to the party (Germany); and
those that remained 'backward' and divorced from the party
(Denmark and France, where the formation of a communist
party was still underway).

This insistence that Russian precedent be decisive for
all other communist youth organizations was also apparent
in policy matters. Shatskin had insisted at Berlin (and
presumably also at the first bureau session) that the policies of the other youth organizations must be determined by
'the experience of the Russian youth league, whose basic
principles are suited to any youth organization under conditions of proletarian dictatorship.'[4] This position would
have been less disturbing to the communist youth elsewhere
if the Russians had remained faithful to its spirit. Russian
experience was claimed here to be relevant *after* the revolution under a 'dictatorship of the proletariat.' Young
communists expected in 1919 that the revolution would soon
spread, so that at Berlin each delegate perceived himself
to be part of a movement in his own country that would soon
be in power and busy installing a 'dictatorship of the proletariat.' Russian experience then would indeed be useful
or illustrative, if not definitive. What the Russians in fact
were doing, however, was going beyond this position and
asserting that Russian policies were suitable even *before*
any revolution occurred abroad.

The Komsomol congresses continued over the years to affirm
an obligation to serve as the model for the entire international communist youth movement.[5] The Komsomol was described
in 1920 as 'the foremost detachment of the international
army of proletarian youth.'[6] At the fourth congress in 1921

4 Quoted in ibid., 55, 101, and 139
5 Ibid. 58, 101, and 139
6 Quoted in ibid., 85

Shatskin again emphasized the leadership role of the Russian representatives in the youth international. Alfred Kurella (writing under the name of Bernhard Ziegler) contributed to the effort to enthrone the Komsomol as a model for all communist youth organizations in his brochure, *Was lehrt uns die russische Arbeiterjugend? (What Can We Learn From the Young Workers in Russia?)*, published by the Executive Committee of the Communist Youth International (ECCYI) in 1920.

The impetus to extend the Bolshevik model to the youth movement came from the controversies over strategy and tactics. In the years preceding the third Comintern congress (June-July 1921), and even later, many of the youth organizations were strong supporters of the more radical, more militant elements within the Comintern. This was particularly so of most of the members of ECCYI, and of those youth functionaries co-opted by ECCYI.[7] ECCYI sympathized with or supported the anti-parliamentary and anti-trade union tactics of the 'ultra-left.' It cooperated with the Comintern's Amsterdam bureau and Vienna under-secretariat in 1919 and 1920, both strongholds of 'ultra-leftist' ideas.[8] ECCYI and the West European communist youth organizations were also supporters of the 'revolutionary offensive,' especially in Germany, during the first half of 1921. Thus, the Bolshevik leaders, by means of the Comintern and the Russian Komsomol, sought to subject the CYI and its members to the discipline of Moscow.

7 Kurella, *Gründung und Aufbau* ... 131-2; Leon Trotsky, *The First Five Years of the Communist International* I, 355
8 The Amsterdam bureau ('under-secretariat') had been formed in January 1920 at a Comintern-sponsored conference in Amsterdam. With communications so difficult between Western Europe and Soviet Russia during 1919, ECCI decided to set up a point of contact in the West with the communist parties and groups in Western Europe and America. As the Amsterdam bureau was under the influence of the 'ultra-leftists,' it did not last beyond the change of line effected by ECCI during the spring of 1920. Its mandate was revoked by ECCI in May 1920, and its functions turned over to the West European bureau set up in Berlin. See the publication of the Amsterdam bureau, *Bulletin of the Sub-Bureau in Amsterdam of the Communist International*. The Vienna bureau was dissolved by ECCI before the third Comintern congress in June/July 1921.

The Russian Komsomol leaders were not able in 1919, 1920, and early 1921 to persuade the communist youth movement outside Russia to accept Russian leadership. The young communists in Western Europe did not see the Komsomol as possessing any special significance as a model for their efforts to foster revolution. The Komsomol had been formed after the Bolshevik revolution, and its experience over the short span of its existence was seen to be of marginal value. Even its post-revolutionary role as an institution for the building of socialism was being criticized.[9] The two Komsomol representatives at Berlin, nevertheless, had behind them the authority of a successful revolution. This did not assure automatic acceptance of their views, but it did tend to make the non-Russian delegates more defensive when asserting their opposition to the Russian positions. At the Berlin congress, the Komsomol representatives had not been able to win acceptance for the program drafted in Moscow without several major modifications. After Berlin, the Komsomol was too busy with its own problems during the civil war to pay much attention to the West European movement. The military and political situation, in any event, was such as to make communication extremely difficult. Meanwhile, ECCYI in Berlin, supported by the German youth organization (FSJ/KJD), the largest and most influential communist youth organization outside Soviet Russia, continued to lead the West European communist youth movement. However, once the Russo-Polish War, the civil war, and Western intervention came to an end, the Komsomol began to devote more time to the affairs of youth movements outside Soviet Russia. Its attempt to assert itself as the dominant force in the CYI lead to a conflict with ECCYI and the young German communists in Berlin.[10]

Different views of the youth movement

The clash between the 'revolutionary vanguardism' of the young communists in Western Europe and Russian centralism began even before the struggle with the centrists had ended. A lively debate over principles was carried on in various

9 See Pawlow and Köres, *Die Aufgaben der kommunistischen Jugendorganisationen nach der Übernahme der Macht das Proletariat* ...
10 Kurella, *Gründung und Aufbau* ... 170-3

journals and periodicals from mid 1920 until mid 1921.[11]
The discussions reflected two quite different conceptions
of the youth movement. The points at issue were the character
of the youth organizations, how they were to become involved
in efforts to improve economic conditions of young workers,
and, most significantly, the relationship of the youth organizations to the parties. As the controversy intensified,
these questions assumed the form of organizational conflicts
with strong ideological overtones - 'Berlin' vs 'Moscow,'
CYI against Komsomol.[12]

The controversy over the form the youth organizations were
to take, and their role in the 'economic struggle,' first
arose in the CYI during the fall of 1920. At issue was
whether the youth were to remain elite political organizations, as they were asserting, or were to confine themselves
to mobilizing mass support for the programs and policies of
the parties and Comintern. The view of the Russian party on
the character of a communist youth organization was set
forth by Lenin in his oft-quoted speech to the third Komsomol
congress in October 1920.[13] Through control of the state and
its instruments of power and authority, the party could now
preserve and maintain the revolution. The young communists
need no longer be concerned with 'revolutionary purity.'
They were, under strict party political guidance and within
the scope of the Komsomol, to devote their efforts to mobilizing the energies of the mass of young people, to raising
the ideological level of the Soviet population, and to becoming the first generation of communist experts and tech-
nicians. This demand that the youth organizations perform
essentially non-political functions was reflected in the
arguments of those endeavouring to shape the youth international on the Russian model. They made no distinction between
the Russian youth organization after the assumption of power,
and other youth organizations in countries where the revolution had not yet occurred.

Opposition to the idea that youth organizations should,
under party political guidance, devote themselves to education and agitation was based on the belief that this was

11 See *Jugend-Internationale (J-I)*, *Internationale Jugendkorrespondenz (IJK)*, and *Die Junge Garde (JG)* from the
latter part of 1919 through mid-1921
12 Kurella, *Gründung und Aufbau* ... 136. For use of the
expression 'Berlin vs Moscow' see ibid., 121
13 V. Lenin, *Die Aufgaben der kommunistischen Jugendorganisationen*

not appropriate for conditions outside Russia. Such an emphasis would be called for only after the takeover of power by the proletariat. Otherwise, the door might be opened to 'revisionism': adaptation to the existing bourgeois system. Most young communists in Western Europe, still struggling to achieve a revolution, were convinced that the youth organizations could not at the same time be a concentration of the most class-conscious youth (a revolutionary elite), and a mass organization (a forum for 'consciousness raising' and the mobilization of support for communist policies). Since they believed that it would be the height of folly for the youth movement to abandon its elite, revolutionary vanguard role at a time when the revolution was still in progress, or imminent, the young communists outside Russia argued that they could follow the Komsomol model, as demanded by the Russians, only after revolution had come to their country.

The debate was complicated only further by the question of how to respond to the immediate demands of the young workers for improved economic conditions. There was agreement that the grievances of young workers really could be remedied only by a radical transformation of society. There was also agreement that these grievances could and should be used as a weapon in the revolutionary struggle. The question at issue was how this was to be done and the priority to be accorded to such work. The Russians insisted that the first priority of the young communists outside Russia was to build mass organizations by taking advantage of the chaotic economic conditions. They wanted the communist youth organizations to promote and lead directly a 'revolutionary economic struggle' by the young workers. The young communists were to go into the factories and other places of work, calling for the immediate satisfaction of the most extreme 'economic demands' as a 'minimum' (for example, four weeks paid vacation, paid time off for apprentices and young workers to attend courses and pursue other educational activities, much shorter working hours and much higher wages). In themselves, these demands were not unreasonable, at least by contemporary standards, but in the conditions of the time it was quite unrealistic to expect their fulfilment. Any improvements in the conditions of the young workers that might, nevertheless, occur under communist leadership could only serve to further the development of mass communist youth organizations. Grateful young worke would see the communist youth organization as a successful promoter of their interests. Whether or not they would become 'revolutionized' simply by enrolling and participating in the youth organizations, or pliant followers when the 'pure' communist leadership called them to revolutionary action, was another matter. In any event, the Russians never really expected these 'demands' to be fulfilled. Rather, they anticipated that young workers would become increasingly radicalized once they had seen that the capitalist system would not respond to their demands. They then would flock to the communist youth organizations, for they would also see that the other socialist factions, including the trade unions, were only accommodating to the system by moderating their demands, or by accepting less than complete fulfilment. To the Russians, the youth organizations (and the parties, too, for that matter, for they were also being urged to pursue this policy) would be useful only as instruments of agitation, and as 'collecting points' for converts to the cause. In the process, the reformist-dominated 'youth sections' that had been established under the trade unions would become 'revolutionized' and thus destroyed. Their members would go over to the communists, thereby weakening capitalism's 'reformist allies.'

The consequence of such a policy would have been to take young communists out of political affairs, for their day-to-day activities would have been wholly taken up by the organization and direction of the 'economic struggle.' If successful, the creation of a mass organization on the Russian model also would have meant an end to the youth organization as a carefully selected, elite group of ideologically motivated young revolutionaries. It would now become a large organization whose main functions were to carry out party policies, suitably adapted to the needs and peculiarities of youth, and to serve as a corps of dissatisfied, anti-capitalist activists at the disposal of the party leaders. The members of the youth organization would be called, and consider themselves to be, communists. They would share some sort of commitment to the transformation of existing society, and perhaps even some general acceptance of Marx's ideas. It would be tacitly understood that they were part of the 'revolutionary elite,' distinct from the 'reformists' and 'opportunists.' Some communists, however, were to be more elite than others. It was to be the party leaders, under Comintern guidance and preserved by the Leninist application of democratic centralism, and *not* the young communists as a 'revolutionary vanguard' who were to be the real leaders of the proletariat.

This image of the youth movement was unacceptable to those who saw the youth organizations as elite, political organizations occupied first and foremost with the strategical and tactical problems of the imminent revolution. This applied to virtually all the young communists in Western Europe, who, however, were themselves divided. Willi Münzenberg was persuaded that the youth organizations should, indeed, become involved directly in the 'economic struggle,' and could do so without sacrificing either their revolutionary elitist character, or the political struggle. On the contrary, the youth organizations could, and should, themselves become 'mass revolutionary elites,' that is, mass organizations committed to and capable of playing an important leadership role in the revolutionary takeover of power soon to occur. As a result of participation in the 'economic struggle' under communist leadership, ever-increasing numbers of young people would not just join the communist youth organizations but would become dedicated, ideologically 'pure' communists. Münzenberg's 'Luxemburgism' led him to assume that the revolution would occur not as a minority coup d'état on the Bolshevik model, but as the result of the efforts of a mass proletarian movement. The relations within this movement between leaders and followers would be one of centralization but not the form it was to take under the developing Leninist interpretation of democratic centralism.

A sizable majority of the other young communists disagreed with Münzenberg. It would be wrong for young communists to become involved directly in any effort even ostensibly designed to improve the conditions of the young workers before the overthrow of a capitalist society. To do so would, contrary to Münzenberg, weaken the revolutionary commitment and rationale of the communist organizations. With youth organizations continuing as political elites, the trade-union youth sections would become useful for reaching the mass of young workers not yet revolutionized. Thus, young communists could, through the 'economic struggle,' develop a mass movement, a corps of supporters, without sacrificing their revolutionary purity or diluting the political purpose of the youth organizations. Any mass revolutionary movement would always need a small, 'pure' elite to provide leadership.

The 'ultra-leftists' would not even go this far. They, too, opposed both the Russian conception of a non-political mass organization, and Münzenberg's notion of a 'mass revolutionary elite.' But they felt that to work, even indirectly through communist nuclei in the youth sections, within the reformist trade unions would weaken revolutionary purity and compromise the political struggle. Political objectives, as well as the mobilization of mass support, could be served best by conducting the 'economic struggle' through separate 'bridge organizations': front organizations under communist control serving to 'bridge' the gap in commitment between the communists and the masses. It was clear that the second CYI congress would have to sort out and reconcile these different viewpoints.

Parties and the youth organizations

The most important subject of discussion in the CYI between 1919 and 1921 concerned the relationship between the young communists and the adults. At Berlin (1919) the Bolshevik view, represented by Shatskin, ran up against the traditions of the socialist youth movement in the West. After a lively debate, an ambiguous compromise emerged. The youth international was not considered a 'sister' organization of the Comintern. It constituted 'a part of the Communist International' and 'stood on the platform of the Communist International.' Individual youth organizations were obligated to follow either the political program of 'that party or faction in their country which is a member of the Third International,' or the political program of the Comintern.[14]

Although political leadership was supposed to rest with the adults, the young communists were to have organizational independence. They understood this to mean the right to decide when and where to hold meetings, what to discuss, and freedom to take positions on party affairs.[15] Association

14 Münzenberg, *Die Dritte Front*, 378
15 The terms 'autonomy' and 'independence' were used in no set pattern by the participants in these discussions. The German words 'Autonomie,' 'Selbstständigkeit,' and 'Uabhängigkeit' are all to be found in the sources, with the first employed somewhat more frequently. In the Russian sources, it is almost always 'samostoyatel'nost',' although one finds 'nezavisimost',' at times. Whichever

168 Revolutionary vanguard

with the Comintern required acceptance of its principles
and guidelines. It was not meant to 'deprive the youth
international [or any youth organization] of its independence in organizational, agitational, or propaganda matters,
or of the right of free discussion of important principles
and policies.'[16]

Relations between the parties and youth organizations,
as between the CYI and the Comintern, remained difficult
and unsettled for some time after the Berlin congress.
Unity was not promoted by the tradition of independent
youth organizations involved in political affairs. Certainly
it did not lead to passive subordination of the young communists to the political direction of their party. The young
communists were unwilling to forgo the hard-won practice
of exercising independent political judgment. On the other
hand, the notion of the youth as vanguard or avant-garde
hardly commended itself to the party leaders. In addition,
the policy or ideological differences in the communist movement did not facilitate harmony. The rationale for joining
the communist movement at this time was that there appeared
to be a 'truly revolutionary' path to socialist power. Some
socialists, it was alleged, had 'sold-out' the proletariat,
some were confused or vacillating, but others had remained
true to the teachings of Marx and were actively committed
to the violent overthrow of bourgeois society. These had
now separated from the 'renegades' so as to retain revolutionary purity. This insistence on a 'correct' way led to
a situation where differences among communist factions had
to be settled with the minority being branded as 'devia-
tionists.' If centralization was justified to ensure unity,
that was only one step toward a situation in which opponents
on tactical issues had to justify themselves by branding
their opponents as misguided and acting counter to 'the best
interests of the proletariat.' It was hard to see how a
youth organization, when it was unhappy with party policy
or orientation, could develop close relations with 'devia-
tionists.'

word was used, the issue remained the same: freedom for
the youth organizations from dominance by their communist parties, and respect for the right of the CYI to
act, within broad limits accepted voluntarily by the
members, on its own as an independent organization.
16 See *The Communist International*, no. 11/12 (1920): 2530

ECCYI left the decision on relations with the parties to
the individual youth organizations, instead of making the
Russian example obligatory.[17] It did so because Münzenberg
and his colleagues in Berlin were the most aggressive pro-
moters of independence for the youth movement. Independence
became a major theme in all CYI publications and statements,
especially in *Jugend-Internationale* beginning in late 1919
and early 1920, even though developments in Soviet Russia,
where the Komsomol accepted subordination to the party, were
held out as 'an example of great significance' for other
youth organizations.[18]

17 Kurella, *Gründung und Aufbau* ... 139. The settling of relations between the Komsomol and the Russian party during
   1919 (complete subordination of the youth) is traced
   briefly in Fisher, Jr, *Pattern for Soviet Youth*, 12-15
18 The Swiss were particularly outspoken on the need for
   independence under all circumstances (see *Neue Jugend*,
   26 January 1920, 9 February 1920, and 8 April 1920, and
   The Communist International, no. 11/12 [1920]: 2314, for
   the Swiss position). They feared control over the CYI by
   the Russians, and were not willing to accept all decisions of the youth international as obligatory for all
   youth organizations. The Swiss wanted the next international congress to declare that only congress decisions,
   and not those of ECCYI, were binding (*Neue Jugend*, 9
   February 1920).
   Edwin Hörnle (also Hoernle), a leading member of the
   communist movement in Stuttgart and active in party educational affairs, argued for complete independence on
   educational grounds as early as November 1919 (*J-I*,
   November 1919, 8-9). His pamphlet, *Sozialistische Jugenderziehung und sozialistische Jugendbewegung*, was published in October or November 1919 when the issue was
   being discussed in the FSJ and at the Berlin congress.
   It had been written in May 1919 while in jail in Würt-
   temburg (Pietschmann, *Die politisch-ideologische Klärungsprozess* ... 11, n.2). Pietschmann suggests that Hörnle
   was drawing back from this position by the end of 1919.
   In the source he cites, however, Hörnle was continuing
   to stress the point that the young communists were not
   to be subordinated to the adults in the party. Rather,
   there was to be, hopefully and desirably, a condition
   of complete equality (Beiordnung) within the entire

The first formal discussion of these issues after the
Berlin congress took place at the first session of the International Bureau in June 1920, shortly before the second
Comintern congress. At that time new theses, again worded
ambiguously but implying considerable autonomy for the
youth movement, were adopted unanimously.[19] The theses,
which were meant to be the position of the youth international in the discussions at the Comintern congress, asserted
that 'the Communist Youth International, while not a party,
is a political organization' and called on each communist
youth organization to work 'in closest cooperation with the
communist party of its country.' The youth organizations
were to give up the right to form their own political program, although they retained their organizational independence. This position remained unacceptable to the Russians,
who wanted more explicit recognition of complete party control.

ECCYI wanted a thorough discussion of the 'youth question'
at the Comintern congress in Moscow in July and August.[20]
However, the congress was too preoccupied with political
and organizational questions. Also, Zinoviev apparently did
not want a discussion of this controversial issue at the
plenary sessions of the congress. The representatives of
several communist parties, notably the German and the Bulgarian, expressed considerable displeasure with the independent behaviour of the youth movement.[21] Over Munzenberg'
objections, the 'youth question' was taken off the agenda
and discussed later by the newly elected Executive Committe

---

communist movement. See also *J-I*, February and March
1920. For the Komsomol as an example see *J-I*, March 1920
13-14, 16.

19 *First Bureau Session*, 25. The theses were also printed
in *The Communist International*, no. 11/12 (1920): 2537-
40, with an editorial note that they were printed for
discussion purposes only. ECCI apparently had not been
able to come to a decision with regard to the youth
movement, for after having discussed the issue in April
it decided to leave a decision to the next Comintern
congress (*Die Kommunistische Internationale* 2. Jahr.,
no. 10 (1920): 239).

20 Kurella, *Gründung und Aufbau* ... 121

21 Ibid., 122

of the Communist International (ECCI).[22] The statute adopted
by the Comintern congress included a provision (Article 15)
that recognized the youth international as a full member of
the Comintern, subordinate to its executive committee.[23]

New theses on CYI/Comintern and party/youth organization
relations were adopted by ECCI after discussions in mid
August.[24] As far as the CYI was concerned, the theses continued the ambiguous compromise between independence and
subordination. It was recognized that 'the CYI is a part
of the Communist International and subordinates itself as
such to the decisions of the congresses of the Communist
International and to the political directives of its executive, and conducts its work independently in the leadership, organization, consolidation, and expansion of the
youth international.'[25] Provisions were made for participation by the CYI at Comintern congresses, with ECCI and ECCYI
exchanging representatives with voting rights.

The relationship between revolutionary parties and youth
organizations was to take different forms, according to the
situation in each country and with each communist party.
Where communist parties were still being built and the youth
organization had only just split from the right-socialist
and centrist parties, the slogan of absolute political and
organizational independence (Unabhängigkeit) of the youth
movement was 'objectively revolutionary.' It was not so,
however, where strong communist parties already existed.
Here, the slogan of absolute independence could be used by
the 'social patriots' and the centrists to lead the youth
astray. In these countries, the young communists worked on
the basis of the party's program. Where 'old and active
communist parties' existed, the youth organization 'accepts
the communist party program [as its own] and works within
the scope of the party's political principles.' At the same
time, the young communists 'determine themselves the methods
of their organizational, agitational, and propaganda activ-

22 *Vtoroi kongress*, 436, 451-2; Münzenberg, *Die Dritte Front*,
   322; Gross, *Willi Münzenberg*, 113; and Münzenberg, *Der
   II. Kongress der Kommunistischen Internationale* ...
23 Degras, *The Communist International* ... I, 166
24 For the theses see *J-I*, October 1920, 29; *Die Kommunistische Internationale*, no. 14 (1921): 311-13; or *Vtoroi
   kongress*, 452
25 *J-I*, October 1920, 29

ities ... discuss general political questions ... [and determine] the place and form of their participation in the political struggle.'[26] All communist youth organizations were to 'come to this relationship with the communist parties not under party pressure, but through the conviction and free decision of the youth organizations.'[27] These provisions did not eliminate all ambiguity. While 'absolute independence' was wrong where strong communist parties did exist, considerable leeway was nevertheless left to youth organizations to conduct their own affairs. Either ECCI did not feel that it should insist on a clear statement of subordination of the youth organizations to the parties, or, more likely, it recognized that it was not possible at that time to do so and expect to be obeyed.

The negotiations on these points apparently had been difficult. The Italian member of the executive committee, Luigi Polano, and Lazar Shatskin had begun discussions in July during the course of the Comintern congress. In a letter of 16 July 1920 to those members of ECCYI remaining in Berlin, Münzenberg was not particularly enthusiastic in his support for the theses which Polano and Shatskin had drafted. He wrote that he had subscribed to them even though he feared they would lead to a premature anticipation of developments.[28] Serious differences of opinion occurred when those delegates who represented a youth organization met in an informal conference after the Comintern congress.[29] After further discussion with ECCI a few days later, an understanding was reached and the new theses were adopted.

26 Ibid. See also Münzenberg, *Der II. Kongress der Kommunistischen Internationale* ... 17–18
27 *J-I*, October 1920, 29
28 Kurella, *Gründung und Aufbau* ... 122–3
29 ECCI, supported by Shatskin but without the approval of ECCYI in Berlin, had invited representatives from the youth organizations to the Comintern congress. The announcement convening the congress had noted that an international conference of communist youth organizations would be held in connection with the Comintern meeting. Apparently ECCI intended this conference to be the second congress of the CYI. Those delegates to the Comintern congress who represented their youth organizations, or ECCYI, met for two days immediately after the conclusion of the Comintern congress, at which 'non-binding discus-

Despite any misgivings, upon his return from Moscow
Münzenberg expressed full satisfacton with the new theses,
as well as with the congress decisions on political and
tactical questions.[30] He viewed the Moscow theses on the
youth movement as recognition by the Comintern of the
necessity for the organizational independence of the youth
organizations. As long as the communist parties continued
to behave as 'the bearers of the proletarian revolution,'
there would be no conflicts over organizational questions
between party and youth organization. The decision to have
ECCI and ECCYI exchange representatives with voting rights
reflected, for Münzenberg, the complete agreement that had
been reached on this point. Not all young communists were
as sanguine as their leader. The Moscow decisions only
stimulated further discussion in the youth organizations.
The reaction almost without exception was critical. Nothing
less than an explicit statement asserting full independence
of the youth movement would do.

The Austrian and Swiss youth organizations, and the young
German 'ultra-leftists,' were highly critical of the provision for the political subordination of the youth organizations to the parties.[31] When the party was a genuinely rev-

sions' took place (Münzenberg, 'Ein Jahr Kommunistische
Jugendbewegung,' *Kommunismus* 2. Jahr., no. 11/12 351).
Without informing ECCYI in Berlin, ECCI, again supported
and encouraged by Shatskin, also had invited the Comintern representative to ECCYI, Albrecht (A.E. Abramovitch),
to the congress. ECCI presumably wanted a commentary on
the youth movement from someone other than the ECCYI
functionaries supporting the 'ultra-left.' This independent action of Shatskin led to his censure by the other
members of ECCYI (Kurella, *Gründung und Aufbau* ... 121).
It also inflamed the already tense relations that had
developed between ECCYI and the West European bureau of
the Comintern (led by Albrecht). The West European bureau
had obstructed the work of ECCYI. It also had taken what
to ECCYI was a far too negative attitude towards the
KAPD (see *IJK*, 30 March 1920 and 30 April 1920, and Gross,
Willi Münzenberg, 107-8).

30 Münzenberg, *Der II. Kongress der Kommunistischen Internationale* ... 8ff
31 *JG*, no. 5 (October 1920): 35-7; *Die Kommunistische
Jugend*, 15 June 1920, 110-11

olutionary party, it was argued, it would naturally exercise a healthy influence upon the youth movement. There was not only no need for a close organizational tie, but rather a positive necessity for the youth organizations to keep their independence. Only in this way could they retain the freedom to rejuvenate a 'slipping' communist party, and prevent it from diluting the revolutionary spirit of the young communists.[32] The Swiss advanced an argument that often was to be heard as the discussion proceeded. The differences, it was said, between the Russian and West European situations called for differences in the relations between the parties and the youth organizations.[33] The subordination and disciplining of the youth movement and the domination of all aspects of life by the communist party were necessary in Russia, said the Swiss, because of the civil war and intervention, then later in order to mobilize the resources of the country for the construction of the new Soviet society. Such a relationship, however, was *not* necessary, or desirable, between the parties and youth organizations in Western Europe. While not part of the 'ultra-left,' the Swiss youth were echoing the views that Gorter used in his response to Lenin's *'Left-Wing' Communism: An Infantile Disorder*.

Evidently having viewed the theses of August 1920 as provisional (until the political situation cleared, communist parties were established in all countries, and the party/youth organization relations were in their 'final stage of development'), the Russian Komsomol in November 1920 placed a new set of theses before the CYI.[34] By this

32 *Die Kommunistische Jugend*, 15 June 1920. See also *Rote Jugend*, no. 1 (1920), quoted in *J-I*, December 1920, 93–4
33 *Neue Jugend*, 22 October 1920. On this theme see also the Austrian, Hugo Zucker, in *Die Kommunistische Jugend*, 15 June 1920, 110–11; the German, Günther Hopffe, in *J-I*, January 1921, 116–19; the Austrian, Richard Schüller, in *J-I*, May 1921, 233–5; and the Austrian, Friedrich Hexman as late as the second CYI congress in *Zu neuer Arbeit; Bericht vom II. Kongress der KJI* ... 61.
34 The theses, allegedly drawn up on the basis of Russian experience, were sent to ECCYI by letter on 10 November 1920 (Kurella, *Gründung und Aufbau* ... 140–1, 237–9). See *J-I*, February 1921, 156–7, and Kurella, 227–30, for the theses.

175 Role of youth

time the campaign to 'clarify' the centrists had passed its
peak. The Russian theses emphasized firm subordination of
the youth organizations to the parties on the basis of
Russian experience, and argued that as revolutionary (communist) parties now existed in almost all countries, there
was no longer a split between revolutionary youth and adults.
The Russians branded the advocacy of independence for the
youth organizations as 'youth syndicalism,' and linked this
idea with the syndicalist concept of decentralization in
the labour movement. The mistake of the advocates of independence, according to the Russians, was that they saw the
interests of communist youth apart from the interests of
the labour movement as a whole.

In December, Alfred Kurella, acting in place of Shatskin
as representative of the Komsomol in ECCYI, provoked what
was to become a 'Berlin-Moscow' split in ECCYI by supporting
the Russian theses.[35] He only made matters worse by defending
the Komsomol against attacks concerning its dictatorial
methods within its own organization, and concerning Komsomol's attempt to impose its will on the youth international.
While in Moscow the preceding summer, Münzenberg had become
involved in an important conflict within the Komsomol. There
was some doubt whether the leadership, including Shatskin,
represented the majority opinion within the Russian youth
organization. The leaders (Dunayevskii and Leontev) of what
was certainly a significant opposition sought Münzenberg's
help against what they perceived to be the dictatorial
methods of the party-controlled leadership.[36] Münzenberg
seems to have found their arguments persuasive. His report
to ECCYI on 30 September after his return from Moscow,
concluded that the opposition charges were justified. In a
speech on 8 October he condemned what he considered to be
'an all too sharp tutelage over the Komsomol by the party.'[37]
This only added to the friction that had developed between
Münzenberg and ECCYI in Berlin, and the Komsomol leaders
in Moscow.

35 Kurella, *Gründung und Aufbau* ... 143, and *IJK*, 10
   February 1921
36 See Fisher, Jr, *Pattern for Soviet Youth* for internal
   developments within the Komsomol, and Kurella, *Gründung
   und Aufbau* ... 123 for Münzenberg's role.
37 Ibid., 124

A certain uneasiness over the behaviour of the Komsomol leaders was growing within ECCYI. The Russians were seen to be exhibiting not only an unfortunate eagerness to subordinate the youth movement to the parties, and (with Münzenberg as witness) a tendency to circumvent the opinions of the Komsomol membership, but as well an inclination to extend their methods to the youth international as a whole. Most ECCYI members saw as evidence of this the statement in the new Komsomol program, adopted at its third congress in October 1920, that it considered itself to be the avant-garde of the youth movement.[38] Kurella only aroused suspicions and resentment when he raised this point, suggesting that the other communist youth organizations had much to learn from the Russians. The Russian experience, said Kurella, showed that the youth organization had to merge with the party in order to 'cleanse' itself of all uncommunist elements.

The differing views in ECCYI only served to intensify the unrest within the individual youth organizations. Münzenberg continued to be chief spokesman for those advocating independence. He acknowledged the need for parties and youth organizations to draw closer together, perhaps with some refinements in the August theses.[39] He refused, however, to make any concessions on basic principles. The Russian theses were good for Russia, where the revolution had already taken place, said Münzenberg, but the youth organizations in other countries, still struggling to carry through the revolution were not working in a situation in which they were ready to go so far as to subordinate themselves to the party.[40] Because of the 'revolutionary instinct and natural enthusiasm for revolution' of communist youth, which contributed so much to the formation of communist parties, Münzenberg insisted that the parties had 'no interest whatsoever in confining in any way the communist youth organizations' organizational independence, which for educational, agitational and *political* [emphasis added] reasons is still necessary

38 *IJK*, 10 February 1921. The statement was in paragraph eleven of the program.
39 *J-I*, June 1921, 287–8. For theses, modelled on the Russian draft, presented by Kurella to a meeting of the KJD 'Zentrale' in January 1921 see *J-I*, June 1921.
40 Kurella, *Gründung und Aufbau* ... 145

today.[41] Münzenberg did not believe that creation of
'strong,' militantly revolutionary communist parties according to the August 1920 theses had as yet been completed.
Münzenberg at this time gave expression to what was clearly
the underlying sense of frustration of the young communist
activists. Acknowledging the necessity for centralism in the
Communist movement so as to concentrate 'the greatest striking power,' he pleaded almost despairingly not to so centralize the movement that the 'revolutionary initiative'
of all true communists was bound and stifled.[42] Having
struggled for so long to get out from under the bureaucracy
of the German social democrats (SPD), Münzenberg and the
young German communists had no desire to substitute a new
communist bureaucracy for the old social democratic one.
The vagueness among the new adherents to communism as to
what precisely centralism meant was now emerging openly.
It had been latent in the youth movement since the Berlin
congress in 1919. Perhaps the young communists themselves
did not yet know what they meant by the term beyond a general commitment to 'unity of purpose' and an avoidance of
debilitating discussion, debate, and indecisiveness. They
were, however, coming out clearly against the efforts of
ECCI to take away their right, hard-won during the war, to
independent political judgments through open discussion,
and to the attempt of the Russian Komsomol to impose Russian
experience and Russian solutions on the entire youth movement. Georg Lukacs gave voice to the developing fears of
many of those in the communist movement, young and old,
when (referring to the youth movement and its exercise of
'autonomy') he argued that 'the revolution' required great
flexibility in organizational questions. Relations between
youth organization and party should be formed so 'that
developments will be guided in the proper direction of
centralization, at the same time, however, as to give these
relations enough elasticity so centralism can never be used
against the interests of the revolution.'[43]

41 *J-I*, June 1921, 280-3
42 Ibid. The tone of this article, important for Münzenberg's
   summary of the problems between ECCYI and ECCI on the
   eve of the third Comintern and second CYI congresses, is
   one of bewilderment and frustration, mixed with hope.
43 *Kommunismus* (Vienna), 15 May 1921, 592

178 Revolutionary vanguard

The Russians connected this question of party/youth organization relations with that of the location of the second
CYI congress, proposing Moscow as the site, and the period
immediately after the third Comintern congress (summer 1921)
as the time. When ECCYI and the West European communist
youth organizations refused to accept this proposal, asserted their independence, and convened the second congress
in Germany in the spring of 1921, the Russians refused to
attend. They called upon ECCI to support their position.
The latter obliged, first by sending a letter over Zinoviev
signature to ECCYI in November 1920 supporting the Komsomol
and then by proroguing the meeting in Germany and shifting
the congress to Moscow for the following summer. This perem
tory action by the Komsomol and ECCI fanned the controversy
even further. Between April and June 1921, as preparations
for the third Comintern and second CYI congresses in Moscow
were underway, the pages of *Jugend-Internationale* carried
a stream of articles on the independence issue. With Münzenberg, Schüller, Georg Lukacs, Edwin Hörnle, Günther
Hopffe, and Luigi Polano speaking out for independence,
only Kurella represented the Russian view.
    Three distinct positions in the debate over party/youth
organization relations had become discernible in the first
months of 1921. Giuseppe Berti and Gino deMarchi, members
of the central committee of the Italian youth organization
and representing the predominant 'ultra-left' Bordigist
view, proposed a set of theses that were extreme in their
demand for absolute political autonomy. At the other extreme were the Russian youth leaders, who proposed that
youth be subordinated absolutely to the parties (except in
minor organizational and administrative matters). In the
middle, attempting to reconcile the need for central direction and firm discipline in the communist youth movement
with the desire to avoid its becoming merely an instrument
of Russian policy, were all the non-Russian members of ECC
    A position close to that of ECCYI, and critical of the
two extremes, was set forth in a brochure by the Italian,
Luigi Polano, in the spring of 1921.[44] Polano criticized
both the Russians and the Bordigists for being too dogmati
He believed a more pragmatic approach was necessary, the

44 Luigi Polano, *Wir weit ist heute eine Autonomie der
   Kommunistischen Jugendorganisationen* ... See also *IJK*,
   30 March 1920

guiding criterion being what form of relationship would be
of greatest advantage for the development of the revolutionary movement. Polano rejected the Italian theses as
absolutely wrong. Berti and diMarchi were said to have
failed to understand that the conditions in which the socialist movement found itself had changed several times
since before the war. Nor did they understand the situation
in the socialist movement just at that time. The young revolutionaries were right to have demanded independence and
separated from the socialist parties during and after the
war. In every country the 'dialectical development of the
class struggle,' which slowly but surely turns into civil
war, had led to the building of communist parties, with
which the youth movement instinctively had associated itself. Where no communist party existed, the youth movement
took the lead in founding one, thus showing its recognition
of the need for a party to lead the revolutionary movement.
In view of this natural development, Polano could see no
need for raising the question of absolute autonomy for communist youth.[45]

This did not mean that the youth movement should give up
exercising a 'progressive' influence on the communist parties. It should continue its functions as a 'vanguard' in
the sense of being a driving force behind the parties, and
should in a certain sense watch over the parties to see that
they always remain on the right path and not deviate into
right 'opportunism.' The form and degree of this work had
changed from the earlier period, however. The young communists would exercise these functions through discussion
and criticism from within. They were to have a presence at
all sittings of party bodies, were to have a representative
on the party central committee, and would speak out when
the party did not remain true to the 'correct' line.[46]

Implicit in Polano's conception of the role of communist
youth was a communist party with free and open discussion
and the existence and tolerance of different points of
view: a *democratic* centralism where centralism was based
on consent because all decisions reflected a true consensus.
However, in Polano's position, and in that of other communist youth who saw 'opportunism' as the main enemy inside
the communist parties, was a view of reality that saw some

45 Polano, 7-9
46 Ibid., 10

policies as 'truly revolutionary,' and others as deviant,
mistaken, or subversive in relation to the 'interests of
the proletariat.' They were thus in the contradictory position of demanding pluralism in the parties to protect their
rights, while arguing against pluralism by asserting that
only their views could be tolerated in the movement.

For Polano, the Russian theses were mistaken because they
stipulated absolute norms and forgot that these do not stand
up in actual practice. Polano perceived the Russian argument
as stating that because a communist party exists, young
communists have nothing more to say. Polano repeated his
argument that the young communists had to have the right
of discussion and criticism. He rejected the Russian notion
that no matter how an individual communist party may have
been created, young communists should give it their full
support. The nature of the relations between the party and
the youth organization in various countries would depend
upon the degree of development of a communist party and the
'revolutionary proletariat' in general. Clear subordination
of the youth organization to the party was necessary only
where the communist movement had to work completely illegally, or where the dictatorship of the proletariat had
triumphed. In all cases, moreover, the youth organization
had to retain its organizational autonomy.[47]

Polano disagreed with Münzenberg and most of the other
ECCYI functionaries that the youth organizations still
represented the vanguard of the communist movement. Polano,
a former Serratiani, was willing to give up a formal avant-
garde role for the communist youth as long as they could
discuss political and tactical issues in their own organizations, and 'drive [the parties] forward' through participation in party discussions and decisions. Others, however,
were not willing to settle for this.

One source of the continued assertion of an avant-garde
role was the militancy within the yough organizations. Often
sympathizing with or supporting the 'ultra-left' where
this tendency had not yet been expelled from the communist
movement, most of the communist youth leaders (certainly
in Central Europe) continued to argue that their independent avant-garde role was necessary to protect the purity
of communism from 'opportunist' tendencies. Contrary to the
Russian view, Richard Schüller argued that 'all the condi-

47 Ibid., 10-12

tions which made the young workers the most revolutionary, most active part of the proletariat during World War I' were still present to govern the relations between youth organization and party.[48] Georg Lukacs expressed the same thought when he argued that as all sections of the Comintern were not yet communist parties in the same sense as the Russian party, the communist youth had to continue to play an avant-garde role.[49]

In his role as spokesman for the Russian views, Kurella wrote that there could be no 'avant-garde within the avant-garde.' There could be no 'best communists.' To Kurella, the communist youth had not performed an avant-garde role because of their age, but rather by the historical happenstance of their being the first groupings of communists in the international labour movement. The youth organizations thus took the lead in breaking the communists away from the socialist parties. Now, with the formation of communist parties everywhere, the youth organizations could get on with their natural educational and cultural tasks among the mass of young workers. The historical episode of an avant-garde role for the communist youth was now over. 'The real history of the youth international,' wrote Kurella, 'begins perhaps now when the youth movement becomes a working part (Arbeitsteilung) of the party movement, and undertakes and develops its special functions inside the Third International.'[50]

Throughout this prolonged discussion on the relations between communist youth and communist parties, Willi Münzenberg remained a stout defender of, and foremost spokesman for, the status quo. The young communists had organizational independence and considerable freedom in political affairs. Münzenberg and the West Europeans, although accepting as desirable close cooperation with the communist parties, struggled to retain this state of affairs. Agreeing with Schüller and Lukacs, he rejected Kurella's contention that the role of communist youth as a vanguard was an historical phase or episode in the labour movement. Even more than during the pre-war and wartime years, said Münzenberg, the

48 *J-I*, May 1921, 233-5
49 Ibid., 231-3; *J-I*, July 1921, 313-14
50 *J-I*, June 1921, 284-7

conditions placing the youth in their vanguard role existed in 1921.[51]

Relations in practice

As this long and spirited debate was going on, the communist youth organizations in many countries were regulating relations with their communist parties to their own satisfaction.[52] The young communists outside Soviet Russia, including the members of ECCYI, were thus developing a feeling of having settled the issue. The Comintern congress could do nothing else than ratify what the parties and the youth organizations had in practice worked out among themselves. Several examples, besides that of Italy where Bordiga left the youth federation to its own devices in return for the support it gave him, can serve to illustrate this process of accommodation.[53] The Russians remained adamant, seeking to impose Russian experience where it was neither wanted, nor (it was argued) applicable.

Switzerland
At its congress in Aarau in April 1920, the Swiss socialist youth organization ratified the actions of its representatives at the Berlin congress and adhered formally to the CYI.[54] The youth organization was declared to be independer

51 Pietschmann, *Der politisch-ideologische Klärungsprozess* ... 211, n. 1, cites an unpublished manuscript from 19(*Von Lenin Geleitet*, in which Kurella argues that Lenin had followed for some time the autonomist tendencies within ECCYI and had commissioned ECCI to take steps against them.
52 See *J-I*, July 1921, 310–12
53 For Italy see the explicit statement by Polano at the youth organization congress in January 1921 that 'the central committee has always subordinated the youth federation to the communist [faction]' (*l'Avanguardia*, 23 January 1921).
54 *Neue Jugend*, 18 April 1920, and 18 May 1920. Three dire tions were evident at this congress: 1) that of the cen tral committee, which urged severance of all ties with the socialist party; 2) an element also for an independent youth organization, but centrist in politics and hoping to retain some tie to the party; and 3) a more

of all parties, for the situation had not as yet crystallized in Switzerland. A small, as yet unrecognized, splinter
communist party had been formed, but the bulk of those who
supported the Comintern remained as a left faction in the
otherwise centrist Social Democratic Party. By March 1921
the left had split from the centrists and were now joining
the 'old communists' to form a united Communist Party of
Switzerland. Following the August theses, the youth organization journal, *Neue Jugend*, declared that the young communists now had 'the right to separate ... from the party-
political struggle and plunge into essentially youth questions.'[55] They would, however, retain the right to discuss
all political questions and participate in all political
activities as they saw fit.[56]

Despite the view of *Neue Jugend*, serious reservations had
existed within the youth organization regarding the August
theses. A long discussion took place at its nineteenth congress in Zurich in May 1921. The strong vanguardism within
the Swiss youth organization manifested itself in the suggestion that 'the communist party does not offer a guarantee

anarchistic group advocating complete independence, no
program, and no statutes. At a congress in Olten in July
1919 the young socialists in both the German- and
French-speaking areas had joined into one organization
and adhered to the new Communist International (see
ibid., August 1919). Emil Arnold and Jules Humbert-Droz
were secretaries of the new organization.
55 *Neue Jugend*, 8 March 1921. This was not to signify a
withdrawal from political affairs, however. The involvement of the youth organization in the day-to-day 'polit-
ical-economic class struggle' would continue. In
November 1920 an expanded central committee had accepted
the Twenty-One Conditions and changed the name to the
Kommunistische Jugendverband der Schweiz (ibid., 20
November 1920). After the left split from the socialist
party in December, the youth leaders had begun to imply
a willingness to give up their avant-garde role. 'Because the communist party is now in existence, the youth
will everywhere give up a greater share of the political
work and pass it over to this party ...' (ibid., 24
December 1920). A united communist party was still three
months away, however.
56 *Neue Jugend*, 18 March 1921

184 Revolutionary vanguard

that in time it will not level off and grow cold in its
[revolutionary zeal]. The independence of the young communists and their influence in the party helps to maintain
within the party an active will to struggle, and presses
it forward. The independence of the youth is therefore in
the interest of the revolutionary proletariat.'[57] The young
communists felt that their subordination (Unterstellung)
to the party would lead to the withering of all initiative.
There were widespread doubts about the party's willingness
to implement aggressively its own programs. After assurance:
from the ECCI representative (the old Swiss leftist, Fritz
Platten), the August theses were approved unanimously.[58]
This decision was accepted by the party leadership, subject
to ratification by the next party congress. Political work
was for the most part to be left to the party. The youth
organization, as prescribed by the August theses, obligated
itself 'by actions and under the strongest discipline, to
comply with the slogans of the communist party' and to forg
the formulation of a program of its own in favour of that o
the party and the Comintern.[59] The young Swiss communists,
nevertheless, went to Moscow in the summer of 1921 as firm
supporters of independence for the youth organizations,
both organizationally and politically.[60]

Germany
Until the fall of 1920, the Freie Sozialistische Jugend
(FSJ) continued to maintain its organizational and political independence while deciding what its relations would
be to the two German communist parties. With the expulsion
of the 'ultra-left' from the FSJ in September, after the
second Comintern congress had rejected the 'ultra-left'
party (KAPD) as a member, relations with the communist
party (KPD) and the issue of the role of the youth movement remained to be settled. Efforts to accomplish this
were complicated by the uncertainty arising from the growi
rapprochement between the KPD and the left-wing centrists
in the USPD, and between the FSJ and the centrist youth
organization (SPJ). With both party and youth organization

57 Ibid., 3 June 1921, 3
58 Ibid., 3 June 1921. For the theses see ibid., 14 May
   1921, 5
59 Ibid., 14 May 1921, 5
60 Ibid., 3 June 1921, 9

in a state of flux, more precise definition of the relations
between them remained in abeyance.

While the self-defined role of the FSJ as the vanguard
of the revolutionary movement surely was not taken too
seriously, it was not openly challenged by the KPD leadership in 1919 and 1920.[61] The FSJ central executive committee
continued during 1920 to assert that the young communists
represented the vanguard of the revolution. At the same time
that the FSJ leadership was repudiating the 'ultra-left'
and the KAPD, it was criticizing, at least by implication,
the KPD leadership for its failure during the Kapp Putsch.
In June 1920, the central executive committee appealed to
the young communists in the FSJ to take the lead in rousing
the masses and in building a 'united proletarian front'
against 'counter-revolution' based on political workers'
councils.[62] The FSJ leadership was unwilling to concede
that the KPD was infused with a genuinely revolutionary
spirit. The youth organization wished to retain its freedom
of action so as to help 'push forward' the German proletariat. Only when the communist party had been strengthened
to the point where it was indeed a revolutionary party could
the FSJ subordinate itself unconditionally to its leadership. One central executive committee member, Günther Hopffe,
asserted that with an increase in their size, there was the
danger of a 'dilution of the sharp class character of the
communist parties.' In the German situation, this was to be
understood as a serious, though mistaken, skepticism on
Hopffe's part about the revolutionary commitment of the new
recruits to the united KPD coming from the left wing of the
USPD.[63] As the most revolutionary elements, said Hopffe,
the communist youth had to strengthen the ranks of the communist party.

With the successful split of the centrist organizations
in Germany in the fall of 1920, and the formation of a
united communist party and a united youth organization in
December, both the party and the young communists took steps

61 Pietschmann, *Die politisch-ideologische Klärungsprozess*
... 52
62 See *JG*, no. 27 (June 1920). For a contemporary criticism
of this behaviour from the accepted Soviet point of view
see Pietschmann, 215ff., especially 216, n.1.
63 *J-I*, November 1920, 53-4. See also *Die Arbeit*, no. 2
(March 1921): 17ff., and *JG*, no. 16 (February 1921)

to stabilize and legitimize their relations. The sixth
(unity) congress of the KPD in Berlin in December adopted
a set of guiding principles (Richtlinien) regarding the
youth movement.[64] As a part of the revolutionary movement,
the young communists were to have a twofold task. In addition to a role in the political struggle, they had to provide a communist education to 'young proletarians.' The
communist youth organization was thus to be a prepatory
school for the party, but in a manner significantly different from the 'recruiting school' concept of the pre-war
social democrats. Because of the special psychological
characteristics of young people, an independent organization was necessary. Provision was made in the party statute
for representaton of the youth organization in the 'leading
party bodies' as the pre-condition for the closest political
cooperation. Implicit, but not clearly stated, was an independent political role of some sort for the young communists
The several references to 'cooperation,' and the acknowledg-
ment of their political role, although unspecified, at least
left it open for young communists to insist on their independence and to assert an avant-garde role, as well as to
claim that the party supported their stand.

The fifth congress of the KJD at the end of December (als
a 'unity' congress) re-emphasized the independence of communist youth.[65] Where no communist party existed, said

64 *Bericht über die Verhandlungen des Vereinigungspartei-
tages* ... 248-9
65 *IJK*, 10 January 1921. See also *Abriss der Geschichte*
... 252-5, 260, 262-3. A new central leadership was
elected by the congress in accordance with a new statute
(Pietschmann, *Die politisch-ideologische Klärungsprozess*
... 242). Heilmann, Hopffe, Richard Gyptner, Franziska
Bergmann, Herman Bergmann, Max Köhler, Otto Unger, Eugen
Schönhaar, and Erich Wiesner were elected members of the
'Reichszentrale,' which replaced the central executive
committee (Zentralausschuss). Heilmann and the two
Bergmanns withdrew 'a few months later,' and Walter
Gollmick (Carl Adler), Walter Schulz, and R. Wissener
were co-opted to replace them (ibid., 243). It is not
clear if this change was due to the response of the KJD
to the March Action, or if it was to open more places
in the central leadership to former SPJ leaders after
unification. Richard Gyptner had been co-opted into the

rapporteur Franziska Bergmann referring to Norway, Sweden, Spain, and Belgium, the youth organization must become the communist party. Where a communist party has been formed, the youth organization must give it full support and cooperation. 'In both cases the youth work completely independently - not only organizationally, but also politically.' With the progressive development of parties to a position of being the leading mass parties, there would occur a *political* incorporation of the communist youth in the fold of the parties. Complete organizational independence would be retained. Finally, 'under the dictatorship of the proletariat the youth, of course, have to subordinate themselves to the proletarian government, i.e. the party.'[66] Here one may observe again the difference in the post-revolutionary Russian experience and the pre-revolutionary situation in Germany and the rest of Europe.[67] In the transitional period, which was said to characterize the situation in Germany at that time, it would be incorrect to speak of the political subordination of the youth organizations. This could occur only after the German proletariat had assumed power through the communist party. In the then-current stage, the young communists had to help promote the fusion process within the new united KPD 'through practical cooperation and through strong, independent criticism.'[68] No objection appears to have been raised at the youth congress to the 'Richtlinien' adopted by the party. The delegates made explicit their assumption of an independent political role, a role that was implicit in the party position. The KPD/KJD relationship was to be one of 'brothers in arms' (Waffenbruderschaft). This remained the situation as both party and youth organization prepared for the Comintern and CYI congresses in Moscow in the summer of 1921.[69]

---

leadership in October 1920 (ibid., 235), and after the fifth congress became the leader of the KJD (*Abriss der Geschichte* ... 260).

66 *IJK*, 10 January 1921

67 One also sees here a drift away from the enthusiasm for the soviets (Räte) as the locus of state power during the dictatorship of the proletariat. It is the party that is equated with 'proletarian government,' not the soviets.

68 *IJK*, 10 January 1921

69 The issue was raised once again in the national committee

France

In France, as in other European countries, the communist party had been formed after the young revolutionary social- ists had organized and had been functioning as an indepen- dent political force. The theses adopted by ECCI in August 1920 remained open and unratified, even after the commu- nists captured the socialist youth organization in early November, because of the unsettled situation in the party. On the eve of the congress in Tours in December, at which the French socialist party opted for the Comintern, the youth organization journal, *l'Avant-garde*, was optimistic in its anticipation that the party would recognize the need for autonomy for the youth organization.[70] It would do so not only for educational/propaganda reasons, but also as a means of countering 'opportunist' elements in the party. Yet the youth organization and the new communist party would have a close understanding because the party would, it was assumed, be both communist *and* revolutionary. This phraseology suggested the scepticism of the youth about the commitment to revolution by some who called themselves communist.

Only at the end of the last day of the congress in Tours, however, was the question raised, and then in the form of a short report on the developments within the youth move- ment.[71] The congress did decide to support the national committee of the Jeunesses communistes (JC) as far as possible, and to open *Humanité* to the youth organization for reports and special articles. The regulation of rela- tions was left to the forthcoming congresses of the two new communist organizations. This left the communist youth leaders unhappy with the way in which the congress at Tours had skimmed over the youth question.[72] Despite talks between Maurice Laporte and the party leaders, agreement on the role and goals of the youth movement had not been reached.

---

in May, with Kurella and Münzenberg presenting the op- posing views. To Münzenberg, the communist party was still not 'developed enough.'
70 *L'Avant-Garde*, 11 December 1920, 2
71 *IJK*, 1 February 1921
72 See Laporte in *l'Avant-Garde*, 15 January 1921

Originally planned for mid March, the first congress of the JC convened in Paris in mid May 1921.[73] During the first part of 1921, the JC had been active in work for which it was to acquire a great reputation and influence: anti-militarist agitation. The occasion was the call-up of the class of 1919, followed by the general mobilization for occupation of the Ruhr cities occasioned by German default on reparations.[74] The question of relations with the party called forth a lively discussion at the congress. A minority arguing for complete and total independence remained dis-satisfied with the Moscow theses of the preceding August.[75] This minority, whose spokesman was Marcel Vandomme, polem-icized against what it saw as an attempt to dominate the

73 See *IJK*, 10 June 1921, 3. Reports issued by the JC on the congress are not available. The congress re-elected Laporte and Camille Fegy as secretaries, and formed a national committee composed of Rosa Michel, Honel, Perche, Lozeray, Auclair, Jacques Doriot, David, Gailard, and Solaire. The critics of the leadership, Gabriel Péri and Marcel Vandomme, were not included.
74 See *IJK*, 20 February 1921 and 20 May 1921, and the issues of *l'Avant-Garde* in the first half of 1921. The JC under-went a crisis over policy and personalities at this time. Because of harassment from the authorities as a result of the illegal and anti-militarist agitation, a small secret committee was entrusted with the underground work among the soldiers and conscripts. Differences developed between the majority of the national committee and the secret com-mittee, with the latter accused of overstepping its com-petence. After a long and ad hominum debate, the congress upheld the majority, abolished the secret committee, ex-cluded its members from the new national committee, and formed a new committee to direct the illegal anti-militarist work under stricter supervision of the new national com-mittee (see *IJK*, 10 June 1921 and 10 July 1920).
75 The division within the outgoing national committee was far closer than among the delegates to the congress. The *majority* in the national committee had consisted of Laporte, Fegy, Auclair, Doriot, Honel, Michel, and Perche; the *minority* of Vandomme, Vidal, Calman, William, and Souques (*l'Avant-Garde*, 15-30 May 1921, 3). The voting at the congress was 4403 for supporting the Moscow theses, 325 for the Vandomme opposition, and 459 abstentions (ibid.).

youth international by the Russian Komsomol. Vandomme argued that this would be a great danger for the communist
youth movement in Western Europe. He saw, correctly, no
guarantee in the August theses or in the resolution of
support for them put forward by the national committee
majority that the parties would not use the slogan of
'party discipline' to suppress the revolutionary enthusiasm of the youth.[76]

As elsewhere, the young communists in France were unhappy
with the attitude of the party leadership. The Comité
Directeur (central committee) of the party, under Frossard's
leadership, was being challenged by the Parisian 'ultra-
left' and the JC for its lack of action and militancy, especially during the Ruhr crisis.[77] 'It is necessary,' said
Vandomme, 'to recognize the impossibility of subordinating
the young revolutionary elements to the adults, whom the
years have made sleepy.'[78] This opposition to the party
leadership was to be expressed at the third Comintern congress by all the JC delegates, and was to come under heavy
criticism from the Bolshevik spokesman on French affairs,
Trotsky.

While the JC leadership was in agreement in its opposition to the Frossard party leadership, it differed on the
purposes of the JC and the consequences of tying the JC
to the party. Thus, at the JC congress the minority argued
that if the JC did not take a firm position for independenc
in principle, it would be 'forging its own chains.'[79] The
minority rejected the view that a claim to absolute independence was 'counter-revolutionary.' Still, while opposed
to subordination to the French communist party the minority
did believe that there should be close collaboration with
it within the Comintern.[80]

76 *L'Avant-Garde*, 15-30 June 1921, 3
77 See Wohl, *French Communism in the Making 1914-1924*, 220
78 *L'Avant-Garde*, 15-30 May 1921, 4
79 Ibid., 15-30 June 1921, 3
80 Ibid. These differences were seen also in the debates
   on the statutes for the JC. The minority was for the
   wording 'is able' rather than 'ought to' in the provision for delegating two national committee members to
   participate in the party leadership ('Comité Directeur'
   The minority wished to have the JC retain the statutory
   right to refuse to have relations with an 'opportunist'
   communist party.

Laporte and Emile Auclair defended the August theses.
Complete autonomy of the youth organizaton had been necessary only in relation to the socialist party, they argued.
Now with a communist party, a closer relationship was both
appropriate and necessary. The JC thus gave up, according
to the August theses, its absolute autonomy and accepted
subordination, in principle, to the political program of
the PCF. In the prevailing situation, however, where there
was no guarantee that the new PCF would be truly revolutionary, the JC demanded independence and sufficient elbow-
room in tactics and policy. 'Active cooperation' was to
characterize the relations between the JC and the PCF, but
in fact there was more coexistence than cooperation.[81] The
'Comité Directeur' of the party did little to fulfil the
pledge made at the Tours congress to support the JC.
    The qualified nature of this acceptance by the JC of
political subordination to the party was evident at the
congress of the PCF, immediately following the JC congress.
Part of one session was devoted to the question of JC/PCF
relations. Laporte, refuting a statement in a socialist
journal that the JC congress had proclaimed the autonomy
of the youth organization, said that 'today there is only
one kind of action, namely communist action - there is no
separate ideology for the Young Communist League. It does
not behoove the latter to go against the dictates of the
communist party.' As both the JC and the PCF had adhered
to the Comintern, they both had accepted the 'principles
of centralizaton.' 'All communist organizations must bow
to the decision of the communist party which alone has the
right to dictate. After action, the Young Communist League
has a free right to criticize, but in the course of action
not to accept the dictates of the party would mean to stab
it in the back.'[82] Thus, centralization and political subordination meant to the JC majority the acceptance of party
dictates in times of action, but freedom to adopt independent views both before and after these actions.
    Frossard accepted, and the congress endorsed, Laporte's
proposal for reciprocal delegation of two members to the
leading bodies of the two organizations. Frossard, in order
to avoid future conflicts, wanted to go further and incor-
porate into the party statutes Laporte's statement that in

81 See Wohl, *French Communism in the Making 1914-1924*, 322
82 *Moscow*, Organ of the III Congress of the Communist
    International, no. 11 (5 June 1921): 3

action the JC was subordinated to the party. There was some discusson on this point, with Auclair very much opposed and Laporte more sympathetic, at least in principle. There was some division among the party delegates as well. Ferdinand Faure said that while all his sympathies lay with the JC, which had been the door through which he had entered the party, 'the pupil wielding the rod was an impossibile position.' The JC should devote itself wholly to the education of its members. Chantereau differed, saying that 'there are times when it becomes imperative to be teacher first and pupil second.' Charles Rappaport was also very sympathetic to the JC and spoke against Faure's notion that the youth should not be concerned directly with political affairs. 'The Young Communist League is a moving power. If it lacks experience, we have perhaps too much of it. We have seen too many things and we are not daring enough. We grew up in a period when enlistment meant more than action. [But] I am certainly not in favour of infantocracy.'[83] In the end, the congress accepted the proposal of Laporte and Frossard that the party central committee and the national committee of the JC jointly draw up the paragraphs in the party statute concerning JC/PCF relations.

Statements by Laporte and Auclair confirming the avant-gardism within the youth movement served to contradict or qualify further the avowed political subordination of the JC to the party program. 'One cannot prohibit the youth, as an avant-garde, from themselves taking on the job of revolutionizing the masses if the party, in a revolutionary situation, does not fulfil its duty.'[84] The JC 'will fulfil its historical avant-garde role: to push the party to action.'[85] Any concern the party might have about the youth drifting away from the centralized communist movement could be assuaged by the knowledge that the CYI, to which the JC was firmly attached, was bound by the decisions of the Comintern. The French thus went to the second CYI congress as outspoken advocates of an independent political position for the youth. A majority accepted in principle political subordination to the party. But as elsewhere, this principle would become operative only when it was clear that, and only so long as, the party was pursuing a genuinely revolutionary policy.

83 All quotations in this paragraph are from ibid.
84 *IJK*, 10 June 1921, 3
85 Ibid., 20 June 1921

Conflict over the location of the second CYI congress

The controversy between the Russian Komsomol and the young
communists in Western Europe was brought to a head over
the issue of the character and location of the second CYI
congress. As early as the first session of the International
Bureau in June 1920, ECCYI had decided to convene the congress in March 1921 in Italy.[86] In doing so, it rejected
a proposal by the Komsomol to hold it in Moscow at the
same time as the second Comintern congress. The conference
of young communists in Moscow in August 1920 confirmed the
decision of the International Bureau. Again rejecting a
Russian proposal to meet in Moscow, ECCYI in Berlin decided
in November to hold the congress in late April 1921.[87] In
its announcement, ECCYI indicated that the political situation in Western Europe was such that it had decided to invite *all* revolutionary youth groups that recognized the
program of the youth international.[88] Thus the second congress was to be a congress encompassing all 'revolutionary
proletarian youth.'
    In a lead article in *Jugend-Internationale* in January
1921, Münzenberg described the congress as he perceived
it. 'The future international congresses of communist youth
must be really congresses, i.e. [in contrast to Berlin
where many were absent] international gatherings which
unite the largest number of representatives possible, above
all delegates from all of the currently existing communist
youth organizations.' It would be necessary to have at the
congress representatives of organizations other than the
communist youth organizations. He sought continuously to
develop as broad a support for the CYI as possible, con-
sistent with a commitment to 'revolutionary socialism' and
the discipline needed to assure unity and firm 'striking
power.'[89] This CYI congress of all 'revolutionary proletarian youth,' being planned when the expectations of a

86 Kurella, *Gründung und Aufbau* ... 120
87 See ibid., 123, and *The Communist* (London), 30 December
    1920, 7
88 *J-I*, December 1920, 90
89 Münzenberg believed that it would be helpful to the
    'clarification process' to have representatives of those
    trade-union youth sections that were 'on their way' to
    the CYI, as well as any centrist youth organizations
    that could be induced or pressured into attending. The

'revolutionary offensive' were reaching a peak, would serve
to bind the masses together and would, Münzenberg hoped,
help the communist youth organizations to become mass revolutionary organizations. Such a meeting would have included
'ultra-left,' syndicalist, anarchist, and all other youth
groups supporting revolutionary action. Because many of these
groups had a political or ideological orientation that had
been condemned by the Russian Bolshevik leaders and the
Comintern, ECCI and the Russian Komsomol were opposed to
holding the congress, especially as it was to be in Western
Europe beyond their reach and control. Münzenberg and ECCYI
insisted on holding the congress in Western Europe where it
would be easier to get 'a larger number of the leading and
most active comrades' together than if the congress were
held in Russia.[90]

Believing in the necessity and possibility of direct revolutionary action under existing conditions, ECCYI and most
of the West European communist youth leaders were supporters
of the 'revolutionary offensive.' This policy called for the
mobilization of all revolutionary forces for direct revolutionary action. Its genesis lay in the optimism with which
Lenin and the Bolshevik leaders viewed the situation in mid
1920 as the Red Army approached Warsaw on the eve of the
second Comintern congress. Despite the failure of the Red
Army to spark the anticipated European revolution, the revolutionary élan and enthusiasm persisted. It had come insti-
tively to the young communists. Although Lenin and others
soon recognized that the revolutionary wave had receded in
Europe, leading them to a policy of 'retreat' in the Comintern during 1921, leading functionaries in the Comintern
continued to adhere to revolutionary orthodoxy and to har-
bour overly optimistic expectations about the possibilities
for revolution. Young communists thus saw the planned CYI
congress as a great political demonstration in support of
revolutionary action.

---

leaders of the latter would only be shown to their members to be 'bourgeois elements masquerading as revolutionaries.' Also to be invited were the communist student
groups and the illegal revolutionary soldiers' organizations.
90 *Fremad* (monthly newspaper of the Danish socialist youth
organization) 15. årg., nr. 3 (July 1921)

The Russian Komsomol, on the other hand, was beginning to assert itself in the youth international. It did not want a broadly based congress, for that would have provided more support for the advocates of independence and for the proponents of the 'revolutionary offensive,' positions that the Russian party, and thus the Komsomol, rejected. A meeting with controlled representation, convened under strict Russian supervision and in a location where leading party figures could exert their influence on the young delegates was essential for the imposition of Russian views.[91]

From the standpoint of ECCYI and its supporters in Western Europe, the presence of communist party representatives in Moscow at the same time was an important factor militating *against* Moscow as a suitable site. As Max Köhler, representative of the German KJD, remarked, 'all comrades who go to Soviet Russia from their [own] countries lose their clarity ...'[92] By this he meant that they fell under the influence of the Russian leaders, and under the spell of their arguments, so that situations became viewed from the Russian party viewpoint rather than from that of the party (or youth organization) leaders back home.

Under continued pressure from the Russians, ECCYI decided to send a delegation to Moscow to discuss the problem with ECCI.[93] The latter had met in mid November, with Shatskin

91 See *Die Kommunistische Internationale*, no. 15 (1921): 601–3, for implicit approval by ECCI for a broad meeting. At a session on 22 December ECCYI approved a list of sixty-two groups to be invited to the congress (*IJK*, 1 January 1921). On 24 January 1921, ECCYI added the German 'ultra-leftists' (KAJ) to the list, to participate with an 'advisory' vote (ibid., 1 February 1921).
92 Kurella, *Gründung und Aufbau* ... 157
93 Ibid., 155–8. In early December, as he was about to leave for Vienna and the first conference of the socialist youth organizations in southeastern Europe, Münzenberg had replied to a message from Shatskin requesting a session of the International Bureau in order to discuss the change of location of the congress. He stated that the site would remain unchanged, indicating that there was no time to hold a meeting of the International Bureau: ECCYI was too busy, its work could not be postponed. He repeated his earlier argument about the difficulties of travel to Russia, and expressed his belief that the time

present to argue for Moscow as the site of the congress, and had approved the Komsomol proposal unanimously.[94] Shatskin was then condemned in Berlin for violating discipline and working against the International Bureau decision to hold the second congress in Italy. The delegation was made up of Kurella and two supporters of the International Bureau position, Max Köhler and Willi Mielenz. If ECCI still refused to accept the youth international decision, a plenum of ECCYI was to meet after the delegation returned to decide what to do. ECCYI made it clear that in any event it reserved the right of independent decision.[95]

The delegation left Berlin on 9 February 1921, arriving in Russia at a time when a food shortage was causing serious unrest. In the last days of February there was a wave of strikes in the Petrograd factories. The Mensheviks and social revolutionaries were calling respectively for freely elected factory committees and soviets, and the convening of a constitutent assembly. Martial law was declared by the Bolsheviks in the face of a 'counter-revolutionary' movement. Probably influenced by Bolshevik arguments that unity and centralization were needed now more than ever if revolutionary gains were to be preserved and extended, Köhler

available should be used to prepare for the congress and not wasted in time-consuming travel (an abridged version of Münzenberg's reply is in ibid., 240-1). By the end of the month, however, it had been decided that the issue was so serious that some discussion with Moscow was required. ECCYI received important support from the fifth KJD congress in December, which adopted a resolution calling for the CYI congress to be in Western Europe and not in Russia (*IJK*, 10 January 1921).

94 *Die Kommunistische Internationale*, no. 16 (1921): 407. See also Kurella, *Gründung und Aufbau* ... 240

95 The delegation was also instructed to investigate the activities of Shatskin, inquiring into whether or not he was properly conducting himself as ECCYI representative in Russia and to ECCI, and to orient itself to the opposition in the Komsomol (i.e. Dunayevskii and the other dissidents; see Kurella, *Gründung und Aufbau* ... 158. After discussion with the Komsomol and ECCI leaders, Shatskin was 'cleared' by the delegation and the opposition elements in the Komsomol condemned as 'mistaken.'

and Mielenz accepted the Russian position on all issues under discussion. Once again, a delegation to Soviet Russia seemed to have 'lost its clarity.' The delegation returned to Berlin in early March to a cold reception, with ECCYI deciding to continue to adhere to an independent line.[96]

The abortive congress in Jena

The Russians and ECCYI remained split as the latter went ahead with plans to hold the second CYI congress in Western Europe. Conditions in Italy, where communists and fascists had become embroiled in constant violent clashes, made it impossible to hold the congress in that country. A decision was therefore made to hold it in Germany instead, but an abortive communist uprising (March Action) created new problems.

The congress was to have opened in Jena on 30 March 1921. With police raids and arrests of communist leaders already underway, and the Russian representatives having failed to arrive, it was decided to postpone the sessions. Rejecting all efforts to change its location to Moscow, ECCYI finally convened the congress on 6 April.[97] Present at Jena, in addition to representatives from all communist youth organizations except Russia, Spain, Portugal, and Asia, were representatives of the communist opposition groups in the Austrian centrist organization (VSAJ) and the Belgian Jeune Garde/Jonge Wacht, as well as two representatives from the 'ultra-left' KAJ in Germany, five from the Jewish Revolutionary Youth Organization of Poland and East Galicia, and representatives from the Austrian communist soldiers' organization, the KPD, and other guests, including Joseph Pepper (Pogany) and Bela Kun as representatives of ECCI.[98]

96 Kurella, 159. Münzenberg appears to have been particularly disappointed with the behaviour of his two spokesmen (Gross, *Willi Münzenberg*, 118).
97 Kurella, 167. In response to a telegram from ECCI designating the meeting only as a 'private conference,' the participants voted 60–48 to recognize the meeting as a 'full decision-making' congress (Sogstad, *Ungdoms Fanevakt*, 299). While ECCI in Moscow was seeking to have the meeting in Jena called off, *Die Kommunistische Internationale* (no. 16 [1921]: 663) was hailing the planned conference as an event of great significance.

The proceedings began on a controversial note with a repor
by Pogany on the world situation, which led to a polemic on
the 'revolutionary offensive.' Pogany and Kun were among the
main proponents in the Comintern of this policy, which had
provided the basis for the revolutionary action in Germany
(March Action) in the weeks immediately preceding the meetir
at Jena. Kun and Pogany had gone to Germany in early March
in order to take the KPD down the path to revolutionary action.[99] Kun argued that a 'revolutionary offensive' was the
only policy appropriate for the conditions of crisis and ter
sion then existing in Germany. Behind the 'revolutionary
offensive' was an aggressiveness that urged all 'real' revolutionary forces (communists) to maintain an offensive aga:

98 Pogany and Kun were two Hungarians who had been active
   in the Hungarian Soviet of 1919, the former as leader
   of the Soldiers' Council and commissar of war, and Kun
   as the guiding force in the abortive revolution. At this
   time they were leading activists in ECCI - Kun for some
   time to remain so, Pogany to go in 1922 to the United
   States and become active in communist party affairs
   there. For a discussion of Pogany/Pepper see Draper,
   American Communism and Soviet Russia, 57-61. Represented
   at the Jena conference were communist youth organization
   from Sweden, Norway, Denmark, Iceland, Finland, Latvia,
   Lithuania, the Netherlands, Belgium, Luxembourg, France,
   Switzerland, Italy, Germany, Austria, Czechoslovakia,
   Hungary, Yugoslavia, Bulgaria, Greece, Transylvania, the
   Banat, Bessarabia, Mexico, North America, and England
   (a representative arrived after the meeting had begun),
   and the socialist youth organization (communist dominated) in Romania (*J-I*, May 1921, 246-52). About 100
   delegates participated. Giuseppe Berti, who was present
   as an Italian delegate, says that the third ECCI representative in Europe at this time (Guralsky) also participated. Michael Borodin, better known for his later
   work in China, was at this time also in Germany illegall
   as the Comintern contact with the KAPD (Gross, *Willi
   Münzenberg*, 116).
99 A good account of Kun's mission, and the controversy
   over the reasons for his having been sent, is in Angress
   The Stillborn Revolution, 119-22. Angress discusses in
   detail the March Action and the situation in the KPD
   before, during, and afterwards.

capitalism. The 'revolutionary offensive' called for action
at all times. It was as important, however, for the psychological state of commitment it sought to perpetuate, as for
its exhortations to practical action. Within ECCI, Zinoviev,
Bukharin, and Kun appear to have been the fathers of the
aggressive policy and efforts to implement it. Support also
came from the communist parties in Austria and Italy, and
the KAPD in Germany. In March 1921 Kun also had the support
of the new leadership of the KPD formed by Heinrich Brandler,
supported by Paul Fröhlich and August Thalheimer, after Paul
Levi had been ousted at the end of February.[100] On March
22-23, a communist-inspired general strike in Saxony began
to turn, thanks to the revolutionary figure, Max Hölz, into
an open and spreading insurrection against the government.[101]
Armed conflicts took place between communist groups and the
police. The KPD undertook action in other places as well -
Hamburg, Berlin, the Ruhr - but it was in central Germany
that the insurrection reached its height. By the end of the
month, however, the communists had been defeated.

As a result of the March Action the authorities instituted
severely repressive measures against the communists, including young communists. 'The communist youth of Germany
had taken a position immediately in complete and basic
agreement with the [March] action, and participated therein
in a prominent way.'[102] The KJD 'Zentrale' had supported

100 Levi, following a cautious policy in recognition of both
the weakness of the revolutionary forces in Germany, and
the limited potential for revolution in general in the
country, had been under attack in the KPD 'Zentrale' by
a left-opposition (Ernst Reuter-Friesland, Ruth Fischer,
Arkady Maslow) that wanted more revolutionary action.
He also came under attack from ECCI when, at the crucial
Livorno congress of the Italian Socialist Party, he supported Serrati and his rejection of the Twenty-One Conditions. Levi resigned as chairman of the 'Zentrale'
after his views were repudiated by a 28-23 vote.
101 See Angress, *The Stillborn Revolution*, chapter five
102 *IJK*, 5 May 1921, 2-3 (resolution from ECCYI on the con-
flict in the KPD sent to the Berlin group of the KJD).
Discussions of the activities of the KJD during the
March Action are in *J-I*, July 1921, 303-5; *IJK*, 1
April and 10 April 1921; *JG*, 1 May 1921, 188 and 1
July 1921, 242.

Levi's united front policy in early 1921. The new Brandler
leadership, however, was more in accord with the basic predisposition of the KJD for more militant action. A majority
in the KJD leadership thus became eager supporters of the
'revolutionary offensive' when it was initiated by the KPD
in mid March.[103] Only a few followers of Levi, who were
expelled at a session of the KJD national committee in May,
had tried to warn against the revolutionary attempt. *Jugend-
Internationale* was banned, and on 30 March the CYI and KJD
publishing house in Berlin was raided by the police. In
many areas of Germany the KJD leaders were arrested, and
the activities of the local and district groups hampered.

Within the CYI, as within the Comintern and the KPD,
there had been a difference of opinion on the theory of
the 'revolutionary offensive.' It had broken into the open
at the expanded session of ECCYI on 5 March, called to
hear the report of the delegation to Russia.[104] Münzenberg,
supported by Valeriu Marcu, was against revolutionary action at that time. While Münzenberg was for continuing the
struggle with the bourgeoisie, he did not believe the time
to be ripe for a direct confrontation with the state. The
three members of the ECCYI delegation to Russia (Kurella,
Köhler, and Mielenz) supported revolutionary action and
opposed Münzenberg. Kurella defended his position on the
grounds that the delegation, just having returned from
Russia, had seen the desperate conditions there and the
need to help the Bolsheviks. Thus they knew better than
the others the need for revolutionary action.[105] Münzenberg

103 *JG*, 15 April 1921
104 Participating were Münzenberg, Kurella, Flieg, and
    Mielenz from ECCYI, Lekai (Hungary), Köhler (Germany),
    Likov (Bulgaria), Valeriu Marcu (Romania) Lieb (Switzer
    land), and Vretling (Sweden); see Kurella, *Gründung
    und Aufbau* ... 164.
105 Kurella later mentioned the Kronstadt revolt and the
    railroad crisis as examples of the difficulties that
    he used at the ECCYI meeting to support his views in
    favour of revolutionary action (ibid., 165). The winnin
    of the ECCYI delegation to Russia to the position of
    Bela Kun, and Kurella's later use of Kronstadt to jus-
    tify revolutionary action, tends to support the view
    of Carr (*The Bolshevik Revolution 1917-1923* III, 335
    n.2 and 338) and Lowenthal ('Bolshevization of the

was criticized for being an 'opportunist,' and his attitude
on the location of the congress condemned as an 'anti-
Moscow' position. Already one could see the frame of mind
that was developing. The KJD committed itself enthusiastically to the March Action because its members were disposed
to militancy. At the same time a subtle self-subordination
to Russian party interests was developing among many communist youth functionaries.

The Jena congress was a major demonstration of revolutionary spirit, despite continued controversy over the
'revolutionary offensive.' Among the delegates, most of the
Scandinavians and a part of the KJD were behind Münzenberg,
while a minority in the Swedish group, the majority in the
KJD, and the Italian, the Austrian, the Swiss, the French,
and most of the other delegates supported the 'offensive.'[106]
A large majority backed Pogany, the insurrectionary activities in Germany, and the 'revolutionary offensive.'

The extensive support for Pogany was evident in the discussion that followed his report on the world situation
(a presentation that was more of an impassioned defence of
the March Action and a justification for continuing support
for the 'offensive' than a report). The dissident voice of
Valeriu Marcu, long a close friend of Münzenberg and a follower of Levi, spoke out against Pogany and the Comintern
tactics in Germany. Münzenberg, while agreeing that the
March Action had been premature, was not ready to go as
far in his criticism as were Marcu and Levi. They not only
rejected the 'revolutionary offensive,' but broke discipline

Spartakus League,' 58) that Kun may have used the conditions in Russia as an argument for persuading the
KPD to take action, but that these conditions, in particular Kronstadt, were not in themselves decisive in
the actual decision in ECCI to send Kun to foment revolution. Evidently Kurella, Mielenz, and Köhler, while
in Russia, had been swayed by whomever it was in ECCI
(Zinoviev, Bukharin, Kun, possibly Radek) that was
responsible for Kun's mission.

106 Kurella, *Gründung und Aufbau* ... 165. Aksel Zachariassen
has said that the Norwegian youth organization was not
informed in 1921 about the conflict within the KPD over
the 'revolutionary offensive.' The Norwegians had not
in principle approved of the March Action; they 'wished
that it had never happened' (interview with Zachariassen).

over this matter of tactics.[107] Nevertheless, Münzenberg
was attacked by Kurella for his refusal to take a more
positive position, as well as for his friendship with
Marcu. What did most to draw Kurella's ire was Münzenberg's
intention of inviting Levi to address the congress.[108]

During these discussions the meeting had to be broken
off because the police were closing in. The participants
all moved to Berlin, where the congress resumed on April
11. It scarcely had begun again, however, when a note was
received from the ECCI representative in Berlin (identified
only as 'J') that caused great uneasiness.[109] It informed
the delegates that on 5 April, ECCI had decided not to
view the ECCYI decision to hold the congress in Germany
as 'binding,' and that the second CYI congress was to take
place in Moscow in connection with the third Comintern congress. Thus, despite (or perhaps because of) the participation of Kun and Pogany, the two emissaries from ECCI, the
meeting in Germany would not be recognized. ECCI in the
process of rejecting the 'revolutionary offensive' in the
aftermath of the failure of the March Action, and under
Lenin's influence moving away from direct action, decided
to step in firmly and bring the CYI into line. There had
been too many displays of independence by ECCYI. The ECCI
representative ('J') insisted that the delegates must obey
the Comintern order. The matter was to be considered, he
said, 'an organizatonal question of the same importance
as the Twenty-One Conditions.'[110] The members of the congress presidium, the members of ECCYI, and Kun and Pogany
discussed the situation and decided to accept the ECCI
order, break off the discussions, and, as demanded, move
the congress to Moscow in the summer.

107 Kurella, *Gründung und Aufbau* ... 168. Marcu later left
    the KPD with Levi. As could be expected from its polit-
    ical colouration, the meeting supported the two Comin-
    tern representatives at the Livorno congress of the
    Italian socialist party in January 1921 (Rakosi and
    Kabaktchiev) and condemned both Levi and Serrati for
    their 'lack of revolutionary ardour' (*Sozialistische
    Jugend*, June 1921, 23).
108 Kurella, *Gründung und Aufbau* ... 168
109 Quoted in ibid., 169. See also *IJK*, 20 April 1921,
    and *Fremad* 15. årg., nr. 1 (May 1921)
110 Quoted from an article by Valeriu Marcu in *Sowjet* by
    Heinz, *Die Entwicklung* ... 13

Only a few, with the Italians in the lead, refused in
plenary session to support this decision. The Italians
had encouraged Münzenberg to stand firm.[111] This he was
not willing to do, however, in view of the seriousness of
such a step. It could have meant a further split just when
the communist movement was getting established, and while
it was still recovering from the failure of the March Action in Germany. Münzenberg was convinced that 'the greatest
possible centralization and discipline in the communist
movement' was necessary, particularly at that time.[112]

The delegates, however, did approve (60-58, with two
abstentions) a statement prepared by Münzenberg on behalf
of ECCYI.[113] ECCI's action was considered to be an abridge-
ment of earlier agreements by which the Comintern had recognized the organizational independence of the youth movement, and (it was asserted) could only have a harmful effect on the work of the youth international. ECCYI was commissioned to find out from ECCI what its motives had been,
and what its intentions were, and to appeal the ECCI decision to the forthcoming third Comintern congress. Shortly
after the Jena congress, ECCYI sent letters of protest to
both ECCI and the central committee of the Russian Komsomol.

The critical moment had arrived and passed for the communist youth movement in Europe. Bowing to the demands of
the Comintern functionaries in Moscow, the delegates dispersed anticipating a settling of accounts with the 'bureaucrats' before the forum of the world congress of the Comintern in Moscow in the summer. By that time, however, it was
too late. The delegates had chosen to accord highest priority to the maintenance of discipline. They did so again,
although reluctantly and not unanimously, at the third
Comintern and second CYI congresses. The consequence of
this virtual obsession with discipline and the avoidance
of conflict was that it opened the door for the Russian
party to impose its own version of democratic centralism
on the entire movement. As the case of Paul Levi was to
show, it was not long before it became impossible to express, legitimately, an independent view and remain within
the communist movement. Rather than putting the 'bureaucrats' in their place, the young communists were to find that
the 'bureaucrats' were taking over the communist movement.

111 Interview with Giuseppe Berti
112 *Fremad* 15. årg., nr. 3 (July 1921)
113 Ibid., nr. 1 (May 1921)

All of the Scandinavian delegates, as an example of the extensive dissatisfaction that followed ECCI's action, had been disturbed by the arbitrary summons from the Comintern executive.[114] They would have preferred the congress to continue, but agreed that one had to bow to a decision of the Executive Committee of the Comintern, 'however inappropriate' it might be, in order to preserve unity and avoid a breach of discipline. All had voted for Münzenberg's statement. For many of the young communists, particularly the Norwegians and the other Scandinavians, Jena had been the 'first direct contact with the revolutionary conditions in central Europe after the war and with the principles of democratic centralism in practice.'[115]

Münzenberg at first had indicated in conversations with some of the Scandinavian delegates that he would resign as leader of the youth international. He evidently changed his mind, telling the Scandinavians that his resignation could not change what the Comintern leadership had decided upon. The only hope he saw for the young communists lay in appealing to the Comintern at large at the next congress.[116] Perhaps what had disturbed Münzenberg most was that no reason had been given for ECCI's intervention, nor was one forthcoming before the congress was reconvened in Moscow. Somewhat apprehensively, Münzenberg noted that 'it is naturally very difficult to argue against a decision whose motives and reasons are unknown.'[117] In an article written not long before he went to Moscow for *Fremad* (nr. 3, July 1921), the monthly newspaper of the Danish youth organization, Münzenberg tried to counteract the more ominous interpretations which apparently had been circulating. He made it clear that he did not see the intervention of ECCI

114 See the report of the Danish delegates upon their return in ibid., as well as Sogstad, *Ungdoms Fanevakt*, 299-300. This information was corroborated in an interview with Aksel Zachariassen.
115 Sogstad, 299
116 See Gross, *Willi Münzenberg*, 120-1. This version of Münzenberg's feelings and the attitude of the Scandinavians was confirmed by Ernst Christiansen, then leader of the Danish youth organization, but not himself at Jena, in an interview and in a radio address he made in 1969 (see *Aktuelt*, 8 November 1969).
117 *Fremad* 15. årg., nr. 3 (July 1921)

as creating a precedent, nor did it 'signify an action
against, and a new position by ECCI towards, the communist
youth movement and its organizational independence.' Events
were to show, however, that his optimism was quite misplaced.
In fact, this step by ECCI did become a precedent, one whose
effects were to extend across the entire communist movement.

Münzenberg provided in this article one of his strongest
arguments for the organizational independence of the youth
movement. This was to mean, above all, the right to convene
congresses and conferences at times and places of its own
choosing. He referred to the recent explicit recognition
of this right in the much more politically significant case
of the KPD, when ECCI had refused to become involved in the
question of convening a party congress. Münzenberg thus
found its intervention in the affairs of the youth international just that much more incomprehensible. 'We see no
reason,' he argued, 'for the Comintern to abolish or cut
off the organizational independence of the communist youth
organizations, and would regard such a step as extremely
harmful not just for the communist youth movement, but also
for the Comintern itself. It would hinder the great drive
and initiative which exists within the proletarian revolution in the West.'

Whether out of miscalculation, or self-delusion is not
clear, but in the article Münzenberg expressed a totally
unjustified conviction that 'all the members of the executive committee of the Communist International are in agreement with us that centralism in the communist movement is
not an end in itself, but only serves as a means to an end,
to increased unity within the communist movement and to
greater ... effectiveness.' Centralism 'must never serve
to curb or block the revolutionary initiative from below,'
as had happened within the social democratic party (SPD)
in Germany before the war. Yet, this was in fact what he
saw happening through ECCI's postponement of the second
CYI congress. Furthermore, by scheduling the CYI congress
after the Comintern congress, ECCI had made it impossible
for the youth international to discuss and determine its
position on the decisions of the second Comintern congress
and the agenda for the third congress. To do so was taken
by Münzenberg to be not simply a right of each member of
the Comintern, but also a duty not to be neglected.

Münzenberg's deep distress at Moscow's intervention, as
noted by Babette Gross, was in no small part due to his

past positions and beliefs, some of which unfortunately were contradictory.[118] These contradictions were to catch up with him in 1921. At the same time that he stoutly advocated independence for the youth movement in 1919 and 1920, he was outspokenly in favour of 'revolutionary discipline,' centralization in the communist movement, and the Twenty-One Conditions for membership in the Comintern. He was thus at the same time committed to both autonomy of political judgment for the youth international and the youth organizations, and the concentration of power in the Comintern. To the extent that he felt compelled to reconcile this contradiction in his own mind, he apparently did so, firstly, by placing equal stress on both aspects of the concept of democratic centralism, and secondly, by assuming that a centralized communist movement would be so 'revolutionary' in outlook and action that in practice centralization would tend to take the form of voluntary submission to 'orders' any good revolutionary could accept unquestioningly.

Münzenberg seems to have been only one of many who joined communist organizations in these years without a full appreciation of the practical, if not logical, consequences of his position. Few seem to have thought through the concept of centralism and what it would mean in practice. Somehow, someway, a spontaneous consensus among all communists, all 'true representatives of the proletariat,' would emerge. This consensus, this unity of will and purpose, would be institutionalized in a centralized and disciplined organization. Differences of opinion would work themselves out through open discussion, after which all would pull together in pursuit of the revolutionary goals. Lower bodies (the parties, for example) would accept as binding the decisions of the higher bodies (Comintern) because these would be accepted by all as legitimate - as democratically determined, as appropriate for the situation. General guidelines would be agreed upon quickly, since they would be more or less self-evident, and each national communist organization would be left to implement general policy in accordance with national conditions. When in fact fundamental differences between communists and communist organizations emerged, centralism became a means not of institutionalizing consensus, but rather a way by which the strongest could

118 Gross, *Willi Münzenberg*, 120-1

impose their views and will on all others; autonomy became
a threat to the vested interests of those exercising authority.

In 1921, Münzenberg was torn. He resisted the steps
whereby the Comintern was curtailing the independence of
the youth. The youth international had in large measure
been his own creation. At the very least he had provided
that dynamism, enthusiasm, leadership, and energy necessary
for it to have held together and developed during World
War I. He most certainly had a deep emotional stake in its
continuation as a significant factor in the communist movement. According to Babette Gross, he appears at the same
time to have reached the conclusion that the Russian party
intended to be more than just the first among equals, that
centralization as defined by Moscow to require domination
of all communist organizations had become irresistible.
The forthcoming Comintern congress was not to prove an
arena in which Münzenberg and the young communists won
ringing endorsement of their revolutionary ardour and their
independent political role. Quite to the contrary, it was
to mark the end of the development toward an independent
radical socialist youth movement that had begun in Stuttgart in 1907.

Support of the 'revolutionary offensive'

The so-called 'Jena theses,' while not formally adopted by
the meeting of the CYI in Germany in April 1921 because of
its abrupt termination, closely reflected the views of the
large majority.[119] After Jena and until the beginning of
the deliberations in Moscow in July, ECCYI worked on the
basis of these 'thesese,' which were later criticized at
the Comintern congress along with the entire theory of the
'revolutionary offensive.'

A large majority in the KJD 'Zentrale' even went beyond
the party in its aggressiveness.[120] Believing that the ob-

119 The 'theses' were an expression of views. The term
   was used to describe the resolution concerning the
   world situation discussed at Jena (see Kurella,
   Gründung und Aufbau ... 241-3).
120 *JG*, 15 May 1921. See also *IJK*, 5 May 1921. The small
   minority of pro-Levi, anti-'revolutionary offensive,'
   KJD functionaries attempted to counteract the aggressive

jective conditions for revolution still existed, it urged the party to create the subjective factor. The party had the duty of sharpening the existing conflict. It had to take steps to bring about a mass strike in order to overcome 'counter-revolutionary' actions by the police. As far as the KJD leadership was concerned, 'the youth are the leaven of the party, it is their task to push forward the weak and indifferent on the path of the revolutionary offensive.'[121] Here once again can be seen an expression of the concept of youth as the 'vanguard' of the communist movement.

The KJD was encouraged by ECCYI to intervene as a revolutionary avant-garde in party debates in defence of the March Action and in support of the party 'Zentrale.' In a resolution sent to the Berlin district organization, ECCYI called upon young German communists to be active inside the party so as to make it 'more capable of future actions.'[122] Only when the mistakes of the party during the March Action (i.e. not enough action) were exposed and discussed, said ECCYI, would the necessary lessons be drawn for future actions.

In early May, the national committee of the KJD rejected by 30-3, a resolution condemning the March Action proposed by Günther Hopffe.[123] It accepted instead a statement supporting the position of the 'Zentrale.' Hopffe agreed with

---

drive by the 'Zentrale' for even more revolutionary commitments. Having approved of the expulsion of Levi from the party, however, disciplinary action was quick taken by the 'Zentrale' against his supporters in the youth organization. At the national committee session in early May it was decided that only those who supported unconditionally the political line of the KJD majority could hold 'leading positions' (*J-I*, July 1921, 303-5). According to *Die Junge Garde*, the East Prussian and Hessian district organizations were the only ones to oppose the 'Zentrale' majority position (*JG*, 1 June 1921, 212-13).

121 *JG*, 15 May 1921
122 *IJK*, 5 May 1921
123 *JG*, 1 June 1921, 212-13. Eugen Schönhaar gave the main address in justification of the 'Zentrale' support for the March Action and for continuation of the 'revolutionary offensive.'

Levi's criticism of the March Action and of the policy of
the 'revolutionary offensive,' arguing that ill-timed aggressiveness could only harm the youth movement by increasing bourgeois repression and disillusioning the mass of
young workers. He did not, however, agree with the public
airing of the differences that had led to Levi's expulsion.
In fact, Hopffe stated explicitly that he would submit to
discipline. Although Münzenberg spoke against Hopffe, he
appears also to have been unhappy with the 'Zentrale's'
aggressive stance. He spoke in support of the ECCYI resolution sent to the communist youth in Berlin, apparently
the product of a compromise in ECCYI. While explicitly
approving of the March Action, and encouraging continued
commitment to the 'revolutionary offensive,' the resolution
also referred approvingly to the Spartakist program that
stressed the need for a mass party and the assumption of
power 'only as an expression of the undoubted will of the
great majority of the proletarian masses.'[124]
  Münzenberg seems to have remained a resolute advocate
of the 'revolutionary offensive' in principle. At the
national committee meeting he said that he 'approved fully
and completely the tactics of the "revolutionary offensive,"
which so far have been the basis for the policies of the
youth international.'[125] Yet he evidently had serious
doubts about the wisdom of turning the principle into action at this time without proper preparation of the masses.
Nevertheless he chose to support the 'Zentrale.' To have
backed Hopffe would have been to repudiate the 'revolutionary offensive.' At Jena in early April, *after* the March
Action that he had opposed in early March, Münzenberg seems
to have been against further steps toward revolutionary
action *at that time*. He saw moves like those called for by
the KJD as undesirable, given the existing situation of
defeat and weakness within the communist forces.
  For Münzenberg, the 'revolutionary offensive' was essentially an attitude or frame of mind. Although he believed
that the objective conditions for revolution were still
present, he recognized the need for broad support and

124 *IJK*, 5 May 1921
125 Ibid. See the last paragraph of the article by W.M.,
    'Die Krise in der Kommunistischen Internationale und
    die Kommunistische Jugend' and the documents that
    follow.

careful planning before communists took further action.
Hence, his opposition to the March Action. And yet, he
continued to lash out at the 'opportunists,' who (he
feared) no longer saw the objective conditions as favouring
revolutionary advance. He fought abandonment of the revolutionary offensive' by the Comintern not because he was
zealous for action, but because he feared that it would
signify loss of the basic emotional and psychological commitment to revolution. Loss of this commitment when the
objective conditions remained favourable would be fatal
to revolutionary prospects. It was the existence of this
commitment, after all, that had justified the formation
of a communist movement in the first place. Münzenberg
believed that without the will to revolution, there could
be no communist movement.

Münzenberg was very critical of the Comintern leaders
for failing to provide adequate safeguards against the
infiltration of 'opportunist' elements into the Communist
International. Writing a few months after Jena, he said
that

> the last year ... has brought proof that the organiza-
> tional obligations [Twenty-One Conditions] do not offer
> sufficient security against the entry and destructive
> influence of the opportunists in the communist parties.
> By the Italian example [ECCI still negotiating with
> Serrati], by the development of the communist party in
> France, and above all by the party affair now dominating
> discussion in Germany [aftermath of the March Action and
> the expulsion of Levi] wider circles in the Communist
> International have also come to realize that in the
> interests of a further rapid development and forward
> push of the proletarian revolution the Communist Inter-
> national must intensify the activity and offensive power
> of the communist parties.[126]

In this same article, Münzenberg spoke harshly of the
French party. 'The Frenchmen Frossard and Cachin represent
[at the second Comintern congress in July-August 1920]
a party that was anything but communist. Indeed, both
pledged themselves to the Communist International after
their return, but even today neither the composition of

126 *IJK*, 5 May 1981

the French communist party, nor its political and revolutionary activities conform to the demands that the Comintern in these days of the revolutionary offensive must direct to all of its members.' Münzenberg was one who looked to the third Comintern congress to rectify the mistakes of the past and to ratify the policy of the 'revolutionary offensive.' He believed that the 'opportunist elements of the right will be cast off from the communist movement.'

The majority in the KJD and the functionaries in ECCYI were by no means the only advocates of the 'revolutionary offensive.' In France, the JC had been considerably more militant than the party leadership in acting to oppose 'the threat of a new war' during the French occupation of the Ruhr cities in March 1921. In April, *l'Avant-garde* was calling for an 'offensive' by the French proletariat and condemning the ECCI campaign against the 'ultra-left.'[127] In May it featured an article by Albert Treint on the 'revolutionary offensive.'[128] At the congress of the party fédération of the Seine, held just before the national party congress, the JC had criticized the party leadership for refusing to recommend desertion from the army during the Ruhr crisis.[129]

The national committee of the JC presented a declaration to its national congress in May calling on all groups to work for the 'revolutionary offensive.'[130] The majority of the delegates stressed the necessity for an 'offensive' tactic. The world political situation was described as being revolutionary, with a party of 'action' required, and the congress spoke of 'systematic preparation for action free from sentimentality [fear of civil war].'[131] Asserting that the time was ripe for revolution, Jacques Doriot, later the leader of the JC and its anti-militarist campaigns, demanded a more active party policy. Gabriel Péri represented the more cautious approach of a minority, disputing Doriot's contention that conditions existed for

127 *L'Avant-Garde*, 25-30 April 1921, 1
128 Ibid., 15-30 May 1921, 2
129 Wohl, *French Communism in the Making 1914-1924*, 223.
    See also *IJK*, 10 June 1921, and *l'Avant-Garde*, 15-30
    June 1921
130 *L'Avant-Garde*, 15-30 May 1921, 3
131 *IJK*, 20 June 1921

an offensive policy.[132] The task of the communists, said
Péri, was to prepare for such a policy.[133] He cautioned
that while there should of course be a commitment to and
preparation for an 'offensive,' one could not jump into
action immediately.[134] The ECCYI representative, Sigi
Bamatter, was outspoken in support of the 'revolutionary
offensive.' Urging the JC to develop support for this policy
within the PCF, he called upon the delegates 'to destroy
the false ideology spouted by the party and to instil in
the masses the necessity for the revolutionary offensive.'[1]

The central committee of the Austrian youth organization
(VKPJ) also spoke out forcefully in defence of the German
March Action, by which the KPD 'had proved itself a communist party.'[136] Although the German party central committee
(Zentralausschuss) was said to have made mistakes, it was
thought to have had a more correct understanding of the
revolutionary potential of the times than had Levi. The
latter was condemned for denying the possibility of a 'revolutionary offensive,' and for breaking communist discipline by publishing his brochure. The lessons to be learned
by all young Austrian communists from the German events was
that 'opportunism' had no place in the communist movement.
All 'incompetent and unwilling' functionaries had to be
weeded out.

The Swiss, likewise, referred to the March Action and the
'revolutionary offensive' in a manner reflecting the 'Jena
theses.' In its report on the Jena congress in mid May,
Neue Jugend repeated the passionate language that had characterized the congress. 'In these historical hours we vow
to do everything we can, never to rest or relax, to double
our forces, to increase our zeal, to increase our efforts,
to fight against every opportunist weakness harmful to the
communist movement, to further all the movements that have
erupted spontaneously because of the misery of the masses,

132 Ibid.
133 *L'Avant-Garde*, 15-20 June 1921
134 Péri was not in the leadership at this time. Because
his position was in accord with that of Lenin and the
new 'retreat' policy of the third Comintern congress,
he was soon to be elevated to a position of importance
in the JC.
135 *L'Avant-Garde*, 15-20 June 1921
136 *IJK*, 1 July 1921

and to introduce and carry through new actions together
with all revolutionaries and communist parties and organizations'.[137]

While the Italian youth organization was busy with the
split with the centrists and with organizational questions,
it was, as has been seen, distinctly left leaning. The support for the 'revolutionary offensive' by the Italians was
made abundantly clear at the congresses in Moscow in mid
1921. They, in fact, were the most recalcitrant elements,
resisting the new policy of 'retreat' and continuing to go
their own way after the Comintern had adopted its new line.
The Scandinavians were the only ones to resist the strong
surge in support of the 'revolutionary offensive.'

As the delegates gathered in Moscow in July 1921 for the
third Comintern and second CYI congresses, there were thus
two sources of controversy between the CYI and the Comintern leaders: first, the demand of ECCYI for more freedom
of movement in organizational questions for the CYI, and
that of the West European communist youth leaders for independence from the communist parties; and second, the
widespread support within the youth movement for the policy
of the 'revolutionary offensive' and the attitudes that lay
behind it.

137 *Neue Jugend*, 14 May 1921, 5-7

7

Decisions in Moscow

The revolutionary, communist movement that had arisen out
of World War I reached a critical point in the summer of
1921. Along with some stunning successes, there had been
even more bitter failures. The new Soviet state in Russia
had succeeded in establishing itself through force of arms.
There were serious economic problems, and the party itself
was torn by strife over its purpose and mission. Nevertheless, in approaching its fourth birthday the new Russian
regime could look to the future with confidence. For communists elsewhere, however, there had been many frustrations
and serious setbacks. The great transformation of existing
society that had seemed so imminent in 1918 and 1919 had
proved more difficult to achieve than had been expected.
The Hungarian and Bavarian soviets had fallen. Revolutionar
uprisings in Germany had failed miserably. Capitalism in
France and Great Britain apparently was recuperating. Revo
tionary discontent within the European working class had
failed to achieve any major successes. The question,
'Whither now?' was conspicuous as the delegates to the
third world congress of the Communist International assemb
in Moscow in June 1921.

Despite difficulties and setbacks, the emotions of the
young communists remained kindled by revolutionary fervour
Supporting the wave of militancy that had gripped many com
munist parties, delegates from the youth organizations expected the Moscow meetings to be great demonstrations in
support of revolutionary activism. They were to be sadly
disappointed. The Comintern congress quickly became the
forum for opposing analyses of the world situation: the
'revolutionary offensive' view that the time for revolution was still ripe, and the cautious retrenchment policy

of Lenin.[1] After much pressure and persuasion, and over
strong opposition, Lenin and the Russian leaders succeeded
in imposing their views on the Comintern. Revolution was
not abandoned, at least formally, but efforts first were
to be made to win more support from the masses. This repudiation of the theory of the 'revolutionary offensive' and
a turn to 'winning the masses' henceforth became the political line for the entire international communist movement,
Comintern and youth international alike.

The young communists were among the most outspoken in
resisting imposition of the new line. They made their opposition clear in the prolonged and heated discussions on
events in the French and German parties, and on future tactics. Despite criticism from Lenin and Trotsky, the young
French communist, Maurice Laporte, continued to attack the
French party (PCF) and to assert that 'only the young communists of France were really imbued with true revolutionary, communist spirit [during the French occupation of the
Ruhr cities in April/May 1921], whereas the party, in spite
of its acceptance of the Theses and the Twenty-One Conditions
of the Communist International, was still far from evincing
any active revolutionary communism.'[12] Münzenberg, too, was
critical of the PCF, accusing it of 'rigidity.'

1 These differences manifested themselves also within the
  Russian party. Although it presented a common front behind Lenin's policies, there had been serious discussions
  within the Politburo and central committee before the
  Comintern congress. Formally, the Comintern congress
  treated the young communists as of some importance. In
  the distribution of votes on a weighted basis by the mandates commission, the CYI was included with the group
  of countries whose parties were to receive the largest
  number of votes (40): Germany, France, Italy, Czechoslovakia, and Russia (*Moscow*, no. 27 [28 June 1921]: 2).
  Of the twenty Russian delegates with a 'deciding' vote,
  there were three Komsomol leaders (Shatskin, Rivkin, and
  Tseitlin – listed eighteenth, nineteenth, and twentieth);
  See *Moscow*, no. 19 (16 June 1921): 2.
2 *Moscow*, no. 25 (25 June 1921): 4. See Wohl, *French Communism in the Making 1914-1924*, 224-8, for a discussion
  of the French question at the Comintern congress. See
  also criticism of the Czechoslovak party from its youth
  organization delegate in *Moscow*, no. 19 (16 June 1921): 2.

Early in the congress Münzenberg declared, in the name of
the youth international, 'complete agreement with the policy
and work of the Executive Committee of the Comintern' (ECCI)
during the events in Germany in the spring, and indicated
'the readiness of the young communists to [give] their full
support [to ECCI].'[3] He had broken, finally, with the 'ultra
left' because of its unrestrained militancy and refusal to
maintain unity. Regretfully, but firmly he spoke out against
the behaviour of the KAPD. Nevertheless, he felt that the
question of the KAPD need not have developed into a prolonged crisis. If the parliamentary fraction of the KPD had
carried through on the decisions of the second Comintern
congress in a resolute manner and really used parliament
for the furtherance of revolution, then the KAPD would not
have had any grounds for splitting with the KPD. He ridi-
culed Heinrich Malzahn, a representative of the Levi opposition in the German delegation, and attacked Levi directly
for his 'passivity.' Münzenberg's break with the 'ultra-
left' was thus by no means a repudiation of its revolutionary enthusiasm. Behind his firm expression of support for
ECCI was the belief that the Comintern, while more sober
and realistic than the 'ultra-left,' would continue to follow an active policy of support for an imminent revolution.
    The tactics to be pursued by the communist movement in
the future obviously were a major point of discussion at
the congress. In the draft theses on this issue sponsored
by the Russian party, the activities of all communists were
directed away from 'dangerous adventurism.' The primary
task was now to turn the communist parties into mass organizations, which in turn required all communists to devote
their full attention to developing the necessary organizational and agitational capabilities. Although he generally
agreed with the theses, Münzenberg thought they were 'too
hard on the left-wing' and showed 'an unnecessary softness
toward the right-opportunist elements.'[4] He openly criticized Lenin for painting the situation as if the left were
seeking to build 'a little party of a few comrades which,
with hand grenades and machine guns, would make a revolution,' and the right as 'comrades who would build a mass

3 In the discussion on Zinoviev's report on the work of
  ECCI (*Moscow*, no. 27 [28 June 1921]: 5-6)
4 Ibid., no. 33 (5 July 1921): 4, and *Protokoll des III.
  Kongresses* ... 587

movement according to great principles and through coura-
geous actions.'[5] Although the masses were needed, and caution in action was indeed called for, the psychological
factor could not be ignored. What was the mood or attitude,
and the expectations, that were to be encouraged? It was
important, argued Münzenberg, to maintain the proper revolutionary perspective. When, as in Western Europe, communist parties were in a daily struggle with the centrists
and social patriots, they could not limit themselves to
propaganda (which he implied would be the consequence of
Lenin's policy).[6] To avoid 'a complete fiasco before the
masses,' all communist parties had to be concerned with
'initiating actions.' Revolutionary action should not be
abandoned at a time when, so argued Münzenberg, the capitalist system was still weak and ready to be overthrown.

Other delegates from the youth organizations were also
critical of the new revolutionary tactics. Luigi Polano
tabled a declaration in the name of the Communist Youth
International (CYI) in which the signatories rejected the
Russian argument that the 'main danger' within the communist movement was from the left. They refused to accept any
criticism of their support for the 'revolutionary offensive.'[7]

Münzenberg and the young communists did not oppose Lenin
on the necessity for mass parties. They had accepted this
even before the Berlin congress. The issue here was what
it meant to say that the communist parties were to be mass
parties. To the young communists, it did not mean an increase in sheer numbers only, at any price. Münzenberg believed that it was not enough that a communist party be a
mass party, it must be 'a revolutionary communist party,
calling the masses forth to fight for the triumph of the
ideals of communism.'[8] Neither Lenin, who was imposing his
'retreat' policy on the Comintern while issuing a call to
consolidate and build up mass support for the communist
parties, nor his opponents rejected either 'revolution'
or a need 'to go to the masses.' The issue was what this
mass party would do, and *when*; how committed was the party
going to be to direct revolutionary actions, and under

5 *Protokoll des III. Kongresses* ... 587
6 Ibid., 586-8
7 Ibid., 670-1
8 *Moscow*, no. 33 (5 July 1921): 4, and *Protokoll des III.
Kongresses* ... 588

what conditions; and at what cost it was to be built.
Münzenberg felt that the opponents of the 'revolutionary
offensive' were going so far as to sacrifice the will to
revolution in order to build their mass party. Once they
had constructed such a party, it would be useless. The enthusiasm and commitment necessary for a truly revolutionary
party would have been allowed to dissipate.

For the young communists in Moscow there were problems
even more serious than defeat on strategy and tactics. The
debate on the role of the youth movement, especially after
Jena, was coming to a head. Was it to retain its independent position, or was it to be brought directly under the
control of the Comintern and the parties on the Russian
model. It was not until the twentieth plenary session of
the congress, on the eve of the opening of the congress of
the Communist Youth International, that the 'youth question
was raised.[9] By this time, however, discussions behind the
scenes had settled the principal issues. Münzenberg's remarks made it clear that he considered the matter closed
and that he had capitulated to the demands for subordination of the youth movement. In a private conversation in
June, Lenin apparently persuaded Münzenberg that it was
necessary for him to drop his demand for autonomy.[10] Münzenberg provides us with an important clue to what Lenin
said in an article written at this time for the daily bulletin of the congress. He noted that at their own congress,
which would soon convene, the young communists would 'become an integral part of the Communist International. They
would thereby show their appreciation of the need for stric
centralization and iron discipline in the communist movement.'[11] Unity and discipline and support for the Russian
Bolsheviks would be the guiding principles. 'In the current
difficult times, only the Russian communist party ...

9 *Moscow*, no. 38 (10 July 1921): 3, and *Protokoll des III.
Kongresses* ... 887–902
10 See Mukhamedzhanov, 'V.I. Lenin i Kommunisticheskii
Internatsional Molodezhi,' *Voprosy Istorii KPSS*, no. 4
(1965): 26
11 See the article by Münzenberg published just after the
formal opening of the CYI congress, but before the work
of the congress had begun (*Moscow*, no. 38 [10 July 1921]
2).

guarantees the continuation of the entire revolution.'[12] The future of the revolution depended upon firm integration of all communist forces. To continue to insist on an independent youth movement would perhaps contribute to a fatal disintegration of the entire revolutionary movement.

The Comintern explicitly laid to rest the notion that the young communists would continue their role as the vanguard of the proletariat. This role was to be given over to the parties. The youth organizations now were to abandon their political independence and accept an auxiliary role. They would be active in organizing the mass of uncommitted young workers, educating them in communism, and enrolling them in the struggle of the communists to promote a revolution. The emphasis was no longer to be placed on direct political activity, but rather on the expansion and strengthening of educational work and the destruction of the centrist and 'social patriot' ideology in the ranks of the working youth. The resolution adopted by the congress stressed the necessity for centralization and unity in the communist movement. The relationship between the youth movement and the Comintern was to be governed by 'iron discipline.' The resolution indicated further that political subordination to the communist parties in matters of program, tactics, and political guidance was to mark the relations between youth organization and party.[13] Because the communist parties still were at different stages of development, however, this principle was to be applied (by ECCI and ECCYI, and not the youth organizations themselves) in accordance with the circumstances in each country. In all cases, organizational independence was to be preserved for educational reasons. The young communists retained the right 'to discuss inside their own

12 *Protokoll des III. Kongresses* ... 254
13 The resolution is in Kurella, *Gründung und Aufbau* ... 220-3. See also *Resolutions and theses of the second congress of the Young Communist International*, 7-9, and *Protokoll des III. Kongresses* ... 905-9. The resolution had been drafted by a three-man committee, apparently consisting of Münzenberg, Shatskin, and a German party leader, Paul Fröhlich (*Protokoll des III. Kongresses* ... 897). Fröhlich stated that in spite of the organizational independence of the youth movement, the whole apparatus of the communist movement had to be very closely bound together from top to bottom (ibid., 904).

groups all political and tactical questions and to take
positions and decisions thereto.'[14] These positions were
to be in full agreement with party decisions; on no account
were they to work against them. The basic qualification
contained in the concept of democratic centralism remained
as a crucial limiting factor: once the party had made a decision, all good communists were obligated to accept and
implement it under severe discipline.

The Second Congress of the Communist Youth International

The Comintern had spoken, and quite decisively at that.
With Münzenberg himself having capitulated, the 'youth
question' had been settled by the time the Comintern congress ended. Thus the second CYI congress was really only
a postscript, ratifying the discussions and decisions of
the Comintern congress. This did not mean that all delegates accepted the great changes that had been imposed by
the Comintern. On the contrary, the young radicals remained
vocal and obstinate. In the end, however, they too acquiesc
at least formally. Ultimately, even they could find no grou
from which to oppose the appeal for unity and discipline.
   The second congress of the Communist Youth International
opened formally on the evening of 9 July 1921 in an atmosphere at once both sober and festive. The delegates assembl
in the Bolshoi theatre to hear greetings and formal remarks
from the leaders of the two internationals, Zinoviev and
Münzenberg, as well as from Shatskin and Efim Tseitlin, the
latter speaking in the name of the Moscow Komsomol. The
delegates were still preoccupied by the serious political
issues that had dominated the Comintern congress and by the
struggle over the role of the youth movement waged behind
the scenes. Outwardly, however, the mood was one of cel-
ebration, in stark contrast to the clandestine affair that
was the first congress in Berlin. On the following day the
delegates, marching and waving red flags and singing revol
tionary songs, participated in a grand youth festival organized by the Komsomol. The foreign delegates were greete
by stormy ovations from the participating young Russians,
and escorted gaily to their lodgings in the Hotel Dresden.
All were treated to an impressive display of fireworks in
the evening. There were other, more verbal, displays of
heat and passion yet to come.

14 Ibid., 899

Questions of Strategy

The results of the discussions during the Comintern congress, and the capitulation of Münzenberg to discipline, were evident from his remarks at the opening session.[15] Given the existence of communist parties to assume the leadership of the communist movement, he declared, the young communists must now turn to new tasks in the spirit of the Comintern decisions. Shatskin pressed home the victory of the Komsomol, asserting that the theory of the 'revolutionary offensive' was dead. He stressed the need for the youth organizations to turn to the task of 'conquering the masses' in accordance with the decisions of the Comintern congress.[16] For this task the experience of the Komsomol, said Shatskin, should be studied and utilized by the West European communist youth organizations.

In an attempt to mollify the radicals, Zinoviev, who himself had been a supporter of the 'revolutionary offensive,' addressed the gathering. Defending the Comintern decisions, Zinoviev tried to assure the delegates that in no way had there been a 'step to the right,' a difficult task indeed, since this was what in fact the Comintern congress had produced. Speaking in a fatherly tone, he chided the radicals for their impatience and sought to convince them that the Leninist position was correct. The bourgeoisie were still the main enemy, but new means were needed in order to attack them. He added a tribute to the service that the youth organizations had already performed for the 'revolution.' 'Never will history forget that the first struggle against opportunism in all the socialist parties of the world was led by the youth, and that we must thank not least the energy of the youth for the victory which we have achieved.'[17]

Bringing maximum pressure to bear, the Comintern recruited Trotsky to face the assembled delegates when they reconvened on 14 July in the Kremlin's former throne room.[18] Trotsky

15 *Zu neuer Arbeit*, 7-8
16 Ibid., 9
17 Ibid., 11
18 The issues included on the agenda (the rapporteur on each item follows in parenthesis) give a good indication of the sort of organization the CYI was considered to be at this time:
The third Comintern congress (Trotsky)
Report of ECCYI (Münzenberg)

agreed that the young communists were the most 'revolutionary minded.'[19] He called on the delegates, however, to accept the fact that the struggle for world revolution might be a long one, 'thus [making] the education of the communist youth [in proper tactics] a question of the first importance.'[20] It must have been hard for the young radicals, infused as they were with hopes and expecations of achieving the revolution in the near future, to hear Trotsky sound such a sober and essentially pessimistic note. In any event, Trotsky was firm that any dissatisfactions among the delegates with some of the Comintern decisions would have to be subordinated to the need for discipline. Nevertheless, continuing doubt about, or outright rejection of, the new Comintern line was manifest in the discussion following Trotsky's speech.

The Italian delegates, Tranquilli and Polano, spoke out against the Comintern decision on the Italian question. To promote a merger between the Serrati-led 'unitarians' and the new communist party (PCI) would only introduce 'confusion' into the minds of Italian workers without yielding any practical results. Both delegates stated that 'the youth [in Italy] cannot be completely satisfied with the

Relations between the youth organizations and the
  parties (Shatskin)
The economic struggle (Münzenberg)
Educational work (Kurella)
Organizational problems
  a. development of the national youth organizations
    (Schönhaar)
  b. international questions and the statute (Flieg)
Children's groups (Hörnle)
The revolutionary youth movements in the Orient and
  among the colonial peoples (Sabirov)
Work among the peasant youth (Kurella)
Propaganda work among the students (Weiss)
Anti-militarism (Lekai)
Election of a new ECCYI and its location
  (ibid., 16)
19 Ibid., 16-19. His speech and closing remarks are found also in Trotsky, *The First Five Years of the Communist International* I, 308-19, without the discussion that occurred in between.
20 Trotsky I, 309

decisions of the [Comintern] congress, and will employ all
means to prevent the opportunists from penetrating the communist party.'[21] Trotsky accused the Italian youth organization of 'sectarianism.' He saw the large group of 'unitarians' as a source of recruits for the communist cause,
to be exploited by appealing to their revolutionary spirit
over the heads of their leaders if the latter refused to
break with the right and join the communists.

Richard Schüller, while approving the 'to-the-masses'
policy of the Comintern congress, was concerned that sufficient steps had not been taken to curb the influence of
'the pacifists and the centrists' in the sections of the
Comintern. He thought that 'the duty of the [young commu-
nists] is, within the scope of party discipline, to act
against the influence of the opportunist elements in the
party.'[22] He also argued for carrying-out 'dynamic actions'
as the only means of winning the masses, to which Trotsky
replied that there had been plenty of 'actions' in recent
years, without much success.[23] It was necessary, said
Trotsky, to prepare properly for these actions so as to
take advantage of existing opportunities. Despite lingering
doubts or die-hard resistance on the part of those communist youth leaders who were the strongest supporters of the
'revolutionary offensive,' the efforts of Zinoviev, Trotsky,
and other Comintern leaders were successful in the end in
getting the CYI congress to accept the new Comintern line,
even though resistance continued within the national youth
organizations for some time.

Having been forced to repudiate his previous positions,
Münzenberg now came under direct and indirect attack for
his past policies. The Russian and German delegations put
forward a draft resolution criticizing not only ECCYI in
general, but also Münzenberg's report to the congress in
particular.[24] It was admitted that ECCYI (i.e. Münzenberg)
had worked under difficult conditions (lack of financial

21 *Zu neuer Arbeit*, 19
22 Ibid., 20. Schüller had supported Münzenberg at Jena on
the issue of independence for the youth international
(interview with Aksel Zachariassen). On the question of
the 'revolutionary offensive,' he was to the left of
Münzenberg with the majority at Jena.
23 Trotsky I, 316
24 *Zu neuer Arbeit*, 27

resources, precarious communications, limited personnel, and the committee's illegal status), and that individual youth organizations had not helped very much. Nevertheless, ECCYI was rebuked for failing to provide leadership to the individual youth organizations, and for failing to exercise its responsibility for watching over all of the activities of its members organizations.

The Russian Komsomol leaders were determined to publicize their self-righteousness at the moment of their triumph. Shatskin said that the ECCYI report showed that ECCYI had not understood the importance of its role. Münzenberg, having been the protagonist of the losing position, was now to be forced to accept an ideological and personal reprimand to emphasize the superior wisdom of the Russians. He was criticized for not having taken proper steps to develop the necessary ties between youth organizations and communist parties, and for having failed to halt the stress in the youth international on the role of youth as the vanguard of the communist movement. The resolution repudiated the 'Jena theses' and censured Münzenberg both for insisting that the meeting in Jena be held, and for allowing the resolution approved there to be published.[25] Despite considerable support for Münzenberg, even apparently including Zinoviev's, the Komsomol bandwagon proved too strong. The congress by a solid majority condemned ECCYI and its leader.[26]

25 Ibid., 27, 28
26 Münzenberg was not without his supporters. Schüller (ibid., 29), the Scandinavians (ibid., 33), and the English, American, and Hungarian delegations (ibid., 35) refused to accept the Russo-German resolution. Münzenberg defended himself, noting that there had been no communication from Shatskin to ECCYI on substantive matters for over a year (ibid., 36-8). For the resolution as adopted see ibid., 39. The total number of mandates at the congress was set at 196 by the report of the mandates commission (ibid., 16). A minimum of forty were directly under the control of the Russian Komsomol (Russia 10, Ukraine 6, Khiva 4, Azerbaidzhan 4, Georgia 4, Armenia 2, Persia 4, and two others), thus giving it a firm, disciplined core of one-fifth of the votes to start with. However, the Russians did not have to rely upon the manipulation of votes in order to dominate the

Role of the Youth Movement
Shatskin stressed that the dispute over the role of the
youth movement must now be considered settled. The youth
movement was to become 'a school of communism for the broad
masses of young workers ... This educational role of the
communist youth movement today stands in the foreground,
and must especially be stressed and realized.'[27] Political
subordination, to Shatskin, did not mean withdrawal from
political activity. Instead, it signified a change in emphasis, toward issues specifically concerning youth, such
as education and protection of the economic interests of
the young workers, and away from tactical questions as in
the past. Young communists were to be active in political
affairs as individuals, under party direction. The youth
organizations, however, would no longer participate in
political actions themselves. They would henceforth serve
only to rally youth behind party-inspired actions. The
Komsomol leaders admitted openly that they were seeking to
tie all youth organizations to their respective communist
parties as the Komsomol had been tied to the Russian communist party.

Even so, the Russians had not subdued everyone yet. The
leader of the young Austrian communists, Friedrich Hexmann,
argued that the decisions of the third Comintern congress
permitted the necessary independence of the young communists.[28] Organizational independence had been recognized
by the Comintern, but this was useless, he pointed out, if
as in the case of Bulgaria, the party could dictate to the
youth organization who it could elect to its central committee and to leadership posts in its local groups. The
Comintern could not have meant, implied Hexmann, to give
a meaningless organizational independence to the youth
movement. Also referring to Bulgaria, the young Swiss communist leader, Emil Arnold, expressed concern that the
pendulum might swing to the other extreme where the party

decision-making process at these international congresses. With all participants commited to 'proletarian
unity' and discipline, and with many spontaneously
accepting Russian moral and political leadership, the
general attitude was not one of searching for majorities
when it came time to vote.
27 *Zu neuer Arbeit*, 40
28 Ibid., 42-3

controlled the youth organization completely.[29] As time was to demonstrate, these concerns were far from unfounded. Arnold proposed, for psychological reasons, a change in language that would have made the relationship between the youth organizations and the parties one of subordination (Unterordnung) instead of subjection (Unterwerfung).[30] Richard Schüller and the Hungarian, Johan Lekai, also refused to give in.[31] The Norwegians 'protested vehemently' the Comintern decision to insist on subordination of the youth organizations, as apparently did the Swedes and Danes.

Shatskin insisted on the Leninist position that new conditions necessitated new policies and new relationships. He thus rejected a Belgian amendment obligating the youth organizations to combat 'opportunism,' a statement that deliberately had been left out of the theses passed by the Comintern congress.[33] Shatskin argued instead that those who were not in agreement with all of the decisions of the Comintern congress would use such a statement to further their own ideas. It would sanction precisely that which just had been prohibited: an independent political line for the youth organizations. By its very nature as a *youth*

29 Ibid., 45
30 'Unterordnung' connotes a voluntary submission to authority, and is perhaps best translated as subordination or submission. 'Unterwerfung' has a much stronger meaning in the sense of subjection as a result of force or innate authority (e.g. it is used to describe the relationship between the conquered and the conqueror in time of war). Arnold's proposal was an attempt by the pro-independence forces to salvage something from a lost battle, an effort to make it clear that the inferior position now being forced upon the youth was one that could be changed at a later date if the youth felt it necessary. Perhaps it was an attempt to have it understood, in principle, that there was no inherent right of the parties to control the youth. Arnold was another of the old socialist youth leaders supporting independence who bowed to discipline and came out after the congress for the new relationship (*Neue Jugend*, 10 October 1921).
31 *Zu neuer Arbeit*, 45-6
32 Sogstad, *Ungdoms Fanevakt*, 300-1
33 *Zu neuer Arbeit*, 45

organization, Shatskin said, a communist youth organization would always emphasize the struggle against the right and support the left. Any encouragement to fight the right would only invite 'leftist deviations.'

Despite the many expressions of disapproval, the congress, by an overwhelming majority, expressed 'unreserved approval' of the theses on the youth question as adopted by the Comintern congress.[34] This explicitly included the political subordination (Unterordnung) of the youth organizations to their parties. The communist youth organizations were 'to discuss political problems, take a position thereon, and participate in party work, but their main tasks demand that the centre of activities be shifted from political and tactical problems [to be settled by the parties] to specific youth problems.[35]'

Having struggled before and during the war to break out of the confining educational and agitational role imposed upon them by the socialist parties who controlled their youth organization (as in Germany), and having defended themselves assiduously against party encroachment elsewhere, the radical socialist youth now found themselves in an even worse predicament. Earlier, they had defended or welcomed a break with the party where necessary for that meant more freedom for growth and political activity. It held out the prospect of participation in the consolidation of all 'truly revolutionary' forces at a time when revolutionary expectations were soaring. Radical socialist youth could indeed afford to break with or attack the party, since there was an alternative. The left within the parties was also in a rebellious mood, and during and after the war was itself to split from the parties. From November 1917, the Bolsheviks in Russia served as a rallying point. An affinity with, or tie to, the Bolsheviks was sufficient justification for the youth to assert their independence. Now, however, the youth organizations had nowhere to go in rebellion except the political wilderness and probable disintegration at a time when revolutionary prospects were dim. The socialist movement had been polarized. To move away from the party now meant either to abandon all pretense of revolutionary socialism and join the social democrats, or to move out of

34 Ibid., 48
35 The resolution is in *Zu neuer Arbeit*, 105-6, and *Resolutions and theses of the second congress* ... 5-7

effective political life. Frustrated and forlorn, reluctantly abandoning their revolutionary enthusiasm for a more disciplined and pragmatic approach, the delegates to the second CYI congress now found themselves deprived of all that they had struggled for over the previous decade and longer. A non-political role in a strictly centralized and regimented movement, directed by the party elite, was not what radical socialist youth had fought for so bitterly.

Meanwhile, the congress had not yet finished with this crucial issue of the role of the youth movement. The success of the Comintern and Komsomol leaders in having their way can be attributed to careful planning and preparation. Thus, the decision to subordinate the youth organizations to the communist parties was not left solely to congressional resolutions of principle. In order to facilitate implementation of the new line, all youth organizations were to be reorganized. As detailed guidelines, the Russians pushed through a set of 'theses on the organizational structure of the national communist youth organizations.' The continuing tension between the 'democratic' and 'centralist' instincts of the communist movement can be seen very clearly in this new statement of organizational principles. 'The free discussion of all questions, the eligibility of all members for election to leading positions (Wählbarkeit), an obligation to make reports, and the publication of the proceedings [of all bodies]'[36] were asserted to be necessary preconditions for both successful organizational work, and the development of the independence of the individual member. The need for stronger discipline was also emphasized, but discipline was to connote as much a voluntary, self-abnegating, self-sacrificing attitude, as a formal submission to orders. One was to 'understand discipline as being not just adherence to a unified party front or conscious subordination under the regulations (Anordnungen) of the highest bodies' (although this was expected), but even more as a frame of mind. 'Partiinost'' was being extended to the entire communist movement.[37]

36 Kurella, *Gründung und Aufbau* ... 248, and *Resolutions and theses of the second congress* ... 17-21
37 The theses went on to say that the heavy responsibilities that lay on the members of all communist organizations demanded of them a serious attitude, a commitment to work energetically and with determination, and to

Alongside what could be argued were democratic features were others emphasizing centralism. In order to become mass organizations, there was to be an expansion of the organizational base of the youth organizations. The 'cell' was now being introduced into the organizational structure of communist organizations. Cells were to be formed wherever large groups of young people were organized – in the factories, schools, trade-union youth sections, sports clubs, opposition youth groups, and elsewhere. These cells were to become the basic units of the youth organizations, and were to form the base of an hierarchical structure rising from local groups (based on residence and controlling the work of a number of cells), through district and/or provincial organizations, to a national committee and a national congress, which would elect the central committee as its executive organ.[38] Authority was thus centralized at the top. Under 'guidance from the party and the Communist Youth International,' the central committees were to be the 'central directors' of the youth organizations.[39] District committees were to be elected by district conferences, but had to be endorsed by the central committee and were subject to its orders. While the central committees were to be elected formally by national congresses, the practice appears soon to have developed of using the congresses simply to ratify

------

seek to fulfil not just the letter, but the spirit of the formal obligations. Thus, one can see the introduction of the Russian party concept of 'partiinost'' into the international communist youth movement. 'It goes without saying,' continued the theses, 'that subordination under the highest bodies permits a free discussion (Behandlung) of all issues in dispute, which, until a decision is taken, is indeed a necessity' (ibid.).

38 *Zu neuer Arbeit*, 78-86. It was recognized that in some countries (Austria, the Netherlands) where the communist youth organization was very small such an elaborate organizational structure would not be necessary (ibid., 84).

39 *Resolutions and theses of the second congress* ... 17-21. See also *Zu neuer Arbeit*, 83, 86. The voting was 106-10, with only the French delegaton supporting amendments offered by the KAJ delegate providing for more decentralization. The KAJ had no voting rights. The organizational statute as adopted is in *Resolutions and theses of the second congress* ... 35-6.

the choice of leaders made by the party and/or ECCYI. By controlling the composition of the central committees of the youth organizations, the CYI and the parties could thus keep the entire youth movement under control. As will be seen, however, this was not accomplished immediately. The youth organizations had not as yet faced the consequences of their general commitment to centralization.

With the main questions of strategy and the role of the youth movement settled, there was little difficulty in securing adoption of the Comintern position on tactical issues. The long debate on the nature of the youth organizations, and on the form of the 'economic struggle,' was now at an end. The youth organizations were to become mass organizations participating directly in, and leading, the efforts of the young workers to improve their living and working conditions.[40] The basis for economic work was to be nuclei (cells) in the factories and schools. At the same time, the young communists were to infiltrate and try to capture the trade-union youth sections. A nine-point program of minimum economic demands was to be put forth as a challenge to the reformist trade-union leaders.

Imposition of Russian control over the CYI was completed when Shatskin's proposal to move ECCYI to Moscow, and to create an under-secretariat in Berlin 'to conduct organizational and propaganda work according to directives from Moscow,' was accepted without formal opposition.[42] A serious behind-the-scene conflict took place, however, in which the Scandinavians, 'together with others,' held out for keeping ECCYI in Berlin.[43] After disagreement on its composition,

40 The theses on the 'economic struggle' are in ibid., 10-
41 There were thus to be no special 'bridge organizations' to conduct the economic work. The Russians, supported by the majority, appear to have had serious doubts about the ability of the communists to control mass economic organizations set up outside the youth organizations. To have placed the main weight of the communist 'economic struggle' on separate organizations would have been to run the heavy risk that communist efforts would be engulfed by a broader movement beyond communist control or influence.
42 *Zu neuer Arbeit*, 97-8
43 See the report of the Danish delegates in *Fremad* 15. årg., nr. 5 (September 1921).

which necessitated the intervention of ECCI, the congress elected a new and larger ECCYI.[44] Besides Vujovitch (Yugoslavia) who replaced Münzenberg as secretary, Shatskin, Sabirov (a Komsomol leader representing the Orient), Unger (Germany), Schönhaar (Germany), Schüller (Austria), Tranquilli (Italy), Kurella (Russia), Münzenberg, Flieg, and a Scandinavian were chosen. Four candidates, among whom were Doriot (France), Tatarov (Russia), and Lekai (Hungary), were also elected.[45] Münzenberg and Flieg never participated in the work of the CYI after the second congress. Despite the presence of at least three of the leading spokesmen for the 'revolutionary offensive' and independence for the youth movement (Schüller, Schönhaar, and Tranquilli), the new leadership was clearly under the control of the Comintern executive committee.[46]

44 Shatskin mentioned this in his report to the fourth Komsomol congress in September 1921 (Fisher, Jr, *Pattern for Soviet Youth*, 102). ECCI intervention seems to have been necessary because of the 'anti-Münzenberg' attitude of the Russians and others, which it appears led them to be reluctant to re-elect Münzenberg and Flieg to ECCYI. Their appearance in the new leadership served to obscure the seriousness of the disputes and changes made by the congress.
45 *Zu neuer Arbeit*, 98. The Norwegian, Ingvald Larsen, was appointed by the Scandinavians soon after the congress (*IJK*, 20 August 1921, 5).
46 The basic principles for work among youth in the colonial world followed Comintern policy (*Zu neuer Arbeit*, 73-4; for Comintern policy see Degras, *The Communist International* ... I, 138-44, and 382-93). Despite considerable effort, the CYI was able to build few serious youth organizations in non-European (or European-derivative) areas. Not only were conservative cultural influences a serious obstacle in these areas, but the colonial regimes and nationalist governments, such as in Turkey and Persia, were very active in combatting all who threatened the status quo. Communism did find an audience, however, among colonial students and young intellectuals who were residing in Europe. The congress also adopted theses on propaganda work among the peasant youth, work among the students, the Jewish question, and a new organizational statute, and approved an anti-

For many of the young communist activists who served as delegates to the Comintern and CYI congresses in the summer of 1921, the weeks in Moscow must have been rather traumatic. Enthusiastic, idealistic, committed, and full of faith in the imminent revolutionary social and political restructuring of Europe, they had arrived spoiling for a showdown with the forces of 'opportunism' within the Comintern. They expected the world congress to provide the guidance and the impetus for the final thrust to power. Instead, they were told to be patient and to restrain their enthusiasm. While the third Comintern congress continued to pay lip service to the prospects for revolution, the emphasis was clearly on organizational consolidation and, for the youth organizations, abandonment of their independent political activities and a turn to the more mundane agitational, propaganda and educational tasks. They were to become one of the 'transmission belts' through which the party would build mass support for the revolutionary overthrow of the established bourgeois society.

The destruction of the Communist Youth International as an institution capable of conducting independent political activity was the heaviest blow that the young communists had to bear - a decision, furthermore, which they were forced in the name of discipline to endorse themselves. By the imposition of authority over the independent communist youth movement, and the subordination of the youth organizations to the parties, the Comintern leaders undid the work of several decades. The long struggle of radical, revolutionary socialist youth to maintain or obtain an independent existence, to concentrate their forces at the international level within an independent organization, and above all, to determine their own role in the 'proletarian struggle,' had come to an end. What remained was to assure that Comintern decisions were implemented, obdurate dissenters removed, cadres trained and oriented toward 'youth tasks,' and the character of the national youth organizations changed accordingly.

Events during the two Moscow congresses, and subsequent developments, made a deep impression on Willi Münzenberg. He had been a product of, and in many ways was most repre-

---

militarist, anti-social democratic 'manifesto to the proletarian youth' (see *Resolutions and theses of the second congress ...*).

sentative of, the evolution of the socialist youth movement
in Europe after 1907. He soon developed a cynicism that was
to colour his attitude toward the Russians and their followers for the rest of his life.[47] What may have disturbed
Münzenberg most was the behaviour of Lenin. Münzenberg had
been very close to Lenin and his circle in Zurich in 1916
and 1917. In fact one could say that Lenin's influence was
a critical element in the development of Münzenberg's political views. At that time, however, Lenin had supported
and encouraged the development of an independent youth
movement. Although he bowed to discipline, Münzenberg was
never really to accept Lenin's argument that conditions had
changed so much that an independent youth movement was
no longer necessary and was, in fact, detrimental to the
further development of the communist movement.

After the CYI congress

The second CYI congress had established new relations
between the youth organizations and the parties, issued
the directives for 'going to the masses,' and given to the
new ECCYI the task of creating a centralized world organization on the Russian model. The period after the congress

47 See Gross, *Willi Münzenberg*, 123. Ernst Christiansen,
an old friend of Münzenberg from the wartime youth international, maintained a continuing correspondence with him,
as well as meeting with him on occasion (interview with
Christiansen). It is his distinct impression that Münzenberg wanted to be the leader of a large and politically important youth movement extending even beyond
Europe. He made no distinction between a 'political
movement' and a 'youth movement.' To further the interests of the young workers the movement had to be political. The Russians made this impossible by insisting
that the youth movement be subordinated to Russian interests and Russian criteria for ideological and tactical
correctness. The increasing discipline within the communist movement offended Münzenberg's independent nature
as the 1920s wore on. It is thus not difficult to understand why, in the 1920s and 1930s, he made such an effort
(on the whole successfully) to dissociate his far-flung
'front organization' and publishing activities in Berlin,
then Paris, from Moscow's usually omnipresent supervision.

was one in which the efforts to carry out the congress
decisions were hampered by opposition within the communist
youth organizations and apathy or hostility on the part of
the young workers. The force of tradition was too strong
for the congress decisions to be carried out immediately,
especially the one about giving up political independence.[48]

The 'leftism' of the communist youth organizations and
the disagreement with the new policy of 'retreat' continued
The opposition at the congress had submitted formally to
discipline, but on return to their respective countries
these delegates often did little to put the new policies
into effect. They were abetted by the disapproval of the
new line by a large segment of either the central leadership, or the membership at large, or both. In addition,
those who had become converts to the new line, like Max
Köhler, the leader of the KJD in Germany, often returned
home to an organization that gave them less than full support. Despite these difficulties, the central leaderships
of the national youth organizations were able in most
cases to win a majority at a national congress for the new
line, but often a disenchanted and discontented minority
remained. The Comintern leaders had their way in that their
supporters managed to secure or retain control of the youth
organizations. However, the generals were soon to lose many
of their most enthusiastic troops. Furthermore, the conflicts within the parties during 1923 and 1924 were once
again to bring the youth organizations into party-political
affairs.

The general weakness of the communist movement after the
political defeats of 1921 also had its effect on the youth
movement. The membership of most communist youth organizations declined during 1921-22, with Denmark as an extreme
example. Numbering almost 12,000 when it joined the CYI in
1919, the Socialdemokratisk Ungdomsforbund i Danmark had
fallen off to a few hundred by 1921 (when the leadership

48 See *Die Kommunistische Internationale*, no. 18 (1921):
53-61. See *IJK*, 16 September 1921 for ECCYI directives
on party/youth organization relations issued after the
second congress. See *Rundschreiben des Exekutiv-Komitee*
der KJI an die Kommunistischen Jugendverbände, 1 August
1921, for the detailed instructions to the youth organizations on how to win the membership for the second
congress decisions.

accepted the second CYI congress decisions, including the
change of name to include the word communist). Most of the
members left to join the right-socialist youth organization.
In many countries the general organizational work of the
CYI came to a standstill during these years.[49] The change
in psychological atmosphere from one of revolutionary anticipation to one of consolidation and the search for broader
support discouraged and frustrated many of the most enthusiastic young revolutionary socialists. A considerable number dropped out of political activities altogether. Except
briefly in 1923 in some countries, there was no compensation
in the form of an increase in the flow of new recruits.

To understand why, despite the large numbers of defections,
so many young communists were willing to accept the new dis-
pensation, one must realize that communist youth had not been
forced to give up an opportunity to give voice to their views
on party/political issues. That was to come later, although
it was foreshadowed at this time by the emphasis that the
new CYI leadership was placing on non-political activities.
What they were not to do was take an independent position
outside the party, certainly not if such a position were
institutionalized within an independent youth organization.
The KJD in Germany, for example, was expected to be concerned
with all party problems, and was to take positions on these
problems. But 'the differences of opinion that emerge in the
communist party cannot be cleared up and overcome by communist youth from the outside, but only through practical cooperation and criticism ... within the framework of the
party.'[50] It was still possible in 1921 for a young communist, in Germany or elsewhere, to accept political subordination of his organization without thereby giving up the
right to express his views or feel that he no longer had
an opportunity to shape party policy. Discipline could still
be reconciled with freedom of discussion. This was not to
last for long, however.

Germany
If the new, acquiescent leadership of the Communist Youth
International was to succeed in imposing the 'new order'
on all the member organizations, it had to assure above all

49 Chitarow (Khitarov), *Der Kampf um die Massen* ... 25
50 *Resolutionen und Richtlinien des 6. Reichs-Kongresses*
... 5-8 (cited hereafter as *Halle Congress*)

that all opposition in the KJD in Germany was overcome. The KJD convened its sixth congress in Halle in mid September in a considerably more subdued mood than had prevailed before the congresses in Moscow.[51] The revolutionary tide had receded, the communists in Germany were still suffering from harassment by various national and local authorities, and the Comintern in Moscow had just cast a chill over the eagerness of the young communists for revolutionary action. Following the example of the communist party at its congress in Jena in the latter part of August, the KJD bowed, over considerable resistance, to the discipline of Moscow and accepted the new line.[52] Some, however, were suggesting that all who were willing to accept subordination of the KJD to the party should be expelled.[53] This resistance continued in the many district conferences held after the Halle congress. The discussion at these conferences was usually led by members of the central leadership (since December 1920, renamed the 'Reichszentrale'). In all cases they succeeded in winning only a far-from-unanimous or enthusiastic approval of the Halle and second CYI congress decisions.[54] Moreover, this was accomplished only at the price of the withdrawal or expulsion of a large part of the membership.

51 *IJK*, 10 October 1921, 4-6. Halle was chosen as the site of the congress as a symbol of solidarity with the communists in central Germany, the most active in the March Action (*JG*, 1 October 1921, 18). In an official history of the German young workers' movement published in East Berlin there is but one short paragraph on this important congress (*Abriss der Geschichte* ... 165).
52 See *J-I*, October 1921, 54-6, for the letter from ECCYI to the congress calling for support for the CYI congress decisions. The letter did not reach the congress in time but was published later 'as an expression of the burning questions of the communist youth movement' (*Die Arbeit*, November 1921, 37-40). The resolution on party/KJD relations is in *Halle Congress*, 5-8. Voting was 128-19-3 for the resolution (*JG*, 1 October 1921, 24). See also *IJK*, 16 September 1921, 2-3; *Der Junge Kommunist*, August 1921 1, 5; and *JG*, 15 November 1921, 71
53 Pietschmann, *Die politisch-ideologische Klärungsprozess* ... 322
54 In some district conferences a large majority remained unsatisfied (see *Der Junge Kommunist*, November 1921, 1-2

An important result of the Halle congress was its approval without discussion of a new organizational statute.[55] The statute, in conformity with the second CYI congress theses, was drawn so as to provide for a firm organization 'to initiate and carry out actions.' All notions of independence were to be eliminated, which meant that there was to be more control from the top through the representation of higher bodies at lower levels. The lower organs were not to consider themselves as representing the membership against the central leadership, but rather as instruments of the latter in carrying out a united policy throughout the entire KJD. Thanks to its wider perspectives, the central leadership was said to be in the best position to decide on tactics. Voting representation of all higher bodies in those sub-

---

and *JG*, 15 November 1921, 71). This issue was finally put to rest during 1922 (see the report of the national committee meeting in August 1922 in *Die Arbeit*, no. 12 [August 1922]). Opposition still existed at the January 1922 national committee meeting, primarily from those supporting Reuter-Friesland. By August, however, the 'Zentrale' was reporting unity. See also *Die Arbeit*, February-March 1922, 71. At the seventh KJD congress in April 1923 it was reported that the Halle decisions were now accepted by all (*JG*, 15 April 1923, 152).

55 The report given at the congress on the statute is in *JG*, 1 October 1921, 25-6; the statute itself is in *Halle Congress*, 21-3. Elected to the new 'Reichszentrale' were Gyptner, Hopffe, Wiesner, and Schulz from the previous leadership, and Emil Birkert, Walter Gollmick (Carl Adler), and Eugen Herbst newly elected (Pietschmann, *Die politisch-ideologische Klärungsprozess* ... 325). The latter three were removed in December 1921/January 1922 because they apparently were following Reuter-Friesland and had signed his declaration in December 1921. Harry Kuhn, Fritz Gäbler, and Eugen Wiedmaier were co-opted to replace them (see *IJK*, 15 February 1922, and *Die Arbeit*, August 1922, 157). It will be noted that Max Köhler, formerly a leading member and advocate of the 'revolutionary offensive' was not reelected. Gyptner remained as chairman. The new organizational norms were elaborated at more length for all KJD functionaries in articles by Gyptner in *Die Arbeit* in November and December 1921.

ordinate to them was seen to be an important means of assuring implementation of centrally determined policy. The
cells and fractions formed within places of work or important social and economic organizations were to form the
'bridge' to the masses under the local groups based on residence (Ortsgruppe).

The first test for the new party/KJD relationship came at
the end of January 1922 when the national committee of the
KJD met in Berlin to take a position on the factional controversy within the KPD.[56] It followed the decision of the
party central committee (Zentralausschuss) and repudiated
Reuter-Friesland's views on KPD/Comintern relations. Where
two years previously (1920) it had been necessary to reject
the 'revolutionary impatience' of the 'ultra-left,' it was
now thought necessary to avoid the path to 'revolutionary
tiredness' advocated by Reuter-Friesland. The national committee came out against both the left opposition (Ruth
Fischer) and the 'right deviation' of Reuter-Friesland and
his followers.[57] The decisions of the party (the Meyer/
Thalheimer/Pieck majority) were to be the 'guiding principle
for the work of the KJD.'[58]

Ever since its formation, the FSJ/KJD had been occupied
primarily with internal political differences. Many district
groups had been concerning themselves so much with political
matters that they had neglected educational and economic
tasks. One result was that the right-socialists (social
democrats) made great gains, thereby surpassing the KJD in
size. Now the KJD leadership wished, belatedly, to remedy
this very serious situation. They felt it necessary to prepare a statement detailing the tasks with which the youth
organization was now to occupy itself in order to expand
its base of support. This was left to an article in the KJD
functionaries' organ, *Die Arbeit*, in February-March 1922.

56 *JG*, 1 February 1922, 122-3
57 *IJK*, 15 February 1922
58 Ibid. Gyptner, giving the report of the 'Zentrale' to
the national committee, refers to four members of the
'Zentrale' as having signed the Reuter-Friesland
declaration. According to Pietschmann, *Die politisch-
ideologische Klärungsprozess* ... 325, only three were
removed. Gyptner mentions the political differences at
this meeting, and the effect that the expulsions and
departures from the KJD had on the strength of the organization (*Die Arbeit*, August 1922, 158).

This statement was co-authored by two leading members of
the 'Zentrale,' Richard Gyptner, the chairman, and Walter
Schulz. It was written as an authoritative declaration of
policy, setting forth the direction and goals of the KJD
now that the political issues had been settled. This had
been made necessary by uncertainty in the KJD ranks over
aims and methods of work in the post-second CYI congress
conditions. More specifically, the authors sought to combat
the ideas of those in the youth organization advocating a
'new way,' that is, those who (at the sixth KJD congress
and at the January national committee session) had offered
a deeply pessimistic appraisal of the prospects for extending
communist influence among young workers in competition with
the bourgeois, religious, right-socialist, and centrist
youth organizations. Many functionaries and local groups
had evidently in practice given up on the 'economic struggle'
because of difficulties and the absence of immediate prospects for success. Gyptner and Schulz criticized as impatient those who wished to refrain from the 'economic struggle'
and to concentrate instead on raising the level of class-
consciousness of the young workers as the precondition for
expansion of communist influence. In order to reach the
young workers many of the local groups were spending their
time organizing hikes, theatre evenings, sports activities,
and the like. Working through the organizational focal point
of the factory cell, the KJD was now to marshal its forces
in the campaign to lead the young workers in a fight for
specific demands.

Openly coming to grips with the weakening of the organization that had resulted from the March Action in 1921 and
the subsequent controversies between the young communists
and the Comintern, the authors admitted that there were
many deficiencies within the KJD. At least half of the members of local groups were fifteen or sixteen years of age.
This meant that the largest groups of members was not yet
of an age at which they could be expected to assume responsible tasks. It also demonstrated the great losses that the KJD
had suffered when large numbers of older members left during
1921, some going into the party, but many others leaving
the movement altogether. The authors noted that the 'communist core' of the local groups had diminished, and that
current functionaries were often untrained. Internal training
programs were to be established to cope with these deficiencies. The year 1922 was thus to be a period of organizational
redevelopment. Outwardly, at least, the KJD turned to its

united-front activities. During 1923 and 1924, however, it was to be caught up again in party affairs.

France
The French communist youth organization (JC) had been a stronghold of the party left since the capture of the socialist youth organization by the communists in late 1920.[5] The majority of the youth leaders supported Souvarine and Loriot, the leading Comintern supporters in the party, against the party secretary, Frossard. Still being young and having entered the socialist movement late in its development, the young communists were not subject to the pull of tradition. They were thus more willing to remake the socialist movement in the successful Bolshevik image.[60]

The second JC congress was held in May 1922 at Montluçon. By this time the leadership felt it possible to seek ratification of the decisions of the second CYI congress.[61] It also sought endorsement of its position regarding the situation in the party. The congress confirmed the strong left tendency of the youth organization. It passed, over some opposition from both those who supported Frossard, and die-hard supporters of the 'revolutionary offensive,' a resolution viewing the 'danger of the right' (Frossard) as still a meance in the party, and demanding 'the ideological, and where necessary organizational, cleansing of the communist party of non-communist, pacifist, and anti-communist tendencies.'[62]

59 Borkenau, *European Communism*, 104
60 See Wohl, *French Communism in the Making, 1914-1924*, 21
61 The continual harassment by the authorities as a result of the anti-militarist activities, and the loss of many functionaries to the army during the annual military call-up, had weakened the JC severely in 1921 and 1922 (*J-I*, September 1922, 46-8).
62 For a discussion of the congress see *J-I*, July 1922, 386-7. The vote on this issue was 2432-394, with 426 abstentions. A new central committee of nine was create a trimming of the old central committee that had had twenty-two members. The provincial districts were to have an opportunity to be heard at quarterly meetings of an expanded central committee, with eight representatives from the provincial organizations added (*IJK*, 15 June 1922). It appears to have been at this time tha

241 Decisions in Moscow

The JC had retained its organizational and political independence from the party, despite the decisions of the
congresses in Moscow in 1921. The leaders of the JC were
unwilling to submit to the 'opportunist' Frossard leadership, and this was tolerated and even encouraged by ECCYI.
The JC was still useful to the Comintern in efforts to impose a more acquiescent leadership on the communist party.
Moreover, the militancy of the JC manifested itself primarily in the one area where the Comintern acknowledged the
desirability of more aggressive policies: anti-militarism.
Thus the left tendency within the JC was within acceptable
bounds. The important point for the Comintern was simply
that the JC leaders, despite differences over strategy and
tactics, had accepted its discipline. Hence, the JC remained considerably closer to Moscow than the leadership
of the PCF, at least until Frossard's exit from the party.[63]
Despite objections that it was not applicable to France,
the JC leaders accepted the united front in principle.
Quietly, they neglected their obligation to seek joint action with the socialist youth organization, but were very
active in the trade unions.[64] They began to make 'economic
work' an important part of the JC's activities. Spurned by
the leadership of the two trade-union federations (CGT and
the new anarcho-syndicalist CGTU), the JC opened a campaign
in *l'Avant-Garde* in support of 'the demands of young workers.'[65] Where possible the young communists, together with
the party, sought to win support from local or district

Jacques Doriot assumed the leadership of the JC. For
preparations for the congress see *J-I*, May 1922, 268-9,
and *IJK*, 1 April 1922. For the post-congress efforts of
the central leadership to assure acceptance of the decision see *J-I*, September 1922, 46-8.
63 See Wohl, *French Communism in the Making, 1914-1924*, 322
64 See *J-I*, March 1923, 205-6, and June 1924, 313-15; also
IJK, 15 August 1922, and 15 December 1922
65 The central committee directed an 'open letter' to the
congress in St Etienne in June 1922, at which the radical trade-union federation, the CGTU, was founded. The
congress, however, dominated as it was by anarcho-
syndicalists, refused to receive a delegation from JC
and announced that its trade unions would have nothing
to do with the JC. See *IJK*, 15 August 1922, and the
issues of *l'Avant-Garde* for June 1922

trade-union groups. They had considerable success in the north of France while also building cells in factories and mines.

In the latter part of 1922 and early 1923 the JC had become very active among French mine workers, whose strike in 1923 was utilized to push for JC economic demands.[66] Of greater importance for the work of the communist youth organization, however, was the occupation of the Ruhr and the resultant economic crisis in Germany in 1923. The main emphasis in communist political propaganda during this period shifted to anti-militarist, anti-imperialist campaigns in which the JC (under Jacques Doriot) took the lead.[67]

Italy

After the communists had asserted control over the Italian socialist youth organization at Florence in January 1921, a sharp decline in the organization followed. Not only did a sizable minority set itself up as the new socialist ('unitarian') youth organization, but the new central committee was arrested, or forced into hiding by government harassment. Most of the provincial and local leaders who went with the communists met the same fate. Still committed to revolutionary action, the Italian youth organization, like the party, reorganized on a basis designed to protect itself against harassment and violence by governmental authorities and the growing fascist movement. Yet, the difficulties of the new communist youth organization were further increased when many of its best functionaries, and about 10,000 members, entered the communist party so as to give it greater strength.[68]

66 See *J-I*, May 1923, 283-4. In 1922 the JC was substantially the largest young workers' organization in France. There were in addition to the communists small syndicalist, anarchist, right-socialist, and centrist youth groups. By their own admission, the most influential of these, the centrists under Pierre Lainé, were a 'laughingly small' organization (*J-I*, June 1922, 307).
67 See, for example, *IJK*, March 1924
68 *J-I*, February 1922, 170-2. The socialist youth organization numbered about 35,000 at the end of November 19. (*Unter dem roten Banner*, 19). The number grew continuously during 1920, and in January 1921 reached 60,000

Under these conditions, and together with the 'ultra-leftism' still present in the youth organization, the decision of the second CYI congress to have all communist youth organizations become mass organizations met with a completely negative response.[69] The youth organization, still supporting Bordiga, would have none of the new 'retreat' policy. It quietly went its own way, ignoring the Comintern decisions on tactics and subordination to the party. While the central committee recognized formally the need to win wider support by going 'to the masses' on economic issues, it refused to cooperate with those ('unitarian' socialists) from whom the communists had just split in an atmosphere of bitterness and recrimination.[70] The central committee took the view that to emphasize joint struggle with the socialists for 'partial economic demands' would be to weaken revolutionary resolve within the working

---

(*IJK*, January 1920, 1921; *Kommunismus* (Vienna) [15 January 1921]: 49–59). After the split of the socialist youth organization at the Florence congress in January 1921, about 12,000 left to go with the 'unitarians' (*Die Kommunistische Internationale*, no. 16 1921 : 645). The communist youth organization went rapidly downhill in 1921 and 1922, reaching a low of about 2000 in December 1922 after the failure of the occupation of the factories in northern Italy (*J-I*, May 1924, 265–6), rising to 8000 in November 1924 with the merger of the communists and 'maximalist-socialists' (*J-I*, November 1924, 81). While the communists were rapidly declining, the 'unitarians' were exhibiting a corresponding growth, reaching 18,000 to 20,000 in 1921 (*IJK*, 20 October 1921; *Die Internationale Sozialistische Jugendbewegung*, 47–9). By the time the 'unitarians' split in January 1923, they had grown to about 50,000, with about 5000 being expelled and setting themselves up as the 'socialist unitarian' youth organization (*J-I*, September 1923, 27–8). Under fascist pressure, the 'maximalist-socialists' (the majority at the congress in January 1923) fell drastically in numbers in 1924 until they were of the same insignificant order of magnitude as the communists, after which the two merged.
69 See *l'Avanguardia*, 16 January 1921
70 See *l'Avanguardia*, 22 and 29 January, 5 and 19 February, and 12 March 1922; and *IJK*, 15 February 1922

class, as well as to open the youth organization to easy
attack and destruction by the fascists.[71]

ECCYI, however, continued to call for the Italian youth
organizaton to find ways of putting the second congress
decisions into effect, without destroying its capabilities
for struggle against the fascists.[72] On the eve of the national congress of the Italian organization in March 1922,
ECCYI called for an end to 'ultra-leftism' in economic
questions. It also wished a change in the basic organizational structure, away from the 'combat groups' (squadri),
which paralleled 'communist groups' in the factories and
elsewhere as a supplementary organizational form.[73] ECCYI,
following the Comintern 'to the masses'and united-front
line developed in 1921 and 1922, wanted the Italian youth
organization to reorganize on a more open basis so as to
facilitate its growth into a mass organization. It thus
called for the military cadres to be subordinated to the
local groups. The basic unit of organization should be inside the factory, with the 'circoli' (clubs, discussion
circles, youth hostels) and military cadres as auxiliary
institutions. A continuation of the organization on a military basis (inquadramento militaire) would condemn the you
organization, according to ECCYI, to being a narrow organization in a period calling for a close tie to the masses.

The young Italian communists held their annual congress
in Rome in late March 1922, a week after the second congres
of the communist party.[74] A lively discussion took place

71 See the article by g.b. (Giuseppe Berti), 'Due Errate
   Opinioni' (Two Wrong Opinions) in *l'Avanguardia*, 26
   February 1922. See also the article 'I fondatori della
   Lega - KIM,' *l'Avanguardia*, 19 March 1922, and the
   editor's comments on an article by V.R. (Viktor Röbig
   [Alfred Kurella]), 'Organizazioni di Mass,' *l'Avanguardia*, 26 March 1922.
72 *J-I*, February 1922, 170-2. See also the article by
   Ziegler (Kurella) in *l'Avanguardia*, 5 March 1922
73 *J-I*, February 1922, 170-2. For the revolutionary spirit
   of the Italian youth leaders as reflected in the discus
   sions over tactics toward the army see *l'Avanguardia*,
   12 February 1922.
74 Having taken over the socialist youth organization, the
   communists sought to profit from emphasizing the continuity with the past by considering the congress to be

on the manner in which CYI decisions should be implemented. Now that a communist party had been formed, agreed the delegates, the youth organization could accept the CYI decision to subordinate itself to the party. As already noted, however, formal recognition of party supremacy in no way inhibited the youth organization from behaving quite independently. The only opposition to the 'going-to-the-masses' principle came from the Florentine delegation, which had to work illegally and in constant conflict with the fascists. While the principle was accepted by the congress majority, it remained a matter of priorities for individual participants: first, protection in a dangerous situation, *then* a broadened organizational form. Even this reaching out to the masses, however, would not be at the expense of a sacrifice of principle or revolutionary purity. The Ordine nuovo delegate, Mario Montagnana, reporting on organizational

the next regular congress (ninth) of the old organization. See *IJK*, 15 April 1922, and *l'Avanguardia*, 9 and 16 April 1922 for reports on the congress. Of the party leaders, only Gramsci appeared and spoke to the delegates. The congress elected a new central committee after some procedural difficulties over who would participate in the making of nominations. Various lists of candidates were circulating and offered to the congress chairman, apparently including one proposed by the outgoing central committee. Pressure from the delegates resulted in the formation of a nominating committee, the majority of whom were congress delegates chosen by the ex officio members (chairman of the congress, the communist party representative, the CYI representative, and a representative from the old central committee). The committee report was accepted unanimously, with no notation in the report of the congress in *l'Avanguardia* of any discussion or debate. Elected were Luigi Longo, Telo', Gorelli, Falcipieri, Frausin, Cianiccieri, Montanari, Berti, Cassita, and D'Onofrio (*l'Avanguardia*, 9 April 1922). There appears to have been a wave of expulsions from the youth organization after the congress in Florence in January 1921, clearing out the 'unitarians.' Berti agreed in response to one speaker that there had been too many expulsions. The process had scared off many prospective members.

and propaganda tasks, stated that propaganda and the effort
to reach the masses were only one aspect of the work of the
youth organization.[75] By seeking to become a mass organization, the youth organization should be careful not to compromise its revolutionary aims. First and foremost this
meant refusal to form a united front with the socialists.
On this issue the communist youth were firm supporters of
the 'Rome Theses' drawn up by Bordiga, which had just been
adopted by the second party congress.

The young Italian communists were unwilling to legitimize
the political and economic status quo in Italy by focusing
their 'economic struggle' on the existing non-revolutionary
trade unions. They also refused to have the youth organization itself lead the 'economic struggle' directly. In clear
contravention of the decisions of the congresses in Moscow
in 1921, they decided that economic work would be conducted
outside the youth organization. Local youth groups would
join with the trade-union departments of local party organizations and form joint committees for action in and out
of the trade unions.[76] A united front would be possible
only at the local level between communist and non-communist
workers.[77]

The form and style of economic work was to vary according
to the region of the country.[78] In Milan and other heavily
industrialized areas, demands for representation of the
young workers in the communist trade-union committees and
for the inclusion of the special youth demands in all strike
and other agitational activities were to be raised in party
circles. In areas of small farms and handicraft industries
the communists were to be active in intervening, through
the predominantly non-communist trade unions, with the
capitalists for the young handworkers. In Sicily, and
other semi-feudal, backward areas where no strong trade
unions existed and 'where the political struggle was not
the class struggle, but rather a personal one,' communist

75 *L'Avanguardia*, 9 April 1922
76 See the article, 'La Gioventi Communista e il fronta
   unico,' *l'Avanguardia*, 14 May 1922
77 There was even some opposition to this limited implementation of Comintern policy. Tranquilli in June 1922 was
   still defending the united front *in principle* from 'put-
   chists' and activists on the left (ibid., 16 June 1922)
78 *IJK*, 15 June 1922

youth were to be active in founding trade unions and co-operatives.

Better prepared than in 1921 for illegal activity, the communist youth organization was able to save much of its organizational structure after the fascist march on Rome in October 1922.[79] The task now was not to go out and do battle, as in Germany in March 1921, because there was no open conflict between the legal authorities and the fascists. The major problem was to preserve the organizational apparatus, and to build up the communist military organization so as to defend the movement. In Bologna, Crosseto, Siena, Aresco, Reggio Emilia, Ferrara, Modena, Mantua, and elsewhere the communist youth organization (as well as the communist party) was completely illegal. The central committee, the sections in the large industrial cities (Turin, Milan, Trieste), and those in southern Italy, Sicily, and Sardinia continued to function normally. Where the working class was too strong for an immediate attack by the fascists on its organizations, or where it was too weak to be of much concern to them, the communists were able to remain operative. Even so, arrests and the prohibition of publishing activities, including Comintern and CYI publications, limited sharply the work of all communist groups.

During 1923, as the fascists successfully strengthened their position in Italy, they bore down more heavily on the communists and the young communists suffered along with the party. Sometime in early 1923 the entire central committee was arrested, including the leaders, Berti, Cassita, and Longo.[80] A secret meeting of the national committee was nevertheless held in Rome in August, when a new central committee was formed, only to be broken up again by further arrests in the fall.[81] Especially paralyzing in 1923 and 1924 for the communist youth organization was the need to assist the party. Because of the decimation of both leaderships, and harassment by the author-

---

79 *IJK*, 15 November 1922. Thus in many ways justifying their resistance to the organizational changes demanded by ECCYI.

80 A report in *IJK*, July 1923, says at the end of May. Berti says that it was earlier, in February, together with Bordiga and Grieco (interview with Berti).

81 *IJK*, October and November 1923

ities, organizational work fell off drastically. Coupled
with a basic disillusionment with communism among Italian
workers at this time, the membership of both the party and
the youth organization declined rapidly. Accordingly, it
was agreed that joint cells would be formed in the factories until such time as the membership grew so that separate cells could be formed again.[82] All legal means for
the defence of the interests of young workers were utilized, especially sports organizations and student movements.[83] Begun in 1923, these efforts were carried on into
the beginning of 1924 when in February the fascists relaxed
their anti-communist repression. The youth organ *l'Avanguardia* was no longer prohibited, as it had been since
early 1923, and reorganization work began to be stepped up

During 1923, the Italian communist youth organization
began slowly to give up its 'ultra-left' policies and come
into line with the Comintern and CYI congress decisions.[85]
As late as the fourth CYI congress in mid 1924, however,
ECCYI was still complaining of 'ultra-leftism' and attacking Bordiga and his supporters in the youth movement.
The major impetus to this movement away from the left came
from the shift in view in late 1922 of Berti and many of
his associates in the leadership of the youth organizatio
Previously a firm Bordigist and an 'uncompromising revolu
tionary,' Berti moved to the right and joined Tasca and
accepted the Comintern position on the united front. The
events in Italy - the March on Rome and the dangers, and
perhaps opportunities, it presented, as well as the decis

82 The fourth session of the International Bureau of the
   CYI in July 1923 viewed these joint cells as being onl
   provisional (*Inprecorr*, 8 August 1923, 1133).
83 *J-I*, February 1924, 73-4
84 *J-I*, November 1924, 81-2. The prohibition was lifted o
   19 February 1924 (*J-I*, March 1924, front cover).
85 *IJK*, June 1924
86 *J-I*, July/August 1924, 335-53 (Schüller report of ECCY
87 Signs of this were evident already in June when Tranquilli wrote approvingly in *l'Avanguardia* of the coope
   ation that had been developing between the 'Third
   International' group in the PSI and the PCI (*l'Avanguardia*, 25 June 1922). See the same issue for an interpretation of the tendencies within the PSI by T.A.
   (Angelo Tasca?).

of the Italian socialist party (PSI) in October 1922, to
expel the reformists (those expelled became known as 'socialist unitarians'; those remaining as 'maximalist socialists') – had influenced Berti. The immediate threat to
the revolutionary left from the March on Rome, as well as
reflection on the consequences of the harassment of 1921,
seem to have led Berti and others to more pragmatic, less
uncompromising views. In any event, in the fall of 1922
Berti admitted that he and the youth organization had been
wrong, that Serrati had not been so mistaken after all in
1919 and 1920. This shift, which developed during 1923 and
1924, facilitated the fusion with the 'maximalist socialist'
youth that took place in 1924. Perhaps Berti went too far
by associating himself with Tasca for, upon his release
from prison, he was sent to Moscow and given the honorific
post of secretary of the CYI so as, according to Berti, to
remove a 'right tendency' from the youth movement.[88] Luigi
Longo became the new secretary of the Italian communist
youth organization.

The national committee in August 1923 took the first steps
to bring the Italian youth organization into line with Comintern policy. The youth organization was to be reorganized on
the basis of factory cells, and to become more active in
economic and educational matters. During early 1924, the
youth organization was busy expanding its work beyond the
large industrial centres, building communist youth groups
throughout Italy. Jointly with the 'maximalist socialist'
youth organization, the communists led an unsuccessful campaign for the 'demands of the young workers' during the
Italian elections in 1924. The merger of the communist and
'maximalist socialist' youth organizations in May 1924
strengthened the communists considerably. This was all an
effort wasted in a hopeless cause, however, as Mussolini
was rapidly consolidating his power. In the fall of 1926,
the communist youth organization was banned, along with
all other organizations opposed to the fascists. What activities the communist youth were able to carry on in
Italy after this time were very limited in scope and
strictly illegal.

Despite continuing difficulties, by the end of 1922 the
Comintern and the Komsomol had gone a long way toward

88 Interview with Giuseppe Berti

translating the second CYI congress decisions into effective control over the youth international. The turn to a new order was symbolized by the formal departure of Willi Münzenberg and Leo Flieg from the Communist Youth International in mid March. The second session of the International Bureau dropped the two from membership in ECCYI. One had provided the energy, vision, and leadership to the revolutionary socialist, then communist, youth movement during its most active years; the other had provided the quiet organizational skills required for the consolidation of the new Communist Youth International from 1919 to 1921. Both had been shunted off after the second congress to other work, but had been re-elected to ECCYI in order to gloss over the subordination of the youth movement to Mosc Ironically, the warm tributes and glowing praise accorded to Münzenberg and Flieg at the International Bureau sessi served only to emphasize the finality of the changes in th youth international.

8

The united front and 'bolshevization'

The two congresses in Moscow in the summer of 1921 marked
the climax of a fateful drama. Only the final scene remained
to be played. No one - not the playwright, not the players,
not the audience - knew for certain what the final curtain
would bring. To a perceptive critic, however, there could
be little doubt. The expulsion of Levi, the subordination
of the youth movement, increasing intervention in the affairs of communist parties, and the growing bureaucratization of the Comintern were harbingers of a new, more restrictive definition of communism. Especially in view of
what was going on within the Russian party and the new
Soviet state, it should have been clear that drastic changes
were in store for the communist movement.

For the emotionally involved participants, however, it
was not immediately apparent that such changes were in the
offing. There was great unhappiness over the turn to a more
cautious 'line,' but the goodwill of the Russian party remained taken for granted. The right of free discussion had
not yet been terminated. Strong currents of opposition persisted within the parties and youth organizations. In fact,
several parties and youth organizations felt free to ignore
the new decisions and go about their business as before.
The Comintern had spoken, and a new 'line' had been adopted,
but differences over strategies and tactics were only beginning to become issues of discipline.

This lack of discipline meant that although the youth organizations were to become, on the Komsomol model, 'transmission belts' through which Comintern and party policy
was to be implemented and the mass of young workers mobilized, it was possible in 1921 and 1922 to relegate the
youth movement only in part to such a subsidiary and non-

political role. The factionalism within the parties over matters of principle and policy, which the Comintern was unable to prevent, provided an opportunity for some youth organizations. They asserted themselves, politically, by supporting a faction within the party either for, or against the Comintern. Even where the youth organization had been purged of all deviant views, it was necessary for it to remain heavily involved in political/factional activities. Thus, while the Communist Youth International and its member groups were trying to carry out Comintern policy as adopted at the third congress, their attention was increasingly being absorbed by internal party disputes.

The united-front policy

As has been noted already, the Russian leaders wanted the Comintern to expand its support within the European working class so as to develop new revolutionary strength. A united front policy was promoted as the best means of accomplishin this end. Following Comintern leadership, the revamped yout international made this the central focus of its activity in 1921 and 1922. By a united front, the communists at firs meant joint action or cooperation with the right-socialists and centrists: the formation of a 'united proletarian effor against capitalism' (against wage reductions, for wage increases, against efforts to increase working hours, and similar actions) in order to improve the lot of the worker.

As developed in practice, the united front has two variations: the 'united front from below' and the 'united front from above.' The former was directed towards winning the membership of the socialist youth organizations away from the leaders. Joint action and cooperation were encouraged at the local levels (local party or youth organization groups, local trade-union organizations, factory councils) so as to create local movements under communist influence. The latter called for overt cooperation between communist and socialist organizations and their leaderships, while at the same time using this cooperation to further the interests of the communists. By getting communists into positions of influence in the special united-front organizatior created, the communists hoped to succeed in undermining the authority of the socialist leaders and, again, in winning the membership away from them. The two forms were usually intertwined in the early 1920s, with the emphasis turning

from 'united front from above' at the outset to 'united
front from below' in 1924.

The united-front efforts were conducted on two levels:
international and national. The Comintern attempted to
sponsor joint activities with the Second International and
the Vienna Union, as did the CYI with the two socialist
youth internationals. At the national level, the communist
parties and youth organizations were to develop joint campaigns with the socialists. The Comintern leaders believed
that few tangible results would follow from these efforts.
Because of capitalist resistance and the unwillingness of
the socialists to fight for 'genuine' improvements in the
workers' conditions, the workers would soon see that only
the communists were prepared to stand up to the capitalist
system. They thus would turn to communist organizations as
their only hope for change. In 1923 the united front was
in Germany to go so far as to mean 'loyal opposition' to
the socialist 'workers' governments' formed during and
after what was meant to be a successful revolution.

The mutual hostility that had developed between the communists and the social democrats doomed the efforts at cooperation from the very beginning. The communists had no
more luck with the centrists. The price paid by the Comintern for domination of the youth international was complete
and final alienation of the young centrists. As the latter
were the only elements with whom a united front could con-
ceivably have been established, the CYI was left with a
policy of cooperation and no one to cooperate with. After
the efforts to develop cooperation failed in 1922 and 1923,
the main thrust of the united front was placed on direct
appeals, over the heads of the socialist leaders, to individual members. In this fashion, the united front was pursued by the Comintern and the youth international from 1921
until 1928, at which time a complete rupture with socialists
at all levels again took place.[1]

1 See Degras, 'United Front Tactics in the Comintern, 1921-
   1928,' in Footman, *International Communism*, 9–22. The
   third congress in December 1922 followed the Comintern
   line and confirmed the united front policy as the basis
   of CYI work (see *Im Zeichen der Arbeit*). The congress
   also confirmed the policy introduced by the second congress of basing the youth organizations on the factory
   cell. Discussion showed that strong resistance had

The reasons for the failures of the youth organizations
were also those that brought about the failure of the
united front efforts of the parties. Cooperation between
right-socialists, centrists, and communists would provide
the facade of unity, behind which the communists would be
taking steps to win the members of the right-socialist and
centrist organizatons. By seeking to establish the united
front on communist terms, and by putting the onus on the
right-socialists and the centrists for any failure, the
communists expected to be able to show to the 'masses' that
the others were not willing to fight for even economic reforms, much less for a radical transformation of existing
bourgeois society. That would 'prove' that only the communists had not 'sold out' to the bourgeoisie. The communists
would appear as the 'real' advocates of working-class unit
and the only proletarian organization concerned with the
interests of the workers. The inherent contradiction betwee
the appeals for 'unity' on the one hand, and the openly
stated intentions of the communists to remain free to pursue their objectives and their attacks on the socialist
leaders on the other, was perfectly obvious to right and
centre socialist leaders. Not surprisingly, they were unwilling to be used by the communists. When it became clear
that the communists were only attempting to exploit the
desire for unity, the centrists turned to the right-
socialists and a new, non-communist socialist unity occurr
- both nationally and internationally. Developments in the
youth organizations followed those within the parties.

---

developed within the youth organizations to both the un
front and the changeover to the factory cell. Oppositio
came, in particular, from the Dutch, Italian, and Germa
youth organizations. In 1924, three years after the fir
instructions had been given to make the factory cell th
basis of the youth organization, there still was heavy
resistance (see Chitarow [Khitarov], *Der Kampf um die
Massen* ... 66-8). The focal point of the united front
for the young communists in Germany was in RAJO (Reichsausschuss der Arbeiterjugendorganisationen), founded
by representatatives of the trade-union youth sections
and the right-socialist and centrist youth organizatior
The young communists tried, quite unsuccessfully, to wi
control of this joint effort to promote the economic ar
social interests of the young workers.

After preliminary negotiations in 1920 and early 1921,
the right-socialists formed the Young Workers' International
(Arbeiter Jugendinternationale) in May 1921 in Amsterdam.
The manifesto adopted by the founding conference called
upon young workers to take a stand against both capitalist
dictatorship and Bolshevik terror, and indicated that the
'Young Workers' International is opposed to the Communist
Youth International, which as a biased political body follows the political aims of the Russian communists and not
the aims of youth.'[2] Likewise, the failure of efforts by
the centrists to create unity in the international socialist youth movement, and to join the CYI on their own terms,
finally led them to form their own international, the Internationale Arbeitsgemeinschaft sozialistischer Jugendorganisationen (IASJ) in Vienna in February 1921.[3] Standing between
the communists and the right-socialists, the IASJ considered
the one as completely political, a tool of the communist
parties and subordinated to the decisions of the Comintern;
and the other as tied too closely to the non-revolutionary
right-socialist parties and giving too little weight to the
independence of the youth organizations. The IASJ was considered by its supporters to be the only socialist youth
international that was both independent, and revolutionary.
By the end of 1922 the right-socialist youth were moving
away from their preoccupation with 'cultural' activities
and becoming somewhat more political, and the centrists were
willing to associate themselves with a party (a basic requirement of the right-socialist position).[4] A common ground

2 *The Young Workers' International* ... 6-8. For the statute
  and standing orders of the new AJI see ibid., 14-18. See
  also Thaller, *Die Internationale* ... 19
3 There was considerable conflict associated with the founding conference in Vienna, for a number of young communists
  from several countries appeared, including Münzenberg from
  ECCYI, and participated in the initial discussions. After
  struggling with the communists, who endeavoured to take
  over the conference for their own purposes, the centrists
  left and met separately to form their own youth international. See *Bericht über die internationale sozialistische Jugendkonferenz* ... and Thaller, *Die internationale* ...
4 The desire of the centrists to preserve a 'neutrality'
  vis-à-vis the parties and the party factions had been
  an important reason for the split with the communists

was thus opening up. When the right-socialist and centrist
youth groups merged in Germany, the way was open for the
merger of the two youth internationals.[5] This took place
in Hamburg in May 1923, at the same time as the two party
internationals merged into the Labour and Socialist International.

Communist youth and the final crisis over centralization

During 1923 and 1924 serious conflicts flared within the co
munist parties. Differences remained over which strategies
and tactics were most appropriately 'revolutionary,' both
in principle, and in the particular conditions of crisis
in 1923. More importantly, they now had become issues of
discipline. In the course of imposing unity and defining
the substance of centralization, the Comintern leadership
increasingly came to intervene in these party conflicts.
It had already begun to do so in 1921 in the case of Paul
Levi.

The youth organizations could not escape the effects of
these party controversies. While attempting to carry out
united-front policies, and while the face presented to thos
outside the movement was one of an activist organization
concerned with anti-militarism, political 'education,' and
the economic rights of the young workers, the communist
youth leaders were in most cases expending the majority of
their time intervening in party conflicts. Behind the facade, even to an extent behind the line separating the full
time functionaries from the ordinary members, the main
topics of discussion and interest were those emerging from

---

in the Freie Sozialistische Jugend (FSJ) in Germany in
   1919.
5 See *Die Internationale der sozialistischen Proletarier-
   jugend*, October/November 1922, and January/February 192:
   The voting at the SPJ congress in October was 92 for
   merger, 20 against, with four abstentions. The minority
   held out for a merger on terms more favourable to the
   centrist point of view, but in the end accepted the
   congress decision (*IJK*, 15 November 1922). The four
   abstainers represented those who followed Georg Ledebou:
   These forces refused to merge with the right-socialists
   met in Zeitz in late January 1923, and reorganized them
   selves as the SPJ (*IJK*, February 1923).

the disputes within the party. In most cases this intervention by youth leaders received encouragement from the executive committee of the youth international because it was
usually, if not consistently, on the side of those party
factions that supported the positions of the Comintern.
In some cases, the youth organizations split along the
same lines as the party. This intervention was given the
Comintern leadership's sanction by Karl Radek at the fourth
session of the CYI International Bureau in mid July 1923
in Moscow.[6]

Germany

The most important party conflict was in Germany, where
the left-opposition (Ruth Fischer, Arkady Maslow) was in
disagreement with the Comintern's united-front policy as
followed by Heinrich Brandler and the 'Zentrale'. The anti-
trade unionism that had lain dormant in the KPD since the
expulsion of the 'ultra-left' in 1920 now surfaced again.
Instead of negotiations with the left-wing socialist leaders, formation of 'workers' government,' and use of the
factory council movement to pressure the trade unions, the
left-opposition wanted a 'united front from below' so as
to revolutionize the membership of the non-communist workers' organizations. These differences were accentuated by
the Franco-Belgian occupation of the Ruhr in January 1923.
More than ever, argued the left, the party should seize
the initiative on its own, arming the workers and preparing
to take advantage of the tension and unrest that would result from the occupation. To tie the KPD to the social
democrats in 'workers' governments' would be to bind the
party to undependable allies.[7] Brandler and the right,
anxious to avoid the consequences of another 'revolutionary

6 See *J-I*, August 1923, 374, for a discussion of this session of the International Bureau. Several changes were
made in ECCYI at this time. Vutchak was moved out and
Schulz elevated from candidate membership. David (France)
and Melnais (Latvia) left as candidate members, the former because of a call-up to military service. Ythe-Lyon
(France), a Bulgarian, and an Estonian were added as
candidate members (*Inprecorr*, 8 August 1923, 1139).
7 In contrast to the universal validity of the united
front policy, the slogan of 'workers' government' was
considered by the Comintern leaders to have a limited

offensive' policy that many had supported in 1921, were
more patient with regard to revolutionary objectives. They
emphasized the need for wider popular support and cooperation with the non-communist workers' organizations.

The national committee of the youth organization, after
long discussions and after hearing both Brandler and a
representative of the left-opposition, decided in mid
February 1923 to support Brandler and the majority at the
recent party congress in Leipzig, and thus to follow Comin-
tern/CYI directives.[8] The national committee apparently
recognized that the views of the left had found considerable support within the KJD, for it felt it necessary to
take steps to 'clarify' the members' attitudes toward the
party's decisions. A major article in *Junge Garde* in
August, as political tensions began to intensify, emphasize
the obligation of each individual member to maintain discipline within the KJD.[9]

The leadership was successful in containing any opposition, as its position was confirmed by the seventh KJD
congress at Chemnitz in April. The position of the left-

application. As a general propaganda slogan, however,
it was useful everywhere. A 'workers' government' was
seen as a way, under certain conditions, of facilitating
a transitional working-class overthrow of the bourgeois
system, on the way to a dictatorship of the proletariat.
Communists could support a 'workers' government' formed
by other socialist parties from outside, or actually
participate in it alongside non-communist working-class
parties and organizations. The theses on the united
front and workers' governments adopted by the fourth
Comintern congress in December 1922 tried to make clear
what it meant, and under what conditions a communist
party could participate. The ambiguities that remained,
however, did not make it easy for the parties to decide
when, and in what way, to apply the policy. See Degras,
The Communist International ... I, 416ff, especially
425-7

8 *J-I*, April 1923, 242-3, and *Die Junge Garde (JG)*, 1
   March 1923, 128.
9 *JG*, 15 August 1923, 248

opposition was rejected overwhelmingly.[10] This KJD congress
was in many ways a replay of the party congress in Leipzig.

10 The voting was on two resolutions: one prepared by the
KJD 'Zentrale,' one by part of the delegation from Berlin
(thus all of the Berlin organization was not with the
left-opposition). One source indicates that the 'Zentrale'
proposal won 'against four votes' (*JG*, 15 April 1923,
152). Other sources say that the voting was 1946-14 (*J-I*,
May 1923, 278-9, and *IJK*, April 1923, 19). The congress
also approved unanimously the decisions of the third
CYI congress (ibid.). See also *JG*, 1 June 1923, 189.

Important changes in the structure and leadership of
the KJD were introduced at the Chemnitz congress when a
new organizational statute was adopted. The 'Zentrale'
was expanded from seven members (the size determined by
the sixth congress in 1921) to fourteen, and an inner
'Büro' of seven was created (*IJK*, 15 April 1923). This
was justified on the ground that it would create a closer
tie between the 'Zentrale' and the local organizations,
and would enable the central leadership to exert stronger
control over their activities. The seventeen elected to
the 'Zentrale' were, in order of listing, Heinrich Pütz,
Fritz Gäbler, Harry Kuhn, Eugen Wiedmaier, Karl Grunert,
Fritz Reinhardt, Erich Wiesner, Theo Lüders, Erich Auer,
Robert Liebbrand, Kurt Schneider, Gertrud Graefer,
Richard Creutzburg, Willi Krez, Conrad Blenkle, Walter
Häbisch, and Martin Klonowski, the last three of whom
were, apparently, candidate members (ibid.). No indication is given of the membership of the 'Büro.' The first
seven mentioned, most of whom were prominently referred
to in the KJD literature of the time, may well have been
its members. The important reports at the congress were
presented by Pütz, Gäbler, Kuhn, Wiedmaier, Wiesner, and
Klonowski. There is some confusion about who was now the
leading figure in the KJD. One source says that by the
end of 1922 Gäbler had replaced Gyptner as chairman
(*Abriss der Geschichte* ... 273). Gäbler had come from
the Thuringian district organization, where after November
1918 he was the leader. Gäbler's position is confirmed
by Hermann Weber in the series of biographic sketches
in his study of the KPD (Weber, *Die Wandlung des deutschen
Kommunismus* II, 130). Gäbler is described as having been

A sign of the importance that the party leadership attached
to the youth movement was the appearance of Brandler himsel
as the main speaker. His objective was to avoid a repetitic
of the tactical conflicts dividing the party, and thus to e
tablish the KJD as a reliable corps of activists supporting
his leadership and policies within the party. In this he wa
relatively successful, at least for the moment. He took a c
ciliatory but firm position towards the left-opposition. Th
party 'Zentrale' would try again to persuade the oppositior
reconcile its views with the majority, but would not tolera
further efforts to replace the policy of the majority with
that of the opposition.[11] The concept of democratic centra:
had come to mean that it was inadmissible for a minority tc
seek to change the policy of the majority.

With the acceleration of economic and political turmoil
in Germany, culminating in August 1923 in the resignation
of the Cuno government and the installation of Stresemann
as chancellor, Comintern doubts as to the feasibility of
a revolution finally were dispelled and belated preparations began for a rising. In early October ECCYI issued a
call to its member sections to prepare for the 'imminent
revolutionary situation.' 'The CYI and all its sections
must and will be on guard, and will exert all efforts to
prepare in revolutionary tempo for the coming events.'[12]
All communist youth organizations were put on a 'stand-by'
status. Those in Poland, Czechoslovakia, and France were

---

chairman of the KJD from 1923 until 1924. However, in
his sketch of Heinrich Pütz, another prominent activist
in the KJD 'Zentrale' Weber says that *he* was chairman
from May 1923 until March 1924 (ibid., 250). In the lis
of those elected to the new 'Zentrale' at Chemnitz,
Pütz is mentioned first and Gäbler second. Pütz had bee
elected to the 'Zentrale' at the meeting of the nationa
committee in August 1922 (*Die Arbeit*, no. 22 [August
1922]). It is not clear whether he was elected only to
fill Gyptner's position on the 'Zentrale,' when Gyptner
was moved out to be KJD representative in ECCYI, or to
fill as well his position as chairman.

11 The left-opposition apparently had made a serious effor
to win repudiation of the Leipzig party congress decisions by the Rheinland-Westfalen-Nord district party or
ganization at its post-Leipzig congress conference.

12 *J-I*, October 1923, 33-4

to be ready to step in to hinder any outside intervention
against possible revolutionary activities. The sternest
tasks in the CYI would fall to the KJD, which would be at
the centre of the battle. 'All other youth organizations
must fashion their work so as to help the German revolution,
as they did during the Russian civil war.'[13] More than ever
before, the work of the communist youth organizations was
to be coordinated with the communist parties. The KJD held
a national committee meeting in early October to set the
tasks for 'the coming great struggle.'[14] Having seriously
misjudged the situation throughout the whole of 1923, however, the Comintern was too late with its attempted uprising. The intervention of the Reichswehr and the overthrow of the 'workers' government' in Saxony, to which the
KPD had agreed to act as a 'loyal opposition,' ended the
revolutionary situation and brought about the banning of
the communists in November 1923.

The 'Zentrale' of the now illegal KJD met in late January
1924 to discuss the implications of the October (1923)
events, immediately after ECCI had met in Moscow.[15] The
Comintern decision to abandon efforts to create a 'united
front from above' was approved by a great majority. Blame

13 Ibid., November 1923, 70-1
14 *IJK*, October 1923
15 *IJK*, March 1924. For the discussion, speeches, and resolutions passed at the ECCI plenum see *Die Lehren der
   Deutschen Ereignisse. Das Präsidium des Exekutivkomitees
   der Kommunistischen Internationale zur Deutschen Frage
   - January 1924* (cited hereafter as *Die Lehren ...*). This
   was also reprinted as a special issue of *Inprecorr*, 27
   February 1924. The ECCI decision was based as much, if
   not more, on the factional controversies within the
   Russian party, as on a dispassionate analysis of the
   German events. The various Russian leaders, for their
   own purposes within the Russian party, developed vested
   interests in supporting or attacking one or another
   interpretation and faction in the German party. Thus, to
   move against the 'right' was to move against Trotsky and
   Radek. ECCYI issued a circular letter on the German
   question immediately following the ECCI session. It was
   made clear that all youth organizations were to accept
   the Comintern decisions. See *Die Lehren der deutschen
   Ereignisse und die KJI*, 50-60

for the communist fiasco in Germany was to be shifted from the Comintern and party leaders to the socialist parties. There was to be no further discussion of cooperation between communists and the 'unreliable' socialist organizations. All relations that remained between communist and socialist leaders were to be broken off. The first priority for all communists was now to be, as the left-opposition had been demanding for some time, the destruction of the socialist organizations by winning away their memberships. As far as Germany was concerned, the united-front effort was hence-forth to be concentrated in the factories and the factory councils as the left has been advocating.[16] The KJD 'Zen-trale' also turned on Brandler and the 'opportunist right deviation.' Having supported the Brandler position during 1923, the members of the 'Zentrale' now did an about-face. They threw support to the centre faction in the party: those who rejected the 'rightist' line of Brandler, and who, as did the left, believed that conditions had been ripe for revolution, but who were more subservient to Moscow than was the left.[17]

The defeat of the German communists in October/November 1923 had consequences more far-reaching than simply the fortunes of the various groups within the German party. The Comintern inquest into the failures of 1923 coincided with the death of Lenin and the beginnings of the succes-sion struggle within the Russian communist party. The Stalin/Zinoviev/Kamenev triumvirate had developed as the effective source of leadership after the onset of Lenin's illness, and it assumed full power after the death of Lenin in January 1924. A major objective of this new lead-ership was to complete the process by which the Russian model of centralization was being applied to the entire communist movement. Begun in 1919 with the CYI, this pro-cess tended to follow developments within the Russian party. As power became concentrated within the party lead-ership, and as restrictions were placed on the right of

16 *Die Lehren* ... 112
17 See both *Die Lehren der deutschen Ereignisse und die KJI*, 61, and Chitarow (Khitarov), *Der Kampf um die Massen* ... 48. The KPD 'Zentrale' had regrouped by the time of the ECCI plenum in January on the following basis: 'right' (Brandler and his supporters), 2; 'centre,' 17; and 'left' (Fischer and Maslow and supporters), 8 (*Die Lehren* ... 95).

dissent and opposition, the Russian party also took steps
to increase its control over the Comintern and the other
parties. This was accomplished by 'bolshevizing' the communist organizations.

The concept of 'bolshevization' was in effect the logical
extension and application of Lenin's concept of organization within a revolutionary party. He had insisted that to
be successful a revolutionary party had to maintain purity
of ideology and unity of purpose. For this, strict requirements for membership and tight discipline were necessary.
His ideas on this issue were a major cause of the split in
the Russian Social Democratic Labour Party between the
Bolsheviks and the Mensheviks. The Leninist ideas on party
organization were first applied to the Communist International in August 1920 at the second congress when the
Twenty-One Conditions for membership and an organizational
statute were adopted. The Twenty-One Conditions had the
objective of creating a centralized world organization on
the model of the Bolshevik party. The European communist
parties, while accepting the Twenty-One Conditions and the
program and leadership of the Bolsheviks in Russia, were
more inclined, because of tradition, toward the democractic
aspects of the concept of democratic centralism. In this
they were closer in fact to the ideas of Rosa Luxemburg.
The Russian Bolsheviks were thus faced (after August 1920)
with the task of getting the European parties that were
members of the Comintern to accept discipline. In practice
this meant the abolition of democratic procedures within
the Comintern, and then within the parties - or at least
reduction of such procedures to an empty formality. This
was accomplished in time by the Russians through utilization of the factional conflicts and through purges. In
early 1924, after the defeats in Germany and Bulgaria in
the fall of 1923, the Russian leaders saw a good opportunity to impose their definition of unity and discipline on
the Comintern and the European parties. This was after the
death of Lenin; thus the content of democratic centralism
came quickly to be shaped by Stalin as he rose to an hegemonic position within the Russian party.

The conflict that grew between the Norwegian Labour
Party and the Comintern, beginning in 1922, was one of a
number of signs of expanding Russian power that followed
subordination of the youth international in 1921. In order
to impose 'discipline,' the new Bolshevik leadership had
to end all factional controversies. There could be only

one approved line, behind which *all* communists had to unite.
The defeats of 1923 provided a plausible opportunity for
intervention in the KPD, and imposition of a new leadership
as a step in the 'bolshevizing' of the German party.[18]

There was to be a role for the KJD in these efforts. In
early March 1924, ECCYI called upon the KJD to support the
centre group in the party, and to work to overcome the
frictions and animosities that the controversies over the
October events had brought forth. All young communists were
to participate in party discussions of 'the lessons of the
October events' and the ECCI resolutions, and to see to it
that the ECCI line was followed.[19] In mid April, ECCYI appealed for support of the Comintern and its tactics, most
especially in the 'bolshevization' of the party and the
youth organization, which were both to be centralized to
an even greater degree and reorganized on the basis of factory cells.[20] ECCYI characterized as an 'extreme-left'
deviation the argument that there was no need for strong
centralization in either the party or the KJD.[21]

18 In addition to Lowenthal, 'The Bolshevization of the
   Spartakus League,' an excellent study of the German
   party is Weber, *Die Wandlung des deutschen Kommunismus*.
   For an example of the unsuccessful attempt by the
   Russians to impose their organizational concept on the
   Norwegian party (NLP) see the works by Knut Langfeldt,
   Per Maurseth, and Trond Gilberg in the bibliography.
   The January 1924 ECCI session had taken the first steps
   toward 'bolshevizing' the KPD when *its* resolution on
   the German events gave to the higher *party* bodies the
   right to confirm the election of all district party
   officers (*Die Lehren* ... 116).
19 See *Die Lehren der deutschen Ereignisse und die KJI*,
   61-9, and *J-I*, March 1924, 212-14
20 See *Die Lehren der deutschen Ereignisse und die KJI*,
   70-80. The communists were allowed to operate openly
   again in Germany from 1 March 1924 (*IJK*, April 1924).
21 The term 'extreme-left' is used here in place of the
   term 'ultra-left,' which was used by the Comintern, in
   order to avoid confusion with the anti-parliament, anti-
   trade union, partially anarcho-syndicalist 'ultra-left,'
   much of which had left the Comintern in 1920 and 1921.
   The old anti-trade union tradition persisted within the
   German party, however, as did a belief in decentralizat

As in the party, factions had arisen in the KJD over the
issues raised by the October defeat. A majority in the
'Zentrale' heeded ECCYI's appeal and supported the Comintern and the centre in the party. It was the minority, however, that more faithfully reflected the mood of the membership. This became evident at the eighth KJD congress, held
clandestinely in late April and early May (1924) in Berlin
and Leipzig and occupied almost exclusively with the party
controversy.[22] Over the objection of the ECCYI representative, the Russian, Rafael Khitarov, the delegates supported
the position of the left on tactics.[23] The left interpreted
the ECCI decision to abandon the 'united front from above'
incorrectly to mean an abandonment of the united front in
principle, and rejection of any and all contact with the
socialists at *all* levels.[24] The left wanted the communists
to leave the socialist-dominated trade unions and to join,
or form new, revolutionary trade unions. However, even
though ECCI had introduced a sharp shift in tactics (to a
'united front from below' and destruction of the socialist
parties), contact, cooperation, and joint action with the
socialists at the local level within the factories, including
within the local trade-union groups, was still to be the
basis of communist policy.

Led by Hermann Jakobs, who had just become chairman of
the KJD when the leader of the left in the party, Ruth
Fischer, forced the preceding chairman out,[25] the left un-

They emerged now in the 'left' as opposition to cooperation with the trade unions (who supported the SPD) and
to ECCI's 'bolshevization' efforts.

22 Chitarow (Khitarov), *Der Kampf um die Massen* ... 48ff.
See also *J-I*, June 1924, 312-13, and *IJK*, July 1924. As
was the case with the KPD congress in Frankfurt in April,
that of the KJD apparently had to be held clandestinely
as several leaders were still subject to arrest.

23 Chitarow (Khitarov), 50. A more recent work incorrectly
says that the 'extreme-left' was not successful in winning
the KJD to its views at the eighth congress (*Abriss der
Geschichte* ... 201-2.) There appear to have been no
rightists at the congress (see *J-I*, June 1924, 312-13).

24 See *Sozialistische Jugend-Internationale*, July 1924, 55-6

25 Interview with Alfred Kurella. See the bibliographic
sketch of Jakobs in Weber, *Die Wandlung des deutschen
Kommunismus* II, 171

veiled its majority when the congress voted 62-42 to support the tactics approved by the left-dominated KPD congress
in Frankfurt in early April.[26] Defying the Comintern further, the young leftists carried the vote to reject the
'bolshevization' theses of the Comintern (ECCI resolution
on organization of factory cells)[27] and the January 1924
ECCI resolution on the united front by 57-45 and 56-45,
respectively.[28] The opposition in the Communist Youth International to the united-front tactics, confined after the
third congress in 1922 primarily to the Italian and French
youth organizations, now emerged in Germany in the KJD.
ECCYI looked to ECCI representatives, members of the party
centre, and supporters of the Comintern line in the KJD,
as well as to the forthcoming Comintern and CYI (fourth)
congresses, to clear up and 'clarify' the differences and
bring the leftists into line.[29] Only by early 1925 had ECCY

26 *IJK*, July 1924
27 Degras, *The Communist International* ... II, 79-82
28 *J-I*, June 1924, 312-13; *IJK*, July 1924
29 Ibid. The leftists did not criticize the old 'Zentrale'
   for having followed a wrong political line, but rather
   because it had demanded the subordination of the KJD
   to the party without retaining the right to exercise
   'independent political views' (Lothar [Hermann Jakobs]
   at the fourth CYI congress, [*J-I*, July/August 1924,
   335-53]). There was nothing in Jakob's comments on the
   right to independent political views, however, to suggest a return to the pre-second CYI congress conditions.
   The youth organization was to be free to express its
   views on political questions *within* the party. According
   to democratic centralism, once the party had decided all
   members were to follow.
      Because the old 'Zentrale' had not continued to go
   along with Brandler, but had supported the new line after
   the January 1924 ECCI session, the changes in the 'Zentrale' were not as 'painful' as those in the party.
   (Chitarow [Khitarov], *Der Kampf um die Massen* ... 50-1.
   See also Schüller in *J-I*, July/August 1924, 312-13). The
   unanimous election of the new 'Zentrale' by the congress
   gave hope that the factional struggles were over in the
   KJD. Conrad Blenkle became the new chairman succeeding
   Jakobs, who had occupied the post for only a few weeks.
   Apparently Blenkle was also at this time a follower of

succeeded in re-establishing its influence over the KJD.
Comintern control over the KPD was not established until
the fall of 1925 when Fischer and Maslow were removed from
the party leadership.[30]

France
The Jeunesses communistes (JC) in France were also engaged
in an intra-party conflict (Frossard vs Souvarine). Large
segments of the congresses in 1921 (Paris) and 1922 (Montluçon) had been devoted to these party matters. There was,
indeed, a conflict of sorts within the youth organization,

---

the 'left,' but was more 'flexible' than Jakobs. The prominent figures in the former 'Zentrale' were re-elected,
among them Gäbler, Pütz, Harry Kuhn, and Erich Wiesner,
in addition to Jakobs, Liebbrand, and Auer, and Gyptner
and Hopffe after an absence. 'Others' were newly elected
(*Abriss der Geschichte* ... 302). The new leadership was
criticized later for having made in 1924 and 1925 many
of the same errors as the Fischer leadership in the party.
The freeing of the KJD from these errors, however, was
said to have been much easier than in the party (Chitarow
[Khitarov], 51). Perhaps this was due to the fact that
the KJD 'Zentrale' under Blenkle eventually moved closer
to the pro-Comintern faction in the party. In 1925, as a
member of the KPD central committee, Blenkle turned
against the Fischer leadership. He was able to maintain
his position, however, and soon became a member of the
KPD Politburo. He was elected as the youngest deputy to
the Reichstag in 1928, and shortly afterwards moved out
as chairman of the KJD (see Jahnke, '"Mein Streben galt
dem Höchsten der Menschheit!" Conrad Blenkle').

30 Comintern control was consolidated at the ninth KJD congress in Halle in October 1925. A 'great majority' of
delegates (but not with unanimity) supported Blenkle and
the new party leader, Ernst Thälmann (*Abriss der Geschichte*
... 319). A new statute (the third since 1918) was adopted,
and the following members elected to the central leadership (now called, on the Russian model, the central committee [Zentralkomitee]): Auer, Blenkle, Gyptner,
Liebbrand, Wiesner, Hans Kiefart, Willi Kress, Fritz
Reinhardt, and Werner Jurr 'among others' (ibid.). For
the central committee elected at the tenth congress in
1927 see ibid., 334.

but seldom in the same form or so drastic as in the party. In general, the youth organization was a firm supporter of the Comintern line within the communist party.

It was stated in early 1923 that the second CYI congress decisions concerning the political subordination of youth to the party 'have in the course of the past year had to experience certain changes in their execution in France.' The young French communists were skeptical of Frossard's commitment to bolshevism. They were critical of his willingness to include what they considered non-revolutionary 'opportunists' in the new communist party. Furthermore, the youth organization, while opposed to its application to France at that time, followed discipline and accepted the united front in principle. Frossard in 1922 strongly resisted the united front. For these reasons the JC felt it necessary to assert its independence from the party. Rationalizing this action with the decisions of the second CYI congress, the JC leaders argued that 'this is not an infringement of discipline, but just the opposite, because we above all lay value on the maintenance of international discipline so as to assure the fulfilment of Comintern policy.'[31] The entire organizational apparatus, as well as the JC press, was assigned to 'clarification' work inside the party.

The third JC congress at Lyon in May 1923 saw the reflection in the youth organization of the party crisis of January and February.[32] Here the JC accepted the new party leadership of Souvarine, while the few remaining Frossard supporters left to follow their leader into the socialist party (SFIO). With the issue of leadership settled, the JC was now to assume its subordinate position to the party. In several articles in *l'Avant-Garde*, both before and after the Lyons congress, the JC leadership endeavoured to make it clear to the membership that discipline now demanded abandonment once and for all of every notion of independence and autonomy. *L'Avant-Garde* stressed that the role of the JC as a 'petit parti communiste' opposed to the party proper was now terminated.[33] The JC was to provide a 'revolutionary education' to young workers and prepare them for admission

31 *J-I*, February 1923, 176-7
32 *IJK*, July 1923, 16-17. See also *l'Avant-Garde*, no. 47 (6-15 June 1923) and no. 48 (15-30 June 1923)
33 See *l'Avant-Garde*, no. 44 (6-15 April 1923)

into the party. Determination of strategy and tactics for the French working class, and the leadership of the revolutionary movement in France, was to be the job of the French communist party (PCF). Nevertheless, a certain 'malaise' remained in the relations between the JC and the PCF, even in the summer of 1923.[34]

As in most other countries, the problem of subordinating the youth organization to the party became enmeshed in the factional struggles within the Comintern and the communist party. In 1924, when the intra-Russian party conflict spilled over into the Comintern, the JC went with the anti-Trotsky forces (Treint and Girault) and turned against Trotsky's main supporter in the PCF, Souvarine.[35] The Treint-Girault leadership suffered the same fate in 1925 as the leftist leadership of the KPD (Fischer and Maslow). Jacques Doriot, leader of the JC, then played an important role in the new PCF leadership. From this time forward, the JC became completely tied to the dominant (Stalinist) faction within the party and Comintern.[36]

Scandinavia
It is in Norway and Sweden, however, that young communists were most deeply involved in party affairs. Here the youth organizations exerted an early and significant influence on important party debates. At issue was how the fledgling communist movement was to develop - not just which conception of the International would prevail, but whether or not the traditions of the Norwegian and Swedish, indeed all national labour movements could and should be maintained. The critical point in time, of course, was mid 1920 when the Bolsheviks imposed the Twenty-One Conditions. Designed to polarize the European socialist movement by splitting the centrists, the Twenty-One Conditions led to a more important result: the imposition of the Bolshevik conception of the International on all member parties. As the youth international

34 Ibid., no. 51 (8-23 August 1923)
35 *J-I*, April 1924, 234. See also Doriot at the fourth CYI congress (*J-I*, July/August 1924, 335-53, fourth session)
36 In the spring of 1929 Stalin placed the chairman of the central committee of the JC, Henri Barbé, in the position of party leader. The central committee of the JC became the leading party body under Barbé. See Borkenau, *European Communism*, 109-10

showed, the Russian party applied its own organizational norms, developed further in practice *after* the 'proletarian revolution' in Russia, to the Comintern and the other national communist parties *before* any revolution elsewhere had occurred. As this became evident, individual members and parties began to come into conflict with the Bolsheviks through the Comintern's executive committee. The issue was the right of national party leaders and bodies to apply and interpret policy on the basis of national conditions.

Even before the end of the war, young socialists in Scandinavia had been active within the socialist parties as spearheads of 'revolutionary socialism.' They found little reason for discontent. The Norwegian Labour Party (NLP) had taken an active part in the Zimmerwald movement and had been one of the first to join the Comintern. The socialist party in Sweden had split in 1917, with the left forming its own party. Supported by the young socialists, it too was one of the first to join the Comintern. Thus, party and youth found common pro-Comintern ground at the outset. What distinguished the role of the young communists in Scandinavia early on was their activity within parties that already were members of the Communist International.

The fact that there was a basic and irreconcilable difference of views between the Russian and Scandinavian party leaders remained obscure for some time. This was so because underlying the affiliation of the Norwegian Labour Party and the Swedish Left-Social Democratic Party to the Comintern were serious misunderstandings and misconceptions. For one thing, the Bolsheviks misinterpreted radicalism in many countries as a firm and dedicated commitment to violent action. In fact, this radicalism was often constrained by the general tolerance, pacifism, and commitment to democratic values of the political culture of a particular country. This was clearly the case in Scandinavia.

Furthermore, the consequences of the commitment to centralization and discipline elicited by the Twenty-One Conditions were seldom thought through either by the members, or their leaders. This was true everywhere, and not just in Scandinavia. Even where serious debates took place over the Twenty-One Conditions, many of those who pressed most vociferously for their unconditional acceptance had an image of a 'centralized' world movement far different from that which was ultimately to emerge. Most apparently never understood that Lenin and the Russian Bolsheviks were committing themselves to a movement in which decision making would be totally and strictly dictated and controlled.[37] This has been seen already in the context of efforts to preserve the independence of the communist youth movement.

By the spring of 1921, however, it appeared that both Scandinavian parties had accepted the Twenty-One Conditions and were members in good standing of the Comintern. At its congress in March, the Norwegian Labour Party affirmed that

37 Some imply that Lenin did not wish to apply the Russian model directly or in all respects to the other communist parties. See, for example, Carr, *The Bolshevik Revolution, 1917-1923* III, 445, 448. What Lenin might have advocated or approved in the way of deviations from the heavily centralized model that he himself had created remains, of course, only speculation. Rejection of item-by-item replication of Russian experience, however, need not have been inconsistent with insistence upon strict centralization and Russian control. Institutional, terminological, and procedural variations on the same theme were, and still are, quite possible. Lenin was committed to assuring a capability for action for the communist parties, and increasingly committed to Russian party control over the determination of strategy and tactics. In his active lifetime, on all occasions when a conflict arose between free discussion and dissent, and unity of purpose or the power of the party, Lenin supported centralization to ensure the latter. He did so in spite of his attempts to make the concept of democratic centralism a synthesis of free discussion and dedicated commitment to unified action (see Meyer, *Leninism*, chapter 5). The question of conscious intent is not of the greatest importance. What is important is what Lenin in fact *did*, and the consequences. And what he did was to approve the strengthening of discipline within the Russian party and the Comintern. With the introduction of NEP at home and in foreign policy in 1921, Lenin was now thinking in terms of preservation of the new Bolshevik regime above all else. Given his commitments and priorities, it was inevitable that he would insist upon strict centralization. From the point of view of the Bolsheviks, this made sense. This developing centralization still left room for acceptance, in principle, of certain national variations on the basic theme of Russian control.

it 'accepts, as a section of the Communist International, the directives, decisions, and conditions as adopted by the International's second congress.'[38] A small minority had left shortly before to form a social democratic party. The Swedish Left-Social Democratic Party accepted the second congress decisions at its congress in May, leading to a more serious split in the party.[39] Having left the social democrats in 1917, the Swedish party was presumably a united revolutionary party. It was divided, however, over the militancy of its revolutionary action and the need for centralization and discipline within the party. The Twenty-One Conditions brought these differences to a head. A considerable minority was expelled for refusing to accept the conditions unconditionally. It was soon to become evident, however, that even those who voted for acceptance did not understand the implications of their action.

Although formally accepting the Twenty-One Conditions, the majority in the Norwegian Labour Party in fact had such serious reservations as to make continued membership impossible. These reservations had been expressed quite frankly at the second Comintern congress. They were the focus of the wide debate before the party congress in March 1921. A resolution accepting the decisions of the Comintern congress not only omitted the word 'unconditional,' but included rather specific interpretations of what the party understood its obligations to be. The democratic aspects of democratic centralism were given precedence over centralism; the party hedged on its commitment to withdraw from the Amsterdam trade-union international; it rejected, in effect the requirement for creation of an illegal apparatus, although it was not opposed in principle; and, most important the party refused to change its form of organization from

38 Langfeldt, *Moskva-tesene i norsk politikk*, 134, provides an excellent analysis of the debate in Norway over the Twenty-One Conditions. He describes the various tendencies within the Norwegian Labour Party in 1920, and argues that the party did not, in fact, accept the full spirit of the Twenty-One Conditions. The following discussion of Norwegian developments relies heavily on Langfeldt and Sogstad, *Ungdoms Fanevakt*.

39 For Swedish developments see Sparring, *Från Höglund* ... and a brief discussion by Sparring in Upton, *Communism in Scandinavia and Finland*.

collective to individual membership as required by the
Twenty-One Conditions.

The NLP took this position with what it thought was the
approval of the Comintern. In October 1920, a Norwegian
delegation had met in Germany with Zinoviev during and after
the congress of the USPD in Halle. The Norwegians returned
home believing Zinoviev had acquiesced in their qualified
acceptance of the Twenty-One Conditions. Addressing the
German Independents, Zinoviev is reported to have stated
that the Twenty-One Conditions were not a catechism, that
the International would be tolerant in their application,
and that he wished to hear from those who opposed them about
which points they considered unacceptable and what they
would propose instead.[40] That this accommodating attitude
was more apparent than real did not become clear to the
Norwegians until later.

What was at first taken to be Comintern acceptance of
Norwegian special conditions was soon to be seen otherwise
by the changes introduced into the structure of the Comintern, beginning with the third congress in 1921.[41] The statutes for the Comintern adopted at the second congress
(1920) had made the annual world congress the sovereign
body, with the executive committee to govern in the interim.
At this time, those national parties allocated seats on
ECCI elected their own representatives. All member parties
anticipated free debate and the taking of decisions on the
basis of consideration for the problems and views of all
members. The prestige of the Russian party, of course, led
all to accord a certain pre-eminence to the Russians, which
was also reflected in the location of the executive committee in Moscow and the larger representation on it for the
Russians. It was not the intention of the member parties,
however, to grant to ECCI the right to issue binding orders
on any subject with which it saw fit to concern itself,
certainly not to the point of removing or installing leaders
of member parties.

40 See Langfeldt, *Moskva-tesene i norsk politikk*, 56, where
   Social-Demokraten, 16 October 1920, is cited as the
   source for Zinoviev's statements.
41 See Degras, *The Communist International* ... passim, for
   changes in the statutory relationships between the Comintern executive bodies and the individual communist parties.

At the third congress, the delegates unanimously accepted
an ECCI-sponsored resolution on 'The Organizational Structure of the Communist Parties, the Methods and Content of
Their Work,' and a resolution on 'The Organization of the
Communist International.'[42] Both of these served to strength
discipline and intensify centralization within the movement. The central institutions of the national parties were
to have greater authority over members and the party
press. Paving the way for future trouble was the introduction of the Russian principle of 'dual subordination,'
whereby the executive organs of national parties were to
be responsible not only to national party congresses, but
also to ECCI. ECCI was enlarged and diluted, thus increasing
the importance of the 'inner bureau,' or presidium. ECCI
was also given the right (although not unanimously) to ap-
point any member of a national party to the 'inner bureau,'
thus by-passing (if necessary) the elected representative.
In early 1922, the practice of convening 'enlarged sessions'
of ECCI was instituted, with the result that they, and the
ECCI presidium, rather than the broader and more representative world congress, became the crucial Comintern organs.

The really serious changes came at the fourth congress in
December 1922. The resolution 'On the Reorganization of ECC
abolished the principle of representation.[43] Members were
not to be appointed by national communist parties as their
representatives; rather, the world congress was to elect
them. Thus, a member of a party could be elected to ECCI,
and participate in the issuing of directives binding on his
party, over the objections of that party or its leadership.
The 'inner bureau,' or presidium, was institutionalized as
a reflection of the Russian Politburo, and an organizationa
bureau and a secretariat were established on the Russian
model. There were several other innovations that brought
forth resistance from elements in the national parties. The
organizational bureau was to supervise the methods of appointment to important offices in the national parties.[44]
It was also to control all illegal work, giving it in principle effective control over the entire policy of those
communist parties that worked illegally. The party congress

42 Ibid., I, 256-73
43 Ibid., 436-42
44 One could not resign from his post without ECCI approval
   for example.

were to be held after and not before world congresses.
Thus, delegates could not arrive for the latter with binding
mandates. The party congresses would only be occasions for
the explanation and ratification of Comintern policy.

These developments helped to dispel any illusions remaining
within the Norwegian and Swedish parties that membership in
the Comintern could be maintained on acceptable terms.
Serious conflicts broke out in 1922 when the Comintern
leadership endeavoured to assure uniform application and
implementation of central policy directives. As these conflicts developed, the affairs of the youth organizations
became even more closely tied to party developments.

It was the issue of how the united-front policy was to
be carried out in Norway that brought the false nature of
NLP membership in the Comintern into the open. The chairman of the NLP parliamentary group and firm supporter of
the Comintern, Olav Scheflo, advocated cooperation with the
bourgeois left and the splinter Social Democratic Labour
Party so as to carry out social reforms. The majority within
the party central committee was opposed to this. Led by
Martin Tranmael, the central committee wanted to pursue a
united front from below, recruiting the masses on an individual basis directly for the NLP. In this Tranmael was
only following what had been NLP policy since 1918: commitment to 'revolutionary socialism,' the formation of one
mass labour party, and cooperation only with working-class
organizations. The youth organization and the opposition
in the trade unions supported Tranmael.

ECCI intervened in June 1922 with a formal declaration
on the 'Norwegian question.'[45] The NLP was called upon to
recognize the right of the Comintern to intervene in the
inner affairs of the member parties. It was also told to
implement the third Comintern congress and subsequent ECCI
decisions as they applied to the NLP. The important question
within the NLP was no longer the united-front policy, but
rather the propriety of ECCI intervention. Was ECCI in a
position to decide policy in Norwegian conditions? In
October ECCI requested the Norwegians to confirm their
willingness to obey a more specific list of instructions
concerning NLP affairs.[46] The fourth Comintern congress in

45 *Kommunisticheskii Internatsional v Dokumentakh, 1919-
1932*, 289-92
46 *Inprekorr*, 31 October 1922, 1444-6

December discussed the 'Norwegian question' and adopted a
resolution over the opposition of the Norwegian delegates.⁴
The congress confirmed the instructions to the NLP issued
by ECCI in June. As a result, the majority in the NLP central committee recommended that the party not remain a
member of the Communist International. This intensified the
debate within the party, which in turn led to the formation
of organized factions, one of which was the group of radical
intellectuals in Mot Dag.

The Norwegian youth organization (Norges Kommunistiske
Ungdomsforbund-NKU) was by now subordinated formally to the
NLP. On questions of strategy and tactics it was close to
Tranmael and the central committee majority. As a member
of the youth international, however, it was also subordinated to the Comintern. With these two at odds, the youth
organization had to face the question of whose views on
organizational procedures it was to accept. The majority
in the NKU central committee, led by Aksel Zachariassen and
Einar Gerhardsen, were firm autonomists; that is, within
the context of general Comintern guidelines, determined
democratically with due regard for the particularities of
each country, the Labour Party leadership should decide
specific communist policy in Norway. Nevertheless, Zachariassen, as chairman, was afraid that the youth organization would be split irreparably if it were to take a clear
stand. The majority position after the June intervention
by ECCI was thus to have the youth organization temporize
and remain outside the fray, while the party and ECCI work
out their differences.⁴⁸ This did not satisfy the pro-
Comintern minority, which wanted the NKU to accept immediately and unconditionally the ECCI declaration and all that
it implied.

The third CYI congress in December 1922 did nothing to
ease Zachariassen's predicament. On the contrary, it only
demonstrated to the Norwegians that the CYI leadership, now
under Russian control, was a firm follower of ECCI directions. In a letter to the Norwegian youth organization,

47 *Protokoll des Vierten Kongresses der Kommunistischen
Internationale* ... 955-6
48 The central leadership was divided into a majority
(Zachariassen, Gerhardsen, Olav Vegheim, Rolf Hofmo,
Edvard Sjølander, and Arnold Hazeland) and a minority
(Ingvald Larsen and Ole Colbjørnsen).

apparently sent some time after the central committee had
decided to avoid involvement in the conflict, ECCYI had
demanded participation of the NKU in the party debates in
support of the Comintern executive committee. It in effect
issued orders to the Norwegian central committee without
even first consulting it. At the CYI congress, Zachariassen
criticized this intervention of ECCYI in Norwegian affairs
as a serious mistake.[49] The Russian spokesman for ECCYI,
however, contended that it was the duty of every youth organization to intervene when necessary in party affairs
in support of ECCI directives.[50] At the close of the congress, during the voting on various resolutions, Zachariassen
followed the lead of the party delegation at the Comintern
congress. He indicated that while the Norwegians did not
approve of the intervention of ECCYI in the 'Norwegian
question,' they approved the rest of the ECCYI report and
thus would vote for the resolution approving the report
'out of duty' (nach Abgabe).[51]

Zachariassen returned to Norway on 21 December 1922, the
day the NLP central committee under Tranmael issued its
statement concerning termination of membership in the Comintern. Having left Moscow under the impression that the
'Norwegian question' had been smoothed out at the Comintern
congress, he returned to find that this was not so.[52] He,
like all others, soon had to make a decision: for the Comintern, or for Norwegian autonomy. While some in the central
committee of the youth organization supported the party declaration, and one, Ingvald Larsen, was against it and for
the Comintern, the majority was still trying to reconcile
NLP unity, NLP autonomy, centralization, and membership in
the Comintern. A hope that the Comintern would somehow
change and relax its demands persisted. These hopes were
dashed by the intransigence of ECCI.

When the NLP congress met at the end of February 1923,
the stage was set for a definitive resolution of the issue.
A large ECCI delegation made its appearance, headed by
Bukharin. The choice of Bukharin was deliberate: he had
spent some time in Norway during the war and had developed

49 *Bericht vom 3. Weltkongress der Kommunistischen
   Jugendinternationale*, 34
50 Ibid., 41-2, 49
51 Ibid., 229
52 Interview with Aksel Zachariassen

good relations with many NLP leaders. His presence notwithstanding, the delegates voted by a slim majority (94-92)
for less guidance and direction from above, and more initiative and freedom for the individual members of working-
class organizations. The majority asserted the right of
members to decide basic policy matters themselves, while
holding leaders under permanent control. This, of course,
ran completely counter to the definition of democratic
centralism now being imposed on the Comintern. The attitudes that lay behind the 'Kristiania proposal' supported
by the majority have been characterized as 'an unconsciou
Luxemburgism.'[53] The congress then elected a new leadershi
strongly opposed to the Comintern demands. The initiative
now passed to the Comintern: to accept or reject continued
NLP membership on these terms.

The NKU congress met in early March, immediately after
the party congress, but had a totally different outcome.[54]
The composition of the congress, arranged in advance by th
pro-Comintern forces, assured a decision favourable to the
Comintern. The desire for action and a need to 'conquer th
party' dominated the proceedings. After long and heated de
bate, the delegates voted 96-33 for the position of Bukhar
The leader of the pro-Comintern forces in the NKU was Pede
Furubotn, who argued very persuasively for democratic centralism and the creation of an organization capable of cor
batting the capitalist enemy. Although such an appeal had
found a less receptive audience among communists over the
previous two years, the urge to action, and a belief in
strength through disciplined unity, persisted for much
longer in the youth movement than in the parties.

Lazar Shatskin, representing ECCYI, insisted that the
NKU not only had a right, but a duty, to participate in
the discussions of party affairs, despite the formal subordination of the organization to the party and its swing
toward non-political tasks. The crucial point was the
party's attitude towards the Comintern. When a party was
at odds with the Comintern, said Shatskin, the obligation
of the youth organization was no longer to the party but
to the Comintern. This view had been virtually unquestion

53 Christophersen, '"Mot Dag" ...' 140. Little was known
   about the ideas of Rosa Luxemburg in Norway (interview
   with Einar Gerhardsen and Peder Furubotn).
54 *IJK*, March 1923, and *J-I*, April 1923, 242

by the young communists in the years 1919-1921, when communist parties were being formed, because they believed
the Comintern to be 'more revolutionary' than many of the
new parties. Now, however, the issue was no longer who was
most revolutionary, but rather what form a 'centralized
world party' was to take. To support the Comintern over and
against their national communist party was, for many young
communists, to give up a fundamental and necessary right.
Within the broad limits of Comintern policies, Norwegian
affairs were to be decided by Norwegian communists on the
basis of Norwegian conditions.

Belief in the need for unity and discipline and support
for Soviet Russian leadership were, however, still strong
in the youth organization. The congress majority thus
stated that it 'not only declares itself loyal to, but
completely in agreement with, the decisions made by the
third and fourth [CYI and Comintern] world congresses.'[55]
While both majority and minority at the congress were represented in the new central leadership, the pro-Comintern
minority in the old leadership now took control. Furubotn
was elected chairman to replace Zachariassen, and a strong
pro-Comintern supporter, Arvid Hansen, became editor of
Klassekampen. Furubotn was then thirty-six; the new chairman of the NLP was only twenty-nine.

With NLP membership in the Comintern still not settled,
the NKU had a major role to play. Under the new leadership,
the youth organization in essence became a pro-Comintern
party competing with the NLP. In June 1923 the 'Norwegian
question' was discussed once again in an enlarged session
of ECCI, with representatives of the majority and the minority in both the NLP and NKU present. The meeting condemned
the majority in the NLP for refusing to accept the Comintern
viewpoint. In its statement, ECCI gave special attention
to the youth organization and its role in support of the
Comintern.[56]

55 Sogstad, *Ungdoms Fanevakt*, 327
56 The ECCI resolution on the Norwegian question contained
    the following paragraph: 'With respect to the youth or-
    ganization, it is subject to the political leadership
    of the central committee of the party, preserving its
    independence in organizational matters. It goes without
    saying that young communists have not only the right, but
    the duty to exhibit a zealous concern with all vital

The NKU leadership now took the lead in arguing the Comintern case within the Norwegian labour movement.[57] A continuous stream of articles appeared in *Klassekampen* supporting the Comintern call for centralization. Persistent efforts to oust the NLP party leadership were, however, firmly repelled. An extraordinary congress of the NLP in November was the scene of the final break. The congress minority soon formed itself into the Norwegian Communist Party, with Furubotn as secretary-general, and was admitted to the Comintern as its Norwegian member.

The central leadership of the NKU proceeded to commit the organization to the Comintern and the new party. All members who remained in the NLP were to be excluded.[58] 'There is no room in the Norwegian communist youth organization for members or organizations supporting in any shape or form the wing [in the NLP] that has broken with the International or that fights the Norwegian Communist Party, the Comintern, or the Communist Youth International.'[59] The victory of the pro-Comintern forces at the NKU congress in March had not, however, reflected the views of the membership at large. A bitter struggle ensued within local groups

questions of the party and the Comintern; to discuss and take positions on these questions corresponding to their own opinions. The executive committee requests the leadership of the Norwegian party to devote attention to the youth organization, and demands, for the education of the members of the youth organization, a significant degree of spiritual (dukhovoi) freedom for them' (*Rasshirennyi plenum* ... 307).

57 For a statement of the ECCYI view of affairs in Norway, and a criticism of the Comintern from the perspective of Mot Dag see *J-I*, September 1923, 5.

58 *J-I*, December 1923/January 1924, 110-11

59 Sogstad, *Ungdoms Fanevakt*, 340

60 There was a serious dispute over possession of the admiistrative offices in Oslo (ibid., 352). ECCYI claimed that of 206 local groups before the split, 146 remained with the Comintern, 54 went to the new youth organization associated with the Norwegian Labour Party, and 3 were neutral (leaving three unaccounted for). Further claims were for 158 groups with 6350 members on 1 Janua 1924; 172 groups with 7000 members on 15 January 1924 (*J-I*, April 1924, 247-8).

Three youth organizations soon emerged, corresponding and subordinate to the three parties of the left: Venstrekommunistiske Ungdomsforbund (Left-Communist Youth Organization) associated with the NLP; Norges kommunistiske Ungdomsforbund (Communist Youth Organization of Norway) tied to the Norwegian Communist party; and the small Norges socialdemokratiske Ungdomsforbund (Social Democratic Youth Organization of Norway) connected with the small social democratic party in Norway.[61] The splitting of the socialist and labour movement initiated by the Twenty-One Conditions in 1920 now had been completed. The result, however, was that the Comintern and the Communist Youth International lost the mass organizations that had been their Norwegian members. The new loyal members in Norway quickly became small sectarian groups. In September 1924 the NKU accepted the fifth Comintern/fourth CYI congress decisions on 'bolshevization,' and became a loyal follower of ECCYI and the Comintern.[62]

The year 1923 also was one of crisis for Comintern supporters in Sweden. As with the Norwegian Labour Party, the Swedish Left Social Democratic Party, led by the long-time revolutionary socialist leader, Zeth Höglund, was concerned about the decisions of the fourth Comintern congress. The Swedish youth organization, however, was unanimous in support of the Comintern positions. Höglund attacked the youth organization in the party press, and soundly condemned ECCYI and its functionaries for an undesirable and unwarranted interference in Scandinavian party affairs.[63] He called the ECCI resolution of the Norwegian question an

61 The first and the last were to join in 1927 to form a new youth organization (Arbeidernes Ungdomsfylking) which has continued to the present day in association with the Norwegian Labour Party.

62 *Inprecorr*, 24 October 1924, 1846. Because of the radical turn in the communist youth movement, especially approval of the revolutionary anti-militarism resolution of the CYI in February 1924 (*IJK*, March 1924), the Norwegian government attempted to arrest the new central committee. All but the secretary, Henry Kristiansen, however, avoided arrest (*IJK*, April 1924). Kristiansen had been elected secretary and editor of *Klassekampen* in February, with Torbjørn Dahl as chairman.

63 See *J-I*, September 1923, 4-5

282 Revolutionary vanguard

incentive for the Norwegian youth organization 'to create
still more confusion' in the Norwegian communist movement,
a step he saw already under way in Sweden. In late 1924,
however, the pro-Comintern forces succeeded, with the help
of the youth organization, in expelling Höglund from the
party.[64] With this step, however, the party lost about one
third of its members. Fresh strength was added by having
the youth organization yield up 'thousands of its best comrades.'[65] The young communists became close followers of
the Comintern line, but at the same time lost much ground
to the social democrats in the struggle for influence over
young Swedish workers.

'Bolshevization' of the communist youth movement

The process of imposing the Russian definition of communis
on the entire communist movement, begun in 1919 with the
youth international, culminated at the fifth Comintern con
gress in July 1924. Through the Comintern, the Russian par
took steps openly and directly to assure that each communi
party became a 'genuine' communist party. That is, a party
was to be acknowledged as a communist party only to the ex
tent that it was formed in the image of the Russian party
on the basis of 'Bolshevik experience.' The basic features
of a genuine Bolshevik party were set forth in general ter
at the fifth congress.[66] However, it remained for ECCI to
elaborate the more specific characteristics in the spring
of 1925. Although a 'mechanical transfer' of Russian experience to other countries was to be avoided, the essence
of 'bolshevization' was the study and application in practice of Russian party experience. The sections of the
Comintern could become, 'in the present epoch ... genuine
communist parties only if they rally under the banner of
Leninism.'[67]
    ECCI asserted that Leninism had 'enriched the general
theory of Marxism' by mastering several problems. Among
other successes, the Russian party had shown under what

64 *J-I*, October 1924, 59
65 *J-I*, September 1924, 2. Moving into the party were Hugo
   Sillen and Nils Flyg, the leaders of the youth organization (*IJK*, June 1924).
66 Degras, *The Communist International* ... II, 154
67 Ibid., 190

conditions, and through what forms, the dictatorship of the proletariat was to be realized. Thus Russian experience provided answers to the questions of how and when all communist parties would seek power, and how they would organize their power once it was attained. Furthermore, events in Russia had demonstrated *the* proper role for a revolutionary, communist party in the revolutionary process. All communist parties would thus inevitably have to follow Russian party organizational norms and forms. Finally, it was asserted that the Russian party had shown how 'the struggle against right-wing social democratic tendencies and also against left deviations in the communist movement' could be pursued successfully. The Russian position on all doctrinal and ideological issues was to be the only sanctioned position. 'Bolshevization' was the full flowering of Lenin's call (in *'Left-Wing' Communism: An Infantile Disorder*) for a universalizing of Russian solutions to problems of the revolutionary transfer of power. Authoritarian control of the entire movement was to rest on the legitimacy of Lenin's ideas, as interpreted by the Russian party leaders, and Russian party experience.

The degree to which the CYI and its member organizations had been brought under Comintern control was evident at the fourth CYI congress. Meeting in Moscow immediately after the fifth Comintern congress, it adapted the Comintern decisions on 'bolshevizaton' to the youth movement.[68] Most of the old figures were missing. Those functionaries who had earlier been active in efforts to maintain the independence of the youth movement had either bowed completely to Moscow, or been shunted aside. Under new leaders such as Richard Schüller, Richard Gyptner, Vuja Vujovitch, and the various Russian Komsomol representatives, the CYI had for all practical purposes become just another part of the Comintern apparatus.[69] The delegates adopted a resolution

68 For the fourth CYI congress see *J-I*, July/August 1924, 333-53. At the Comintern congress, a German member of ECCYI, Otto Unger, reported on the youth movement (*Inprecorr* 4, no. 55 [5 August 1945] and theses were adopted on 'the tasks of the youth' (ibid., 687).
69 The third CYI congress in December 1922 had expanded ECCYI from nine (not counting Münzenberg and Flieg, who never participated) to eighteen: Shatskin, Schüller, Kurella, Doriot (France), Vujovitch, Bamatter (Switzerland),

stressing the necessity of spreading the principles of
Leninism among the younger generation.[70] The history of

Vretling (Sweden), Unger and Gyptner (Germany), Tseitlir
Tarchanov, and Petrovsky (Russia), Cassita (Italy),
Michalec (Czechoslovakia), Jackson (America), Paasonen
(Finland), Fucak (the Balkans), and Yang Ta-lai (China)
with Young (England), Schulz (Germany), David (France),
Vegheim (Norway), and Melnais (Latvia) as candidate
members.
  At the fourth congress, a new and enlarged ECCYI of
twenty-two members and six candidates was elected:
Shatskin, Schüller, Vujovitch, Gyptner, Berti, Hessen,
Chaplin, Vartanyan, Katalynov, Muratbaev, L.I. Mil'chak
Blenkle, Jakobs, Michalec, Paasonen, Lambrev, Williamse;
Doriot, Chasseigne, Gorkic, Wilde, Vegheim, Vretling,
Hrschel, and two from the Far East (leaving two unaccounted for). The new ECCYI met immediately after the
congress to discuss the organization of its work (*J-I*,
July/August 1924, 361). A secretariat of three was
created, along with standing commissions to supervise
the work of the various youth organizations (German-
speaking areas, Latin countries, Scandinavian, the
Balkans, the Orient, the border countries and Poland,
and the Anglo-Saxon countries). Several functional departments were also created (organization, economic/
trade-union work, anti-militarism, press, education,
rural areas, children, sports, the opponents). Of the
twenty-eight members and candidates of ECCYI, seventeen
were to work in Moscow, four were to act as representatives to the national youth organizations upon demand,
and seven were to work in their own youth organizations
ECCYI was to meet at least once a week, with plenary
sessions (of all members) as often as the political
situation demanded. The Russian Komsomol was to be continuously represented through one of its secretaries.
ECCYI was expanded once again at the fifth CYI congress
in 1928 to an unwieldy 55 full and 32 candidate member:
70 *Draft Program of the Young Communist International* contains the 'Resolution on Propagandizing Leninism.' See
also *J-I*, July/August 1924, 335-53, thirteenth session.
Included were 'the lessons of the union between theory
and practice' provided by Lenin, as well as Lenin's
ideas on imperialism, the national question, the coloni

the 'struggle of Lenin against opportunism and leftist deviations' was to be an important part of the theoretical
studies of the leaders and functionaries of the youth organizations. The works of Stalin, Safarov, Adoratsky, and
Bukharin were to be used as examples of Leninist thought,
and special, cheap editions of Lenin's works were to be
published for young readers.[71]

An essential aspect of 'bolshevization' was the restructuring of all communist organizations on the basis of factory cells. The CYI congress demonstrated great reluctance
to accept the need for converting the youth organizations
into mass organizations based on this principle. Many young
communists still perceived communist organizations as elite
institutions of professional revolutionaries whose ideological purity had to be preserved from the diluting effect
of mass membership. Stubborn resistance to the factory cell
remained in the youth organizations. Some felt that the
economic structure of their country made it inappropriate
to place the full weight of the work of the youth organization into the factory; some believed that to do so would
harm the youth organization by driving members away without
corresponding gains from the factories; and some feared
the reorganization would only strengthen the growing bureaucratization and Russian dominance of the communist movement.

Most youth organizations were only taking the first steps
toward building factory cells. As the bulk of the members
of communist organizations continued to come from *outside*
the large factories, it became impossible to change completely to the factory cell as the basic organizational unit.
Despite a major effort, the communists found it hard to
increase their strength in the factories. Even where this

----

question, the State and the dictatorship of the prole-
rariat and Soviet power, the role of tactics and strategy, and the basis of the organization of the party.
Some indication of what was to be considered the substance of Leninism was seen in two articles by Stalin
('Fundamentals of Leninism,' *J-I*, May 1924, 263-5, and
July/August 1924, 331-3), his first contribution to
Jugend-Internationale.
71 See *Draft Program of the Young Communist International*,
and Chitarow (Khitarov), *Der Kampf um die Massen* ...
188

could be done, local communists were under severe pressure from the state, the employers, and social democratic trade-union leaders.[72]

The 'Bolshevization' campaign served also intra-Russian party purposes. The triumvirate (Stalin/Zinoviev/Kamenev) wished both to have the complete support of the European communist parties against its opponents (Trotsky and his allies), and to take away from its opponents all sources of support within the European parties. The Comintern was to be used to support the triumvirate. It was not to be a source of strength from which its opponents could work to unseat it, nor was it to be an outside arbiter. Writing in the Comintern journal, *International Press Correspondence*, in November 1924, Zinoviev praised the young communists for standing by the Comintern at the CYI congress in the struggle to 'bolshevize' the parties.[73] According to Zinoviev, a member of the ruling triumvirate, those 'old Bolsheviks' who had 'freed themselves of the social democratic ideology only during or after the war' (Trotsky) tried at the fifth Comintern congress to turn the youth against those 'old Bolsheviks,' the earliest supporters of Lenin, who had been struggling since 1914 for the ideas of the Comintern. As part of the anti-Trotsky campaign, the Russian triumvirate portrayed him as not being a true Bolshevik. Thus, the remedy for ridding all communist organizations of deviants was 'bolshevization': separate those adhering to 'true Bolshevik' principles from those who did not.[74]

72 See Borkenau, *World Communism*, 358–66
73 *Inprecorr* 4, no. 80 (20 November 1924): 2004
74 In 1923 and 1924 Trotsky served in Russia as a source of inspiration to the students in the technical institutes and the universities in their protest against the bureaucratizing of the party, as well as against party economic policy (Carr, *The Interregnum, 1923–1924*, 325–328). There was also support for Trotsky within the international communist youth movement at this time. Two important members of ECCYI, Vujovitch and the Czech Michalec, were expelled at an expanded session in November/December 1926 as Trotskyists (Chitarow [Khitarov], *Der Kampf um die Massen* ... 95). Vujovitch was in fact a close follower of Zinoviev (interview with Giuseppe Berti). The degree of support for Trotsky within the

After the fourth congress, the leadership of the Communist Youth International worked to assure that member organizations undertook the new tasks of 'bolshevization' as set by the Comintern: deepening educational work 'in the spirit of Leninism' by indoctrination in Leninist principles of revolution and party organization, further developing the youth organizations into mass organizations, and continuing 'the struggle against reaction and the danger of war.' These goals were all designed to keep the young communists primarily occupied with non-political activities, such as propaganda, education, and protection of economic interests. The youth organizations were to become involved in party affairs only when ECCYI, following ECCI directives, decided it was useful to have them intervene. When the young communists had subordinated themselves to the parties and the Comintern in 1921, they had retained a recognized right and duty to take their own positions on political issues and party affairs. With 'bolshevization,' this last remnant of independence was to be eliminated. The only position of the youth movement was to be that of the Comintern.

After the second CYI congress, the communist youth organizations had ceased to be independent political organizations united by a belief in the imminence of revolution. They became, instead, recruiting grounds for the parties, instruments for the dissemination of party and Comintern positions among young people, and revolutionary training schools. They were no longer organizations formed spontaneously and expressing the attitudes of the most politically active young workers. Instead, they became instruments of adult tutelage and appendages to the communist parties. In this role they displayed little similarity to traditional youth movements. Support for the Soviet Union, while awaiting more favourable revolutionary conditions, became their major political objective. In the meanwhile, those with

---

communist youth movement is difficult to ascertain, but it appears (despite an official attitude denying the importance of Trotsky's influence) to have been considerable (see ibid., 96-8, for acknowledgement that the youth organizations had to devote most of their attention in 1926 and 1927 to the struggle against Trotskyism). A more revealing study of this issue would be very useful, but the difficulty in finding source material is enormous.

the abilities and attributes for more responsible tasks
and eventual elevation to the party were sifted from the
parade of members passing through the ranks. Cadres were
selected and trained in preparation for future revolutionary activity. The best the communists could do outwardly
was to maintain a persistent, if not always heavy, pressure
from the extreme left on other political youth organization
Communist ideas and programs, at least the Comintern variet
were propagated in a manner calculated to draw the attentic
of their opponents, forcing them to respond and thus to tak
the communists seriously. However, all these changes in the
nature of the communist youth organizations had been far
from foreseen in 1919.

After its fourth congress in 1924, the Communist Youth
International became not only politically but also organizationally a firmly subordinated part of the Comintern
complex.[75] Shatskin had been elected to ECCI as the CYI
representative at the second Comintern congress in 1920,
Münzenberg and Lekai at the third congress in 1921, and
Schüller and Shatskin at the fourth congress in 1922.[76]
After the fifth Comintern congress in 1924 ECCYI had three
voting representatives in ECCI, including one on the presidium for most of the time and one in the organization
bureau.[77] ECCYI also had representation in the 'common-

75 See the discussion on the organizational development of
the CYI after the third congress in *From the 3rd to the
4th: A Report on the Activities of the Young Communist
International* ... 37-45. See also the draft of a new
statute for the CYI in *J-I*, October 1924, 53-4.
76 Degras, *The Communist International* ... I, 453-5.
Schüller and Shatskin were added to ECCI after the
third Comintern congress as representatives of the
actual leadership of the CYI.
77 *J-I*, September 1924, 29. At times Shatskin, Hessen,
Vujovitch, and Schüller are mentioned as members of ECC
Vujovitch was a member of ECCI (as well as ECCYI), but
was not specifically identified as a CYI representative
Besso Lominadze was co-opted into ECCYI in April 1925
and served until 1927. Completely new leaders moved int
the CYI after 1928 and the end of the anti-Trotsky campaign. The Russians Rafail Khitarov and Vasilii Tchemo-
danov, as well as Michel Wolf and the Frenchman, Raymon
Guyot, served for varying periods up to World War II as
CYI secretaries.

action committee' set up by the Comintern and the Profintern, in the Krestintern Council, in the Red Sports International, and in the International Red Help.[78] The congresses of the CYI became irregular, always following those
of the Comintern, while ECCYI plenums also always were held
after those of ECCI. Close contact and cooperation existed
between all ECCYI departments (both geographical and functional) and their corresponding bodies in ECCI. The Russian
Komsomol also exercised its decisive influence in international communist youth affairs: from the second CYI congress on, there was always at least one Komsomol representative in the inner leadership of the CYI and one as a CYI
representative in ECCI. Moreover, the heads of Komsomol
functional departments collaborated with the departments
and commissions of ECCYI.

  This political and organizational subordination of the
Communist Youth International was a major contributing
factor to its failure, despite very impressive initial
successes, to win the 'struggle for supremacy' in which
it had been engaged since 1919. It had not only failed to
win a majority of young workers, but the year 1923 had
seen the fusion of the right-socialist and centrist youth

78 For the Profintern (Red International of Labour Unions)
   see Lorwin, *Labor and Internationalism*; for the Krestintern (Red Peasant International) see Jackson, *Comintern
   and Peasant in East Europe, 1919-1930*; for International
   Red Aid (MOPR) see Münzenberg, *Solidarität, zehn Jahre
   Internationale Arbeiterhilfe, 1921-1931*.
   The CYI acknowledged its losses at the fourth congress
   in 1924. The Russian Komsomol, with 30 per cent more members than the Russian party, and 40 per cent of all young
   workers in the country, was held up as a model. ECCYI
   complained that the membership of the strongest youth
   organization outside Russia was only 10-15 per cent of
   its party's membership, and 'only a very small part' of
   the young workers in this country were in the communist
   youth organization. The only exceptions were Sweden
   (where the youth organization was stronger than the
   party) and Italy (where the membership of the youth organization was 30 per cent of the party's). See 'Resolution on the Report of ECCYI' at the fourth CYI congress
   in *Resolutions adopted at the 4th congress of the Young
   Communist International*, and Chitarow (Khitarov), *Der
   Kampf um die Massen* ... 178

internationals into a united socialist youth international strongly opposed to the communists. The Communist Youth International was never able to hinder the growth of the socialists, and it soon ceased to be a serious competitor for influence among the mass of young workers. Even more than the parties, the communist youth organizations declined during the balance of the 1920s and early 1930s, both in numbers and significance. It is true that to some extent this was the result of the harassment, often persecution, of the communist youth movements, but the basic cause remained the inability, and perhaps the unwillingness, of the communist youth organizations to reflect adequately the desires of young workers. The strength of the communist youth movement in the period 1918-1921, with a brief resurgence in 1923 and 1924, had been the result of a radical mood and economic hardships. Then, with improvements in material conditions, communist youth organizations, as all other communist organizations, rapidly lost influence. Their revolutionary strategies and Leninist organizational norms found little reception, even among the younger generation.

9

The revolutionary vanguard
in perspective

The Communist Youth International (CYI) is generally and
often patronizingly dismissed, to the extent that one is
even more aware of its existence, as an arcane footnote to
the history of the communist movement. This is understandable, although short-sighted. It is true that over the
whole time-span of its existence, from 1919 to 1943, its
contributions to the development of communism were meagre.
It exerted almost no influence on the course taken by the
communist movement in the inter-war period, did not succeed
in building a mass movement among the young workers, and
was in no way able to provide to the 'world proletariat'
the stimulus to revolution that it had once seen as its
raison d'être. And yet, the same might also be said of the
parties themselves. Despite its failure to make a lasting
mark, the communist youth movement did, for a few turbulent
years, become a 'revolutionary vanguard.' It has been the
purpose of this study to describe how and why it came to
occupy such a position, what it meant, and what the consequences were.

The Comintern and party leaders accepted explicitly the
argument of the young communists that they were in the vanguard of the revolutionary forces during and immediately
after World War I.[1] The argument between the Comintern and
the CYI was over the necessity of continuing this role once

1 See the resolution on the youth movement adopted by the
  third Comintern congress (*Protokoll des III. Kongresses
  ...* 905-9). The resolution also stated that the economic
  position and psychological make-up of the young workers,
  who 'show more enthusiasm for revolution' than the
  adults, 'makes them easier converts to communist ideas.'

communist parties had been formed in all countries. The young
socialists had been the most resolutely anti-war of all socialist organizations. After November 1917 the youth organizations became noticeably more pro-Bolshevik than the parties. The latter were more cautious and aware of the differences in principle and practice that separated the various
socialist tendencies. The young socialists were much less
critical; the Bolshevik revolution, in fact, came to be the
major event shaping the attitudes of those adhering to the
youth organizations. They were unfamiliar with pre-war socialist or syndicalist traditions. They had no perspective
from which to judge alternatives. In the absence of any serious knowledge of other interpretations, socialism meant
bolshevism. Their understanding of what bolshevism meant,
however, was not well defined. Thus, serious conflicts
developed as the dimensions of Bolshevik elitism, which ran
counter to the traditions of the young socialists, became
clearer.

These traditions included an intense idealism, impatience,
self-assertiveness, and a general reluctance (which turned
into stubborn refusal) to accept adult tutelage or paternalism. Acquisition or preservation of full independence from
the parties became almost an obsession with young socialists
This persisted, in fact intensified, as the radicalized young
socialists became young communists after World War I.

Vanguardism was the response of a younger generation to
the failures of adult socialists. For fifty years the parties had been struggling in vain to bring about a socialist
revolution. In the course of time, many were seen to have
fallen along the way - to have abandoned the revolutionary
mission and accommodated within the existing system. To the
young socialists, the weaknesses of the adults - their willingness to compromise, their reluctance to make sacrifices,
their softness when it came to violence, their parochial
visions, and their growing scepticism of the validity of
Marxism - had led the working class astray, away from a
'genuinely' revolutionary path. These weaknesses had also
permitted the 'bourgeois imperialists' to raise the level
of exploitation to new heights, to an unbelievably destruc-
tive and debilitating World War. The parties thus could not
or would not, do anything to end the war or to promote a
socialist revolution.

This attitude was not altered by the formation of communist parties. Many adult communists appeared, to the young

communists, to have unwarrantedly pessimistic expectations of the prospects for revolution. This was seen as leading the adults into the same sort of 'opportunist' compromises to which the socialist parties had fallen prey. If the adults, having lost their revolutionary mission, could not be relied upon to provide leadership to the working class, the young communists would have to provide it themselves.

Believing that by nature they were more revolutionary than the adults, more firm in their commitment to revolutionary *action*, the young communists asserted the right (and assumed an obligation) of moral leadership. The young communists knew best, knew instinctively what was genuinely revolutionary and what was not. Youth organizations would not replace communist parties, or assume day-to-day political leadership. They would, however, persist as separate identities. They would follow general party political leadership as long as the party was 'truly revolutionary.' Existing independently of the parties, the youth organizations would be the judge of a party's 'revolutionariness.' From their position as revolutionary vanguard, the young communists would always be leading the adults, the entire working class, towards the revolutionary objective. Steadfast and true, independent youth organizations could serve as a rallying point from which to push 'slipping' parties back on the revolutionary path.

Several specific consequences inevitably flowed from the vanguardism of the young communists. It led them to overestimate drastically the prospects for revolution in Europe after World War I; it led them into far too uncompromising support for the 'revolutionary offensive' in 1920 and 1921; and it led them into a hopeless crusade for autonomy within the communist movement. Most serious of all was the failure of the communist youth organizations during the years of 'revolutionary vanguardism' to equip themselves and their members to cope psychologically and emotionally with existence in a non-revolutionary environment. This was soon to have a catacylsmic effect on the future of the youth organizations.

Frustration of revolutionary spirit

The character of the communist youth organizations underwent an important change after 1921. This was not due, as some allege, simply to crass suppression of youthful revolutionary enthusiasm by a dictatorial bureaucratic elite, an elite more interested in the fortunes of the Soviet state than in external revolutionary change. Rather, it was in the nature of things. Because they perceived themselves to be, and behaved as, instruments of revolution, the life of the Communist Youth International and its member organizations had been dominated in its early years by political and organizational issues. The traditional concerns of a youth movement (economic, educational, cultural, recreational affairs) were defined in political terms. All activities were to be directed toward immediate political ends. All problems, all inequities in the conditions of young workers were reduced to the single factor of class rule. No improvement could be accomplished within what was by definition an exploitative capitalist class system. Therefore, all young workers had to join in overthrowing the existing order. With the working class in power, all ills could be remedied. Until 1922, most of the young communist activists believed that this revolution was imminent. There seemed to be an unspoken fear of letting the objective moment slip away.

The Communist Youth International admitted reluctantly at its second congress in 1921 that the possibilities for revolution were dim, and formally abandoned the 'revolutionary offensive.' It only succeeded in discouraging its most enthusiastic members. If there was to be no commitment to revolution *now*, no expectation that it could be achieved in the foreseeable future, why belong to the communist youth movement? Why be active in a cause when the rewards were to be achieved in some indefinite future? The attraction of the communists was their promise of some immediate success, or at least the opportunity to be active in a way that could be interpreted as meaningful by young people craving to work against the established order. Youthful radicalism, impatience, and enthusiasm were not suited to a prolonged struggle for a revolution that would only occur 'some day.'

What had begun before the end of the war as a spontaneous turn to radicalism among the younger generation in Europe had only too shallow roots. Soviet Russia aside, the membership of the communist youth organizations fell drastically beginning in 1921. In most cases they became small uninfluential sects. Only in Germany, France, and Czechoslovakia were the communists able to maintain youth organi-

zations of any size. Hidden was the extensive communist
strength in Italy and Bulgaria that was suppressed in the
mid 1920s by authoritarian regimes of the right.

New recruits, it is true, did continue to come to the
communists. These were barely enough, however, to maintain
the existing low numbers. Radicalism became less attractive
and less imperative in a more stable environment. The
existing order was not paralysed; in fact, economic recovery
began rather rapidly. A new, post-war generation grew to
political awareness. The horrors of the war and the turmoil
in its aftermath were not part of their experience. Age
limits in the youth organizations naturally pushed members
out, either up to the communist parties, or into more apolit-
ical pastimes. A most important consequence for the CYI was
that after 1921 the youth organizations lost most of the old
leaders, and thus lost contact with the traditions that had
been built up before the war.

The early leaders encountered a variety of fates. Münzenberg was moved out of the CYI in 1921 and developed the communist publishing empire in Berlin, and later in Paris. He
also introduced the 'front organization' as a practical and
successful instrument. He fell, apparently to a Stalinist
assassin, in France in June 1940.[2] Lazar Shatskin remained
active in the Komsomol and the CYI until the late 1920s,
when he ran afoul of Stalin and was purged as a 'Trotskyite.'
He had formed, with several other Komsomol leaders, a 'left-
opposition' opposed to the growing bureaucratization of the
party. Shatskin seems to have been caught, as had Münzenberg
and others, in the consequences of an earlier commitment to
centralization and discipline. He perished in the late 1930s
but was rehabilitated in the early 1960s. Alfred Kurella
fled to the Soviet Union in 1934, where he was active in
the National Committee for a Free Germany. Returning to
Berlin in 1954, he was for some time the member of the central committee of the East German communist party (SED)
responsible for cultural affairs. Leo Flieg, 'a small,
delicate man ... formal and reserved' by nature, functioned
for many years as the 'grey eminence' of the German communist party.[3] He remained a close friend of Münzenberg until
called to Moscow in 1937, where he was shot in 1939 during

2 For details of Münzenberg's last days see the Carew-Hunt
  and Schleimann works cited in n.17, chapter three.
3 Weber, *Die Wandlung des deutschen Kommunismus* II, 120-1

Stalin's purges. Luigi Longo went on to become leader of the Italian communist party; Peder Furubotn to be leader of the Norwegian party; and Henri Barbé to a short-lived tenure as leader of the French party. Vuja Vujovitch and Richard Schüller became active in the Comintern apparatus, the former to become another victim in Stalin's purges. Giuseppe Berti, Luigi Polano, Richard Gyptner, Friedrich Heilmann, Gabriel Péri and many others became important functionaries in their communist parties. Gyptner held several high diplomatic posts, including ambassador in China and Poland for the East German government; Polano was a communist member of the Italian Senate.

Einar Gerhardsen and Aksel Zachariassen both left the Norwegian youth organization when the pro-Comintern forces took control, the former to become for many years leader of the Norwegian Labour Party and prime minister of Norway. Nils Flyg in Sweden, and Jacques Doriot and Maurice Laporte in France, moved all the way to the extreme political right in the 1930s. Secondino Tranquilli turned to literature and journalism and became known as Ignazio Silone. Emile Auclair after playing an important role in France in 1920 and 1921, soon fell into political obscurity.

Even more than in the parties, there was a continual turn-over of membership in the communist youth organizations. They were perfect examples of what Annie Kriegel, referring to the French communist party, has called the 'sieve-like' nature of a communist organization.[4] A 'frustration in fruit-less activism' affected the young even more than the adults. The impatience and desire for action that had led the typical recruit into the communist youth movement was not compatible with a stabilized environment and diminishing expectations of revolution. Those most attracted to the radical cause of communism in 1919 were also the first to leave when communism began adjusting to post-war capitalist stability. The militant 'ultra-left,' unwilling to make any compromises in strategy and tactics, had already split off in 1920.

The great crisis came in 1921, when the 'revolutionary offensive' was repudiated by the Comintern. Young communist were forced to reassess their commitments. Membership in the communist meovement and full-time participation in revolutionary activities filled a need that could be satisfied in few other places. It was not just that the young radicals

4 Kriegel, *The French Communists* ... 36

wished to be active; they wished to have a sense that their
activities were of some foreseeable benefit. The needs of
most of the first young communists could not be satisfied
within a movement, ostensibly revolutionary, but in which
the basic activities were to be organizational development
and agitation and propaganda. Few could make the transition
from the streets to the factories; from a life of demonstrations, rallies, and planning for the takeover of power to one
of persuading and enticing the young workers to revolution.

After 1921 the communist youth organizations were no longer
institutions a part of, and active in, a movement for imminent revolutionary change. They became arenas in which alienated and idealistic young people acted out their self-
identity crises. The communist youth movement continued to
present a revolutionary image, to subscribe to the same
universalistic and apocalyptic doctrines as before. Like
the young radicals of 1919 and 1920, those young people who
continued to join did so for reasons involving rebellion
against their environment - perhaps a lashing out against
the authoritarianism and paternalism still pervading most
European institutions at this time. Those who found no further outlet for their rebelliousness in revolutionary agitation, or in activities in support of the interests of
Soviet Russia, soon left. And yet, some did stay; 'bolshevization' and all that it implied was accepted with little
or no protest.

There were several reasons why some supported the Russian
party and strong centralization, even when it ran against
their own instincts for independence and autonomy. In the
non-revolutionary conditions after 1921 there was a feeling
of dependence on Russian leadership. There also was simple
opportunism; ambitions were best satisfied by going along
with those who had power. More deeply, perhaps, there was
the psychological need for unity and belonging. Many had
a strong belief in the need for international solidarity,
at least of all the 'true' revolutionaries. The undesirable
features of Bolshevik central leadership were seen as the
lesser of evils, certainly preferable to the chaotic pre-
1914 conditions under the Second International. Finally,
Comintern positions and policies simply were accepted by
many as correct and necessary.

In its early years under Münzenberg, the CYI wished to
become a mass movement capable of effecting a revolutionary
seizure of power. The two objectives were not compatible.

In the Luxemburgist tradition, most communist youth leaders in 1919 were committed to revolutionary action only on the basis of wide support. This was true, as well, for many of the first members of the Comintern. The young workers, because of their natural radicalism, were seen to occupy a key political position. It was taken as self-evident that an overwhelming majority of them would come over naturally to the communist movement. This, of course, did not happen, even though initially the communists made great gains. Nor, as has been seen, did the revolutionary commitment of most of those who did join extend beyond the ability of the existing order to re-establish itself and revive the economy. The young communists could not, or would not, accept the fact that a majority of young workers, like the adults, would never rise above 'trade-union consciousness.' The idealism, or rebelliousness, of most young workers either never became intense enough for them to join the revolutionary movement, or found other outlets.

When economic stability began to return to Europe in 1921, when the broad mass of young workers did not come to the communists instinctively or naturally, the communist youth leaders did not recognize that their assumptions required reassessment. A mass movement could not be built simply on the basis of a call to revolutionary action. If the young workers were to be won, they had to be wooed. This meant a choice: the young communists could maintain the revolutionary movement in its existing form, as an elite of dedicated and 'ideologically acceptable' activists but only at the price of remaining small sectarian groups; or they could take the steps required to expand the membership by offering genuine enticements to the young workers to join. Instead, the young communists were putting forth 'demands' with no hope of acceptance by the existing system and without the means to force their acceptance. At the same time, the reform-socialists and the trade unions were working to provide jobs, a weekly wage, and less dramatic but still tangible improvements in working conditions. The young workers were not willing to fight for the 'revolution' when perceptible improvements in their way of life were being realized.

The more the young communists remained true to their revolutionary principles, to the drastic and radical transformation of society through a violent seizure of power, the more estranged they became from the very masses they

sought to win. To have played the game of genuinely working
for realizable improvements in the life of young workers,
however, would have cut at the very raison d'être of the
youth organizations. To work within the system, to compromise with the bourgeoisie and cooperate with the reform-
socialists, would have been a denial of the very alienation
and radicalism that had led to the formation of communist
youth organizations in the first place. It would have been
an implicit admission that there was not, in fact, any
moral difference between a communist and a reform-socialist,
and that there were no 'truest' revolutionaries who could
be distinguished from either other communists, or those
who were traitors to the working class.

The dilemma was never resolved. The Comintern tried without success in 1921, with its 'retreat' policy and a turn
to the united front, to break out of the impossible situation of building or maintaining a mass revolutionary party
in a non-revolutionary environment. It wished to use the
existing system without, in the process, according it any
degree of legitimacy. To this day, communist organizations
have never been able to cope with this dilemma. The capacity to do so, in any event, was taken out of their hands
by the mid 1920s. When the Russian party, then Stalin, acquired control over the communist movement, the purpose of
communist organizations ceased to be to sponsor a revolution. The preservation and promotion of the interests of
the Soviet State/party became the effective communist definition of 'proletarian internationalism.' Obedient, even if
small, organizations were more useful than large and politically influential, but independent, ones. Through the
years, greater involvement in the existing order on the
part of most non-ruling communist parties has led to considerably less obedience. It also has come to mean only
formal adherence to the traditional revolutionary commitments, or, more pertinently, to a re-definition of the process of revolution such that the old differences with other
socialist tendencies begin to disappear. To the extent that
communist organizations remain faithful to their earlier
conceptions of how, and through what forms, the change from
a 'bourgeois' to a 'socialist' society must take place,
especially their commitment to Leninist organizational
norms, they remain isolated from effective, positive
political life.

There was really little chance in 1920 and 1921 that young
communists could have successfully preserved their political
identity. An organizational separation between party and
youth organization was supported by all. Young people had
to be left at least the illusion of independence. Those who
were sympathetic or receptive to the communist position, but
who had not yet reached the point of making a firm commitment, were enrolled more easily in a separate youth organization than directly into a party. An element of paternalism
was also involved. Separate organizations would avoid the
inconvenience of having teen-agers intruding at party meeting
and roaming through party premises. Let the young have their
own apparatus and their own meetings. But on no account were
the youth organizations to retain a separate political identity. The adults knew best and would decide policies, while
the youth organizations would carry them out as appropriate

In a pre-revolutionary environment, the reduc ion of the
communist youth organizations outside Soviet Russia to the
role of 'transmission belts' and instruments of mobilization
on the Komsomol model was, with a few exceptions, accepted
as natural by all the communist parties. Even though there
were those who sympathized with and admired the dedication
of the young communists, there was no need for the Russian
party to exert pressure. Even during the factional struggle
in the 1920s, the youth organizations did not have much
scope for independent initiative. The factions and the
Comintern leaders used them for their own purposes. No
party group ever indicated a willingness to return to the
pre-1921 conditions in which the youth organization occupie
a distinctly separate and independent *political* position.

It would have been too much to expect the parties to have
allowed their fortunes to be decided by the adolescent members of a youth organization. The parties certainly were
not impressed by the argument of the young communists that
they *in principle*, and at all times, represented the vanguard of the revolutionary forces. The enthusiasm of the
young was applauded. It perhaps was accepted as natural.
It was not always appreciated in practice, however. The
leaders of neither the Comintern nor the parties wished
to allow young communists to decide who was a 'true' communist and who a deviant 'opportunist.'

Once the critical period in which communist parties were
founded was past, the parties ceased to pay the youth movement much attention. This was precisely one of the frustra-

tions of the youth movement; the party and Comintern leaders
would not take it seriously. This attitude put off the average member, and certainly galled those independent and
anti-bureaucratic leaders and functionaries who still remained. The members thought themselves part of a spontaneous
movement leading the parties, if only by example and enthusiasm, to an imminent revolution. The leaders perceived
themselves as political forces to be reckoned with, at the
pinnacle of what could be a strong and dedicated mass movement. They had a vested interest in maintaining the youth
movement as a distinct entity. Münzenberg and most of the
others responsible for creating the Communist Youth International were in their twenties or thirties. They had developed a power base of sorts within the youth movement, and
took positions on all important questions within the communist movement. The youth movement was a useful vehicle
by which to further these positions. In building up the
youth movement, these leaders acquired a self-importance
they would not have had otherwise. Subordination to the
Comintern and the parties meant not simply a smothering of
youthful zeal and the loss of independent participation in
the preparation for revolution, but a blow to their pride
as well.

The priority of power

Aside from a natural reluctance of the parties to take it
seriously, there were other reasons for the loss of a separate political identity for the youth movement. For one
thing, Lenin and the leading Bolsheviks were too committed
to organizational centralization to have permitted an independent youth movement to exist. If the younger generation
had any value at all, then it had to be enrolled with all
other communist forces behind a single leadership on the
basis of democratic centralism: one political movement with
one political voice. Even the young communists recognized
this point in principle. Their strong commitment to unity
and centralization led them to be firm supporters of the
Twenty-One Conditions. It also led many to accept the Comintern decisions on the role of the youth movement. The
terms 'unity' and 'centralization' had acquired a distinctly
emotional meaning for committed communists in 1921. It was
enough to be accused of, or even appear to be, 'disrupting
unity' or contravening the centralist ties that bound

communists together to find oneself on the defensive. Münzenberg serves perfectly to typify the dilemma of the young
communists. He wanted to preserve an independent political
youth movement, but not at the expense of a split with the
Comintern. When it was clear that there would have to be a
choice, Münzenberg came, reluctantly, to the conclusion
that preservation of the integrity of the young and embat-
tled communist movement had first priority.

Although events reinforced this commitment to unity by
so many young communists, difficulties in application of
the principle remained. Internal difficulties in Soviet
Russia, and the increasingly dim prospects for extension
of the revolution abroad, were to lead Lenin in 1921 to
the New Economic Policy at home and the 'retreat policy'
in the Comintern. Thus committed to certain policy lines,
Lenin insisted that measures be taken to ensure that all
communist organizations would follow these policies. There
could not be a situation in which the Comintern and the
parties went one way, and the CYI and the youth organizations another. To avoid communist organizations drifting
toward 'left-extremism,' or slipping back into the 'opportunism' of the reform-socialists, discipline had to be
made strict and deviants expelled. The young communists
were all for discipline and the explusion of deviants, and
for all communist organizations proceeding in one direction
only. They were at best, however, cool to Lenin's conception
of the conditions upon which unity would be based. Their
response to events also emphasized the need for unity, but
it implied policy lines quite different from those offered
by Lenin. The major problem, of course, was how to define
orthodoxy, and thus heresy - or more precisely, who would
do the defining.

Although it would have been too much to have expected the
Comintern and the parties to have acknowledged an independent political role for the youth movement, the young communists did have some important grievances that could have
been accommodated even within a highly centralized system.
There was, for instance, no need to interfere in the organizational activities of the CYI. There also was no need
for the Comintern's executive committee (ECCI) to insist
on determining the location, timing, and agenda of CYI congresses. Nor did ECCI need to control the membership of the
Executive Committee of the CYI (ECCYI), and, through ECCYI,
the leading organs of the youth organizations. Not unless

the Russian Bolsheviks insisted, as indeed they did, on exporting their own definition of centralism to the whole Comintern. But there was nothing inherent in the situation, other than Bolshevik ideological and organizational commitments, that led logically to this end. Bolshevik concerns for 'security' and preservation of the revolution need not have been threatened by a less restrictive definition of centralism. The young communists ultimately were willing to accept political subordination. They were willing, despite their talk of communist youth as an avant-garde, to have the CYI follow the political leadership of the Comintern. Less willingly, they even came to accept the demand that the youth organizations follow their respective country's party.

The young communists thus agreed that one could not have communists running off in all directions. This had been clear at the outset, when the founding congress in Berlin in 1919 rejected the concept of the youth international as a 'sister organization' of the Comintern. As understood by the young communists, unity meant leadership by the Comintern in political matters, with freedom for the CYI to call its own meetings, choose its own leaders, and carry out the political program of the Comintern in its own way. Furthermore, it was expected that the political line of the Comintern would be unequivocally revolutionary and determined democratically. A revolutionary policy was taken for granted. But, to the extent that thought was given to the decision-making process, and very little was, it also was assumed that all communist parties and the youth international would have proportionally equal rights in determining Comintern policies. The influence of the Russian communist party would be great, and its position one of moral leadership, but it would not, as was actually the case after the 'bolshevization' of the international movement, dictate to the Comintern.

In accepting the decisions of the second CYI congress in 1921, the young communists were not committing themselves consciously to Comintern interference in the affairs of the youth movement. No one believed that he would be deprived of the right to free discussion, or of the right of his youth organization to meet when it chose, to select its own leaders, and to organize itself, within the general guidelines of the Comintern's program and principles. To submit to the Comintern and the parties was not at this time to submit to bureaucratic, authoritarian institutions. There was still free debate within the parties, as there was in the Comintern. It was still possible to form groups and factions inside the parties.

Writing in 1917, Antonio Gramsci attempted to overcome this contradiction between independence and centralization by arguing that

> to join a movement means to assume part of the responsibility for coming events ... A young man who joins the Socialist youth movement performs an act of independence and liberation. To discipline oneself is to make oneself independent and free. Water is pure and free when it runs between the two banks of a stream or river, not when it is dispersed chaotically on the soil.[5]

All may not have seen their acceptance of discipline in quite this light. The typical young communist at this time perhaps justified the need for discipline in more pragmatic terms. The need for all revolutionary socialists, for all those set on destroying the capitalist order, to stay together and speak with one voice so as to maximize their power and protect the 'family' was a strong motivating force. Nevertheless, Gramsci was touching on an important psychological point. To have meaning one's life must have some direction. It is not enough to have an idealistic, visionary goal. Like a river, suggested Gramsci, one's life must be contained and channeled by outside forces. The life of each young communist needed that riverbank of communist discipline if it was to reach its idealistic goals. And yet it needed freedom of movement and expression within the confines of communist discipline if it was to reach its full revolutionary potential.

At the outset, Comintern domination of the CYI was not seen as something to be feared. It was, after all, through the Comintern that the Russian Bolsheviks were promoting extension of the revolution. Furthermore, the Comintern did not, until 1921, take any steps to abridge the independence of the CYI, even though Shatskin and the Russian Komsomol were arguing for complete subordination. In fact, the Comintern tended, at least by its neglect of the youth movement, to confirm the image the youth organizations had of themselves as an important, independent political force.

5 Quoted in Cammett, *Antonio Gramsci* ... 46

The parties, however, were another matter. The young communists feared what they perceived to be the weak commitments of the parties to 'genuinely' revolutionary tactics. Contact between the youth organizations and the parties was continual and much more visible than that between ECCYI and ECCI. The basic conflicts over tactics between the young communists and the parties were more acute than the differences between the CYI and Comintern. CYI/Comintern relations only became important once it became clear that party/youth organization relations depended on the Comintern's attitude.

The early years of the communist youth movement tell us a great deal about more recent problems of the international communist movement; about why it has become increasingly inappropriate to speak about an 'international movement.' In analysing the course of developments within international communism, one is tempted to view the year 1953, or perhaps 1956, as a watershed or turning point. The death of Stalin in March 1953, and Khrushchev's 'secret speech' and report to the twentieth congress of the Communist Party of the Soviet Union in February 1956, released forces that have worked since to destroy the highly structured and controlled political movement created by Lenin and developed by Stalin. But these forces did not materialize out of thin air. They had been present ever since the formation of communist parties in countries other than Russia, albeit submerged under the pressures for centralized control. The early years of international communism were in fact years of great diversity. There was no precisely established orthodoxy representing a consensus of values. More important, there was no agreement on strategy and tactics - on how the imprecisely articulated dogma, in which all purported to believe, was to be transformed into practical, effective action.

Many of the early European communists believed that a considerable degree of local autonomy was necessary. Centralization was seen not so much as an organizational norm as agreement on basic principles, goals, and directions. Given such unity there would be considerable scope for local initiative and decision making. This orientation was swept aside by the Russian Bolsheviks as incompatible with a world party structured on increasingly bureaucratic lines. For them, only the latter represented genuine proletarian internationalism. 'Bolshevization' became necessary primarily because the parochial attitudes of the European communists would not disappear. Thus, the character of international

communism under Stalin became such as to becloud and repres
persistent autonomist influences over many decades.

The experience of the Communist Youth International provides evidence of the intensity of these pressures both for
and against autonomy and independence. The rise of revolutionary forces to dominance in the socialist youth movement
during and after World War I and the struggle of the new
Bolshevik regime in Russia to control these forces illustra
the spontaneous sources of diversity present in the international communist movement from its inception. The attitud
of the Bolsheviks towards their young supporters in other
countries, on the other hand, their response to youthful
self-assertion, radicalism, and revolutionary 'purity,'
foreshadowed the later development of authoritarianism in
the Communist International.

From the Russian point of view, insistence on discipline
and a bureaucratic definition of centralization could well
be understood. As leaders of a self-proclaimed socialist
state, existing in an isolation in good part imposed by
themselves and feeling encircled by hostile forces, the
Bolsheviks (and their successors) defined 'security' as
direct control over whatever friendly forces they could
find. Leaderships ready to comply with their wishes had to
be found within the ranks of their supporters abroad. The
situation became complicated further by the leadership
struggle within the Russian party itself. To support and
justify its position at home, each Russian faction wished
to install a secure and loyal leadership in other parties.
Eventually unity came only on the basis of subordination
to a single dominant faction within the Russian party, and
then finally to one man.

The lament, 'if only Lenin had lived!' is often heard
from old communists who left in disillusion in the Stalini
era, as well as from those younger ones who today seek a
return to the 'original,' purportedly pure, communism of
Lenin's day. Lenin's speech at the fourth Comintern congre
in December 1922 is cited as evidence that he foresaw the
dangers of Russian control and of an extension of the
Russian model to other parties. Yet when he criticized certain decisions as being a too mechancial application of
Russian experience, and too difficult for other communist
parties to understand, what he was challenging was not the
substance, but the *form*, of these decisions.[6] There is no

6 See Lenin, *Collected Works* 33, 430-2

evidence to indicate that he opposed further restructuring
of the Comintern and other parties on the Bolshevik model.

One is inclined to interpret the wistful references to
Lenin as reflections of a frustrated humanitarian and democratic conception of revolutionary socialism. The fact that
there is no such political movement of any significance is
rationalized by referring to Lenin's untimely death. These
views overlook the course of developments in Soviet Russia
and the international communist movement even under Lenin.
Indeed, there undoubtedly would have been some differences
in inter-party relations had Lenin lived, for his presence
would have created conditions different from those that in
fact developed. It is doubtful, however, whether Russian
dominance would have been any less evident, or whether
early members of the communist movement such as Tranmael,
Höglund, Reuter-Friesland, or Frossard would have remained.
Each of these individuals represented important nationalist,
autonomist forces within the Comintern, and left, taking
most or a considerable portion of the membership of their
party with them. In all cases, the departure occurred, or
the crisis developed, while Lenin was still active. Other
autonomists, such as Levi and Serrati, and even the 'ultra-
left,' were excluded even earlier. Certainly, however one
views the growth of Stalinist bureaucratic control - whether
as an iron necessity in defence of the Bolshevik revolution,
or as a perversion of the revolution, or as the inevitable
result of a commitment to the principle that unity is more
important than consensus - it was not responsible for the
subordination of the youth movement. This issue had been
debated and settled by 1922.

The experience of the Communist International and the
Communist Youth International demonstrates that the essential problem in relations among and between communists and
communist organizations has been the basis on which unity
is to be achieved. Given the impact of diverse national
traditions and cultures, neither command, nor a shared commitment to certain vague goals and a particular interpretation of history have been sufficient for maintaining unity
within a political movement that lays claim to universality.
Stalin's monolithic control mechanism was an artificial
solution that had become overstrained even before his death.
A relationship between governing parties, each facing different circumstances and problems, established on the basis
of commands issued by one of them was untenable once the
established source of authority was removed. The prolonged

postponement elsewhere of the expected revolutionary confrontation between 'the capitalists' and 'the proletariat'
served in the short run to make it possible for Stalin to
define unity by establishing his personal control over the
national communist movements. In the long run, however,
the persistence of a gap between promise and reality,
between proletarian revolution and the continued stability
of capitalism, was bound to place each non-ruling communist
party under increasing pressure to adapt to reality, to its
national environment, or run the risk of political irrel-
evance. Each such party as a practical matter is thus impelled to go its own way. This raises the question of how
unity is to be achieved in such circumstances.

Lenin's answer was the concept of democratic centralism,
a term he introduced in 1906. The attraction of the concept
in the post-World War I period was that it appeared to com-
bine two fundamental, but opposite, desires. More so than
the Bolsheviks, European communists believed that democrati
organizational forms were necessary for any proletarian organization. Only the proletariat itself could define its
true interests, and it could do so only if given freedom
of opportunity. Only if policy were an actual expression
of these interests could it be assured of support and fulfilment.

And yet, if a revolution was to be won against the strong
entrenched, and ruthless forces of capitalism, all 'true
revolutionaries' would have to remain united and under
strong discipline. Lenin and others assumed that acceptance
of democratic centralism by all communists would assure bot
the necessary unity, and the desired freedom of expression
and broad participation in decision making. But what, in
practice, the concept means, what specific rules and regulations, structures, and norms of behaviour it demands, was
never clearly thought out by the first adherents to the
Comintern and the CYI. Lenin himself was not precise in his
definition, and what he did say was expressed too broadly
to be self-evidently applicable once large, open parties
had been formed.

Before the Bolshevik revolution, the ambiguity of democratic centralism was less evident.[7] Lenin spoke of the
need for democracy, and insisted as early as the London
congress of Bolsheviks in 1905 on additions to the party

7 See Meyer, *Leninism*, chapter 5

statutes to emphasize the democratic nature of the party.
Yet, in practice the democratic restraints on central authority tended to be overridden. Lenin himself was not above
excluding those with whom he had fundamental disagreements.
Despite this, considerable freedom existed to put forth
differing views and to criticize those of others. A sufficiently viable synthesis appears to have existed to enable
the Bolsheviks to profit from Russian conditions in 1917.
Being out of power, the Bolsheviks had no responsibilities
of governing, with their many potential sources of conflict.
The instrument of the state was not available for enforcing
discipline, compelling Lenin and other leaders to rely more
on persuasion. Most importantly, perhaps, there was neither
a clearly established 'line' that all party members were
expected to follow, nor a norm for decision making by which
it was understood that the average party member would have
little or no effective voice in determining policy. The enthusiasm and dedication of the party members, certainly in
1917, made the question of discipline of subsidiary importance. It was enough that all could rally around the cause
of revolution. Sufficient acceptance of discipline seems to
have been inherent in the commitment made by the individual
member joining the party. After the revolution, this was no
longer true: only the personality, prestige, and authority
of Lenin served to limit conflict and maximize unity.

The need for a more precise definition of democratic centralism became evident as soon as the Bolsheviks acquired
power. The party grew enormously, and the issues it took
to itself for decision multiplied many times over. By 1920
and 1921, the Comintern had been founded and communist parties were being created in many countries. Democratic centralism had to be given a meaning that could take all these
developments into account. It was in the Communist Youth
International that the issue of democracy and centraliam
first was raised outside of Russia, as early as November
1919, but without any clear outline of the alternatives and
consequences. The young communists grappled with the issue
intuitively. There was never a clear statement of the problem, nor a conscious effort to solve it. The intense struggle
to form communist organizations was absorbing the attention
of all communists. Only the young communists, seeking to
preserve a distinct role for themselves, came up squarely
against the problem of organizational structure, and thus
of defining democratic centralism.

The early history of the Communist Youth International demonstrates the latent ambiguities and contradictions in a concept that is at the core of Marxism-Leninism. From the start, democratic centralism in practice has been an unstable method of regulating relations between individuals and groups within an organization. It implies a 'non-conflict' situation, a condition of continuing consensus and a sharing of values, goals, interests, and, especially, an interpretation of the significance of events and a prescription for coping with them. The non-recognition of inherent conflict results in the absence under democratic centralism of any legitimate and effective means for resolving disputes. Differences in definition and interpretation often, if not usually, become infused with an ideological content leading to the establishment of 'orthodox' and 'deviant' positions, to the postulation of 'a true Marxist-Leninist line' and 'a false and herectical line.' So far no means have been found for handling such conflict short of expulsion or withdrawal.

The need to justify actions on the basis of membership in a unified world movement representing the 'true interests' of the proletariat meant that in the Comintern a 'one-party, one-vote' position, or even some form of weighted voting, was not a practical solution to the question of coping with conflict. If there was to be 'one truth,' then negotiation and bargaining were illogical. Each faction or party had to seek a way to make its views the orthodox views. In the absence of self-evidently appropriate strategies and tactics, and adaptations and extensions of doctrine, i.e. in the absence of a continuing consensus, no communist party was willing to let others determine its policies. No group or faction claiming the 'correct' interpretation was willing to submit to another, which of necessity and by definition must be in error. Control thus came to mean the ability to impose on others one's own views and policies in the name of orthodoxy.

As the Russian party came to impart practical content to the concept of democratic centralism through its own action in Russia, it moved to impose its definition on the communist organizations of other countries. This process of 'bolshevization' (or 'Leninization') is formally dated from 1924 and associated with Stalin's rise to power. Observers usually refer to Lenin's *'Left-Wing' Communism: An Infantile Disorder* and the second Comintern congress as the

first steps, taken in 1920, toward imposition of the Russian
model of organization. A study of the Communist Youth International shows that the imposition of the Russian model can
be said to have begun as early as mid 1919. It shows, as
well, that contrary to the view of E.H. Carr there was a
considerable element of design behind the Russian approach
to the organization of the Comintern and the other communist movements.[8] From the very beginning there were differences in organization between the Russian party, the Comintern, and other communist parties, yet the experience of
the youth international provides persuasive evidence that
these differences were able to persist only because the
Russian model itself was still in process of development in
the years 1919-1922. That part of the model that concerned
youth had been defined by 1919, while others were to take
somewhat longer. Even so, there was a logical imperative
in Lenin's views on revolution, on the role and organization
of the party, and on the exercise and justification of power
that led inevitably to the universalization of Russian experience, even before the rise of Stalin.

The application of the Russian model to the communist
youth movement outside Soviet Russia was only delayed by
the attitudes of the young West European communists. In
the early years they had demonstrated whole-hearted support
for unity and centralization, *before* democratic centralism
had acquired its bureaucratic and autocratic character.
Resisting the imposition of the Russian model and definition of the concept, they conceived of democratic centralism in more idealistic terms. They were committed to a
'humanitarian communism' more responsive to the masses in
the Luxemburgist tradition. As Lenin saw, the centralism
part of the concept tended in practice to give way to
youthful anti-elitist instincts, despite a belief in the
need for centralization and discipline.

Today, organized factions still remain prohibited in all
definitions of democratic centralism, but the de facto
existence of 'tendencies' has come to be accepted by many
parties. The major problem is still to ensure that all tendencies will give unstinting support to a policy that they
may have fought, and perhaps bitterly, once a majority has
determined the basic line. But to legitimize tendencies,
even unofficially, runs the risk that minorities will devote

8 See Carr, *The Bolshevik Revolution, 1917-1924* III, 198

their time and energy not to implementation of majority
policy, but to efforts to change that policy. Resolute and
united action against the common external enemy is weakened
The old dilemma thus remains. To deny the right of differer
views to be heard, of minorities to meet and discuss their
opposition, and to be active in persuading the membership
at large to support them in forming a new majority, is to
move back towards the bureaucratic centralization of the
Stalinist years.

A new revolutionary vanguard?

There are other important questions that emerge out of the
experience of the CYI. To what degree is faithfulness to
'first principles' by the members of a revolutionary movement related directly to age? Is there a simple correlatior
to the effect that the younger the partisan, the more dedicated and committed he is to 'the revolution'? Does one ter
to lose enthusiasm with age, and become more open to re-
defining the revolution in less than the original militant
terms? Certainly, the young communists in 1919, 1920, and
1921 thought this a real danger. The young radicals of
more recent times apparently also believe this to be so.
Many have been vehement critics of the communist parties,
condemning them for having abandoned their revolutionary
origins. The point at issue is not the ultimate goal, but
rather the means by which to achieve it. There is surprisingly little disagreement among radicals over the need
for a fundamental transformation of the existing order.
What the young revolutionaries, past and present, have argued is that the parties end up pursuing policies that lea
to an accommodation with existing society. Where the parties see this as a necessary and reasonable utilization of
the 'bourgeois democratic' system for revolutionary purpos
the youth equate accommodaton with an abandonment of the
cause of revolution. The younger generation of 'Marxist-
Leninists' is organized for the most part outside the traditional communist parties. At the same time, a significan
segment of today's young revolutionary socialists has gone
even further and jettisoned much, if not all, of the Lenin
accretions to Marx's ideas.
    The proponents of the 'de-radicalization' thesis (those
who argue that the communist parties, as all Marxist movements, have abandoned their revolutionary commitments and

lost their revolutionary identity) confuse changes in means
with abandonment of ends. Or, they assume that changes in
means, or movement away from a rigidly Leninist definition
of the revolutionary process, leads to loss of revolutionary
commitment and identity. Thus, it is said, or implied, that
a communist party can remain a communist party and retain
its revolutionary identity only if it adheres to this rigid
Leninism. It is assumed further that working within the
existing 'bourgeois' system is incompatible with revolutionary goals. This latter assumption is the subject of much
dispute within the revolutionary socialist movement today,
but remains an open, empirical question of which time can
be the only judge. There may be a definitional reason for
this alleged incompatibility, but no historical or logical
one. While it may be argued very persuasively that a process of 'de-Leninization' has been underway within the non-
ruling communist parties, this is not necessarily the same
thing as 'de-radicalization.'

A fusion of the general social analysis and vague prescrip-
tions for action of Marx and Engels with the idealism, enthusiasm, impatience, and instinctive radicalism of those
young students and workers who are most politicized appears
to be a sure impetus to action against the status quo,
against the 'establishment' - whether capitalist or communist. It is a condition that first acquired popular dimensions in the years 1914-1924 when ideologically inspired
political movements had their first great impact on youth
and students. The intensity of youthful radicalism and activism, of commitment and involvement in political and
social issues, during the war and the early post-war period
was the result of specific circumstances. The Bolshevik
revolution, conditions in Europe during and after the war,
indeed the war itself, and the ideological and moral conflict of the era all served to enflame much of the younger
generation. They had a vision of a better society and were
promised a role of leadership in achieving, or at least
actively working toward, that goal. The Bolshevik revolution
and the new regime's efforts to build a socialist society
served as an inspiration to many. The formation of communist
parties and youth organizations provided a means by which
many young people thought that the Russian experience could
be repeated within their own society. It is disillusionment
with the Russian experience, among other things, that under-
lies the defection from communist organizations by the most

militant elements and is reflected by the 'anti-communism' of the New Left today.

For a variety of reasons, not all of which are yet clear, the conditions necessary for a re-emergence of radical activism among youth developed in the 1960s. From the late nineteenth century until after World War II, the vehicle of discontent had been the political youth organization. The arena of youthful unrest shifted in the 1960s to the universities and student organizations. While they are not unimportant, youth organizations that are today associated with political parties and traditional ideologies have been subsumed into a far wider, far more unstructured, far more chaotic phenomenon. If the experience of the radical youth groups of the past has anything to tell us about the future however, it is that each young generation of revolutionary socialists acts to keep alive a faith in the original ideal and ultimate utopias, and to serve as a conscience for political parties. Above all, it demonstrates that even (or perhaps especially) in the traditionally ideological political movements the impatience and pristine, uncompromising idealism of the young remain the primary sources of an *active* revolutionary commitment.

One could interpret the abortive efforts of the first young communists to promote a socialist revolution as testimony to the enthusiasm and high idealism of youth. Their actions and attitudes, however, should serve as a reminder that 'where there is a will, there is *not* always a way.' So far, at least, a commitment to the overthrow of the status quo, to a utopian transformation of society related in some way to the ideas of Marx, Engels, Lenin, and/or Mao Tse-tung, has not shown itself to be a sufficiently viable or appealing prescription for the problems of modern industrial or post-industrial society.

Bibliography

Many sources that would be of great value for any study of
the Communist Youth International (CYI) have not been accessible. The archives of the youth international went to
the Soviet Union in 1921, at the time that the executive
committee (ECCYI) was moved from Berlin to Moscow. The archives were not accessible for research; in fact, the Soviet
authorities deny any knowledge of them. The main sources
have been the publications and periodicals issued by the
CYI, by its predecessor, the Internationale Verbindung sozialistischer Jugendorganisationen (IUSYO), and by its
rivals, the right-socialist (Arbeiter Jugendinternationale)
and centrist (Internationale Arbeitsgemeinschaft sozialistischer Jugendorganisationen) youth internationals; selected
publications of various national socialist or communist
youth organizations; and interviews with individuals who
had been active in the communist youth movement. For the
period covered in this study, the working language of the
socialist and communist movements was German, thus sources
in the German language predominate. The available Russian
sources of this period that concerned themselves with the
CYI, or with Komsomol activities within the CYI, were for
the most part either translations from the German, or general surveys used for agit-prop purposes within the Komsomol itself. A collection of articles and documents by
Lazar Shatskin, *Pervye gody Kommunisticheskogo Internatsional Molodezhi; sbornik statei i dokladov* (Moscow 1926)
has not been available.

There is no comprehensive work on the early development of the
of the socialist youth movements. There are individual studies of national movements such as those noted below in the
bibliography for Austria, Slovakia, Germany, Italy, the

Netherlands, Sweden, Norway, and Denmark. Considerable information is available in the reports of the bureau of the
IUSYO published before World War I: for the period up to
1907, *Die internationale Organisation der sozialistischen
Jugend; Bericht des Sekretariats der internationalen Verbindung der sozialistischen Jugendorganisationen, August
1907* (Leipzig 1907); for the period 1907-1910, Robert
Danneberg, *Die Jugendbewegung der sozialistischen Internationale* (Vienna 1910); for the period 1910-1914, Robert
Danneberg, *Die Rekrutenschule der internationalen Sozialdemokratie* (Vienna 1914). The secretariat in Vienna also
published the *Bulletin der internationalen Verbindung der
sozialistischen Jugendorganisationen* (Vienna) from 1907 to
1914. There also are useful discussions in Willi Münzenberg,
*Die sozialistische Jugendorganisationen vor und während des
Krieges* and Richard Schüller, *Von den Anfängen der proletarischen Jugendbewegung bis zur Gründung der Kommunistische
Jugend-Internationale,* as well as Georgij Tschitscherin
(Chicherin), *Skizzen aus der Geschichte der Jugend-Internationale.* The bibliography in Münzenberg's *Die Dritte
Front* is also quite helpful.

There has never been a detailed study of the Communist
Youth International in English. A very short and highly
tendentious summary of the early history of the CYI was
published by the Young Communist League of Great Britain
in the late 1920s. Very brief discussions of the CYI are
available in E.H. Carr, *The Bolshevik Revolution, 1917-
1923* III (London 1953) and *Socialism in One Country, 1924-
1926* III, part two (London 1964), and in Ralph Talcott
Fisher, Jr, *Pattern for Soviet Youth* (New York 1959). The
only study of the CYI in any detail is a history, in
German and Russian, published by the executive committee
(ECCYI) in three volumes in 1929, 1930, and 1931, and reprinted in German in 1970. In 1961 this history, authored
by Richard Schüller, Alfred Kurella, and Rafail Chitarow
(Khitarov), was not listed in the open catalogues of the
major libraries in the Soviet Union, and in fact was noted
as being 'non-recommended literature' in one brief work in
Russian on the CYI. The discussion of issues and personalities in this history, particularly in the first two volumes
follows quite closely the course of events, although it is
tendentious and suffers from omission of much important detail. These volumes thus go beyond the bounds of accepted,
hagiographic Soviet historiography during the later Stalini

times as represented in the entry for the CYI (*Kommunisti-cheskii Internatsional Molodezhi*) in the *Bol'shaia sovet-skaia entsiklopediia* XXII, second edition, 267-9.

From the early 1930s until the early 1960s very little attention was paid in Soviet historical literature to the Communist Youth International. Beginning in 1962, however, a number of articles appeared in Soviet historical, party, and Komsomol journals. Among the more interesting are three by V.V. Privalov: 'Bor'ba V.I. Lenin i Bolshevikov za soz-danie kommunisticheskogo internatsional molodezhi', *Vestnik* (Leningrad Universiteta), Seriia Istorii, Vypusk 3, no. 14 (1962): 5-19; 'Vlianie Bolshevikov na mezhdunarodnoe dvizh-enie molodezhi v gody pervoi mirovoi voiny,' ibid., no. 20 (1962): 153-8; and 'Lenin i internatsional molodezhi,' *Molodoi kommunist*, no. 8 (1966). Also see M.M. Mukhamedzhanov, 'V.I. Lenin i Kommunisticheskii Internatsional Molodezhi,' *Voprosy istorii KPSS*, no. 4 (1965), and 'V.I. Lenin i mezh-dunarodnaia sotsialisticheskaia molodezh' v gody pervoi mirovoi voiny,' *Novaia i novyeshaia istoriia*, no. 2 (1967): 3-13; a reprint of the 1923 reminiscences by Lazar Shatskin, 'Lenin i RLKSM,' *Iunost'*, no. 7 (1965): 66-7; *Blizhe vsekh. Lenin i iunye internatsionalisti. Sbornik dokumentov i ma-terialov* (Moscow 1968); S.M. Goncharova and G.E. Pavlova, 'Kommunisticheskii Internatsional Molodezhi - vernyi pomosh-chnik Kominterna (1919-1943),' *Voprosy istorii KPSS*, no. 12 (1969); and A. Zinoviev and M.M. Mukhamedzhanov, 'Rol' ross-iskogo komsomol v sozdanii kommunisticheskogo internatsio-nala molodezhi,' *Informatsioni biulletin*, no. 5-6 (1969). A longer study in book form of the early years of the CYI appeared in 1968: V.V. Privalov, *Obrazovanie kommunistiches-kogo internatsional molodezhi* (Leningrad 1968). A standard Soviet party study of the international socialist movement during and after World War I dismisses the youth interna-tional in one or two unrevealing short paragraphs: *Istoriia mezhdunarodnogo rabochego i natsional'no-osvoboditel'nogo dvizheniia*, two volumes, Vyshaia Partiinaia Shkola pri TsK KPSS (Moscow 1959 and 1962).

Although remaining essentially exercises in imposing a priori definitions and explanations upon historical phenom-ena, these more recent studies of the CYI have been be-coming more responsive to the actual historical issues. In part this has been a positive consequence of the 'de-Stalinization' process. Other, external forces appear to have been present as well. The Soviet party apparently felt a need to develop a stronger historically grounded position from which to defend its definitions of Marxism-Leninism, revolution, and the role of the youth movement. The author of a recent work, A.P. Zinoviev ('Bor'ba RKSM za preodolenie avangardistskikh tendentsii v Kommunisticheskom Internatsional Molodezhi [1919-1921gg]', *Voprosy istorii*, no. 12 [1971]: 43-57) indicates that he is studying the problem of 'avant-gardism of the youth' in the CYI in the early 1920s so as to 'expose the various falsifications [of the revolutionary, historical process] by bourgeois and social-reformist ideologues,' in particular the 'false, pseudo-revolutionary ideas' of Herbert Marcuse and the New Left. Western historians, or 'bourgeois ideologues,' discussing the early years of the CYI are condemned, also, for 'falsifying the nature of the relations between the Russian Komsomol and the CYI in the years 1919-1921' as part of a 'struggle against Marxism-Leninism, against an increase in its influence on the minds of young people.' Nevertheless, the author treats the subject as historical reality, offering his own interpretations and explanations. Previously forbidden references to certain individuals and authors, and to ideologically 'false' positions, are now to be found. Lazar Shatskin already has been rehabilitated by the party. Whatever 'errors' Münzenberg later may have committed, he is portrayed in sympathet terms in the recent literature, although condemned for his 'mistaken' views. Kurella's volume is cited approvingly, with reservations concerning his discussion of the role of the Komsomol, and documents from Komsomol archives are quoted. There is still no recognition of the existence of the CYI archives, although several citations leave the impression that they are now part of the Komsomol archives.

A serious gap also exists in the literature and sources concerning the various national communist youth movements. This is gradually being remedied for the Soviet and German youth organizations, with many studies being undertaken in the Soviet Union and East Germany of various aspects of the emergence and development of the Komsomol and the KJD. Few studies exist of young communists elsewhere. An early study of the Italian youth organization in Russian by Giuseppe Berti (Dzuzheppe Berti, *Ital'ianskii komsomol* [Moscow 1925]) has not been available. In many cases, some or all of the basi ources - newspapers, journals, protocols, and the like - have been lost. Furthermore, few of the importan former participants in the events covered by this study are still alive. As many as possible of those who were alive and available when the research for this study was undertaken were interviewed. The comments of others not available for interview are included in many of the East German studies.

Conferences and Congresses: Proceedings, Resolutions, Decisions, Reports

Am Werk! Protokoll 1. Internationale Konferenz der sozialistischen Jugendorganisationen Süd-Ost-Europas. Vienna 1920

Beretning, 1921. Norges kommunistiske ungdomsforbund. Kristiania (Oslo) 1922

Beretning, 1922. Norges kommunistiske ungdomsforbund. Kristiania (Oslo) 1923

Bericht über die erste internationale Konferenz der sozialistischen Jugendorganisationen, abgehalten zu Stuttgart vom 24. bis 26. August 1907. Berlin 1907

Bericht über die internationale sozialistische Jugendkonferenz, abgehalten zu Wien vom 26. bis. 28. Februar 1921. Vienna 1921

Bericht über die erste Sitzung des Büros der Kommunistischen Jugend-Internationale, abgehalten am 9. bis. 13. Juni 1920 in Berlin. Berlin 1920. (Cited as *First Bureau Session.*)

Bericht vom 3. Weltkongress der Kommunistischen Jugendinternationale, vom 4. - 16. Dezember 1922 in Moskau. Berlin-Schöneberg 1923

Bulletin des 3. Kongresses der Kommunistichen Internationale. Moscow 1921

Bulletin des IV. Kongresses der Kommunistichen Internationale. Moscow 1922

Fourth congress of the Communist International: Abridged report of meetings held at Petrograd and Moscow 7 November - 3 December 1922. London 1923

Im Zeichen der Arbeit. Resolutionen und Beschlüsse des 3. Kongresses der Kommunistischen Jugend-Internationale. Berlin 1923

Internationaler Sozialisten-kongress zu Stuttgart, 18. bis 24. August 1907. Berlin 1907

Internationaler Sozialistischer Jugendkongress in Hamburg vom 24 Mai bis 26 Mai 1923: Die Verhandlunger und Beschlüsse der Tagung. Berlin 1923

Minutes of the 3rd Congress of the Young Communist International ... 1922. Berlin 1923

Pervyi kongress KIM; stenograficheskaia zapis' podgotovil k pechati A. Kurella. Moscow 1930

Premier Congrès National des Jeunesses Socialistes-Communistes de France (Paris, les 15 et 16 May 1921): Rapports et Thèses présentés au Congrès National. Paris 1921

Postanovleniia IV kongressa KIM. Moscow 1925

Protokoll der Reichskonferenz der Opposition der Freien Sozialistischen Jugend Deutschlands (28. und 29. August 1920 in Leipzig). N.p., n.d.

Protokoll des III. Kongresses der Kommunistischen Internationale (Moskau, 22. Juni bis 12. Juli 1921). Hamburg 1921

Protokoll des vierten Kongresses der Kommunistischen Internationale. Petrograd-Moskau, vom. 5. November bis 5. Dezember 1922. Hamburg 1923

Protokoll des 5. Kongresses der Kommunistischen Internationale. Hamburg 1924

Protokoly kongressov kommunisticheskogo internatsionala. Vtoroi kongress kominterna, iul'-avgust 1920g. Moscow 1934. (Cited as *Vtoroi kongress.*)

Rasshirennyi plenum Ispolnitel'nogo Komiteta Kommunisticheskogo Internatsionala (12-23 iiunia 1923 goda); Otchet Moscow 1923

Resolutionen und Beschlüsse der 3. Bürositzung der KJI. Berlin-Schöneberg 1922

Resolutionen und Richtlinien des 6. Reichskongresses der Kommunistischen Jugend Deutschlands vom 10. bis 12. September 1921 in Halle. Berlin 1921. (Cited as *Halle Congress.*)

Resolutions adopted at the 4th congress of the Young Communist International. Stockholm 1924

Resolutions and Theses of the Fourth Bureau Session, Published by the Executive Committee of the Young Communist International. Berlin-Schöneberg 1923

Resolutions and Theses of the Second Congress of the Young Communist International, Moscow 14-23 July 1921. New York 1921

Results of Two Congresses: 5th Communist International and 4th Young Communist International. N.p. 1924

Sie ist nicht tot! Bericht über die internationale Konferenz der sozialistischen Jugendorganisationen 1915 zu Bern. Zurich 1915

The Young Communist International: Report of the First International Congress Held in Berlin from 20-29 November 1919. Contains manifesto, program, and report of the actual stand of the YCI. Glasgow/London 1920
Unter dem roten Banner: Bericht über den ersten Kongress der Kommunistischen Jugend-Internationale. Berlin 1920
Zu neuer Arbeit: Bericht vom II. Kongress der KJI, abgehalten vom 14. bis 21. Juli in Moskau. Berlin 1921

Books, Pamphlets, Brochures, Articles, Dissertations, Manuscripts, and Archival Materials

Abriss der Geschichte der deutschen Arbeiterjugendbewegung (Entwurf). Teil I, Von den Anfängen bis 1945. Berlin (East) 1966. Published as *Geschichte der deutschen Arbeiterjugendbewegung, 1904-1945.* Berlin (East) 1971
Am Aufbau: Dokumente des Exekutiv-Komitees [of the Communist Youth International], volume 1 (November 1919 – August 1920), Berlin 1920; volume 2 (September 1920 – February 1921), Berlin 1921
Angress, Werner. *The Stillborn Revolution.* Princeton 1963
Die Arbeiter-Jugend-Internationale. Ihr Werdegang und ihre Ziele. Berlin 1921
Aufwärts: Bericht des Exekutiv-Komitees der Kommunistischen Jugendinternationale an der Weltkongress der revolutionären Proletarierjugend. Berlin 1921
Barbé, Henri. *Souvenirs de militant et de dirigeant communiste.* Unpublished manuscript, the Hoover Library, Stanford, California
Bericht des ersten Staatsanwaltes A. Brunner an dem Regierungsrat des Kantons Zürich über die Strafuntersuchung wegen des Aufruhrs in Zürich im November 1917 (Vom 9. November 1918). Zurich 1919
Böhny, Ferdy. 'Die sozialistische Jugendbewegung des ersten Weltkrieges als politischer Faktor.' *Der öffentliche Dienst (Zeitung des Schweizerisches Verbandes des personals öffentlicher Dienste),* 57. Jahr. 1964, nos. 45-59
Bericht über die Tätigkeit des Präsidiums und der Exekutive der Kommunistischen Internationale für die Zeit vom 6. März bis 11. Juni 1922. Hamburg 1922
Berti, Giuseppe. *I primi dieci anni di vita del PCI*
– 'Problemi di storia del PCI e dell'Internazionale Comunista.' *Revista Storica Italiana* LXXXII, no. 1 (March 1970)
Bock, Hans Manfred. *Syndikalismus und Linksradikalismus von 1918-1923.* Meisenheim am Glan 1969

Borkenau, Franz. *European Communism*. London 1953
- *World Communism* (Ann Arbor Paperback). Ann Arbor, Michigan 1962
Brandt, Willy and Richard Lowenthal. *Ernst Reuter. Ein Leben für die Freiheit. Eine politische Biographie*. Munich 1957
Brupbacher, Fritz. *Zürich während Krieg und Landesstreik*. Zurich 1928
Buber-Neumann, Margarete. *Kriegsschauplatz der Weltrevolution*. Stuttgart 1967
- *Von Potsdam nach Moskau*. Stuttgart 1957
Cammett, John. *Antonio Gramsci and the Origins of Italian Communism*. Stanford, California 1967
Carr, Edward Hallett. *The Bolshevik Revolution, 1917-1923* III. London 1953
- 'Radek's "Political Salon" in Berlin, 1919.' *Soviet Studies* 3, no. 4 (April 1959)
Chitarow (Khitarov), R[afail]. *Der Kampf um die Massen: vom 2. bis 5. Weltkongress der Kommunistischen Jugend-Internationale*. Volume three of *Geschichte der Kommunistischen Jugend-Internationale*. Berlin 1930
Christophersen, Jens. '"Mot Dag" and the Norwegian Left.' *Journal of Contemporary History* 1, no. 2 (1966)
G.D.H. Cole. *Communism and Social Democracy, 1914-1931*. London 1958
Crossman, Richard (ed.). *The God That Failed* (Colophon edition) New York 1963.
Danneberg, Robert. *Die Jugendbewegung der sozialistischen Internationale*. Vienna 1910
- *Die Rekrutenschulen der internationalen Sozialdemokratie*. Vienna 1914
Degras, Jane. *The Communist International 1919-1943. Documents*. Volume I (1919-1923), London 1956; volume II (1924-1928), London 1960
Deutschlands Junge Garde (Zusammengestellt und bearbeitet von Wolfgang Arlt, Manfred Heinze, und Manfred Uhlemann). Volume I, *Erlebnisse aus der Geschichte der Arbeiterjugendbewegung von den Anfängen bis zum Jahre 1945*. Berlin (East) 1959
Drachkovitch, Milorad M. and Branko Lazitch, *The Comintern: Historical Highlights*. New York 1966
Draft Program of the Young Communist International. London 1924
Draper, Theodore. *American Communism and Soviet Russia*. New York 1963

Dunajewsky, W. *Die Frage der sozialistischen Reorganisation der Arbeit*. Published by the Executive Committee of the Communist Youth International, n.p., n.d.
Egger, Heinz. *Die Entstehung der kommunistischen Partei und des kommunistischen Jugendverbandes der Schweiz*. Zurich 1952
Engelhardt, Viktor. *Die deutsche Jugendbewegung als kultur-historisches Phänomen*. Berlin 1924
Fainsod, Merle. *International Socialism and the World War*. Cambridge, Massachusetts 1935
Fischer, Ruth. *Stalin and German Communism*. Cambridge, Massachusetts 1948
Fisher, Ralph Talcott, Jr. *Pattern for Soviet Youth*. New York 1959
Flechtheim, Ossip K. *Die KPD in der Weimarer Republik* (Mit einer Einleitung von Hermann Weber). New edition. Frankfurt am Main 1969
Footman, David (ed.). *International Communism*. St Antony's Papers, no. 9. London 1960
Frobenius, Else. *Mit uns zieht die neue Zeit; eine Geschichte der deutschen Jugendbewegung*. Berlin 1927
From the 3rd to the 4th: A Report on the Activities of the Young Communist International since its Third World Congress (by the Executive Committee of the Young Communist International). Stockholm 1924
Fundamental Problems of the Young Communist Movement. Berlin 1922
Gankin, Olga Hess and H.H. Fisher. *The Bolsheviks and the World War*. Stanford 1940
Gegen bürgerlichen Militarismus und Sozialverraterei. Berlin-Schöneberg 1924
Gilberg, Trond. *The Soviet Communist Party and Scandinavian Communism: The Norwegian Case*. Oslo 1973
Globig, Fritz. *... aber verbunden sind wir mächtig*. Berlin (East) 1959
– *Was wir wollen!* Berlin 1929
Graf, Georg Engelbert. *Jung und Alt in der proletarischen Jugendbewegung*. Berlin 1921
Gross, Babette. *Willi Münzenberg: Eine politische Biographie*. Stuttgart 1967
Gruber, Helmut. *International Communism in the Era of Lenin*. Ithaca, New York 1967
– 'Willi Münzenberg: Propagandist For and Against the Comintern.' *International Review of Social History* X, part 2 (1965)

Grünberg, Carl. *Die Internationale und der Weltkrieg.* Part 1, *Vor dem Kriege und während der ersten Kriegswochen,* Leipzig 1916; Part 2, *Die Zimmerwalderbewegung 1914-1919, von Angelica Balabanoff,* Leipzig 1928

Gyptner, Richard. *Vom Verein zur Klassenorganisation, die Betriebszelle der kommunistischen Jugend.* Berlin 1923

Haas, Leonhard. *Carl Vital Moor, 1852-1932. Ein Leben für Marx und Lenin.* Zurich 1970

Hansen, Arvid; Eugene Olaussen; and Aksel Zachariassen. *Den Røde Ungdom i Kamp og Seier.* Kristiania (Oslo) 1923

Hanssen, Andreas. *Kristiania og Moskva.* En Utredning av den 3. Internationales Betingelser og Vigstigste Teser. Gjøvik Norway n.d. [1920]

Harmsen, G.J. *Blauwe en rode jeugd.* Amsterdam 1961

Heinz, Karl. *Die Entwicklung der Kommunistischen Jugendinternationale.* Vienna 1922.

– *Kampf und Aufstieg.* Vienna 1932

Heinzelmann, Paul. *Die Organisation der sozialistischen Jugend.* Berlin 1919

Herrle, T. *Die deutsche Jugendbewegung in ihren wirtschaftlichen und gesellschaftlichen Zusammenhangen.* Gotha 1921

Höglund, Zeth. *Minnen i fackelsken.* Four volumes. Stockholm 1951-60

Honay, Karl. *Proletarische Jugendbewegung und Politik.* Vienna 1919

Hopffe, Günther. *Die Internationale Jugendtag und seine Bedeutung* (herausgegeben von der Zentrale der Kommunistische Jugend Deutschlands). N.p. 1921

Hörnle, Edwin. *Sozialistische Jugenderziehung und sozialistische Jugendbewegung.* Berlin 1919

Humbert-Droz, Jules. *Mon Evolution du Tolstoisme au Communisme, 1891-1921.* Neuchatel 1969

Instructions on the building up of the nuclei and their practical work as the basic units of communist organization. Stockholm 1924

Die Internationale Organisation der sozialistischen Jugend: Bericht des Sekretariats der Internationalen Verbindung der sozialistischen Jugendorganisationen (August 1907). Leipzig 1907

Der Internationale Jugendtag. Vienna 1925

Die Internationale Sozialistische Jugendbewegung. Berlin 1924

Jackson, George D. Jr. *Comintern and Peasant in East Europe 1919-1930.* New York and London 1966

Jahnke, Karl-Heinz. 'Die Beziehungen zwischen dem Komsomol und der revolutionären deutschen Arbeiterjugend im ersten Jahrzehnt der Sowjetmacht.' *Zeitschrift für Geschichtswissenschaft* XV. Jahr., Heft 6 (1967)
- '"Mein Streben gal dem Höchsten der Menschheit!" Conrad Blenkle.' *Beiträge zur Geschichte der Arbeiterbewegung* 15. Jahr., Heft 1 (1973)
Jahnke, Karl-Heinz, and Horts Pietschmann. 'Zur Gründung der Kommunistischen Jugendinternationale und ihrer historischen Bedeutung.' *Beiträge zur Geschichte der Arbeiterbewegung* 12. Jahr., Heft 1 (1970)
Die Jugend der Revolution. Drei Jahre proletarische Jugendbewegung, 1918-1920. Berlin 1921
Kampf gegen die Verelendung der Arbeiterjugend! Berlin 1922
Koestler, Arthur. *The Invisible Writing.* New York 1954
Korn, Karl. *Die Arbeiterjugendbewegung. Einführung in ihre Geschichte.* Three volumes in one. Berlin 1924
Kriegel, Annie. *The French Communists. Profile of a People.* Chicago and London 1972
- *Aux origines du communisme français, 1914-1920.* Two volumes. The Hague 1964
Kurella, Alfred. *Gründung und Aufbau der Kommunistischen Jugend-Internationale.* Volume two of *Geschichte der Kommunistischen Jugend-Internationale.* Berlin 1929
- *Unterwegs zu Lenin.* Berlin (East) 1967
Langfeldt, Knut. *Moskva-tesene i norsk politikk.* Oslo 1961
Laqueur, Walter. *Young Germany.* New York 1962
Lazitch, Branko, and Milorad Drachkovitch, *Biographical Dictionary of the Comintern.* Stanford 1973
Die Lehren der deutschen Ereignisse. Das Präsidium des Exekutivkomitees der Kommunistischen Internationale zur deutschen Frage - Januar 1924. Hamburg 1924
Die Lehren der deutschen Ereignisse und die KJI. Berlin-Schöneberg 1924
Lenin, V.I. *Collected Works.* Second edition. Moscow 1960-
- *Sochineniia* [Works]. Second edition. Moscow 1926-32
- *Die Aufgaben der kommunistischen Jugendorganisationen.* Berlin 1920
- *'Left-Wing' Communism: An Infantile Disorder.* New York 1940
Lenin i Stalin o molodezhi. Moscow 1938
Liebknecht, Karl. *Militarism.* New York 1917
- *Militarismus und Antimilitarismus unter besonderer Berücksichtigung der internationalen Jugendbewegung von Dr Karl Liebknecht.* Berlin 1907

- *Speeches of Karl Liebknecht.* New York 1927
Lindbom, Tage. *Den socialdemokratiska ungdomsrörelsen i
Sverige.* Stockholm 1945
Lorwin, Val. *Labor and Internationalism.* New York 1929
Lowenthal, Richard. 'The Bolshevization of the Spartakus
League,' in David Footman (ed.). *International Communism.*
St Antony's Papers, no. 9. London 1960
Mahrholz, Werner. *Ein politische Programm der deutschen
Jugend.* Berlin 1922
*Manifest, Programm, und Statut der Kommunistischen Jugend-
Internationale.* Berlin n.d.
*Die Masken herunter! Das wahre Gesicht der Schäffer einer
gelben Jugend-Internationale.* Berlin n.d.
Material zum Jungarbeiter-Weltkongress. Berlin 1922
*Material zur Diskussion des Programms der Kommunistischen
Jugend-Internationale.* Berlin-Schöneberg 1923
Mattmüller, Markus. *Leonhard Ragaz und der religiöse Sozia-
lismus.* Two volumes. Zurich 1968
Meyer, Alfred. *Leninism.* New York 1962
Maurseth, Per. *Fra Moskvateser til Kristiania-forslag. Det
norske Arbeiderparti og Komintern fra 1921 til februar
1923.* Oslo 1972
Münzenberg, Willi. *Die Dritte Front.* Berlin (Neuer Deutsche
Verlag) 1930; Berlin (Universum Bucherei) 1931
- 'Ein Jahr Kommunistische Jugendbewegung.' *Kommunismus*
2. Jahr., no. 11/12 (1 April 1921)
- *Ein Jahr der kommunistischen Jugend-Internationale (Novem
ber 1919 - November 1920).*
*Nehmt euch der Kinder an! Die Aufgaben und der gegenwärti
Stand der Sozialistischen Kingergruppen in allen Ländern.*
Zurich 1917
Nieder mit Spartakus! Chemnitz 1919
*Programm und Aufbau der sozialistischen Jugend-Interna-
tionale.* Stuttgart 1919
*Die proletarische Jugendbewegung bis zur Gründung des
Kommunistischen Jugend-Internationale.* Berlin 1929
*Solidarität. 10 Jahre internationale Arbeiterhilfe. 1921-
1931.* Berlin 1931
Die sozialistische Jugend-Internationale. Berlin 1919
*Die sozialistischen Jugendorganisationen vor und während
des Krieges.* Berlin 1919
Unser Programm. Rede auf dem Gründungskongress. Berlin
1919

- *Der II. Kongress der Kommunistischen Internationale und die Kommunistische Jugend-Internationale.* Berlin 1920

Nasonov, I. *Istoriia KIM (v kratkom izlozhenii).* Moscow 1930

Nettl, J.P. *Rosa Luxemburg.* Two volumes. London 1966

Nicht wollen oder nicht können? Briefwechsel des Exekutiv-Komitees der Kommunistischen Jugend-Internationale mit dem Vorstande des Verbandes der sozialistischen Arbeiter-Jugend Österreichs. Vienna 1920

Ollenhauer, Erich (compiler). *Von Weimar bis Bielefeld. Ein Jahr Arbeiter jugendbewegung. Zum Reichsjugendtag in Bielefeld Ende Juli 1921.* Berlin 1921

Pawlow, W. [Lazar Shatskin] and B. Köres [Johann Lekai]. *Die Aufgaben der kommunistischen Jugendorganisationen nach der Übernahme der Macht durch das Proletariat, aus der Praxis der kommunistischen Jugendorganisationen von Russland und Ungarn.* Berlin n.d.

Pietschmann, Horst. *Der politisch-ideologische Klärungsprozess in der kommunistischen Jugendbewegung Deutschlands zur Durchsetzung marxistisch-leninistischer Auffassungen über die Jugendarbeit Februar 1919 bis September 1921.* Phil.Diss., Ernst Moritz-Arndt-Universität, Greifswald May 1969

Polano Luigi. *Wie weit ist heute eine Autonomie der Kommunistischen Jugendorganisationen in der Kommunistischen Bewegung notwendig und möglich?* Berlin 1921

Das politische Grundwissen des jungen Kommunisten; Leitfaden für den politischen Grundunterricht der kommunistischen Jugendverbände. Edited by B. Zeigler [Alfred Kurella]. Berlin-Schöneberg 1924

Program of the Young Communist International. (Adopted by the 5th congress.) New York 1929

In den Reihen der Gegenrevolutionen. Briefwechsel KJI - Internationale Arbeitsgemeinschaft sozialistischer Jugendorganisationen. Berlin 1923

Reimann, Paul. *Geschichte der Kommunistischen Partei der Tschechoslowakei.* Berlin 1929

Richter, Friedrich. *Die Jugend und die sozialistischen Parteien.* Berlin 1919

Rühle, Otto. *Neues Kinderland; ein kommunistisches Schul- und Erziehungsprogramm.* Basel 1920

Schiller, Paul. *Die Betriebsorganisationen der Jugend.* Berlin 1919

328 Bibliography

Schönhaar, Eugen. *Der Internationale Jugendtag.* Berlin
1922; Vienna 1925
Schorske, Carl. *German Social Democracy, 1905-1917.*
Cambridge, Massachusetts 1955
Schlamm, Willi *Einstation Hamburg, oder 2 + 2½ = 2, an
die Sozialistische Arbeiterjugend Österreichs.* Berlin
1923
Schleimann, Jørgen. 'The Life and Work of Willi Münzenberg
Survey (London), no. 55 (April 1965)
Schurer, H. 'Karl Moor: German Agent and Friend of Lenin.'
Journal of Contemporary History 5, no. 2 (1970)
Schüddekopf, Otto-Ernst. 'Karl Radek in Berlin.' *Archiv
für Sozialgeschichte* II. Bind (1962)
– *Linke Leute von Rechts. Die nationalrevolutionären
Minderheiten und der Kommunismus in der Weimarer Repub-
lik.* Stuttgart 1960
Schüller, Richard *Von den Anfängen der proletarischen
Jugendbewegung bis zur Gründung der Kommunistischen
Jugend-Internationale.* Volume one of *Geschichte der
Kommunistischen Jugend-Internationale.* Berlin 1931
A Short History of the Young Communist International.
London n.d.
Sieger, Walter. *Die junge Front. Die revolutionare Arbeit-
erjugend in Kampf gegen den ersten Weltkrieg.* Berlin
1958
Sinowjew (Zinoviev), Grigorij. *Die Kommunistische Jugend-
Internationale und ihre Aufgaben.* Speech to the fourth
congress of the CYI, 1924. Vienna n.d.
H. Gordon Skilling. 'The Comintern and Czechoslovak Commu-
nism, 1921-1929.' *The American Slavic and East European
Review* XIX, no. 2 (April 1960)
– 'The Formation of a Communist Party in Czechoslovakia.'
The American Slavic and East European Review XIV, no. 3
(October 1955)
Sogstad, Per. *Ungdoms Fanevakt. Den Socialistiske Ungdoms-
bevegelsens Historie i Norge.* Oslo 1951
*Die sozialistische Proletarierjugend Deutschlands und die
Kommunistische Jugend-Internationale: ein offenes Wort
an die Mitglieder der sozialistischen Proletarierjugend
Deutschlands.* Berlin 1920
Sparring, Åke. *Från Höglund till Hermansson. Om revisionis
men i Sveriges kommunistiska parti.* Stockholm 1967
*Staatsarchiv des Kantons Zürich. Verhöre und Lebenslauf
von Willi Münzenberg.* P239. 14 Nr. 24 and 25

Steiner, Herbert. *Die Kommunistische Partei Österreichs von 1918-1933. Bibliographische Bemerkungen.* Vienna 1968
Die Tätigkeit der Exekutive und des Präsidiums des E.K. der Kommunistischen Internationale vom 13. Juli 1921 bis 1 Februar 1922. Petrograd 1922
Thaller, Leopold. *Die internationale sozialistische Jugendbewegung.* Vienna 1921
Thesen über die Arbeit auf dem Lande; Materialien zum II. Weltkongress der Kommunistischen Jugend-Internationale vom Kommunistischen Jugendverband Russlands. Petrograd 1921
Tkadeckova, H. *Dejiny Komsomolu na Slovensku (1918-1938).* Bratislava 1964
Toft, Frode. *Kampens ungdom. 50 års socialistisk ungdomsbevegelse i Danmark.* Copenhagen 1956
Toward Singing Tomorrows. The Last Testament of Gabriel Péri. With an introductory essay by Louis Aragon. New York 1946
Trotsky, Leon. *The First Five Years of the Communist International.* Two volumes. New York 1945, 1953
Tschitscherin [Chicherin], Georgij. *Skizzen aus der Geschichte der Jugend-Internationale.* Berlin 1919
20 Jahre der Jugendinternationale. Vienna 1927
25 Jahre Jugendinternationale. Berlin 1932
Upton, A.F. *Communism in Scandinavia and Finland.* London 1973
Urquidi, Donald William. *The Origins of the Italian Communist Party, 1918-1921.* Ph.D. dissertation, Columbia University 1962
Der Verband der Sozialistischen Arbeiterjugend Deutsch-Österreichs und der Weltkongress der revolutionären proletarischen Jugend. Berlin 1921
Vom III. zum IV. Weltkongress der Kommunistischen Jugend-Internationale: Bericht des Exekutiv-Komitees über die Tätigkeit und die Lage und Entwicklung der KJI. Berlin-Schöneberg 1924
Vom IV. zum V. Weltkongress der Kommunistischen Jugend-Internationale: Bericht des Exekutiv-Komitees über Kampf und Arbeit der Kommunistischen Jugend-Internationale. Berlin 1928
Was ist und was will die Kommunistische Jugend-Internationale? Vienna (Süd-Ost Undersekretariat der KJI) 1920, and Berlin (EKKI) 1921
Weber, Hermann. *Die Wandlung des deutschen Kommunismus.* Two volumes. Frankfurt am Main 1969

Westphal, Max. *Unser Wirken. Die Arbeiterjugendbewegung 1921.* Berlin 1922
Wohl, Robert. *French Communism in the Making, 1914-1924.* Stanford, California 1966
The Young Communist International between the 4th and 5th Congresses - 1924-1928. London 1928
The Young Workers' International. Programme, Rules, Manifestoes. Berlin 1922
Ypsilon [John Rindl and Juliam Gumperz (Rindl is a pseudonym for Karl Volk, Gumperz for Jules Humbert-Droz)]. *Pattern for World Revolution.* Chicago and New York 1947
Zehn Jahre Kommunistische Jugend-Internationale; kurzer Abriss der Geschichte der KJI. Berlin 1929
Zur Geschichte der Arbeiterjugendbewegung in Deutschland. Eine Auswahl von Materialien und Dokumenten aus den Jahren 1904-1946. Berlin 1956

Periodicals and journals

Die Arbeit (Zeitschrift für Theorie und Praxis der Kommunistischen Jugendbewegung). Published in Berlin by the Kommunistische Jugend Deutschlands, 1921-25.
Arbeiterjugend. Monthly organ of the German social democratic youth organization. Berlin 1909-?
Arbeiterjugendinternationale. Monthly organ of the right-socialist youth international from October 1921 to June 1923. Berlin
Arbeiterpolitik. (Wochenschrift für wissenschaftlichen Sozialismus). Organ of the radical opposition in Bremen, 1916-19.
Arbeiter-Rat. Organ of the workers' councils in Germany, 1919-1920. Berlin
L'Avanguardia. Organ of the Italian socialist, then communist, youth organization.
L'Avant-Garde ouvrière et communiste (l'Avant-Garde). Organ of the Comité de l'Internationale communiste des Jeunes, September 1920 - October 1920. Organ of the Fédération Nationale des Jeunesses Socialistes-Communist de France, section français de l'Internationale Communiste des Jeunes, November 1920-?
Basler Vorwärts. Organ of the Swiss social democratic part in Basel, from February 1921 of the Swiss communists.
Berner Tagwacht. Organ of the Swiss democratic party in Bern, 1893-1918.

Bulletin der internationalen Verbindung der sozialistichen Jugendorganisationen (six times a year, except for 1907 and 1914). Vienna 1907-14

Bulletin of the sub-bureau in Amsterdam of the Communist International; two numbers published: February and March 1921.

Bulletin, Internationale sozialistische Kommission zu Bern, 1915-17

The Communist International. English-language edition of the organ of the executive committee of the Communist International.

Freie Jugend. Organ of the social democratic youth organization in Switzerland, 1911-18. Zurich

Freie Jugend (Jugendschrift für herrschaftlosen Sozialismus). Anarcho-syndicalist youth periodical published in Berlin, then Vienna, 1919-?

Fremad. Monthly newspaper of the Danish socialist youth organization, 1907-22.

Internationale Jugendkorrespondenz. Published by the Executive Committee of the Communist Youth International, Vienna 1919-24. The first number was in December 1919, mimeographed in fifty copies. From February 1920 until the end of 1921 it was published three times a month, then on the first and fifteenth of every month, later as a monthly until it ceased publication in September 1924. It appeared also in French, English, and Russian editions.

Inprecorr (International Press Correspondence). Published by the Executive Committee of the Communist International. Berlin, Vienna, London 1921-43.

Inprekorr (Internationale Presse-Korrespondenz). German edition of *Inprecorr*, 1919-33

Die Internationale der sozialistischen Proletarierjugend. Organ of the centrist youth international. Vienna, August 1921 to July 1923.

Jugend-Internationale. Published by the Internationale Verbindung der sozialistischen Jugendorganisationen (September 1915 - November 1919) and by the Communist Youth International (November 1919 - June 1941). Zurich, Berlin, Vienna. A quarterly until May 1918, when it ceased publication until July 1919. Resumed as a monthly. From December 1919 to June 1941 in Russian (frequency varies; from 1925 to 1928 it was superceded by KIM [Kommunisticheskii Internatsional Molodezhi]). Also published in

Swedish (*Ungdoms-Internationalen*), Italian *(l'Internazionale della Gioventu)*, French *(l'Internationale des
Jeunes)*, English *(International of Youth)*, Hungarian
(Ifjamunkas Internationale), Hebrew, Romanian, Czech,
and Serbian.

Jugend-Internationale; Die 11 historischen Nummern der
Kriegsausgabe 1915–1918, Moscow n.d. Reprint in book
form of the eleven wartime numbers. Published also in
a Russian edition.

Der Jugendliche Arbeiter. Organ of the socialist youth in
Austria, 1902–?

Die Junge Garde. Organ of the Freie Sozialistische Jugend
(October 1918 – September 1920), then of the Kommunistische Jugend Deutschlands. Berlin, October 1920–33.

Der Junge Genosse. International organ for working childre
published by the Executive Committee of the Communist
Youth International. Vienna 1921–24.

Der Junge Kommunist (Mitteilungsblatt der KJD, Bezirke
Berlin/Brandenburg)

Der Jungsozialist. Organ der sozialistischen Jugend Süd-
deutschlands. Edited by Willi Münzenberg and Edwin Hörnl
Stuttgart 1918–19

Der Kampfer. Organ of the KPD in Chemnitz.

Kommunismus (Zeitschrift der Kommunistischen International
für die Länder Südosteuropas). Vienna 1920–21

Der Kommunist (Organ der Internationalen Kommunisten
Deutschlands). Edited by Johan Knief. Bremen 1918

Der Kommunist (Flugzeitung der KAPD). Dresden 1919

Der Kommunist (Mitteilungsblatt der KPD [Spartakusbund]
Bezirk Wurttemburg). Stuttgart

Der Kommunist (Tageszeitung der KPD [Spartakusbund] für
Mitteldeutschland). Erfurt

Kommunistische Arbeiter-Zeitung. Organ of the KAPD. Hambur
February 1919–? Published also in Essen and Berlin in
different editions.

Die Kommunistische Internationale. Organ of the Executive
Committee of the Communist International. Petrograd-
Moscow, Hamburg-Berlin 1919–33

Die Kommunistische Jugend. Organ of the Verband der Kommunistischen Proletarierjugend Deutsch-Österreichs. Vienna
January 1919 – August 1920.

Moscow. Organ of the III Congress of the Communist International. Moscow 1921

Neue Jugend. Organ of the socialist youth organization in Basel from 1919 to 1920; succeeded *Freie Jugend* when it was prohibited in Zurich in 1918; then in 1920 became the organ of the Swiss communist youth organization.

Proletarier-Jugend. Published by the Zentralstelle der sozialistischen Proletarierjugend Deutschlands in Leipzig from 1 January 1920; succeeded *Freie Jugend*, which served as the organ of the USPD youth in the FSJ from June 1919 until January 1920.

Das Proletarische Kind. Information organ for teachers and friends of communist children's groups. Published by the Executive Committee of the Communist Youth International. Vienna 1925

Die Rote Fahne. Organ of the KPD. Berlin 1918–33

Rundschreiben des Exekutiv-Komitees der Kommunistischen Jugend-Internationale an die Kommunistischen Jugendverbände. Berlin, August 1921–?

Rundschreiben der Zentralstelle für die arbeitende Jugend Deutschlands. No. 7 (1 January 1915) – no. 14 (31 December 1916). Berlin

Sbornik Sotsial-Demokrata. A collection of issues of *Sotsial Demokrat*. Geneva 1916

Sozialistische Jugend (Zeitschrift der Sozialistischen Jugendorganisation in dem deutschen Gebiet der Tschechoslowakei). Teplitz (Teplice), January 1921–?

Sozialistische Jugend-Internationale. Organ of the Socialist Youth International. Berlin, October 1923–?

La Voix des Jeunes (nouvelle série). Organe mensuel de Propagande et d'Education Socialiste. Organ of the French socialist youth organization, 1918–19.

Zirkularschreiben der Internationalen Verbindung sozialistischer Jugendorganisationen. Zurich, Basel, March 1918 – April 1919.

Index

208, 211, 234; and 'bolshevization' 275-6, 282, 283f;
imposition of Comintern line 233f, 241, 244, 251, 264-5;
membership 101-2, 112, 231, 257n, 283n, 284n, 288; moved
to Moscow 230; Norwegian question 276f; directives on
party/youth organization relations 234n
- finances 111-12
- independence (*see also* youth organizations *and* Münzenberg
167f, 169n, 178, 213, 219, 220, 226n, 235, 279n, 280n
- International Bureau 101, 113, 195n, 196; 1st session
(1920) 73n, 119, 120-1, 124, 128, 137, 160, 170, 193;
2nd session (1922) 250; 4th session (1924) 248n, 257
- and Komsomol 174-8, 196n, 197, 203, 230, 284n
- membership 97, 108, 109n, 155, 281
- relations between youth organizations and parties 99,
100, 101n, 167f, 219-20, 222n, 225-30, 232, 234, 251-2,
256-90, 300, 305
- revolutionary strategy 115, 200, 221-4
- united front 252-6, 266
communist youth organizations (*see* youth organizations
and groups)
Creutzberg, R. 259n

Dahl, T. 281n
Danneberg, R. 11, 12n, 14, 15, 19n, 22, 28n
David 189n, 257n, 284n
Draft Declaration of Principles (1916) 28-9
Decree on Peace (Bolsheviks) 46
democratic centralism/centralization ix, 78, 87-8, 101n,
144, 153, 155, 158-9, 162, 166, 179, 203-4, 206, 220,
228-9, 260, 262-3, 266n, 270, 271n, 272-5, 278, 301,
303, 306, 308f
diversity in the communist movement viii, 305-7
D'Onofrio, E. 245n
Doriot, J. 189n, 211, 231, 241n, 242, 269, 283n, 296
Die Dritte Front 54n, 57n, 61n
'dual subordination' 274
Dunayevskii, V. 175, 196n

Ebert, F. 13
'economic struggle'/economic work 163, 164-7, 222n, 230,
239, 241, 243, 246, 249, 256
'education' 5, 7-8, 10, 28, 37, 92-5, 143, 219, 227, 232,
256, 287
'extreme left' 264, 265n

339 Index

350
Winarsky, L. 11n
Windau 141n
Wissener, R. 186n
Wohl, R. 133
Wolf, M. 288n
Wolffheim, F. 72, 84
workers' councils 3, 6, 39, 131
Wynkoop, D. 116

Yang Ta-lai 284n
Young 284n
Young Workers' International 255
youth: belief in centralism 101, 177, 220, 235, 268, 278-9,
  301f; enthusiasm for action 46, 51-3, 59, 71, 74, 81, 145,
  157, 190, 194, 214, 222-3, 228, 232, 244, 292f, 306;
  idealism x, 3, 107, 110, 141, 232, 292; radicalism 8, 17,
  20, 30, 45f, 51, 88, 103, 106, 108-9, 143f, 154, 161, 176,
  207, 214, 292f, 306, 313f; radicalism frustrated 235, 293f
  support for 'ultra-left' and 'revoltuionary offensive'
  110, 207-13, 215, 217, 222-3, 243f; World War I, effect
  on 45, 64, 109-10, 140
youth organizations and groups
- Austria: (VJA) 4, 6, 11n, 14, 28n, 29, 32; (VKPJ) 33, 71n,
  98n, 114n, 115n, 123-5, 173, 198n, 201, 212, 229n; (VSAJ)
  32-3, 71n, 114n, 122-5, 134, 197
- Banat communist 198n
- Belgium (Jeune Garde/Jonge Wacht) 4-5, 14, 34, 155, 187,
  197, 198n, 226
- Bessarabia communist 198n
- Bulgaria communist 114n, 120n, 198n, 225, 295
- Czechoslovakia communist 198n, 215n, 260, 294; Czech
  (Kladno) 71n; Czech communist 114n, 155; German-Czech
  socialist 114n; Slovak communist 114n, 120n
- Denmark communist 198n, 204, 226, 230n, 234-5
- Denmark social democratic 25-6, 28n, 71n, 154, 160, 226
- England communist 198n, 224n
- Finland communist 120, 198n
- France communist (JC) 50n, 115, 131-3, 155, 188, 198n,
  201, 229n, 260, 268, 294; anti-militarism 189, 240n, 241,
  242; at 3rd Comintern congress 190; 1st congress 189, 267;
  2nd congress 240, 267; 3rd congress 268; and CYI 241;
  crisis within 189n; factionalism 189, 190, 267-8; leadership 189n, 212n, 240n, 241n, 269n; 'leftism' 240-1;
  relations with communist party 188-92, 211, 240f, 267-9;

Ziegler, B. (*see* Kurella)
Zimmerlich, W. 143n
Zimmerwald Commission (ISC) 19, 27n, 28n
Zimmerwald conference (1915) 16, 19n, 34n, 270
Zimmerwald left 25, 27n, 60n, 61, 76n
Zimmerwald majority 26 (*see also* centrists)
Zinoviev, G. 19n, 71, 81, 83, 85, 102n, 116, 151, 170,
   178, 199, 201n, 216, 220, 221, 223-4, 262, 273, 276n,
   286
Zucker, H. 174n